SCARABS AND CYLINDERS WITH NAMES

FIVE GENERA OF BEETLES IMITATED IN HISTORIC TIMES.

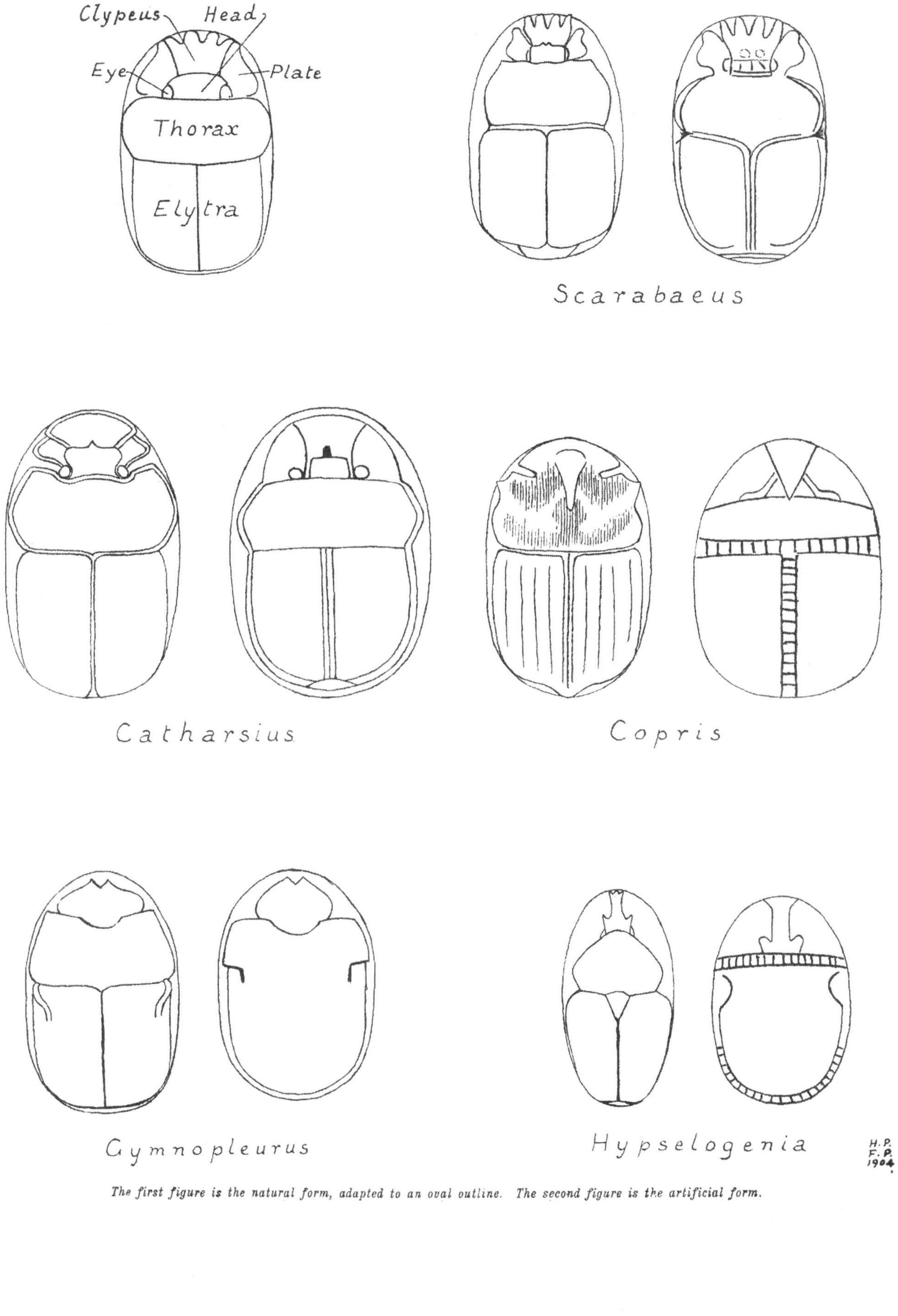

The first figure is the natural form, adapted to an oval outline. The second figure is the artificial form.

SCARABS AND CYLINDERS WITH NAMES

Illustrated by the Egyptian Collection
in University College, London.

SIR W. M. FLINDERS PETRIE

OXBOW | books
Oxford & Philadelphia

This edition published in the United Kingdom in 2023 by
OXBOW BOOKS
The Old Music Hall, 106–108 Cowley Road, Oxford, OX4 1JE

and in the United States by
OXBOW BOOKS
1950 Lawrence Road, Havertown, PA 19083

Paperback Edition: ISBN 979-8-88857-002-9
Digital Edition: ISBN 979-8-88857-003-6 (epub)

First published by the British School of Archaeology in Egypt, 1917
Facsimile edition published in 1974 by Aris & Phillips Ltd

Oxbow Books is grateful to the Petrie Museum for their collaboration in bringing out these new editions

Printed in the United Kingdom by CMP Digital Print Solutions

For a complete list of Oxbow titles, please contact:

UNITED KINGDOM
Oxbow Books
Telephone (0)1226 734350
Email: oxbow@oxbowbooks.com
www.oxbowbooks.com

UNITED STATES OF AMERICA
Oxbow Books
Telephone (610) 853-9131, Fax (610) 853-9146
Email: queries@casemateacademic.com
www.casemateacademic.com/oxbow

Oxbow Books is part of the Casemate Group

Front cover: String of beads, scarabs and amulets. From Naqada South Town (Tomb 1), Egypt, Dynasty 19 (*c.* 1295–1186BC). Petrie Museum UC29133. Image © Mary Hinkley, UCL Educational Media.

CONTENTS

INTRODUCTION

CHAPTER I

RELIGIOUS ASPECT OF THE SCARAB

CHAPTER II

THE VARIETIES OF SCARABS

CHAPTER III

THE MAKING OF SCARABS

CHAPTER IV

THE EARLY CYLINDERS, PLS. I—VII

CHAPTER V

THE OLD KINGDOM, PLS. VIII—XI

CHAPTER VI

THE EARLIEST AGE OF SCARABS

CHAPTER VII

THE MIDDLE KINGDOM

CHAPTER VIII

THE NEW KINGDOM

CHAPTER IX

ETHIOPIANS AND SAITES

ERRATA IN PLATES.

xix, 4th line: 1 to be under 1st of Queen Ana.

xxxvi, 6th line: Names of the Aten begin at 45.

liv, 3rd line: 13 to be 1; 1 to be 2; 2 to be 3, 4; 4 to be 5; 5 to be 6.

The British School of Archaeology in Egypt has been making a collection for a war fund since 1914. We undertook to raise £1,000 for the Officers' Families Fund, and achieved this in about a year. We are now collecting entirely for the Scottish Women's Hospitals, to maintain Dr. Elsie Inglis' two Field Hospitals, which are serving the Serbian division of the Russian army in Rumania, and are greatly valued by our allies (Hon. Sec. S. W. H., London Units, Hilda Flinders Petrie). It is hoped that all subscribers will help to make this the special War Work of our organisation. We have no hesitation in continuing to receive usual subscriptions to the School, as such are invested in War Loan, and thus pass into the National Savings for the present. Our students are now all serving their country, but when that sad duty is passed, they will again turn to the School to support their researches. Meanwhile our supporters, by their subscriptions, ensure getting the volumes of this catalogue, which will be continued for the years of the War. The volumes are :—

Amulets (previously issued by Constable).
Scarabs, for 1915.
Tools and Weapons, for 1916.
Funeral Statuettes (Shabtis) } for 1917.
Weights and Measures }

Following volumes will be on Ornaments and Toilet Objects; Stone and Metal Vases; Scarabs with designs and Button Seals; Prehistoric Egypt; Games and Writing Materials; Glass and Glazes (in colours); Beads (in colours); and ten or twelve other subjects.

At a time when all our energies are required for our defence, it is needful to state the conditions under which any historical work is produced. At the beginning of the war the writer of this volume offered to resign University position until peace, but was officially instructed to retain it; and the most direct duty of such position is the present catalogue of College collections. His offer also, in two official enquiries, to take the work of other men in public service, has been refused. The printing of this volume has been left to be produced entirely as deferred work, only taken up to level the output of the printers and plate-makers; thus equalising the conditions of labour, without employing more workers than are otherwise needed. The splendid early volunteering of over 250 men from the firm of printers, shows that they do not hesitate at complying with the national requirements. Great delays in printing have necessarily occurred, and it is doubtful if volumes beyond this, and that on Tools, can be issued till after the war.

SYSTEM OF THE CATALOGUE

The current description of the plates, and discussion of the materials.
The HISTORICAL Index, and general census of scarabs in the principal collections.
The TEXT Index.
The PRIVATE NAMES Index (lithograph).
The TITLES INDEX (lithograph).
The CATALOGUE plates and description of all early cylinders accessible, and of all scarabs with names in University College.
The TYPES OF BACKS of scarabs.

The order of the scarabs under each king is (1) Falcon name; (2) Nebti name; (3) Hor-nubti name; (4) Throne name with phrases, or with titles, or plain, proceeding from the longest to the simplest; (5) Personal name in similar order. Other objects with names follow after the scarabs under each person. Private scarabs, etc., are placed as nearly as may be in their historic position. Heart scarabs are all together between the xxth and xxist dynasties.

The system of numbering is not continuous throughout, as that does not indicate the period at sight. Each object has the number of the dynasty, the king, and of the object under that king. Thus 18·6·23 is the xviiith dynasty, 6th king (Tehutmes III), and his 23rd scarab. The drawings of scarabs outside of this collection are only inserted to complete the series, and are not numbered or catalogued. The colour stated is the original colour wherever any part of it can be found, regardless of the general change in such cases. The letter and number after the colour refer to the types of backs.

In the plates of backs LIX—LXXIII the references below each drawing are the dynasty, king, and number, as above stated. Where there is more than one reference, the underlined reference is the source of the drawing, which the others resemble. The top number of each drawing is that of the type, and is used with the type letter of the class for reference in the Catalogue pages. Occasionally two drawings have the same number when the type is alike, and they only differ in work.

References are made to the following works:—

Hall, H. R., Catalogue of Egyptian Scarabs, etc., in the British Museum, 1913.
Newberry, Percy E., Scarab-shaped Seals (Cairo Catalogue), 1907.
,, ,, Scarabs, 1906.
Ward, John, The Sacred Beetle, 1902.
Frazer, George, A Catalogue of Scarabs, 1900 (now in Munich).
The Golenisheff Collection (photographs privately issued).
Petrie, W. M. F., Historical Scarabs, 1889.

PREFACE TO THE 2023 EDITION

In the 1970s, a much-anticipated new series of publications illustrated objects and themes related to the excavations of the archaeologist William Matthew Flinders Petrie (1853–1942) in Egypt, and aspects of the collection of University College London's Petrie Museum of Egyptian and Sudanese Archaeology. A young couple setting up in business in the early 1970s, Aris and Phillips published these works, written by members of the UCL Egyptology Department, in their *Modern Egyptology* series. Building on Petrie's own observations, the authors of these volumes aimed to complete the great task of publishing the Petrie Museum of Egyptian and Sudanese Archaeology's vast collection, and to present some of the research that Petrie himself was not able to address in his own published works during his lifetime. As the current Curator of the Petrie Museum, it is a great privilege for me to support Oxbow Books in their mission to republish the series, which remains a key source of information for all those interested in object-based approaches to the study of the ancient world.

The Petrie Museum, part of University College London (UCL), is home to one of the largest and most significant collections of Egyptian and Sudanese archaeology in the world. Free to visit, this extraordinary collection tells stories about the lives of ordinary people who lived along the Nile Valley thousands of years ago. Originally set up as a teaching collection, the Petrie Museum comprises over 80,000 objects housed together with an internationally important archaeological archive. It is a collection of world firsts and 'oldests': the oldest woven garment; the oldest worked iron objects; the first known depiction of loom weaving; the oldest known written document about women's health; the earliest veterinary treatise; the oldest will on paper. The Museum has Designated Status from Arts Council England, meaning that it is considered to have outstanding resonance and national cultural significance. The collection has a substantial, visible international reputation for research, supporting hundreds of researchers every year, both remotely and in person.

The Petrie Museum is named after Flinders Petrie, who was appointed in 1892 as the first Professor of Egyptian Archaeology and Philology in the UK at UCL. Over three-quarters of the material in the Museum comes from excavations directed or funded by Petrie, or from purchases he made for university teaching. In 1880 at the age of 26, Petrie travelled to Egypt to survey the Great Pyramid. For the next five decades he was at the forefront of the development of archaeology in Egypt and later in Palestine, and his detailed methodological approach continues to shape the discipline today.

Petrie worked at more sites, with greater speed, than any modern archaeologist: seeing his life as a mission of rescue archaeology, Petrie aimed to retrieve as much information as possible from sites that were shrinking dramatically in size as Egypt modernised during the late 19th and early 20th centuries. He published a large part, but not all, of the finds from his excavations in his illustrated typological volumes, arranged according to object types and themes. Today, much of the Petrie Museum's collection is displayed and stored in a way which reflects these publications: for example, several storage cupboards are dedicated to the material illustrated in the 'Objects of Daily Use' volume, and objects in the drawers are arranged according to the order of the published plates. This offers a unique opportunity for researchers to engage with Petrie's typological and methodical approach to archaeology, as well as with the history of museum collections.

The first catalogue to be published in the *Modern Egyptology* series was *Amarna: City of Akhenaten and Nefertiti* in 1972 by Julia Samson, Petrie Museum Honorary Research Assistant. As official publishers to the UCL Egyptology Department the series went on to produce facsimile reprints of eight of Flinders Petrie's most important site reports and many of his object catalogues, originally published through the British School of Archaeology in Egypt. The substantial annual royalties from these reprints were paid into the 'Petrie Fund' at the time, which provided special grants to students in financial need.

In many ways, the new reprints of this classic series can be seen as the latest layer in a vast 'publication stratigraphy' of the thousands of finds from Flinders Petrie's excavations, which now live in museum collections around the world. On reading these volumes, I hope that readers will also be inspired to learn more about the Petrie Museum collection and its fascinating history.

Dr Anna Garnett
Petrie Museum of Egyptian and Sudanese Archaeology,
University College London
January 2023

PUBLISHER'S PREFACE

Oxbow Books is pleased to present this title in our *Classics in Egyptology* series. This series of facsimile re-issues is comprised of two sub-series. The first consists of 16 typological catalogues produced by W.M. Flinders Petrie based on his massive collection of Egyptian artefacts. Mostly excavated by Petrie during many seasons of campaign in the last years of the 19th and early decades of the 20th century, they now reside in the Petrie Museum at University College London. Published between 1898 and 1937 and long out of print, the catalogues were re-issued in facsimile by publishers Aris and Phillips in the 1970s. These were followed in the next 15 years or so by publication of a number of newly commissioned titles, based on more recent examination of elements of the Petrie Collection by contemporary experts, under the name *Modern Egyptology*. A selection of these additional titles forms the second component of our own series.

The archaeology of Egypt continues to fascinate. Multi-disciplinary investigation and research continues unabated, encompassing methodologies, scientific and data processing techniques, theoretical approaches, and even whole paradigms that were unheard of in the 1970s and undreamt of when Petrie was working in Egypt. Yet all the titles included in this series continue to be invaluable sources of basic data, providing an unparalleled resource that can easily be cross-referenced with the actual materials they describe and discuss. They remain within the Petrie Collection where they may be accessed and re-examined as new research flourishes. As historic documents, the Petrie catalogues stand as exemplars of the craft of typological classification, the backbone of modern archaeology – much of which, though refined by absolute dating and another 100 years of research, still stands the test of time.

A note on presentation

The facsimile titles of Petrie's catalogues re-issued in the 1970s were produced from scans of the original publications. Scanning technology at that time was not of the standard or resolution of today. The scans are no longer available, nor has it been possible to obtain, and in doing so destroy, original copies of the Petrie catalogues. These titles have therefore, of necessity, been rescanned from the 1970s re-issues. Where necessary the pages have been digitally enhanced for clarity of reading and to ensure the good quality of the plates, though inevitably a few are not of the standard we might wish, because of the quality of the previous scan, and occasional blocks of text are not precisely 'straight' or evenly situated on the page. However, some pages in the 1970s re-issues had been inserted in the wrong order and this has been corrected. The originals were produced at a folio size. The pages have been reduced slightly to standard A4 for ease of shelving and because this has the effect of slightly improving the scanned images. In some cases, illustrations were presented to scale and the original scale is given on the plate. There were also no digital files available for titles included in the *Modern Egyptology* series, so these too have been scanned from printed copies.

SCARABS

INTRODUCTION

1. THE little amulets of beetle form, which are the most usual production of Egyptian art, have fascinated the amateur collector for a century past, but have not yet fully received the scientific attention which is due to them. The most obviously interesting class of them are those with names of kings, of the royal family, and of officials. These carry with them in most cases a dating, which fixes their historical position. They stand thus to Egyptian history much as coins stand in relation to Western history. They often add historical matter which is otherwise lost to us; and the style of their art and manufacture serves as an index to the changes which went on in the civilisation. In the present volume we only deal with the scarabs —at University College—which bear names; and to these are added the cylinders, plaques, and other small objects with names, as they are closely similar in work, and stand on the same footing. In another volume the scarabs of other kinds will be dealt with; but their dating must depend mainly on comparison with the styles of those here described.

2. At first sight it might be supposed that the subject was boundless, when looking at the hundreds of scarabs that lie in the Cairo shops. But this is far from being the case. The named scarabs are only a small proportion of the whole, and the greater part of those are of Thothmes III. Any one can form a collection of that king's scarabs in a year or two, as readily as of coins of Constantine, and very few of them would be of any interest. To acquire the variety of different periods, and the rarer names, needs a very long search. When I first went to Egypt I used to buy about a hundred name-scarabs each year, and only included those of Thothmes III which were of interest. Latterly about thirty each year is all that I can get that are worth having.

So far from the subject being boundless, there are only about 300 different kings and royal relatives who are thus commemorated on scarabs, cylinders, and seals. Of that 300, there are at University College over 240 different royal persons, about 150 at the British Museum, about 90 in Paris, 70 in Cairo, and various minor selections in other museums. Thus the collection here described is by far the most varied in its range; and in order to make the view more complete, drawings are here inserted of the scarabs, cylinders, etc., of persons not represented in this collection.

Turning to the total numbers of scarabs, cylinders, rings, and plaques with royal names, the limits of the subject are also well in view. Apart from the overwhelming commonness of Thothmes III's objects, there are rather over 5,000 named objects in all the public collections together. Of these there are over 1,600 in this collection; the same in the British Museum, about 300 in Paris, and fewer in Cairo and elsewhere. Practically a third are here, a third in Bloomsbury, and a third in all the rest of the museums. Thus the subject is quite within reach, and can be dealt with tolerably completely, with this catalogue and that of the British Museum. Of course there are many scattered in private hands, and some collections of note; but it is seldom that much of importance is seen on going over such gatherings. In stating this, the scarabs and seals with private names are not included, as they are not so fully published for comparison. They form, however, only a small minority of the whole, probably not 5 per cent. of the name-scarabs in most collections, and generally much less. There are about 330 in this collection, and a little over a hundred in the British Museum, but no other collection has more than a few dozen.

A considerable part of the illustrations were prepared, more than a dozen years ago, from photographs by Mr. Nash; this unfortunately has entailed a loss, as the cost of blocks was then double of the present amount. The drawings of backs were also partly done then, and the classification of the types. In the last two years the collection—now largely increased—has been worked up to date, and the text completed, and rearranged to suit the present form of publication. In this manner the illustrations and catalogue are always together, while the advantage of finer paper for the figures is obtained.

CHAPTER I

RELIGIOUS ASPECT OF THE SCARAB

3. THAT various kinds of beetle were venerated in Egypt from prehistoric times is clearly proved, both from the preserved animals, and from the images of them. So far back as S.D. 53, in the earlier part of the second prehistoric civilisation, two jars in a grave contained numerous dried beetles (grave B 328, *Diospolis*). Rather later, in S.D. 66, a grave (B 234) contained a jar with scarab beetles. Of the same age another grave (B 217) contained a jar with dozens of large desert beetles, and an immense quantity of small beetles. Another grave, undated (B 17), had thirty-six beetles in a jar.

Not only are the dried animals thus found, but the intention with which they were buried is vouched for, by the models of beetles pierced to be worn as amulets. At Naqadeh two beetles of green serpentine were found, of prehistoric age, copied from the long bright green beetle now found living in the Sudan (*Naqada*, lviii). Other beetles of the same kind cut in sard, and one in crystal, have been found in graves at Tarkhan, about S.D. (Sequence Date) 77–8. In another grave (1552), of S.D. 77, was a group of amulets with two desert beetles cut in opaque green serpentine. Of S.D. 77 also, was a translucent green serpentine beetle found in the lowest level of the town of Abydos (*Ab.* i, li, 7). Slightly later, but before the ist dynasty, was another long beetle found in the temple of Abydos (*Ab.* ii, xiv, 282). Of S.D. 78, just before Mena, there is the most striking instance of a reliquary case, to be worn as a charm, made of alabaster in the form of the true *Scarabaeus sacer* (grave 27, *Tarkhan I*, iii, 4, xiv, 19). About the time of King Den (S.D. 81) in a grave at Tarkhan (120) was a jar containing many large desert beetles. Passalacqua found the *Buprestis* beetle embalmed at Thebes. The variety of beetles here mentioned, beside the commonly recognised *scarabaeus*, is what is to be expected, as we find that four other genera are clearly copied in the scarabs of later times, and are alluded to in papyri for magical use.

4. What then must we conclude as to the Egyptian view of the beetle, before the engraving of designs upon it? It was certainly sacred or venerated, as shown by the many amulets, and especially the amulet case or reliquary in the form of *Scarabaeus sacer*. It was, by the same examples, certainly worn as an amulet. This being the case, we have no right to dissociate it from the very primitive idea which we find connected with it in later times, that the sun is the big ball rolled across the heaven by the Creator, and hence the scarab is an emblem of the Creator, Khepera. The scarab is figured with the disc of Ra in its claws in the xiith, xviiith, and later dynasties. Such a symbolism is assuredly primitive, and would not arise after the anthropomorphic gods filled the religion of Egypt; moreover Khepera is called "the Father of the Gods" (LANZONE, *D. Mit.* cccxxx). This symbolism of the beetle is a part of the primaeval animal worship of Egypt. The idea of the word *Kheper* is "being," existence, creation, or becoming; and the god Khepera is the self-existent creator-god.

On turning from the material remains to the inscriptions, we find that the importance of the scarab emblem was transferred from the Creator to the soul which is to be united to him. In the Pyramid texts it is said, "This Unas flieth like a bird and alighteth like a beetle upon the throne which is empty in thy boat, O Ra." Teta is said to "live like the scarab." Pepy is "the son of the scarab which is born in Hotept."

The scarab also passed to the other gods as a creative emblem. Ptah Sokar has the scarab on his head; so also Ka, "father of the gods," has a scarab on his frog's head. Horapollo refers to Ptah having a scarab.

5. We are now in a position to see the Egyptian idea which underlay the immense popularity of this form in historic times. We need not suppose that the original amuletic purpose and theologic allusion ruled entirely; mere habit of association was perhaps all that was commonly in the thoughts. We know how in Christian times the cross was popularised, and was used so incessantly that at last a higher value had to be attached to the emblem by forming the crucifix, in order to renew the solemnity of it. In somewhat the same spirit, after the scarab had become too familiar in common use, it was resanctified in the xviiith dynasty by being carved in a very large size, with a purely religious text upon it, and placed in a frame upon the breast of the dead. On this frame it is often shown as adored by Isis and Nebhat. It is said to be the heart of Isis, who was the mother of the

dead person, thus identified with Horus: to be the heart which belonged to the transformations or becomings of his future life, in order to give soundness to his limbs; and to be the charm which should ensure his justification in the judgment. Such were the high religious aspects of the scarab in the later times, removing it from the almost contemptuous familiarity to which it had been degraded, as the vehicle of seals and petty ornament.

On passing to the xxiiird dynasty and later, we see the winged scarab placed on the breast of the mummy, as the emblem of the Creator who should transform the dead; and associated always with the four sons of Horus, as guardians of special parts of the body.

From this time, and specially from the xxvith to the xxxth dynasties, many scarabs were placed on the mummy, usually a row of half a dozen or more, along with figures of the gods. Such scarabs are almost always carved with the legs beneath, and are never inscribed.

On reaching gnostic times we see on amulets three scarabs in a row, as emblems of the Trinity, with three hawks as souls of the just before them, and three crocodiles, three snakes, etc., as souls of the wicked driven away behind them (see *Amulets*, 135). Thus the function of the scarab as emblem of the Creator Khepera was transferred, and it became in triple group the emblem of the Trinity.

6. Turning to the documents of that age, there are descriptions which throw much light on the way in which it was venerated. Pliny says of the scarabaeus, " The people of a great part of Egypt worship those insects as divinities; an usage for which Apion gives a curious reason, asserting as he does, by way of justifying the rites of his nation, that the insect in its operations pictures the revolution of the sun " (xxx, 30). Horapollo (i, 10) explains this allusion, saying that the scarab " rolls the ball from east to west, looking himself toward the east. Having dug a hole, he buries it in it for twenty-eight days; on the twenty-ninth day he opens the ball, and throws it into the water, and from it the scarabaei come forth." This description applies to the most usual place for the scarabaeus insect, the western desert edge. There we may frequently see the scarab rolling its ball toward the rise of sand to bury it, and holding it between the hind legs, pushing backward with its face to the east. The same description is given by Plutarch (*Isis and Osiris*, 74).

There was regard for various kinds of beetles in Roman times, as previously on the carved scarabs, and the prehistoric amulets. Pliny (xxx, 30) says, " There is also another kind of scarabaeus which the magicians recommend to be worn as an amulet—the one which has small horns thrown backward. A third kind also, known by the name of *fullo*, and covered with white spots, they recommend to be cut asunder and attached to either arm." This method of use is described in the Demotic Magical Papyrus (xxi, 18); " you divide it down the middle with a bronze knife . . . take its left half . . . and bind them to your left arm."

Horapollo (i, 10) states, " There are three species of beetles. One has the form of a cat, and is radiated, which is called a symbol of the sun . . . the statue of the deity of Heliopolis having the form of a cat, and the scarab has also thirty fingers like the thirty days of the month.

" The second species is two-horned, and has the form of a bull, which is consecrated to the moon.

" The third species is unicorn, and has a peculiar form which is referred to Hermes like the Ibis."

This third species is evidently the *Hypselogenia*, which has a long beak in front; this seems to have been compared to the long beak of the ibis, and hence was referred to Tehuti. Of the two-horned scarab there is a bronze figure in the British Museum; it may be that known to us as the stag beetle. To the cat-shaped beetle we have no clue; from being put first it may be supposed to be the *Scarabaeus*.

Another account of varieties is in the Demotic Magical Papyrus (xxi, 10), where for a love-potion " you take a fish-faced (?) scarab, this scarab being small and having no horn, it wearing three plates on the front of its head, you find its face thin (?) outwards—or again that which bears two horns."

Whatever may be the modern equivalents of these various descriptions, it is certainly evident that five or six different kinds of beetles were all venerated, and used for their magical properties.

7. We have now seen that the scarab and other beetles were regarded as sacred or magical, from the earlier part of the second prehistoric age down to the Christian period. The religious texts that we have of the vth, vith, xviiith, and xixth dynasties all refer to it as an emblem of the Creator-God, as a symbol and guarantee of his assistance to the deceased, or as an emblem of the apotheosis of the deceased. In the xiith dynasty this emblem

came into common use, and served as a seal, doubtless owing to the name of the person being placed on it, to ensure that its powers should be given to him. Just as the use of the divination arrows drifted down into the vulgarisation of gaming cards, or the cross became used for various unseemly purposes, so the personal amulet of the scarab became treated commonly as the seal for everyday use. This did not however prevent the symbol being most generally employed with a religious significance.

The purely utilitarian view of the scarab as a seal was true enough in some instances; but the facts of its actual use show that this was not the main purpose, even if we had not the use of it vouched for as a sacred amulet in the earliest, as in the latest, times. In the first place, the scarabs were originally nearly all coated with glaze, which has since perished from the majority, leaving the lines clear. But, when the glaze remains, we see that a large part of the lines were so filled with glaze that no impression could be taken from them. As to the actual use for sealing, we know of very few instances of such except in the xiith dynasty; hardly any scarab sealings of the xviiith to xxvith dynasties are found, although scarabs were commonest at that age. For signets it would be required that the name and title of the person should appear, as on many that are known. Yet such name-scarabs of private persons are very rare, except in the Middle Kingdom, and even these are but a small minority of all that were made. Further, those with kings' names are, in some cases, later than the rulers whom they name, and could not therefore be used for official seals, but must refer to the claim on the protection afforded by the deceased king to the wearer, like the medals of saints worn by the devout.

A somewhat similar change of usage is seen in the cylinders of the late prehistoric age. Though cut in one of the softest materials, black steatite, it is seldom that they show any wear. They can never have been carried on the person in most cases; the few that have been so used are so much worn as to be scarcely legible, and even hard scarabs of later times show much wear if they have been carried on the finger, owing to the prevailing grit and sand. The subjects generally engraved on the cylinders bear this out, as in the earlier classes they are seldom titles. The usual subjects shown are the seated figure with a table of offerings—as on Memphite tomb steles subsequently, or the *aakhu* bird, emblem of the soul—as on Abydan grave steles subsequently. Names of gods are also usual. Apart then from any question of the reading of these cylinders, the subjects show that they are funerary in character. The absence of wear upon them shows that they were not usually carried during life, but were engraved to place as amulets with the dead. Thus the cylinder—like the scarab—was essentially an amulet, and usually for the dead. Subsequently the titles were added, and then the cylinder developed in the ist dynasty into an article of daily affairs. We should note the contrast that while hundreds or thousands of impressions of the business cylinders are known, but scarcely a single actual cylinder; yet, on the contrary, over a hundred early cylinders of the funerary type are known, but not a single impression of such. The complete contrast of usage shows that the early cylinders were entirely different in purpose to the business cylinders of the ist dynasty and onward.

CHAPTER II

THE VARIETIES OF SCARABS

8. WE have already seen that the Egyptian fully recognised several varieties of beetle, all included in the sacred class. Both among the animals preserved, and among the different kinds described by authors, the variation is unquestionable. When we turn to the artificial figures of scarabs, we find a similar variety. Not only are there great differences in the workmanship, and in the attempt at imitating nature, but the models that were followed were clearly quite distinct.

Having started from many varying models the conventional types naturally tended to become confused and parts copied from different genera were mixed together. In the same way the Egyptians mixed elements of the papyrus and lotus together in their architectural forms. To gain any rational classification of the various types, it is necessary to follow the various genera separately. Yet this must not be done slavishly; as, owing to the mixture of forms, it is often needful to follow some one detail as a means of clear classification, even though it may run across two or three genera.

The designs of scarabs are generally unique. Common as may be the scarabs of any one king, yet it is very seldom that an exact duplicate can be found of the name and titles. The backs are equally varied, and seldom will a drawing of one scarab represent a second specimen efficiently. It is only when endeavouring to make a set of type drawings for reference, that the extreme variety of detail can be realised.

One of the first considerations in arranging any scheme of classification of types for reference, is that the critical points shall be clear and quickly settled, so as to be able to run down any type to its right place for identification as soon as possible. For this purpose all distinctly different elements must be brought forward, while keeping the natural differences of genera as much as possible in use.

9. In order to clear up the questions, it proved needful to work over the scarabaei and allied beetles in the Natural History Museum, South Kensington, and to draw from those for the frontispiece, as there is no efficient publication of these genera. Not only the form but also the distribution must be taken into account; it is useless to compare forms that are unknown in the Old World, but South- and Central-African genera may well have been known in Egypt, looking at the great zoological recession from North Africa in historic times.

It appeared that the varieties of form could not be accounted for without recognizing five genera (see Frontispiece). The main genus is the generally recognized *scarabaeus*—classes E to N—with a serrated clypeus, and a usually lunate head. The species *Scarabaeus venerabilis* is marked by ribbed elytra, see pl. lxxiii, 13, 16. A definitely square head seems to belong to *Catharsius*, classes S, T, the next most common genus. Occasionally the clypeus extends far back in a pointed form over the head, apparently imitated from the horn of the *Copris*, U. The presence of marked side notches, turning in above the elytra and then downwards, is characteristic of *Gymnopleurus*, V, W; and probably the deep collar where the head joins the pro-thorax, belongs to the same. Lastly, a long beak is probably copied from *Hypselogenia*, classes X, Y.

10. The details of workmanship which may also serve for distinctions are: (1) the feather pattern on the edge to imitate the hairy legs; (2) the head of lunate form, or (3) deep form, or (4) merging into the clypeus; (5) notched clypeus; (6) smooth clypeus; (7) V-shaped marks at the top of the elytra; (8) curling lines on back.

On the basis of these various distinctions twenty-three classes may be formed, which can almost always be quickly distinguished so as to find any given type. (See plates lix to lxxi, where all the varieties of form are drawn.) The types are classified as follows:

			General range.	
With legs on underside (not in this catalogue)				A, B
Feathered legs		fore and aft	X—XIII	C
		one way only	X—XV	D
Scarabaeus	V notches on elytra	lunate head	XVIII—XXVI	E
		deep head	XVIII—XXV	F
		merging	XVIII—XXV	G
	notched clypeus	lunate	V—XIX	H
		deep	XI—XIII	J
		merging	XI—XXVI	K
	smooth clypeus	lunate	III—XXV	L
		deep	IX—XVIII	M
		merging	IV—XXV	N
Scarabaeus venerabilis, ribbed elytra			XIX, XX	O
Scarabaeus ? ribbed head			XXV, XXVI	P
Curl on back			XII—XXV	Q
Quadruped heads, and peculiarities			XIX—XXV	R
Catharsius		square head	XII—XIII	S
		A head	XIII—XVI	T
Copris			XIII—XVI	U
Gymnopleurus		side notch	XVIII—XXV	V
		collar	V—XXVI	W
Hypselogenia		regular	XII—XVIII	X
		modified	VI—XVIII	Y
Scaraboids				Z

11. It may seem surprising that such a variety of types should have had so long a range of use. We might have expected that only a few types would have been fashionable in one age, and would not have recurred later. Yet there can be no question that six of these types were usual from the xiith to the xxvth dynasties at least; while on good grounds some of them, as we shall see, go back to the Old Kingdom. With such ranges of date commonly over thirteen dynasties, it is evident that vague statements of resemblance between a given scarab and others of a known date are of

no value. The only way to reach results for discriminating dates, is to look for any characteristics of workmanship—often quite trivial—which are only found over a short range of time. The general type is not a question of date but of locality.

Some types with a short range are already clear. The scarabaeus with feathered sides for the legs belongs only to the xth to xiiith dynasties; limited to the front or to the back legs, it was in use till the xvth dynasty. The Catharsius head begins in the middle of the xiith, and extends down to the xiiith and xvith dynasties respectively. Another of short range is the Copris, which only belongs to the Hyksos age, xiiith to xvith dynasties. The Hypselogenia is rare in the xiith dynasty, and is not found later than Rameses II. Minor details may also have but a brief range; the deep Y outline of the elytra is only found on scarabs of Khofra and Zedra (? Dad-ef-ra); the nearest approach to it is at the close of the xiith, and the xiiith dynasties, but that is less deep, and the form of the head and clypeus is then different. The palm-branch pattern on the back, in Class J, is only known from late xith to xivth dynasties, and in a one-sided form in the xvith. The curling lines on the back, Class Q, begin at the end of the xiith dynasty, and end in the xxvth. It is in tracing the limits of such distinctions as these that progress may be made in dating scarabs, and hence in fixing the age of burials which have no kings' names.

12. On examining the various small differences statistically, some strong preferences for certain types are found in some periods, though not exclusively of one age. The notch marks on classes E, F, G, vary in form. The V or I line from the girdle line (as E·7, E·28) is early and continues late. The V from the girdle to the side line (as E·9) begins in the xiith dynasty. The diagonal line from the girdle to the side (as E·4) begins under Thothmes III. The loop on the girdle (as E·17 and F·20) does not begin till Rameses II.

The number of lines in the girdle, or in the division of the wing cases, is not exclusively characteristic of age; but certain types prevail at different times. One girdle line and two or three vertical, and two girdle with two vertical lines, prevail in the Middle Kingdom. Two girdle lines with one vertical is chiefly of Old Kingdom and Saite ages. The double girdle with three vertical lines is mainly of xxist to xxvth dynasties.

13. The local sources of smooth and lined backs may be examined by various tests. On separating the *bati khetm* from the *deshert khetm*, there is presumably a local separation of Upper and Lower Egyptian scarabs. The numbers are:

Total.		Smooth.	Per cent.
8	*bati khetm*	1 =	13
22	*deshert khetm*	16	73

These percentages—as we shall see below—are the same as 13 per cent. of smooth backs in the xviii–xixth dynasties, mainly Theban, and 77 per cent. smooth backs in the Hyksos period, mainly Delta.

Another test is the use of names compounded with Sebek, that god belonging to the Fayum, Manfalut, Silsileh, Ombos, and Syene, but not prominently to the Delta. Of such scarabs, presumably of Upper Egypt, there are—

Total.		Smooth.	Per cent.
13	Sebek names	1 =	8

Another test is that of Amen names, also presumably Upper Egyptian, there are—

Total.		Smooth.	Per cent.
7	Amen names	0 =	0

Taking now the general review of the numbers of smooth backs in each of the main periods, there are in—

Dynasties.	Total.	Lines.	Smooth.	Per cent.
iiird to viith	33	21	12 =	36
ixth to xith	40	21	19	47
xiith to xivth	316	196	120	38
xvth to xviith	86	20	66	77
xviiith	350	306	44	13
xixth	165	143	22	13
xxth	51	38	13	25
xxist to xxiiird	83	59	24	29
xxivth to xxvth	86	71	15	17
xxvith to xxxth	55	48	7	13

It is obvious that the xvth to xviith dynasties were the special period of Delta scarabs, there being practically none then of Upper Egyptian rulers, and most or all of the scarabs coming from the Delta. This is the period when smooth backs are far commoner than at any other time. On the other hand the period of special Theban importance, the xviiith and xixth dynasties, has a smaller number of smooth backs than any other age. It seems, however, that smooth backs decrease in the later periods, regardless of locality, as the Ethiopian period at Thebes and the Saite in the Delta hardly differ in the proportion.

As a whole we must conclude that until the late times the smooth back was the product of the Delta, and the lined back that of Upper Egypt.

Another feature is the crescent line on the head, usually on about one in thirty of all periods; but on one in eight of scarabs in the Ethiopian and Saite age.

The ribbed head, P, is very rare in the xviiith and xixth dynasties, about 1 per cent.; the only other age of it is in the xxvth and xxvith, when it appears on one-quarter and one-third of the scarabs, and is the commonest type of all. The square Catharsius head, S, is the commonest type in the xiith and xiiith dynasties, appearing on one-fifth of all. The pointed Catharsius is scarcely found outside of the xiiith to xvith dynasties; it is on one-sixth of the xiiith dynasty and on two-thirds of the xvith. Type U, which is similar, is only found in the xiiith and xvith, with a stray example in the xviiith.

The form of the girdle line, and its junction with the vertical, has many varieties, but they seem to have been used more or less through all periods. On the whole there was a far more continual usage of varied types than might have been expected. General impressions are only of use as suggestions for research; the conclusions here are from tabulating every well-marked difference throughout the whole collection.

14. For the sake of ready comparison of scarabs with the plates lix to lxxi, the system of arrangement should be here explained. From the preceding table it will be seen that the points on a scarab back to be successively noted are as follows:

(1) If legs are feathered at side. If so, then C on the whole length, or D on the back legs only. If not feathered, then

(2) By the head distinguish scarabaeus E–N, *S. venerabilis* with ribbed elytra O, ribbed head P, curl lines on back Q; wide legs or mammalian heads R, square heads, A-head T; Copris U; Gymnopleurus side notch V, or collar W; Hypselogenia X, or modified Y; Scaraboids without animal pattern Z.

(3) If scarabaeus, then with V notches on girdle (E-G), or with clypeus notched (H–K) or smooth (L–N): and each class divided into three according as the head is lunate, or parallel-sided, or merging into the clypeus.

After thus discriminating the class, each class is subdivided into sections as follow:

C and D, being small classes, are grouped by the form of the head, in the order of the different genera. E is divided by inner crescent on head 2–29, Λ on head 32–40, double lines for eye 42–49, single line for eye 52–64, plain deep head 67–78, lunate head 80–98. F is divided by inner crescent on head, 1–9 double eye, single, or none; angular head 11–19—eye, or none; slope-sided head 20–30—eye, or none; square head 31–53—double lines for eye, single, or none; barred head 55–67—double lines, single, or none; long head 69–99—double, single, or no eye, and in order of length. G in order from widest base to narrowest base for head. H in order of inner crescent on head; double line eye; single line; plain curved head from deep to shallow. J in order of inner crescent; double line eye, single line, on sloping head; double line, single, or no line, on square head; barred squared; long head with double, single, or no eye lines. K hour-glass head, wide below, equal, round eyes with straight clypeus, sides sloping more to end with narrow base. L in order of E. M sloping-sided head; square head; long head with square eyes, round eyes, or no eyes. N hour-glass head, wide below, rounded eye, equally divided, round clypeus, head proceeding to narrower base. P back lines increasing in number. T, U, complex forms, see key at the foot of the plates.

By following the regular order of discrimination an example can be run down to the nearest drawing in much less than a minute. The range of date of each type is marked by giving the reference to the examples in the form of dynasty number, king number, figure number; thus 18·6·47 means xviiith dynasty, 6th king (Thothmes III), 47th scarab of the king. This mode of numbering serves to show at once the date of the example. In the case of private scarabs, or kings that are undated, they are grouped together in periods and designated by the dynasty number and a letter as, 12 R, or 30 AM. If the reign is approximately known (as by style in the xviiith dynasty) the king's number is also included, as, 18·6·c. Thus the numbers give an indication of the age, and the letter distinguishes the example, and shows that it is not precisely dated.

CHAPTER III

THE MAKING OF SCARABS

Materials

15. THE usual material is variously termed stea-schist, fibrous steatite, or schist. It varies in quality from a smooth, translucent steatite to a hard, fibrous schist. All kinds have the valuable property of being superficially hardened by the fusion of a glaze over the surface; thus after the coat of glaze has entirely decomposed and perished, the face of the stone remains glass-hard. The result seems to be due to part of the magnesia of the stone combining with the silica of the glaze, thus changing the surface from soft soapstone to hard magnesia-hornblende. This material is so general for scarabs that it is not specified separately to each in the catalogue; so, where only a colour is named, it means glaze of that colour upon a steatite or schist body.

16. Various other materials were occasionally used for scarabs; the dynasties in which I have observed examples are here stated after each material. Clear quartz crystal is rarely used (xiith, xxvith); white quartz rock is also rare (xith); blue glazing on quartz was made in the prehistoric age and onward, and used for scarabs (in xiith); translucent green quartz is very rare (xxiiird); chalcedony is very rare (xixth) and agate was seldom used (xxvith); amethyst began to be used in xth or xith, but is nearly all of xiith, and rarely of xixth.

Carnelian began to be used in xiith, but is most usual in xviiith and xixth. Jasper of various colours was employed; red in xixth, yellow in xviiith and xxvith, green in xith, xiith, brown in xiith and xxvith, and black in xith, xiith, xviiith.

Felspar was usually green, and its source is as yet unknown. It has no relation to beryl or "mother of emerald," with which it is often confused. It was used in xith, xiith, xviiith, xxvith. Red felspar was used in xiith, xixth. Beryl or emerald is unknown in scarabs, and was only worked after the cessation of scarab making.

Black obsidian was a favourite material for fine work in xiith, but is very rare later (xixth). Diorite is rare (xith, xiith). Peridot occurs once (xviiith). Serpentine was occasionally used, and is mainly late. Black steatite was the usual material for early cylinders, down to the vth dynasty, and sometimes later (xviiith to xxiind). This is the natural colour of the stone, and is not due to smoke, as has been strangely supposed. Jade was used for large heart scarabs (xixth), but seldom—if ever—for small name-scarabs. As the use of this material has been doubted, it should be said that it has been mineralogically identified by all tests, especially specific gravity. Basalt was rarely used, the brown kind is seen in the cylinder of Khufu. What is usually termed "green basalt" is really a metamorphic volcanic mud, much like slate in composition but not in fracture; as there is no recognised name for it, I have termed it Durite (in *Amulets*). This is very usual for heart scarabs, but too dull and coarse usually for the more delicate cutting of small scarabs.

Lazuli was known from the prehistoric age, but seldom used for engraving; scarabs and amulets of it occur in xiith, xviiith, xixth, xxvth, and xxvith. Turquoise is very rare in scarabs, though it was a staple material in jewellery of the xiith dynasty. It has no connection with malachite (which has been confounded with it owing to both occurring in Sinai); of the latter I have only seen one scarab, uninscribed. Haematite was very rarely used for engraving, probably always under Syrian influence.

Limestones were favourite materials in late times, the hard coloured varieties, green, yellow, red, and brown, appearing in the Saite ages. The pure calcite, or Iceland spar, was far too soft for wear (though called "glass-hard" in a recent work), and it only occurs in a cylinder of Pepy, filled with blue paste, and here (18·9·166) in a large bead of queen Taiy. It was used for beads in xxiind, xxiiird. Shelly brown limestone occurs in about xth dynasty, and xviiith.

Of metals, gold scarabs rarely appear in xviiith, and inscribed gold plates were applied to plain stone scarabs in xiith. Silver appears for scarabs in xiith (scroll patterns), xviiith (silver plate of Akhenaten) and xxvith (Shepenapt). Bronze is very unusual, but there is one here of xxth.

17. Glass first appears as a light blue imitation of turquoise, used for an *uzat* of Amenhetep I; after that, clear blue and opaque violet glass scarabs appear in xviiith, and dark blue glass in xixth.

A rich Prussian blue transparent glass was used about xxiiird, and on to Persian times. Glazing was the most usual surface for scarabs, of all colours, as stated in this catalogue throughout. The blue glazes were very liable to fade away to white under the influence of damp; the green glazes, which contain some iron, decompose to brown of varying depth, which is the commonest appearance of scarabs. Coloured paste begins in the xiith as light blue, hard and finely finished. It is darker in xviiith, xixth, and very common as a soft paste in xxvith. A soft yellow paste was also usual in xxvith.

Pottery scarabs were made of the usual siliceous paste, bound together by a coat of glaze; they were incised in the xiith and xxvith, but often moulded in xviiith, xixth. Under Saptah they were made in two moulds, back and face; the groove for the hole was cut, and the two halves joined together, and united in the glazing. Ushabtis were also made in the same way.

Wood is very rare; but there is a large wooden scarab here (12·2·5), a wooden seal (12·5·13), and a delicate scroll-pattern seal of hard wood (all xiith). Fossil wood is once found used for a scarab (xixth?). Amber was rarely used, but two scarabs (U.C.) which are uninscribed will be published with the nameless scarabs.

Engraving

18. Though the surface of steatite is rendered glass-hard by the action of glaze being fused upon it, the interior of the mass is quite unaltered by the heat to which it has been subjected. On broken scarabs and objects it is found that an ordinary bronze needle of the xviiith dynasty can cut into the steatite freely; on the schist it is more difficult to work, the siliceous particles glint the metal, but yet lines can be cut with sufficient ease. There is therefore no question about the cutting of all the stea-schist scarabs; bronze in the xviiith dynasty, hardened copper in the earlier ages, and possibly flint splinters, would readily do the work.

The question of the hard stones is quite different. We know certainly that sawing and drilling of granite with copper tools and emery was practised on the largest scale in the ivth dynasty. Copper and emery were familiar materials from prehistoric times, and such would suffice for dealing with all the materials used for scarabs. The forms of the tools can only be inferred from the results, as no such tools have been found.

19. Nearly half a century ago an article on "Antique Gems" in the *Edinburgh Review* (Oct. 1866), debated when the wheel was first used for gem engraving. The opinion that its work begins to appear under Domitian was questioned, and the evidence of the stork of Dexamenos was quoted in favour of dating the wheel a few centuries earlier. When we here turn to the evidence of Egypt, we see that the question is of thousands, not hundreds, of years.

We may start from the onyx bearing a head of Ptolemy Soter (?), which is clearly cut with the wheel, and we may see it also plainly used under Shabaka on lazuli (25·3·14), as under Amenardas (25·2·6); along with the drill on green quartz (23·H), with the ball drill on jasper under Usarken I (22·2·1); on jade heart scarabs (*Ab.* 20, 21); on large durite heart scarabs (*Ab.* 7, 8, 9); on jasper of Rameses X (20·8·5); on jasper of Rameses II (19·3·37); on sard of Amenhetep III (18·9·101); on black jasper of Tehutmes IV (18·8·13); on black granite of Tehutmes III (18·6·129); on black jasper of Tetanefer (18·6 B); on carnelian of Hotshepsut (18·5·10); on blue glass of Amenhetep I (18·2·15); on brown jasper of Meny (12 A E); and most brilliantly shown on the earliest example, a private scarab of Onkhy son of Mentuemhot (10 M) in green jasper, probably of the xith dynasty, certainly not later than the xiith.

20. Side by side with this there was the older system of graving with a hard point, and scraping out lines; also sawing out lines with copper edge fed with emery, and grinding holes with a point and emery. Beginning with the earliest, we see the hard point scraper and the emery saw on the crystal of Aha (1·2); the point graver on the diorite of Khosekhemui (2·9). The Khufu cylinder of basalt (4·2·5) shows the use of a hard point graver, and a pecking out of the bases of the hollows; similar pecking can be made on this material with a quartz crystal point, which was therefore probably the tool used. On the chert slab of Assa (5·8·3) a point graver was used, probably fed with emery. The jasper scarabs of the xth dynasty (10 C, 10 G) show a hard point scraper. In the xith dynasty the amethyst scarabs (10 T, U), quartz (10 H), and green felspar (10 L) show a point, with both scraping and graving action. The obsidian scarabs of the xiith dynasty were not cut by the wheel, but by a copper edge-tool fed with emery, and a scraping point, perhaps of rock crystal. The jasper cylinder

of Khondy—probably made by a Syrian—shows a point scraper to have been used. When we reach the xviiith dynasty, the point only appears on softer stones, as the limestone pebble of Sataoh (18·2·55), and the wheel was universal for hard stones. It seems then that the older graver and scraper overlapped the use of the wheel, from the xith to the xivth dynasty; while before that the point alone, and after that the wheel alone, were used on the harder stones.

What mechanical arrangement the Egyptian had for the wheel cutter is not known. Probably it was developed from the bow drill, and would be on a vertical axis worked by a bow.

CHAPTER IV

THE EARLY CYLINDERS

(PLATES I–VII)

21. THE early cylinders of black steatite have been hitherto neglected, because they belong to a stage of the writing when the recognised canons had not yet become fully regulated; and they need to be studied by inter-comparison, rather than by the same rules as the developed inscriptions. The present renderings given here are only a first attempt; and for the detailed reasons of the readings, reference should be made to the preliminary articles in *Ancient Egypt*, 1914, pp. 61–77, 1915, pp. 78–83.

In order to reach any conclusions, it is needful to have as much material as possible for comparison. The University College Collection already contained by far the largest series of such material; my best thanks are due to the Rev. W. MacGregor, for kindly lending me his cylinders from which I took casts, and also to Mr. Blanchard for supplying me with casts of all his cylinders; thus the two other principal collections are here shown in photographs. Beside these I have drawn all those published by Dr. Reisner from Naga ed Deir, and also obtained many drawings from other sources. Thus there is here practically a *corpus* of such remains, which will enable them to be compared for the first time.

22. The cylinders are classed here under the following divisions: seated figures, phrases, *Aakhu* figures, titles, later phrases, columnar inscriptions, figures, early dynastic titles. These classes are in the apparent order of their origination, but of course they largely overlap in their dating. Within each class the order is that of the apparent date, grouping together those of similar style. As to definite ages for these, there are a few fixed. No. 81, of ivory, is of S.D. 65–76 (*Diospolis*, pl. x), a little before the Tarkhan cemetery and the earliest known kings. No. 56 is of S.D. 78–80, the beginning of the ist dynasty (*El Amrah*, pl. vi, p. 39); this by the style of the band on it carries with it No. 39, which is obviously later in style than the simpler work of most of those on pl. i. No. 95 is dated by the name of King Athet, the third of the 1st dynasty. The more complex and detailed style of the Naga ed Deir cylinders, as 32–35, is well dated by the pottery and stone vases found with them, of S.D. 81, or the middle of the ist dynasty. The dating by the forms of the tombs—on the strength of which several are assigned to the iind dynasty—is dependent on the theory of two forms of tomb not being used simultaneously; the pottery shows conclusively that these tombs are all contemporary, as it continuously changed, and differed from this style in the later period. Thus it seems that the titular cylinders may belong to the ist dynasty; while the religious types, even of advanced forms, are before the ist dynasty, and probably go back to the incoming of the dynastic race. There is no ground for assigning any cylinders to the predynastic race, before dynastic influence entered the country.

The cylinder impressions found in the Royal Tombs of the ist dynasty quite agree with the dates above stated. They are of more advanced style than most of these cylinders, and would quite imply that these were earlier than Mena. They do not serve to explain these, as they are entirely connected with the royal estates and property, whereas these are concerned with private devotion or religious service. The royal sealings are not included in this series, as they do not serve to explain these, and they have been already fully published in *Royal Tombs* i and ii.

23. Before considering the style of inscriptions found on these cylinders, we should glance at the ideas of such an age about language. The early Greek supposed that truths about ideas, and the nature of things, could be reached by arguing over the words by which he expressed himself; he took words as equivalent to thought, whereas we recognise now that they are a very inefficient expression of thought. Looking further back we see that the

historic Egyptian valued words even more; he believed in creation by the word, the greatest of intentions was supposed to take effect only through spoken words; no object really existed without a name, the word gave it reality; plays upon words meant to his mind a hidden connection between the realities named. It is therefore to be expected that in a still earlier stage the word would be still more important; inversions of a word giving different senses, plays upon words, slightly varied repetitions of words, would all be supposed to have special value and meaning. We should expect to find this manipulation of words in any inscriptions which had a religious or magic purpose, in the same manner in which we actually see it upon these cylinders. Another consideration is that in early historic inscriptions the regular position of writing was not yet systematized; on the panels of Hesy, the tombstones at Abydos, and the variations of duplicates of the royal labels, we see that the rules for position were by no means certain. So long as all the elements were there, the value of them was the same in whatever order they stood. Hence the confused arrangement and inversions here seen on the cylinders are only an earlier stage of this unregulated writing which still prevailed in the first two dynasties.

The forms of some of the signs show how remote the usages were from those of even the ist dynasty. The mouth was distinguished sometimes by a side view of it open, showing the teeth, as in Nos. 2, 3, 74. At other times it was shown in front view with the teeth as in Nos. 1, 5, 31, 32, 62, 108A. The hand is shown with all the fingers spread, as in 113, 114. The mat, *p*, is drawn with loose ends, as in 101, 102, instead of a square, as on 132. *Onkh* is very rarely found, as the future life was certain, and only its welfare was prayed for; but it occurs on 123 in a very different form to any known later, with short, wide-spread ends—compare the normal form on a much later style of cylinder, 133.

CHAPTER V

THE OLD KINGDOM

(PLATES VIII–XI)

24. THE question raised by assigning to a later origin all scarabs with names earlier than the xiith dynasty, can best be considered after reviewing the material which exists, and will therefore be discussed in the next chapter.

Pl. viii. The scarabs with the word *Ra·menas* are obviously late, and whether they are intended to commemorate Mena is uncertain. The scarabs reading *Heseptu mäot kheru* are certainly not contemporary, as the signs are corrupt; they may be modern attempts copied from the form in Lepsius, *Todtenbuch*, pl. 53. With Nebkara begin the scarabs which may be contemporary. The second and third here might perhaps be of Ra-neb-kau Khety of the ixth dynasty. The fourth is probably later, by the style.

The square plaque of Khufu (4·2·4) shows the first instance of the winged sun. That next appears over the figure of Unas at Elephantine. There is a sign among the pot-marks of the ist dynasty, which looks as if the winged sun was already designed (*Royal Tombs*, i, xlvii, 169, and perhaps l, 483–485; *R. T.* ii, lvA, 104, etc.).

The cylinder seal (4·2·5) of the great pyramid, is one of the most interesting seals known. It is in perfect condition, carved in the brown basalt which was used largely for building in that reign. The basalt has slightly altered, as it does in the course of ages, and fine fissures vein the surface. These fissures are the absolute guarantee of antiquity, as they isolate portions of the signs, which could not now be cut without breaking up the stone. The cylinder was found at Gizeh, probably in the tomb of an official which was opened just before I bought it. The seal was apparently intended for sealing documents and produce belonging to the endowments of the great pyramid.

The piece of a large alabaster vase of Khufu (4·2·6) I bought at Koptos; it doubtless belonged to the furniture of the temple there. The plummet of hard limestone (4·2·7) I obtained at Gizeh; probably it was used by workmen of Khufu.

Pl. ix. The scarabs of Khofra are commoner than those of Khufu. There are twenty-two known of Khufu, twenty-six of Khofra, but none that can be equally clearly attributed to Menkaura; those with the inscription Ra·men·ka probably belonged mostly to the age of Menkara the vassal of Shabaka (25·3·18–22). Two Menkara scarabs at Aberdeen, and one in the British Museum, seem to be of the Old Kingdom by their simple, bold style. Now that we have evidence of Menkara and Menkheperra as vassals of Shabaka, the scarabs formerly supposed to be re-issues by Hotshepsut (*Historical Scarabs*,

936–953) may probably be assigned to these later kings. The plaque from Marathus with both names together is clearly of the Shabaka age (*H. S.* 1951). The Zedefra scarab is probably a forgery; but condemned scarabs have so often been proved to be ancient by similar ones being discovered, that unless a scarab is of a well-known class of forgeries it should be left in suspense. The Ra·zed scarab appears to be early, and so may be of this reign. The Shepseskaf has the best and most naturalistic work on the back, far better than anything after the xviiith dynasty. The private scarab of Hetep·hers shows by the name that it must belong to the ivth or vth dynasty. It is the earliest private name-scarab known.

25. In the vth dynasty the cylinders almost supersede the scarab. A systematic resemblance is seen between the falcon names and cartouches in this dynasty, Nefer·kho·u = Nefer·ra, Men·kho·u = Hormenkau, Zed·kho·u = Zed·ka·ra. Now a second name of Sahura is yet unknown, but as the falcon name is Neb·kho·u we might expect to find Neb·ra or Neb·khou·ra. Hence the scarab Neb·-khou·ra is here assigned to Sahura. It is true that the name Sahura is treated as a throne name, by both the Sinai inscription and Manetho; but as no separate throne- and personal-names had yet been started in Egypt, it might well be that at first Sahura was the sole name, and later he adopted Neb·kho·ra as a throne name parallel to his falcon name.

The clay sealing placed after those of Sahura bears a Horus name which is yet unidentified, but by its style seems to be of this period. The scarab of Shepseskara is the first one known in this dynasty. That of Ne·user·ra An appears to be royal by the title "son of Ra"; the large central disc to the Ra belongs to this age, as on the tablets of Sahura and An at Maghara. The cylinder of Zed-ka-ra is fixed by the Horus name; the cartouche looks more like Zedefra, and was so described by Wiedemann (*Geschichte*, i, 187) who saw it at Luqsor; after being lost for some years, I bought it in Cairo. The metal is a peculiar hard white alloy. The name on the chert ink-slab, 5·8·2, is lightly incised on the base, the only part shown here; the whole slab is exquisitely cut and polished, with perfectly flat planes and sharp edges. The scarab of Zedkara with spirals cannot belong to Shabataka in the xxvth dynasty, as there are no spirals of any kind after Ramessu II, nor any spirals of this form after the xiith dynasty. The first two scarabs of Unas seem to be contemporary, by the style and inscriptions. The others may be also of this age.

26. Pl. x. Of Meryra Pepy there are many scarabs known, including a very fine amethyst scarab (Murch), on which the *mer* has the longer side uppermost as on Merenra here, a curious irregularity unlike later usage. The scarab of Merenra (6·4) is of dark blue pottery, identical in colour with glaze of the vith dynasty. The Horus Nefer-să is known in a papyrus at Cairo; but, though early, the historical connection has not yet been found. This alabaster block of the king is part of some large object. Many alabaster vases and lids of this age are known, belonging to temple furniture dedicated by the kings, as of Teta and Neferkara here. A fine perfect vase in this collection, naming the *sed* feast of Pepy, is among the stone vases, and will be published with those.

A special feature of the reign of Pepy I is the number of large cylinders of officials. Three are figured here, and four others are in the British Museum. They all appear to have been made at one time as insignia of office, usually without the personal name of the official.

27. Reaching the viith dynasty we are in a period which was so obscure, that it is very unlikely that any attention would be subsequently given to re-issuing scarabs of this age. The name of Neferkara might refer to Pepy II, but the style—with central spot in *ra*—entirely forbids dating so late as the reign of Shabaka. Nekara, who appears in the Abydos list, here appears on another cartouche plaque, along with Nub-neb-ra, who is otherwise unknown, probably a vassal or suzerain. The cowroid reading Er·ka·nen·ra. is perhaps of the same king. The seal with a handle, of Tereru, belongs clearly to the successor of Ne·ka·ra; his throne name, Nefer·ka·ra, is given here by *nefer*, and *ka* arms raised by a figure. The signs *ha* and *neb* may be read "Lord of the north," or Delta. It is impossible to separate this name from Tereru of the viith dynasty, and the form of a seal with a handle also agrees with the button seals of that age; it therefore gives a valuable standard of the engraving and style of the time, for comparison with scarabs.

The large scarab of Seneferonkhra Pepy seems to rank beside the king Neferkara Pepy·senb of the viith dynasty; and the wide-spread tail to the *onkh* is not seen in the xiith dynasty or later scarabs.

The name of Pepy as the great figure of the vith dynasty was copied in the viith; just as Amenemhot —the great name of the xiith dynasty—was copied in the xiiith. The important evidence of the drawn scarab of Pepy we shall notice later. The private name Pepe-nos-es appears on two scarabs, which have the deep indigo-blue glaze of this age.

Of the ixth dynasty there is one scarab here, with the *mer* turned long side up, as figured on the scarabs of Pepy I and Merenra. There is also, at Paris, another Merabra scarab, here drawn. It seems very unlikely that this obscure king should have been commemorated in any later period, when he is not in any of the monumental lists. Of Khety II, Neb·kau·ra, there is the fine jasper weight. On this his throne name omits the *ra*, giving only Neb·kau; this is like Tereru, above, being named Nefer·ka, without the *ra*. Probably of the xth dynasty is the scarab of King Shenes (Brit. Mus.), as it bears the epithet or wish *Uah onkh*, which belongs to the xth and xith dynasties, and is not found after the xiith.

28. Pl. xi.—We now reach a class of small hard-stone scarabs, of rather irregular work, which cannot be paralleled in the xiith dynasty or any later period. By several of these having the epithet *Nefer ka uah* it appears that they must belong to the ixth to xith dynasties; compare with this the Uah·ka princes of Antaiopolis. The title of the first (10 A), *uortu*, is usually found combined with "the prince's table" or "the capital city," and the latter was the higher title, held by great nobles. It cannot refer to a courier; and the clue seems to be given by the scope of another word for leg, *sebeq*, which also means "to re-unite," "to assemble together." The word therefore which seems to agree best with this is "marshal." The "marshal of the dykes" here would have the duty of marshalling all the material at the inundation; the "marshal of the prince's table" would organize the court precedence; the "marshal of the city" would manage the public assemblies and processions, and therefore be of high rank.

The scarab 10 B has the title royal sealer, followed by a name, as the determinative shows. This appears to be "beloved of Merto"; "Mer" or "Merto" was the goddess of inundation at Oxyrhynkhos (Brugsch, *Dict. Geog.* 617, 1197, 1364). The confused writing of 10 D seems as if intended for *re*, mouth or speech, and possibly *khetet* by abbreviation for *nekhtet*; the *hetep* sign is partly worn away, but the *tep* below indicates it. The circular bead, with flat-domed back, 105, by the perfection of its spirals cannot be later than the early part of the xiith dynasty, and may well be of the xith. The lazuli scarab of the high priest Antef, 10 K, with equally fine spirals, is probably late xith. Likewise the next two, with names of Antef and Mentuemhot, by the hardness of the stone and bold work, are of the same age.

A very definite class are the scarabs with the epithet *Ka · nefer · uah*, "the good ka is established," which was used much like *maot-kheru*, "justified," or *uahem onkh*, "living again." The names found with this epithet, or prayer, are of the type before the xiith dynasty—Khety (ixth), Beba (viith), Athy (viith), Nebhat·nefer·ka (see Ra·nefer·ka, viith), Mentu·hetep (xith), Mer (vith); only one is distinctively as late as early xiith, Ameny. The hard stones mostly used in this class were not generally worked after the middle of the xiith dynasty; and the epithet is practically unknown on the great mass of steles which begin with the xiith dynasty. 10 N is of the very flat domed form which belongs to the xith and early xiith dynasties. For the use of Antef as a female name in 10 U there are other examples (Lieb. *Dict.* 146, 161).

29. The kings' names are resumed in the xith dynasty, with Neb·taui·ra. The first, 11·5·1, with the crown, is clearly of the king. 11·5·3 and 4 are difficult in reading. Oryt was a place where Hathor was worshipped, probably Alyi, which was nearly opposite to Deshasheh. In the abbreviated style often found on scarabs, Oryt alone might be used for Nebt·oryt, or "She of Oryt." It is curious that two examples of this should be found, a cowroid, and a prism which is similarly inscribed on two sides.

The scarab 11 A is so obviously of the type and style of work of 11·7·1 following it, that it must be intended as a variant of Antef V. On reaching this king we should note the difficulty in the fashionable view of placing him in the xvith dynasty. Nothing in that period is at all comparable with the work of these scarabs—such hard-stone scarabs with such fine engraving are unknown from the middle of the xiith to well into the xviiith dynasty. To attribute them to the most degraded time under the Hyksos is like ascribing coins of Hadrian to the Byzantines. The details are dealt with more fully below. One reason for the later date, on which the main stress has been laid in England, is the reference to an enemy of Antef being received at Koptos. But a similar state of things is shown on the stele of Zara, who in the xith dynasty under Uah·onkh Antef "fought with the house of Khety in the domain of Thinis" (*Qurneh*, 17). The Antef princes were continually at war with northern neighbours, and an enemy being at Koptos does not prove any connection with the Hyksos, and may just as well have been in the xith dynasty.

The name of Nub·seshesht·ra is allied to those of two Antef kings, Seshesh·her·her·măot·ra and Seshesh·up·măot·ra. The work of his scarab is of the same group as those of Antef V. The work of the scarab of Dadames resembles that of Antef V in 11·7·3. Mentuemsaf has the fine circular spiral which is not seen in royal scarabs of fixed date after Senusert I (12·2·1), or in a poorer form under Senusert II (12·4·2). The scarab of Neb·hapt·ra Mentu hetep has a light blue glaze like that of the early xiith dynasty (12·2·11); the colour, the work, and the sign all forbid attributing it to a supposititious name, Neb·ab·ra, of late date. The scarab of Sonkhkara is of very delicate, refined work, like that of Amenemhot I (12·1·4). These are not like the style of any later period.

CHAPTER VI

THE EARLIEST AGE OF SCARABS

30. In the preceding description we have noticed various indications of the scarabs being contemporary with the kings named on them. This is however denied by some other writers on the subject. Prof. Newberry states "that scarabs were not employed in Egypt before the end of the Sixth Dynasty, and then only very rarely" (*Scarabs*, 69). Mr. Hall makes a greater reservation: "Blue glazed steatite scarabs, of rude form and with roughly geometrical designs upon their bases, occur contemporaneously with the Button-seals [that is vith to viiith dynasties]. But the manufacture of fine scarab-seals does not begin till the xith dynasty, to which period belongs the scarab of Aatshet. . . . No contemporary scarab bearing the name of Amenemhat I, the first king of the xiith dynasty, is known" (*Catalogue of Egyptian Scarabs*, xiii). After such sweeping statements, made on the alleged ground of style, it is needful to bring together the various facts bearing upon the question, and so to see if scarabs were commonly made before the xiith dynasty.

First we may clear the ground of many of the supposed re-issues of scarabs in later times. Of the commonest of all names, Menkheperra, a large part have been supposed to be later than Tehutmes III. By far the greater part of those here published are clearly of his reign; but many are later, and not only the scarabs, but also the kings whose names they bear, are later. There were at least three Menkheperra kings after Tehutmes III. The high-priest of the xxist dynasty is named on one scarab with his daughter Astemkheb (Cairo 37426). Another Men·kheper·ra appears to be named Khmeny, on his stele in Paris (*Stud. Hist.* iii, 293). A third Menkheperra was Nekau I, father of Psemthek I (statuette pl. liv). With these in view it cannot be said that any posthumous scarabs of Tehutmes III were ever made, except those associated with the name of Sety I and Ramessu II (pl. xxxix, xl). When we see, besides the many kings who copied the name of Ramessu II, also Uasarken III copying Pasebkhanu I, Pefdabast and Shabaka copying Pepy II, Nekau I = Tehutmes III, Psemthek II = Nefer·ab·ra (xiiith), Psemthek I and Uah·ab·ra = Aoab (xiiith), Naifoarud = Merneptah, Nekhtherheb = Senusert I, and Ptolemy II = Sety II, it is impossible to ascribe any scarabs to re-issues of earlier kings on the ground of late style, however clearly proved. Among the multitude of petty kings of the xxvth dynasty there may have been some who took any name of earlier times. It is only when one scarab bears a double name, such as Senusert III and Hotshepsut, in an age clear of vassal kings, that any certainty of a re-issue can be settled. Such a group of uniform scarabs as those of Khofra, Kho·nefer·ra (Sebek·hetep III) and Men·kheper·ra (Tehutmes III), all found together by Mr. Quibell (pl. lii), is also a good evidence of re-issue. In looking, then, at the scarabs of kings before the xiith dynasty we must remember that proved re-issues are very rare, and were probably connected with historical events; that of Senusert III, by Hotshepsut and Tehutmes III, refers to the worship of Senusert in the temple of Kummeh built by those later rulers. The *onus probandi* therefore lies in all cases upon the proof of re-issue, and it is at least 100 to 1 against such copying.

31. Before attributing scarabs to late periods, we should see what are the characters of the suc-

cessive ages. Broadly speaking, there is a continued degradation of work from the xiith dynasty onward; none of the various revivals reach as high a point as the best of the period before. Circular spirals were in perfection under Senusert I (12·2·1), poor under Senusert II (12·4·2), and only appear once afterward in a clumsy form under Amenhetep II (*Hist. Scar.* 1097). The oval scrolls, which disappeared under Senusert III, were revived at the end of the xiiith in one case, Nehesi-ra, and by Khyan of the xvth and the earlier Hyksos kings. They occur in the xviiith dynasty and under Ramessu II; but after that not a single dated scroll-pattern scarab is known. In general style there is a poverty seen under Amenemhot II, worse under Senusert III, and clumsy, coarse work in nearly all of Amenemhot III. The xiiith dynasty continues increasing in coarseness down to the xivth. The earlier Hyksos reverted to the style of the middle of the xiith dynasty; but rapidly degraded to work even worse than the xivth. In the xviiith dynasty, Aohmes only occasionally shows some fine work. The best of Amenhetep I and Hotshepsut are good, but not comparable with the best work of the early xiith dynasty. After that, continued degradation went on till the xxvth dynasty revival. The best work of that age is under Shabaka, and that does not equal the early xviiith-dynasty style. Later, the degradation progresses, and the Saite period was noted for the small size and poor work of most of its scarabs. One of Nekau II (26·2·1) is the only scarab which could stand by those of Hotshepsut, and even that is inferior in the forms of the signs, and in the work of the back.

Thus, judging by the abundant material with positive dates, it is futile to ascribe fine work like that of the xiith dynasty to the later ages, or to assign fine circular spirals to the degradation of the xivth or later dynasties. Nor can any hard-stone scarabs be found dated between the xiith and xviiith dynasties, except under the Syrian kings Khenzer and Khondy. The detail and delicacy of the work on the back and head of the scarab goes with the work of the front, excepting for a naturalistic revival limited to a very few scarabs of Akhenaten. The certainly dated material—which is the only basis by which to judge—therefore firmly limits the possibility of ascriptions to later re-issues.

32. The latest group of connected scarabs before the xiith dynasty is the Ra-kheper-nub series, of a king who used to be called Antef V, but whom some have recently shifted to an undefined place near the xviiith dynasty. On his scarabs there is an attention to details of signs, like the elaborate sculptured work of the xith dynasty, which is quite unknown in the xiiith or later dynasties. The legs of the *kheper* are notched, as seen on 11 A, 11·7·3, 4, 5, 6, 8; exactly the same detail is used under Senusert I, 12·2·1, 7, 8; a little under Senusert II, 12·4·3, 4; and only once later, under Tehutmes II, 18·4·6. Such detail is entirely foreign to the coarse work of the late xiith to xviith, and on the scarab of Mer·kheper·ra 13·36 the sign is

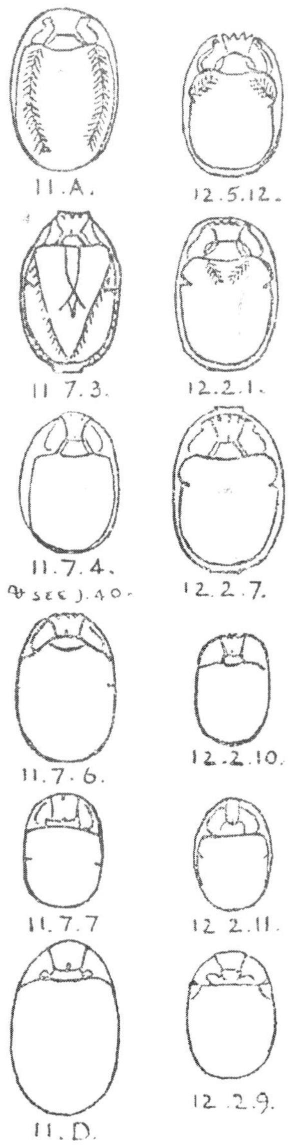

ANTEF. SENUSERT.

quite simple. On referring to the backs, it will be seen that there are two general types, the elaborate head, often with branches on the back, and the plainer head (placed below). Those in the left half are of the Antef group, all of those in the right half are of Senusert I. It is evident that both types run across the two columns. Each type belongs doubtless to a different centre of work, but the scarabs of Antef V and Senusert I were obviously made in the same style at both places. It may be said that these styles were continued later, but the fine work of the fronts is quite unknown later, and bars our placing these in the xiiith to xviith dynasties. Another dating point is in the white quartz scarab 11·7·1, with rich peacock-blue glaze. The cutting of hard stone scarabs is practically unknown on any dated examples between the middle of the xiith dynasty and the xviiith; I have none, nor any references to such in that period. The back of this scarab accords with the early date of it, as it is beautifully worked with curves at the junction of the elytra. There is nothing known at all approaching such work after the middle, or even the beginning, of the xiith dynasty.

Thus the external evidence of age of this group, is rather for its preceding and not succeeding the xiith dynasty. Dadames, whose scarab 11·D is like others here, 11·7·6, 11·7·7, placed his name amid *graffiti* of Pepy. The scarabs of Senusert I in this group indicate that Dadames was near his time, in the xith dynasty.

It might be supposed that the symmetric scarab 11·7·6 was evidence of a later date for Ra-kheper-nub. But the same system appears in the beautifully cut scarab of Senusert I, 12·2·11, the brilliant sky-blue colour of which is characteristic of the early and middle xiith dynasty. Similar to that again is another symmetric scarab, 12·2·10, which has a double reading Ka-ra-kheper, Ra-kheper-nub, the names of Senusert I and of Nub-kheper-ra Antef united. The scarab 11·7·5 has unfortunately lost the head, so that the type of it cannot be settled; but it has a fine feather pattern on the leg, which begins in the xith and is rare in the xiiith dynasty. It cannot be supposed to come in shortly before the xviiith, where Antef V has otherwise been placed.

Another scarab of this group, 11 B, reads Ra-nub-seshesh, with two hawks below wearing crowns of Lower Egypt. This recalls the Ra-seshesh-up-mäot Antef-oä and Ra·seshesh·her·her·mäot of the xith dynasty.

It has long been generally recognized that Ra-nefer-zad Dadames is closely connected with Ra-zad-onkh Mentu-em-saf, whose name is found in the same place, at Gebeleyn. The scarab Ra-zedui-onkh, 11 E, is probably the same king. It has a very fine circular scroll round it, quite unknown after the middle of the xiith dynasty, and most closely like scarabs of Senusert I, 12·2·1, 2, and the high priest Antef, 10 K.

The name of Mentu belongs specially to the xith dynasty, and the form . . . em saf is like Mehti-em-saf of the vith dynasty. The probabilities from the name are therefore rather in favour of the xith than of later dynasties, and the evidence of the work may be allowed full force in favour of the xth or xith dynasty. There seems no reason why Mentu-emsaf and other kings may not have belonged to the xth dynasty, contemporary with the earlier part of the xith, before the forty-three years of supremacy of the xith which is stated by Manetho.

33. Another considerable class which belongs to this same age is that of the *Ka-nefer-uah* scarabs. This epithet of private persons is not found on steles, and therefore probably belongs to an age when steles are rare. It appears to be parallel to the *uahem onkh*, "live again," which was used at this time; and it is also connected with the favourite name Uah-ka, of the Middle Kingdom. The *ka* and *nefer* are always more closely associated than either of them with *uah*. The *ka nefer* was therefore parallel to the *ka aäkhet*, "illuminated or glorious ka" of the 1st dynasty steles. We must read it then as a prayer or assertion that the excellent ka is established or multiplied. The age of this class is shown by the names, as we have noticed, belonging to the viith to xith dynasties. Five of these, however, are of ruder work than the others, 10, N, O, P, Q, R; and as the xith dynasty passed on into the fine work of the xiith, these cannot be put after the others. The rude ones probably precede the others, and may reasonably be placed in the xth dynasty. The *ka-nefer-uah* precedes the name on these earlier examples (N, O, P, Q), but succeeds the name on the later and fuller scarabs.

The hard-stone scarabs of small size form a distinct class, merging into more elaborate scarabs of larger size. There does not seem to be a single hard-stone scarab which can be fixed between the middle of the xiith, and the xviiith dynasties. The names in this class, of Se-khenty-khati, Antef (twice), and Mentuemhot, are probably of the xith dynasty. The backs of 10 D, 10 E are of very fine work, highly polished, indicating the close of the xith or early xiith dynasty. The other scarabs of this class are all ruder in cutting, and less elaborate, and must be placed before the xith rather than in the xiith. We may conclude then that these begin in the ixth or xth dynasty, and run on to the beginning of the xiith. Rude as the small examples are, yet the heads are well cut and natural.

34. Between the xth and vith dynasties a few pieces claim a place. Mer-ab-ra Khety of the ixth dynasty has a scarab of good work 9·1; the back of it is of the same type as the two little scarabs of Neb-taui-ra Mentuhetep of the xith dynasty, but is of better and earlier style. The Merabra scarab in Paris cannot be attributed to any later king, and points thus to the symmetric border beginning well before the xiith dynasty.

A cartouche plaque of Nefer-ka-ra (7·4·2) cannot be placed in the xxvth dynasty, as the loop ends to the *ka* were never used as late as that age. The Ra has a central mark, which is much more usual before than after the xiith dynasty. As no king of this name is known between the viiith and the xxvth dynasties, it seems that this should be put in the viith or viiith dynasties. The cartouche form of amulet is known under Senusert I, and on to the end of the history, so it may well occur in the viiith. The cartouche plaque of Ra-ne-ka may well be of the king of that name in the viith dynasty; the form is known, as we have just seen, and the rounded coarse work in pottery is much like the scarab of Merenra of the vith, which is agreed on by Prof. Newberry as being contemporary. The oval Ra-ka-enen may perhaps be also of the same king, as the form is closely like two already dated to the xith dynasty.

An important scarab is the large one with the names Senefer-onkh-ra Pepy. This name is like the viith to viiith dynasty king, Nefer-ka-ra Pepy-senb. Pepy being the most celebrated king of the vith dynasty, was copied in the following dynasty, just as Amenemhot was copied in the xiiith dynasty. Here there seems to have been another king called after Pepy, and therefore probably of the viith dynasty.

A very remarkable scarab belonging to Mr. A. L. Payne of Manchester is shown here in drawing. The style might at first be put to the Hyksos age; but it is far too good for the work of Pepa-Shesha, beside being distinctly Pepy and not Pepa. The cutting is like that of Senusert I, 12·2·7; and in 12·2·11 there is a guarantee that a similar arrangement is as early as Senusert I. With the plain name of Pepy on it, we should give much weight to its being made under that king. Other scarabs of his differ from this, because of local workmanship; the present example, by its resemblance to Hyksos types, is evidently of the eastern Delta. There seems no reason why this should not be a Delta scarab of Pepy II, or possibly of some king of the viith dynasty called after him. Thus we see that three objects with symmetric borders claim place in the viith to ixth dynasties—No. 7·9·2, the Payne Pepy, and the Paris Merabra. They belong to three separate kings, and each is placed here independently by reason of the names, and the similarity to examples not far distant. Until other evidence may show that other kings of those names also recurred later, we ought to accept these in the only position legitimate for them.

In the stamp of Teruru, with a loop behind, we have a well-fixed point of comparison of style. This very obscure king, of whom nothing is known beyond the list of Abydos, cannot be supposed to have had re-issues of a stamp in later times. The reading Teruru Neferka clearly belongs to Nefer-ka-ra Teruru. The use of seals with a loop behind belongs to this age, of the vith to ixth dynasties.

We now reach the vith dynasty, where the small indigo-blue glazed scarab of Merenra (6·4) is so closely like other glazed work of that age, that the contemporary date of this scarab is accepted as likely by Prof. Newberry. Moreover the type of the back agrees with that of Atmuhetep (10 H), which we have seen belongs to the xth to xith dynasty; and the *mer* turned with the curve upward is seen on the scarab of Khety in the ixth dynasty, and Pepy I of the vith dynasty. The two scarabs here of Mery-ra Pepy are not distinctive in their type.

35. In the vth dynasty there is an important group of Unas and Shepseskaf, which are connected. The main feature is that two scarabs of Unas are of closely similar work, with the large hare, and must be of the same age. One (5·9·1) has *Neter nefer neb taui Unas hotep*, "The good god, lord of both lands, Unas is satisfied," and there can be no doubt of this referring to the king, and pro-

bably during his life. The other (5·9·2) reads *As·un*, which is as good a form grammatically as Unas, or even better; it is a birth-exclamation, "Behold the being." Such an inversion would be quite likely while the name was fresh, but would never be started in later ages when the old royal name was fossilised in the lists. There seems, then, no chance of these being later re-issues. Turning to the Shepseskaf scarab (4·6) we see a finer edition of the same head as the Unas-hetep scarab; the detailed treatment of the head, the minute eyeball, and the curves of the elytra, are finer work than any scarab after the very best of the xith and early xiith dynasties. Such work would be a miracle amid the far ruder design and cutting of all later ages; it stands almost alone for its perfection. Hence by its isolation of refinement, and its appearing the prototype of the Unas backs, it seems that there is no other conclusion except that it is of the age of the king whose name it bears.

Regarding the other Unas pieces, the flat-backed ovoid (5·9·3) is exactly the shape and size of one with the name Senusert (12·2·26), probably of Senusert I by the style. This therefore need not be after the xiith dynasty, and might well be of the vth. Another stands or falls with one of the Khofra types.

36. Coming to Zad-ka-ra Assa, the scarab cannot possibly be placed to Shabataka of the xxvth, nor after the early xviiith dynasty, as the *ka* arms end in loops. The back of it is of the same family as some of the Unas and Khofra scarabs, having a slightly curved girdle line, two lines between the elytra, and—as in Khofra—a border line round the elytra but not round the thorax. The head is practically the same; only as the notching is not visible on the broken clypeus, the Khofra is classed as L, while the others are in H. The decomposed glaze on scarabs of Khofra, Assa, and Unas, is of a peculiar bright ochreous red, not seen later until Psametek, to which age these cannot possibly belong, by the style and forms of hieroglyphs. This group, then, carries with it the small plain scarab of Unas 5·9·4. It has been objected that the spiral pattern on 5·8·4 is unknown so early as the vth dynasty. But finely developed spirals appear in the xith dynasty (Antef, 11·7·5, and Mentuemsaf, 11 E); a precisely similar spiral is on a scarab dated by pottery to the xth dynasty (*Heliopolis*, pl. xxvi, p. 32); and on the animal seals of the button seal class (certainly between the vith and xiith dynasties), there are not only spirals but degraded spirals of squared form, showing that the design was familiar. There is, then, no reason against a simple form of spiral being one or two dynasties earlier than these. Of the ivth or vth dynasty must be Hetep·hers (4·C), as the name is unknown in any other period.

At the close of the ivth dynasty is the scarab of Shepseskaf, the work of which is finer and more detailed than any others, even of the best age of the xith to xiith dynasty. As we have noted, the Unas scarabs show the same type, but less detailed and perfect; and those are shown to be contemporary, by the title *neter nefer*, and the inverted spelling As-un. In default of any later scarabs comparable to this, it is the most probable that it belongs to the finest period of sculpture, the ivth to vth dynasties.

Among the Khofra scarabs are several signs of early date. The Ra sign is large (4·3·1, 4·3·3) with a central disc, a form very rarely seen after the early xiith dynasty, but frequent in the Old Kingdom; one in the British Museum has the same form of centre. The *f* sign in 4·3·4, 7, 8, is thick and slug-like; this is the original early form, but is not usual in late times.

The Khufu scarabs are not well represented here. The beautiful small bright blue ones of the Grant Collection (Aberdeen) are quite characteristic, and unlike anything of any other age; the *Ur-hemt-khet* scarab here (3·9·A) and Nebkara (3·1·1) are of the same class. Details agree to the early dating of most of these; the chick upon 4·2·2 has the beak slightly open; a characteristic of the young chick, which might be copied in an early period, but never later. The Turin scarab has the short slug-like *f* sign; and in general the *f* signs agree closely with others of Khofra, so that the dating of each group supports the other. Of course some re-issues of Khufu, of a totally different kind, were made—as under Kashta; but there is no later age in which scarabs were made with the style of signs or of work which belongs to these Pyramid kings.

The iiird-dynasty scarabs hold together as a group. On the thorax of 3·9·2 there is a border line (Q 73) curving into a curl on each shoulder. It is present, though rather less curled, on 3·9·1 (see J·20). The same, though more roughly done, is on the back of Nebkara 3·1·1 (see L·24). Though such a curled line is found at various later periods (see Q), yet there are no scarabs in those periods at all like these in their fabric or inscription.

37. It seems, then, that from the xiith dynasty back to the iiird, we find in each group well-marked details which unite them, and point to contemporary manufacture, while no group can be paralleled in any later period. In most instances the workmanship is far better than in later ages; this is not likely to be the case with re-issues, those of the living king probably receiving the most attention. The theory of an extensive issue of scarabs by late kings in commemoration of kings who left none, seems to depart along with the theory of all statues of early kings being works of the Saite age. A sense of style will save us from all such fallacies.

When we turn to scarabs which are certainly late issues, such as the Khufu found with Amenardas, and the group found by Mr. Quibell (here pl. lii, copied from *Excavations at Saqqara*, 1905–6, p. 31, pl. xxxvii) the styles are quite unlike those which we have considered above. The Khufu is of coarse pottery with indigo-blue glaze, and the Saqqara group is of the soft paste class, like the scarabs of Pama and others of the Delta.

It has been urged sometimes that no scarabs of the Old Kingdom are recorded as having been found in tombs. Looking at the scarcity of them, that is not to be expected. If we take dynasties in which they are equally scarce, say xviith, xxist, xxiiird, probably not a single scarab has been found in a tomb. The number of tombs is not the question here, but the number of scarabs dated to certain periods. Another way of looking at the matter is that cylinders and sealings are as usual as scarabs of early kings. Yet there is only one instance of a cylinder found with a burial of the ivth to vith dynasties, and therefore the scarabs are not to be expected in the range of recorded groups. There is at least one record of two scarabs, found with pottery which must be earlier than the xiith dynasty, and is probably of the xth dynasty. See *Heliopolis*, p. 32, pl. xxvi xxvii, and coffin of tomb 509, pl. xv.

CHAPTER VII

THE MIDDLE KINGDOM

(PLATES XII–XXII)

38. Pl. xii. The styles at the beginning of the xiith dynasty were somewhat mixed. The sculptures of Koptos show what delicate work was done under Amenemhot I, comparable with the delicately engraved scarab 12·1·4. The rather clumsy but detailed work of the xith dynasty survives in the style of 12·1·3. The rough work of some districts crops up in the scarabs, 12·1·1—2, which have the writing in order of the speech, Sehetepabra and Sehetepraab. Notwithstanding the dogma that there are no scarabs made under Amenemhot I, it would be very difficult to parallel these in a later reign. Only one scarab is clearly late, in every respect, 12·1·5. The name Amen Ra stamps it as being after the xviiith dynasty; the back is like one of Sheshenq I, K·50, and it is probably of xxiind to xxvth dynasties.

The scarabs of Senusert I hardly need remark, except as to the use of two *nefer* signs in place of *ra*. Some thirty years ago this equivalence was suggested by Mr. Wilbour, and the examples strongly confirm it. The intermediate stages can be seen here. In 12·2·16 there is a greatly enlarged *ra* with *nefer* inside it; the other signs are normal, of the style of the best, 12·2·1, and the scroll border is as 12·2·3. The next scarab (17) has a large circular body to the *nefer*, like *ra*, with a small top; and in No. 18 the work is the same, only two *nefer* signs appear in place of *ra*. All of these show a contemporary style; but different work is seen in the next two, 19, 20, bearing the same inscription. The fronts and the backs are unlike any other scarabs of this period: and the source of them is shown by a scarab 18·7·31 with closely the same work and name (with *kheper* on its side), but with the name of Amenhetep II added. Hence we can date these, 19, 20, as a re-issue of his reign. A very different class to all others are 23, 24, 25 with very perfect work but blundered inscriptions. The cylinder seals were revived under Senusert I, and lasted on into the next dynasty.

Pl. xiii. Of Amenemhot II there is a scarab, 12·3·5, with the name Senuser added, written as spoken, and not inverted as Usertesen. This gives contemporary evidence of the spoken form of the name, and is parallel to the spoken forms on 12·1·1—2. It was doubtless made in the coregency during three years of Amenemhot II and Senusert II. The very large stone beads, 7, 8, seem peculiar to this reign. Under Senusert II there are two variant writings; 12·4·2 with *neferui* for *ra* and inverted order of the signs; and 12·4·4 with the same inversion, and the uraeus in place of *ra*.

39. Of Senusert III there is a plaque and two *uzat* eyes (12·5·18–20), the latter seeming by the style to be of the xxvth dynasty. The name of this king was also commemorated by Hotshepsut and Tehutmes III in connection with the revival of his worship in the rebuilt temple of Kummeh. But the scarabs which formerly were attributed to such re-issues (*Historical Scarabs*, 936–956) must be reconsidered in view of the names of Menkara and Menkheperra recurring in the xxvth dynasty. The couchant sphinx with double plumes, and holding the *hes* vase, seems to be restricted to the xxvth. A walking sphinx with double plume is on three scarabs in the British Museum (3996, 16808 of T. III; 38585 of Amenhetep II), also a couchant sphinx with double plume (3997 B·M), and a couchant sphinx with a *hes* vase on 18·6·51 here. These are all of the xviiith-dynasty style, whereas the couchant plumed sphinx with the *hes* vase is of xxvth-dynasty style. Referring to the numbers in *Historical Scarabs*, it seems that 941 is of Shabaka; 938, 939, 948, 951, 953, 954 of vassals of Shabaka. But the straight-barred uraei seem to belong to the Hotshepsut age, and thus 936, 937, 949, 950, together with 946, belong to her time. These commemorate Senusert III on 946, 949, and Menkaura on 936. The curious-looking ligature across from arm to arm of the *ka* represents the bases of the three *ka* signs conjoined, This mode of making a plural was already started in the xiith dynasty, see *H.S.* 236. Another here, made by Tehutmes III, is 12·5·15.

Of Amenemhot III, though some neat work remains, as 12·6·1, 12·6·5, the prevalent style in pl. xiv is coarse and even rude. The last two pieces of this king are animal figures—hawk and crocodile—inscribed on the base.

40. Pl. xiv. *Private Scarabs.*—These form the most important class of the Middle Kingdom scarabs. For reference they are here thus classified; spiral patterns, numbered 12 and a letter; and without spirals, numbered 13 and a letter. Many of the latter class are of the xiith-dynasty period; the number is only used to distinguish broadly those with and without spirals. The spirals are classed as follows: first, round spirals, continuous, then only at sides; oval scrolls continuous, then only at sides, joined over; or, next, not joined from side to side. The plain scarabs begin with linkages top and base, twisted lines, rope borders, and then plain border lines, which are subdivided according to styles of work. The various classes are in their general order of age, but of course they overlap in periods.

41. So far as the titles are well understood the catalogue will suffice; but some which are dubious we shall notice here. *Ur res mobă* occurs on 12 F, Y, Z; 13 B, X; it has not been well explained as yet, and there are difficulties in the rendering as "chief judge."

The meaning of this title must depend on the actual use of it, and its connections, indicating whether it is judicial or administrative.

In the Old Kingdom there are twenty-five instances of it, quoted in *Names and Titles.* These are associated with other offices in the following frequency:

15 *onz,* administrator of a nome;
14 *tep kher nesut,* viceroy, chief under the king;
12 *an mutek,* priestly (of the kingship);
11 *nest khentet,* throne of the south—Nubia;
11 *her seshta ne hez medu nebt ent nesut,* secretary of the enlightening, or explaining all words of the king;
never *her seshta ne per duat,* secretary of the cabinet;
never *her seshta ne het ur,* secretary of the palace;
8 *mer katu nebt ent nesut,* over all works of the king;
only 3 *tăit, săb, thăt,* chief judge and vizier;
never *khetm bati,* chancellor;
never *nekheb her tep,* chief of Hierakonpolis;
never, high priest of Memphis, priest of Ptah, or priest of Sokar.

Thus the titles are distinctively not of the home-office, secretary of the cabinet or palace, or chief judge and vizier, or chancellor, or Memphite priesthoods, or over Hierakonpolis. This seems to exclude the headship of the thirty judges. On the contrary the commonest additional offices are viceroy, over the nome, the throne of Nubia, and the Foreign Secretary; all of these point to the position of prince of the southern chiefs or districts.

In the Middle Kingdom the title is scarcely ever associated with any other; of twenty-six in the catalogue of Cairo steles, one is a *meti ne să,* and in eight at Aswan one is *repoti hot.* The frequency of the title on the rocks at Aswan bears out the connection with Nubia.

When we reach the New Kingdom this title

entirely disappears. A new title arises, *să nesut ne kesh,* "royal son of Nubia," as viceroy in the south.

These connections of titles point to *mobă,* meaning chiefs or a district, and in Nubia rather than Upper Egypt, as it is never linked with Hierakonpolis. It hardly seems possible that *măbă,* harpoon, might be related to a harpoon sign being perhaps used for a chief on the tablet of Narmer. The titles "great *met* (10) of the south, great *met* of the north," however, belong to Taharqa as viceroy over Egypt; these seem to show that *met* was the title of a chief or sub-ruler, and *moba* might therefore be taken as referring to the Nubian chiefs.

42. In 12 H appears the epithet *măot kheru,* which has been variously rendered. It is now recognised as having a judicial sense of acquittal, and "justified" seems to be the best translation. As it often recurs, it is denoted as M·K· in transliteration, and is omitted in the translation. 12 O and 12 AA are the earliest examples here of the title *neb amăkh*; this has been rendered in many ways, usually as devoted to, or worthy of, the lord of the person. Yet being without the possessive *f,* it seems rather as if it was analogous to the various other expressions relating to the person, as *măot·kheru, uahem onkh, nefer ka uah*; thus *neb* would refer to the person, and the whole mean "the worthy lord."

This is confirmed by its never being applied to a woman, in any published here or by Prof. Newberry; except in one case (Newberry, xliv, 4) where it is in the feminine, *nebt amakh,* "the worthy lady."

43. 12 P has a rare title, scribe of *sekh,* "to beat," determined by a fist, or punishment. 125 might be supposed to be a blundered form of Amen·ra; but as the back is certainly of the xiith dynasty this is impossible, and it must be a proper name.

Pl. xv. 12 AC has a remarkable title, Guard of the 110 Amu; this recalls the 37 Amu who were thought worthy of very full record at Beni Hasan; the 110 Amu were probably another immigrant party who had this Egyptian officer over them. 12 AG, AH, the rendering of *uortu* as "marshal" has been considered under 10A. In 12 AS the sign like *onkh* seems to be a form of the seal *khetm*; the *m* after it is used when expressing a thing sealed, a treaty or fortress. Here with *oper,* to provide or supply, it appears to refer to sealed contracts of supply, probably the assessments of food-rents from different places. On 12 AV the title is quoted by Pierret (*Vocab.* 509), but his reference seems wrong, and I have not been able to follow it. 12 BC has a title apparently derived from *patu* food, perhaps "caterer." On 12 BG the *uortu neteru* would be the marshal of the sacred processions. The class 12 BK to BP is puzzling; it is not at all certain that they are not modern inventions. It is difficult to see what the signs were originally before repeated copying, ancient or modern. The bird at the top on BL, BN, is corrupt on BM, and thence changes to BO and BK. As BN seems best, we should accept the plant sign *ha* as the origin of the *nesut ka* on the others. The two following signs may be the head following *ha,* and *t* feminine. Below these may be *neteru,* and *măot·kheru* at the end. It might possibly be a wish *neh ha neteru măot·kheru,* "having confidence behind the gods, being justified." The materials of this class are never glazed, but of bare stone, which is suspicious; or the other hand BK is of a hard stone unlikely to be used by a forger, and the diversity of the blunders does not seem as if they had all been made together by a modern fabricator. BQ can be dated to the close of the xiith dynasty, as it is much like 12·7, Amenemhot IV, pierced with three holes from end to end, and with deeply-cut legs. Another scarab dated by the same features is BU of Har, of whom many plain scarabs are known, 13 BU to CE.

44. Pl. xvi. Though this section is named as 13, that only refers to the majority of the class of unbordered scarabs. Some such are found undoubtedly of the xiith dynasty, as A, H, S, AB, AC, AG, on this plate. The twisted border of 13 G occurs also on an Aswan scarab (Fraser, 83) and one of a *nebt per* Neferu (Ward 224). 13 H is remarkable for an epithet fuller than usual, "living again eternally." 13 N is of very rare work, entirely hollowed out, with the back pierced in open-work. The head is human, and arms and legs, apparently belonging to it, occupy the thorax. The elytra are figures of Taurt. The front, however, is not unusual in work. 13 T is a group of cat and kitten, belonging to Se·hetep·ab·ra·onkh, evidently of the beginning of the xiith dynasty. The enlargement of the central spot of the *ra,* converting the sign into a ring, is very peculiar, and occurs on the inscription of Antef V (*Koptos* viii); this is an additional reason for the dating of that king to the xith dynasty. AC has an unusually long inscription giving the parentage,

of which I only know of one parallel. The next, AD, is also of very rare design, giving a figure of a prince Nefer·ra, hunting. The three scarabs, AL, AM, AN, are a remarkable class, for the size of the body and the hieroglyphs. The title on AL is new to us, General of the Memphite army of Ptah, mentioned by Ramessu II (*Stud. Hist.* iii, 51). AM has a rather confused reading; from the sacred stand, it seems that a god's name is present, and this must be Unnefer; the previous signs must be read "the leader of the youths," referring to some religious corporation of youths consecrated to Osiris Unnefer. The name appears to be the *uzat* or eye of Tehuti, namely Aoh the moon. AN is of a rather similar style to the preceding class. The cylinder AQ is perhaps unique as a private cylinder of this age. AV has on the back a style of pattern familiar in decorated scarabs of the xiiith or xivth dynasties, but not otherwise associated with inscriptions; by the coarse cutting, it may have been engraved later than the front.

Pl. xvii. AY is a later and coarser example of the soldered wire hieroglyphs seen on the electrum pectoral 12·6·26. The royal sealer Häar, 12 BU, 13 BT to CE, has left far more private scarabs than any other man. The age is of the beginning of the xiiith dynasty, as the best of these, 12 BU, is of the peculiar fabric of Amenemhot IV. 13 CO, CP, CQ of Peremuah appear to be of the Hyksos age, judging by the border, which seems to be derived from that of the later Hyksos kings. The rudeness of these would agree with that date.

45. The various indications of the age of the private scarabs may now be summed up. Seeing the cessation of circular spirals on kings' scarabs at the middle of the xiith dynasty, all the scarabs 12 A to 12 L must be of the first half of that dynasty. Of the same age, by the style and names, must be 13 T, 13 AG. The work of these will carry with them also 12 AA, 12 AC, which seem as early as Senusert I. Of the middle of the xiith dynasty are probably those of good work, but not fine, such as 13 A, 13 AB, 13 AC, 13 AE.

The next clear date is that of Häar, 12 BU, which is pierced with those holes from end to end like 12·7 of Amenemhot IV, and is therefore of the end of the xiith dynasty. This must carry with it the much rougher scarabs of the same man, 13 BT to 13 CE, which may be put to the beginning of the xiiith dynasty. Seeing how poor these are, we may well accept nearly all the scroll scarabs as being of the xiith dynasty, and the well-cut scarabs of pls. xvi and xvii.

Next a peculiar type of back will give a date. There is a class of scarabs with long and deep body, straight sides, straight girdle lines, and double line between the elytra, see pl. lxxii. This type is dated to the Princess Kema, mother of Sebekhetep III, and to Sebekhetep II her contemporary. With these go also 12 AJ Snooab, 12 AK Sekhru-ab, 13 P Senb, 13 W Antef, 13 AU Semekh, 13 AX Sebekhetep, all coarse in work. Immediately after, the type changes to a deep groove between the elytra; and this is dated to Ha-onkhef, father of Sebekhetep III, Neferhetep, and Sebekhetep III. With these go also 12 AV, 13 S, 13 X, 13 BC, 13 BH, 13 BJ, 13 BK, 13 BO, 13 CF, 13 CN, and King Ay. These in turn will take with them others of similar engraving, as 13 R, 13 Y, 13 AA, 13 BB, 13 BC. All of these must belong to the middle of the xiiith dynasty.

Other rude ones are later, and we again touch ground with Peremuah, 13 CO, CP, CQ, which, by the side pattern of CO, belong to the latter part of the Hyksos age. Thus we have reached a useful number of fixed points, by which most private scarabs can be placed in the correct dynasty.

46. Pl. xviii. At the beginning of the xiiith dynasty are placed scarabs of unknown queens of the xiith and xiiith. These of Erdaneptah and Khensu must, by the scrolls, belong to the xiith. Nubti·hetep·ta has the back of the time of Neferhetep. Resunefer is like this in work of the face. Sat·sebek is like 13 U, 13 V, which are also about this date. Uazet seems too good to be later than mid xiith dynasty; the back is exactly that of 12 Z, 12 AL, agreeing to this date.

After a worn scarab (13·2) which seems to be of Sekhem·ka·ra, there are others of similar style of Onkh·neferu·uah·ra and Nefer·onkh·ra. These must be early in the dynasty by the good work, and they may be the names of Amenemhot and Aufni, of that age. But the scroll work seems too good to be after the xiith dynasty. Next is Seonkh·ab·ra, whose great quartzite altars are familiar in Cairo. Two of Sehetep·ab·ra are too rude for Amenemhot I, and must be placed to the second of that name. The beautiful cylinder in the Amherst collection, of Amenemhot·senbf, must also be early in this dynasty. The half cylinder 13·15·1 is fixed to Sebekhetep I by the falcon name *Khe bau* (see NAVILLE, *Bubastis*, pl. xxxiii, 1);

this cylinder gives the *nebti* name, otherwise unknown, *zedui renpetu*. The reading *hes her* on 13·15·4 suggests the xxvth dynasty. Hetep·ka·ra is only known from this cylinder; it might be the 9th, 18th or 38th name in the Turin list, all ending in *ka*. Another of these three names may be Se·beka·ka·ra, of whom here are two cylinders. Of Sebekhetep II, a large gold bead is formed in two halves, soldered together; they seem to have been impressed from a mould or die. The parents of Neferhetep and Sebekhetep III (13·20·3, 4) are well known on their scarabs (13·21, 1–6; 13·22·1, 4); from their independent scarabs we see that Haonkhef was a royal sealer or chancellor, and Divine father (13·20·3), who married the heiress, the king's daughter, Kema (13·20·4). These give good dating points of style of signs and of back among private scarabs. Of the small scarabs of Sebek·hetep III there is no question that some are late, as one with *Kho·nefer·ra* occurs in the group of xxvith dynasty work found by Quibell at Saqqareh. So 13·22·18 to 22 of small neat work, mostly in paste, may be put late. Yet we must not at once call them all re-issues, as the name was used in the xxvth dynasty, where there were two Sebek·hetep princes, a son of Zinefer of Abusir, and a son of Tafnekht II (*Stud. Hist.* iii, 322). Some of these scarabs might well have belonged to one of those princes.

Pl. xix. The cowroid of Kho·ka·ra differs from the style of Senusert III, and might be of the king of this name in the xiiith dynasty. The scarabs of Queen Ana are put here next to King Ana, as being probably his wife or daughter; the style shows they belong to this period. The lion with the name Neb·măot·ra cannot be of Amenhetep III, by the style; it may belong to ... *măot·ra* Aba 13·41. Nehesi, 13, 53, shows an unexpected revival of scrolls, which had disappeared since the beginning of the dynasty.

The king's son Antef (14 B) must be of about the middle of the xiiith dynasty, as the back of the scarab has the deep groove between the elytra; the rough style of work agrees to this date. The other scarabs of kings' sons seem clearly later, like the Hyksos scarabs of the xvith dynasty; compare Nehesi and Sepedneb with Apepa I, and also Nebneteru with Yekeb·bor. Tur might be of the beginning of the xviiith dynasty, compare Turs, wife of Amenhetep I. The style of Kho·sebek·ra and Uazed approaches most to that of the earliest Hyksos, so they may well be of the end of the xivth dynasty.

47. The scarabs of the xivth dynasty are of very coarse work. Those of Suazenra are not common (14·69·1–5) and there is only one of Nefer·ab·ra (14·76), which agrees with the Hyksos style. Of the same age are Khenzer and Khondy, two kings of eastern origin. Khenzer has apparently the same name as the later Babylonian king Ukīn·zēr, Khinzēros in Ptolemy; and Khondy represents the Syrian taking precedence of the Egyptian. Khenzer is best known from his stele in Paris, showing him as a pious Egyptian king who restored the temple of Abydos, and had the throne name Ne·măot·ne·kho·ra, modified from that of Amenemhot III. Beside the two scarabs here, three others have been attributed to this king. The Fraser example (65) has a second cartouche User·ka·ra, which raises a difficulty; and the *zer* is so different from that on the stele and on these scarabs, that it seems a doubtful reading; possibly it is Er·khnum, a shortened form in which *da* is understood, "By Khnum" (he is given). The British Museum example (42716) is very confused, *oă kho* being inserted in the name, and a title of an official added,—a construction to which there is hardly a parallel; the supposed *zer* sign is also quite different to the form on the stele or other examples. The scarab attributed by Ward (219) is of Amenemhot III, with Nefer·ka·ra added. None of these others therefore can be safely assigned to Khenzer. Of Khondy the cylinder here shows much. He was king of Upper Egypt, by the crown; his rule over Syria (or Mesopotamia) was his main dominion, as the Syrian takes precedence; the Egyptian—called *hen*, the "servant,"—who follows, bears a papyrus with a nesting bird, a symbol of the Delta. The king had the Egyptian attribute of giving life to his subjects, "life of the Living One"—the king. The style of the twist pattern and the row of ibexes is Mesopotamian rather than Egyptian; the jasper cylinder with figures belongs to Babylonia, and is quite unknown in Egypt. One scarab is known of this king, rather differently spelt (Blanchard), and it is of haematite, a characteristic material of Syria. It seems certain that in Khondy—and probably also in Khenzer—we have easterners entering Egypt, and taking over rule, probably by peaceful means, before the harsh confusion of the Hyksos triumph.

48. Pl. xx. On many scarabs are groups of

signs, of the same character as the royal names. It is probable that these are the names of some of the host of kings who are only known by their total number in the xivth to xviith dynasties. On scarab 14 O the name may be Sekhem-ra, and *zet onkh* equal to *onkh zetta,* "living eternally," as on 16·C·16. The border of 14 P is like that of 13 Q; but the name Kems, on the latter, is so usual in the Middle Kingdom that it does not give a closer dating. On 14 Q, R, the sign *sma* seems fairly distinct from *nefer*; yet, on the other hand, R has the marks on the body of the sign like *nefer*; and it would be unlikely that T, V, and X should not be intended to show *nefer*. Perhaps then Q, with the stem widening upward, is the only *sma* sign. It would seem impossible to attribute all the Nefer-ra scarabs to one king. On X the work is very good, and the circular spirals appear to belong to the early part of the xiith dynasty; while on W the system of the surrounding hieroglyphs belongs to the earlier part of the xvith dynasty (*Hyksos and Israelite Cities*, pl. li). The Nefer-ra scarabs, then, are more probably only acts of devotion to Ra, and not belonging to a king. Rather the same conclusion is shown by the diverse periods of the Nekara scarabs. While AN is clearly of the age of Apepa I, see 15·5·12, the fine circular scrolls on AP and the playing with *Ra* and *nefer* signs (as on Senusert I, 12·2·16, 17) indicate the early part of the xiith dynasty.

The long cylinder of Ka·zed·uah·ra has two separate scenes upon it, placed base to base; one of these is here reversed, so that both read upright. The essential key to the reading lies in the signs in the second cartouche, which contains *bat nub*, probably to be read as a title, "victorious king" (like *Her nub*, the "victorious Horus"); followed by *Uah-neferui* as a name, and *ur*, "the great," as a following adjective. Now on the first half is a figure with *Uah-neferui* around it, intended therefore for the same name as is written with titles in the cartouche. The first half shows this ruler Uah-neferui, with apparently a son, and wife kneeling, before a larger figure holding a lotus, who has the cartouche behind him, Neferui·ka·zed·uah. By the usage of the Middle Kingdom *neferui* is equivalent to Ra, at the beginning of a cartouche, so that Ka·zed·uah·ra must be the throne name of the larger figure, who is doubtless the suzerain of the lesser ruler. In the field behind the larger figure and also behind the larger figure on the second half, is Ka·onkh·er·nefer·kho, which appears to be the personal name of the same. Thus we have here the record of a suzerain Ka·zed·uah·ra, Ka·onkh·er·nefer·kho, with a subject ruler Uaz·ra, who takes the titles "victorious king" and "great," and who has a son, and a wife named Hathor, or priestess of Hathor.

49. Pl. xxi. Although the exact order of the Hyksos kings is unknown, the general positions are shown by the many stages of degradation of the border designs, as tabulated in *Hyksos and Israelite Cities*, pl. li, repeated in *Historical Studies*, pl. vi. Only two of them can be connected with literary statements, Apepa I with the mathematical papyrus, and with Apophis of Josephus, and Apepa III with Apepa of the Seqenen-ra papyrus. By the time of Apepa I, the fourth or fifth of the great Hyksos kings, they had taken up much of the Egyptian civilisation, as shown by his erecting columns and a bronze gate for the temple at Bubastis; but the violent stage of the conquest is reflected in the titles of Ontha here, "Prince of the Desert, the Terror." By the style of his scarabs he stood at the beginning of this dynasty; and this title, together with the fluctuation of his name—Ontha or Ont·her—well agrees with this position. The supposed scarab of Nubti (Brit. Mus. *Cat.* 301) is probably of Tehutmes I, see 18·3·1.

The scarabs of Apepa I are remarkable for their variety of design and frequency. Here on 1 is the human-headed uraeus and *nefer*, the Agathodaimon; and the uraeus as royal emblem also appears on 6 and 7. The *nub* sign at the head of scarabs, as on 4, 6, 7, and below on 12, may well be the emblem of Set, as in his title Nubti, and the Horus on *nub* title. The twist of cord, on 3 and 4, is a Mesopotamian design; but the old Egyptian design of the entwined Nile plants was adopted, as on 11. The Agathodaimon type appears again under Oanebra, 16·A·1, 2.

50. The scarabs of Pepa were at one time assigned to Pepy of the vith dynasty. As the Hyksos types became recognised, it was seen that these were of that period; and on the strength of the long form of the signs, as on 10, 13, 14, the reading Shesha was generally adopted. But lately, guided by the names Teta and Pepa occurring in the xviith dynasty, the name has again been acknowledged as Pepa. What seems to be the best reason for the reading is the variation according to the style of the scarab. On those of the best work,

as c. 1 here, the form is quite square, and finely ribbed with three vertical strokes, unmistakably the *p* and not the *sh* sign. The scroll borders are the best class of these scarabs, and the form is nearly square on these. The most elongated form is with the most debased borders as 13, 14, 15. Thus the *sh* form must be looked on as a degradation of the *p* form.

51. Pl. xxii. As the degradation of style progressed, the reading of the names becomes more difficult, and can hardly be settled without comparing several examples. On touching the xviith dynasty, however, an entirely new departure appears under Apepa III, whose two cartouches are on a piece of chert vase of fine work in the British Museum. The style of the scarab is thick, and the signs are large and clear; the hard green paste is also revived after a long eclipse. Of the same style of scarab and hieroglyphs is the large scarab of Nub·onkh·ra, which must therefore be assigned to this period.

Another sudden change is the rise of small, clearly cut, scarabs, certainly of this age, as dated by those of Rahetep (pl. xxiii). The names of Neb·neferui·ra, Nub·sma·ra, Nub·peh·ra and Nub·hetep·ra would all well accord with the Hyksos forms.

Pl. xxiii. Rahetep was followed by Men·hetep·ra, according to an ostrakon of the xxth dynasty. A scarab here with the crowned uraeus on *nub* and Ra·men might belong to this king. A clearer example is that in Aberdeen with Ra·men·hetep, and a figure of Taurt with *onkh* (here drawn).

The name Khnem·taui·ra is in a debased border closely like that of 18·2·18. Khu·uaz, by the size, seems more like the Rahetep group. Neb·ka·ra is clearly a name, by the scarab of the same in a cartouche surrounded with *zed*, *nefer*, *onkh*, and *nub* below. (*Cairo Catalogue*, pl. v. 37082.) From the style of the border it might be of the xvith dynasty, but the xviith is more likely, on comparing the small size and square form with the plaques of the xviiith.

The xviith dynasty is only known by the names of the later kings, of whom there are very scanty remains. The royal pectoral shell of gold of Seqenen·ra is the only such object, until we reach the jewellery of Queen Aoh·hetep at the end of the dynasty. Kames, who is known by that group of jewellery, appears here on a finely-cut scarab with gold mounting (Kames 1); the signs *neter nefer da onkh* at the sides are a reminiscence of the Hyksos arrangement, and the double feather on the top is interesting as the earliest example of such on a cartouche, though seen later under Amenhetep I, Heremheb, and onward. The plaque of blue paste (2) belongs to the earlier period when Kames only claimed to be the *heq* prince, not a king.

CHAPTER VIII

THE NEW KINGDOM

(PLATES XXIII–L)

52. The xviiith dynasty opens with a rough style of scarab, none of Aohmes or Nefertari showing good work. The best cutting is that of 18·1·8, rather like that of the middle of the xiith dynasty; another echo of that age is the ball bead with titles of the queen, 18·1·25. The coarsely painted blue glazed *menats* begin in this reign (27, 28).

Pl. xxiv. Rather better work appears under Amenhetep I, though many of his scarabs are of barbarous style. The gold ring 18·2·1 was brought down to Cairo by a dealer from Thebes, a few days after the tomb of that king had been identified, by vases being found in the clearing of it. Probably therefore this was found in the course of opening the tomb. The style is quite consistent with that age; the double feather was already used by Kames, and the *ka* with the hands turned outward appears in the next reign, see 18·3·13. The form of the name is peculiar, with *zesert* for *zeser*. Light blue glass imitation of turquoise begins to appear in this reign for amulets, as in 18·2·15. The best work is on square plaques, 41 being fairly well cut.

A fresh interest begins now with the habit of making scarabs of the royal family. These were probably to be worn by officials of the households of the princes and princesses, as shown by 18·2·50, which has the name of Sat amen on one side, and that of the "keeper of the palace, Ao·ne·bau" on the other side.

Pl. xxv. Under the xiith dynasty the sub-names of the kings were sometimes placed upon scarabs; this custom was resumed by Tehutmes I and his successors, and the Horus name, Hor-nubti, and Nebti names are often found in this dynasty. On the scarab 18·3·1 is the Nebti name; and a scarab in the British Museum of similar work has a variant of this, *peh oă* (*Cat.* 301).

On 18·3·2 is a name of Tehutmes I which does not appear on other monuments. The scarab type is dropped, in 18·3·4, for a kneeling figure, which probably represents a Syrian with tribute in each hand; unfortunately the detail is worn away. A type which has not been explained yet is shown in 15 and 16. It belongs to the Thothmes age, between I and IV, by its style; yet no such name as Neferkara is known then. The explanation seems to be that the *oă* and *nefer* signs are often made much alike (see 18·3·20), and have here been confounded. Thus these would read Ra·oă ka·kheper, mer·oă·amen, "Tehutmes, greatly beloved of Amen." No. 21, with both names of the king, is very unusual in this reign.

The objects with private names are classed along with the period to which they probably belong. Nos. 22–25 appear to date early in this dynasty.

The scarabs of Tehutmes II are unusual. 18·4·1 is of the most brilliant light blue paste, only equalled by one of Hotshepsut. This has the falcon name, and No. 2 the Hor-nubti name.

53. With Hotshepsut the great diversity of the scarab begins, which characterized Tehutmes III. The falcon name on No. 1, the Nebti name on Nos. 2 and 3, and the Hor-nubti name on No. 4, are all found as at Deir el Bahri. Historical allusions begin to appear, as "setting up monuments" on No. 7. The *uzat* eye in place of the scarab, as on 13 and 34, begins a type often found later.

Pl. xxvi. No. 37 is certainly of this reign, by the close similarity to No. 39, of Nefrura. The formula of 45 is very unusual, *măot kheru kher Asar*, "justified from Osiris," or "with" or "under Osiris."

With Tehutmes III came the greatest age of the scarab, when it was most common and most varied. It has often been supposed that the name of Men·kheper·ra was engraved in later times merely as a favourite amulet. On looking over the series here of 150 selected examples, it does not seem, however, that any large number can be assigned to the styles of later times. The great majority are clearly contemporary. As we know, for certain, at least three kings named Men·kheper·ra after Tehutmes III (the priest-king, Khmeny, and Ṇḳau I), the small proportion with this name which are after the xviiith dynasty are probably contemporary scarabs of these (or perhaps other) later kings. A few here, 130–148, are left as later scarabs, as there is nothing to prove to which of the subsequent kings they belong; but all of these may be contemporary with later kings of this name.

The sub-names continued in favour, No. 1 has a new falcon name, *kho em aăkhut*, "rising in the horizon," parallel to *kho em măot* and *kho em uast* of this king. A pretty variant has the child Horus in place of the hawk, see Brit. Mus. *Cat.* 666; compare 1016. The Nebti-name, *uah nesuty*, is on No. 2. An abundance of interesting types now begins; the youthful king shooting (4), the king adoring an obelisk (12), the birth of the king at Thebes (13), the man of Qedesh making obeisance to the royal name (14), the Syrian girl lying crouched in place of the scarab, with the record of the "smiting of Qedesh" (15), the invention of hunting on horseback to capture animals (16), the setting up monuments and obelisks in the temple of Amen (17–20). Pl. xxvii. Note the titles "king of princes" (22), lion of princes (23), the divine son (34), the prisms, 57, 58, with joint names of the king and Nefru·ra, which seem to prove their marriage, and the figure of Set (65). On pl. xxvii, see the bull's head as a protector (74), the revival of scroll borders (87–93, 125), and their degradation as circles (94, 95). Pl. xxix. The queen Hotshepset Merytra appears here with the spelling Hotshepsi (150). Among the private names the cylinder of Senmut, with his titles, is of most interest (18·6·A).

54. Pl. xxx. Amenhetep II abandoned using sub-names on scarabs, but otherwise continued the style of his father, with the inscription "born at Memphis" (18·7·1), and many references to the gods. The design of four uraei which begins under Tehutmes III (18·6·46, 86) was usual in this reign, as on 26, also two uraei on 14, and 21; and continued under Tehutmes IV, see 18·8·9 and 10. The *uzat* eye continued in place of the scarab, as 18·7·10, 37, and 18·8·12. Oval plaques for rings, inscribed on each side, came into favour, as a substitute for the clumsy cartouche plaques of Hotshepsut (18·5·1, 5, 6, 22). Tehutmes III began the use of an oval plaque, as 18·6·10, 27, 46, 47, 49, 56, 115; and it was prevalent under Amenhetep II, 18·7·11, 12, 16, 17, 18, 20, 21, 22, 24, 32, 39. Under Tehutmes IV it was more usually square, as 18·8·3, 4, 5; later under Amenhetep III

these fashions almost vanish, and cowroids, *uzats*, and rings come into use. The scroll pattern was well made under Amenhetep II, as on 30; along with it was the degradation of rows of circles, which we can date to this reign by the upper name on 31, where it accompanies the *Neferui·kheper·ka* form of Senusert I, and so dates the curious later scarabs of this style, 12·2·19, 20. Nos. 18·8·13 is important as giving the name of a queen Nefertarti who is otherwise unknown.

55. Pl. xxxi. As the scarabs of Tehutmes III show the greatest variety and number, so those of Amenhetep III are of unparalleled size. Not only are there the big scarabs with long historical inscriptions, but also an extensive class of scarabs of usual types, but of two or three times the usual size. Examples are here of the lion-hunt and marriage scarabs and part of a tank scarab. The marriage scarabs are of better work than the hunting type, and have double or triple lines between the elytra, in place of single lines.

Pls. xxxii–xxxiii. The scarabs of less monstrous size 18·9·10 to 52 scarcely ever contain any historical statements, but almost all refer to the gods. Nos. 10–13 bear falcon names; 14 has the Nebti name. 16 shows that the king was born at Thebes, 17 refers to seizing Singara in Mesopotamia; otherwise they are to us mere matters of ostentation.

Pl. xxxiv. On the small scarabs there is nothing of note. The references to the gods are much fewer, and the subject of the scarab is reduced to the mere names, as in the beginning of this dynasty.

Pl. xxxv. Of queen Taiy there are many scarabs, cowroids, and rings, the fashionable shapes of the reign. There is nothing beyond the baldest titles with the name.

56. Pl. xxxvi. The revolution of Akhenaten left a great mark on the portable objects. At the beginning of his reign, scarabs of the orthodox form were usual, see 18·10·3, 4, 6, 7, 8, and the plaque was retained, No. 2. Even large scarabs were made down to the beginning of the Aten worship. On No. 1 the king is kneeling upholding the names of the Aten, while he has the cartouche name Amenhetep, which was subsequently ground out. After his conversion there is not a single scarab, except—strangely—the most personal of all, his own heart scarab 18·10·33. Rings of gold, bronze, and glazed pottery entirely superseded the scarab in private use. Pendants and rings with the queen's name are usual. The cartouches of the Aten were only worn on plaques with little rings attached, in order to stitch them on the white muslin dresses, as represented on the royal statues.

Pl. xxxvii. The use of rings continued during the Aten worship, under Smenkh·ka·aten·kheperu, and the earlier period of Tut·onkh·aten. But on his abandonment of the Aten, he ordered the worship of "his gods" (18·12·21), and scarabs re appear (20). Ra, Amen, and Ptah were all reverenced, and the royal name was changed to Tut·onkh·amen. In the next reign, of Ay, scarabs are as common as rings.

Pl. xxxviii. Under Heremheb the taste and skill, which had atoned for the previous poverty of idea in the scarab, have gone, and clumsy signs and bad spacing mark the beginning of decline. Scarabs and rings are about equally usual.

57. The xixth dynasty brought the scarab back to full use, and rings were henceforth uncommon, and became rare after Saptah. Of the brief reign of Ramessu I scarabs are not unusual.

Pl. xxxix. The cylinder, which had almost ceased to be made since the Middle Kingdom, reappears in a large form, with rather misproportioned signs (19·2·1). The large ovoid No. 2 has a rough unglazed back, as if for inlaying; it may have been inserted in a wall, like the cartouches of Sety II. The back of the plaque 17 is curious, inscribed "a thing of the king." The colour and work of this looks most like that of the xxvth dynasty. Ramenkheper was often associated with the name of Sety, and from the style it does not seem that these scarabs were issued by any of the later Men·kheper·ra kings, see 35–40. No. 43 seems of late work, about the xxvth dynasty.

Pls. xl–xlii. Sety I was often commemorated by Ramessu II, probably at the beginning of his reign. Sometimes the cartouches are side by side (19·2·45), but usually conjoined Ra-user-men-măot. Ramessu also commemorated Tehutmes III (19·2·54).

Ramessu II was rather scarce to find, in scarabs, thirty years ago, but has of late years become nearly as common as Amenhetep III. The reign is a turning-point in this, as in all artistic work, having occasionally good work at the beginning, and drifting to barbarous roughness half a century later. There are no historical types, and the only interest is in the arrogant vanity of the king. He is figured walking hand in hand with Set and Amen (No. 3), while on the Turin scarab his chair of state is carried by Set and Ra. The harvest goddess Rennut appears (15, 16, 17), though never figured in other reigns. A scroll border, and its degraded copies in circles, yet survive (45–51, 102), and then vanish finally after this reign. Rarely a delicate piece of work appears, as in 90, 91, 99, 100, which are better than almost all of the previous dynasty. The scarabs of queen Nefertari are distinguished from those of Aohmes Nefertari by the thinness and poverty of the style.

Pl. xliii. The private seals and amulets are the redeeming feature of this time. The variety of titles, and the personal interest of these seals, gives them precedence over the bald names of the kings. Some plaques are of very fine work, and were doubtless the personal seals of the high officers, as 152, 154. Others are roughly moulded in blue-glazed pottery; these must have had an original block engraved, and it seems therefore that such moulded copies were given to the sub-officials of a great officer to seal documents in his name, see 151, 153, 156.

58. Pl. xliv. There appears to have been some revival of work under Merneptah, as in 19·4·4; but most of his scarabs are of rough moulded pottery. He revived the name of Tehutmes III, associating it with his own, Nos. 9–14. According to the latest evidence found, it appears that Saptah and Tausert preceded Sety II, who was followed by Ramessu Saptah; this order is here adopted. Of Saptah I, scarabs were very rare until I found the deposits of his temple with pottery scarabs and rings. The same is true of Tausert; her scarabs, however, had been overlooked, owing to the factitious arrangement of her cartouche to resemble that of Ramessu II.

Sety II is fairly common on scarabs and plaques, but these are destitute of any additions to the bald name, except devotion to Amen and Ptah on the larger plaques (19–23). These glazed plaques are peculiar to this reign, and the purpose of them is suggested by a row of holes of similar size, running all round the walls of the court at the temple of Luqsor, four or five feet from the ground. The holes contain plaster at the back, and have evidently contained objects. Probably these plaques, or similar ones, were inserted in the holes, forming a kind of dado line of colour.

Saptah II was formerly known as Ramessu IX, Sekhoner and was supposed to come in the xxth dynasty. The discovery of a papyrus of accounts in which he follows on at the close of the reign of Sety II, proves that the xixth dynasty is his place. As it would be confusing to change all the numbers of the xxth dynasty, by inserting the name Ramessu III here, it is best to call him by what was probably his current name, Saptah. Strange to say, immediately after the papyrus was published, the excellent scarab (19·9·2) with the double name, turned up in Cairo.

59. Of Ramessu III all that can be said is that degradation progressed; nearly all his scarabs are worse than those of Ramessu II. Ramessu IV shows some more care in work, as in 20·2·1 and 10, but of a very poor style.

Pl. xlvi. Ramessu V may be said to patronise this collection, as the seventeen examples here comprise most of those known of his work. Ramessu VI is also fairly usual. The scarab here attributed to Ramessu VII has, *meses, neter heq an*, and *a*; the latter abbreviation is only found in this king's name. Ramessu VIII is very rare. Ramessu IX is yet unknown, as the king formerly here is transferred to the xixth dynasty, as Saptah II. The number may however well be left open for a king Ramessu Mery·atmu, whose name was seen by Brugsch at Heliopolis. Ramessu X, Neferkara, is well represented here on scarabs and other objects. Ramessu XI is fairly identified by the peculiar name Kheper·măot·ra, and Ramessu XII seems indicated by the name Ra·men·neit, as well as Ra·men·măot. The *kheper* on 20·10·3 seems as if it were an error for the vertical *neit* sign on No. 2. The four following scarabs, 20·10·A, B, C, D, seem to be Ramesside, but cannot yet be identified. This is the most complete series of the xxth-dynasty scarabs, and contains most of those that are known of Ramessu V–XII.

60. Pls. xlvii, xlviii. The class of heart scarabs is here put together, though they probably extend through the xviiith to xxiiird dynasties. They are arranged as nearly as may be in order of date, judging from the names and the work. The backs are drawn on pl. lxxiii. How soon the work became formal is shown by the coarse cutting of one of the age of Akhenaten found at Riqqeh (*Riqqeh*, xvi). The most notable scarab is No. 6, of the Aten period, showing how the old system was adapted to the new Aten worship; the soul was to be guarded by Aten, and to feed from the endowments of the

temple of Aten; thus the theory of temple endowments became changed to a sustentation fund for the deceased. The scarab 20, of hard green stone, has been mineralogically proved to be true jade by all tests, especially specific gravity. This is the first determination of jade from Egypt, and carries with it many similar specimens, including one on the Kennard board of amulets. The type of names, Zed·ptah·auf·onkh, etc., shows that the series descends to the xxist dynasty or later. A fixed point is given by No. 28, for Petpetur; his father was of the household of Setnekht, and this dates it to about the close of the xxth dynasty.

61. Pl. xlix.—Of the divided xxist dynasty there are very few small objects, either of the Tanite or Theban line. The scarab of Nesi·ba·neb zedu, whose cartouche was copied a century later by Sheshenq I, is fixed to the earlier king by the bright green colour and the work, which resembles that of Painezem I. The scarab reading Thent·amen·neb·apt must be of about this period, being too delicate for the next three dynasties, and it may probably belong to the queen Thent·amen. The foundation plaques of Pasebkhonut came from Mariette's work at Tanis, and I obtained them in exchange for rarer things of mine kept at the Cairo Museum. They are curious for having had the cracks in the glaze filled up with blue paste. Of Sa·amen the scarabs are fairly common, usually with the two figures of Amen or Atmu seated facing: the throne-name scarabs (21·5·1, 2, 3) are perhaps more certainly of this king. The copper plaque from Tanis also comes from Mariette's work. The scarabs of Sa·amen with Men·kheper·ra (21·5·9, 11) doubtless refer to the contemporary priest king at Thebes, as do some in the British Museum (*Cat.* 2394, 2395).

The Theban line has left scarcely any small remains. Of Painezem I there is the ivory knob of a staff (21·1·1) and three scarabs (2, 3, 4) which by their style cannot be placed to Senusert II. The interesting scarab in Cairo, drawn here, names Men·kheper·ra and his daughter queen Ast·em·kheb; it has nothing to do with Piankhy, to whom it is placed in the Catalogue.

62. The xxiind dynasty considerably revived the use of the scarab; those of Sheshenq I are as common as those of Ramessu III or Heremheb. The Hor-nubti name reappears; but the work is poor, the signs are disjointed and out of proportion,

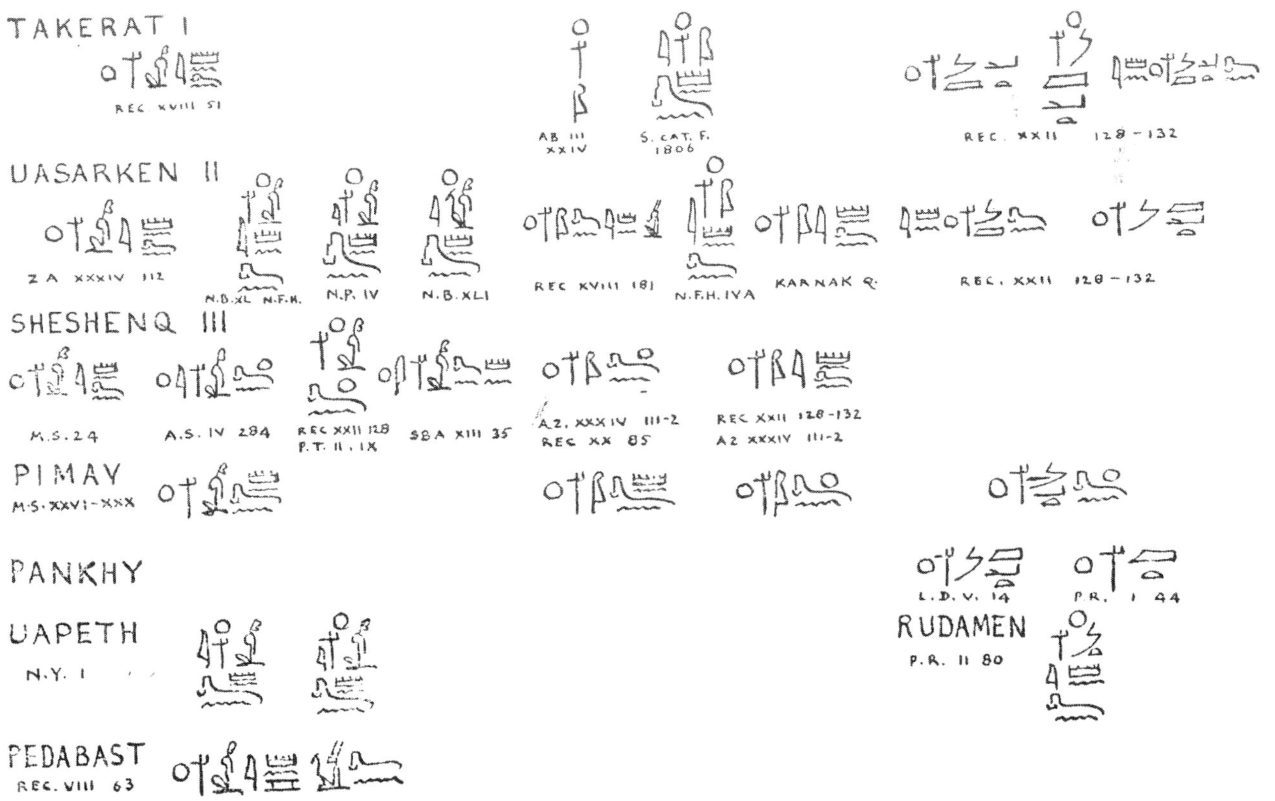

and the style is worse than anything since the late Hyksos.

Pl. l. In this dynasty we meet with one of the most difficult groups of scarabs, those of the User-măot-ra kings. In order to disentangle these, it is needful to keep closely to what we have from other monumental sources. We do not get any help from other collections, for at Cairo there is but one of this class, and that assigned to Ramessu II, and at the British Museum they are not classified quite in accord with the details of the cartouches on dated monuments, and no system is stated that will help in historical discrimination. The twenty-two User-măot-ra scarabs here, of late date, must therefore be studied apart; those of Ramessu II and III being of styles sufficiently distinct to separate them from the later ones, which range from Takerat I to Rudamen, 901–670 B.C.

The variant forms actually found on monuments are as shown on preceding page.

From these variants we may learn a few criteria.

(1) Takerat I is the only king who placed *a* and the feather *măot* in parallelism.

(2) Sheshenq III and Uapeth are the only kings to place *a* and the goddess *măot* parallel on either side of *user*.

(3) Pamay is the only king who dropped the *a* of Amen, and put only *men*.

(4) The feather *măot* is not used after Pamay.

So far as style goes we can only separate three periods:

(A) Takerat I and Usarkon II, 900–854 B.C.

(B) Sheshenq III and Pamay, 832–781 B.C.

(C) Piankhy, Uapeth and Rudamen, 748–720 ? B.C. (See *Ancient Egypt*, 1914, p. 40.)

Referring now to the scarabs there is first a group, 22·3·1–7, which by the parallelism of *a* and *măot* is to be placed to Takerat I. The backs of these are of the types F·63, 69, 74, 76, 97, T 54. Of these F 63 is like Sheshenq I E·16; F 69, 74, 76 are like F 69, and F 97 like F·96 of Usarken II. Further the V marks on the elytra are made as loops U on F 63, 76, and this peculiarity is found earlier, on Ramessu XI E·17 and XII F·76, but not on scarabs of Sheshenq III or later kings.

The next group, of 3 (22·4·1–3), has the figure of Măot; the *a* of Amen is large, and sunk down halfway to the level of *setep*. This agrees with the style of Usarken II, as at Bubastis. The backs are of E 37, F·97 and G 22; of these E·37 compares with E 72 of Usarken II; F 97 is the same as in the previous reign; G·22 is the same as in Usarken I; hence all these are against any later dating.

The next group of four (22·7·1–4) has a minute *a*, while *men* continues full size; this approaches the abolition of *a* found under Pamay, and hence is probably of his predecessor and co-regent Sheshenq III. The backs are of G 48, 76, and one broken. These are almost the same as those of Pamay, next following, G 60, 68, 76.

Next are three (22·8·1–3) without any *a* of Amen, a peculiarity of Pamay, which fixes these to his reign. Another very rude one, R 26, may be compared with J·69 of Menkara, a vassal of Shabaka, which would place it as late as is possible for its type. Another has the sickle *mă* and *setep ne ra*, a combination only found under Pamay.

Of the square plaques (22·7·5, 6) two with the goddess *măot* and *setep ne ra* can only be paralleled under Sheshenq III. No. 7 with the feather and a dwarfed *a* for Amen seems by the last detail to be of the same reign. The green glazed plaque, No. 8, may be put to this reign, as the other three come here. The king Men-neh-ra must come here by the similar style of his plaque.

It does not appear, therefore, that any of these can be placed to the Pankhy group. The piece of a statuette, 25·1, might be of Takerat I, Usarken II, or Pankhy, by the plain form of the name. The style is more like that of the later time, and the writing with the arm before the cubit sign is peculiar to Pankhy, so that it should probably be attributed to him.

It should be noted that the series of scarabs reading *hez her ma pa* are not of Pamay, as shown by the variants, which will be published with the nameless scarabs.

Pl. li. The two kings with Ra·oa·kheper name, Sheshenq IV and Usarken III, have objects differing from any of the xviiith-dynasty kings by their rude work. The reign of Usarken at Thebes is entirely included in that of Sheshenq IV at Bubastis (see *Anc. Eg.* 1914, 40); hence the difference, if any, in their work must be that of place and not of time. One scarab is distinctive; Usarken placed uraei pendant to the *ra* in his name, and such are used here on 23·2·3. This has only *Ra·kheper*, and hence we may assign to this king the scarabs on which *oă* is dropped. A stamp, 23·2·1, belongs also to this king, as he is called *setep ne amen*, an epithet never assumed by Sheshenq IV.

Three pieces seem to be connected, with a name Kheper·neb·ra. A, reading *Măot·neb, Ra·oă·kheper·neb*; B, *Ra·kheper·nub, mery măot*; C, *Ra·kheper·neb, mery măot*. The smooth back of the last is like J 4 Usarken III, and J 49 Painezem; the square plaque was used by Sheshenq III; the *ra* with uraei belongs to Usarken III; hence these are of about the close of the xxiind dynasty. It may be that only the Ra·kheper is the name, and the other signs are titular; if so these are all of Usarken III.

The Sheshenq *Ra·uas·neter* must be called Sheshenq V; he appears to be the later ruler of Busiris, named as a vassal of Pankhy. Other vassals here are Pema of Mendes, Onkh·her of Hermopolis, and probably Ptah·nefer, perhaps short for Ptah·nefer·her. The priest of Amen Her, named on the plaque H, had a sister Ast·urt, who married Her·să·ast, the founder of the xxiiird dynasty at Thebes (see *Ramesseum*, 16, 18, pl. xvi). The plaque is finely cut in green moss quartz.

The electrum pectoral of Uasa·ka·uasa is a very unusual object. The high priest Au·uar·uath, who was his father, was son of Usarken (III?), see Karnak quay (*Z.A.S.* xxxiv, 113); hence Uasa·ka·uasa probably lived about 680 B.C.

CHAPTER IX

THE ETHIOPIANS AND SAITES

(PLATES LI–LVIII)

63. THE earliest piece that we can attribute to the Ethiopian kings is the part of a statuette of Pankhy (25·1). The form of the cartouche is more like that of Pankhy than like any earlier *User-măot-ra* king; and the blue-grey stone ware is quite unlike anything of the xxiiird dynasty, but to all appearances of the xxvith dynasty or later. Of Kashta there are some scarabs of pottery, all alike, with the name of Amenardas (25·2·1). No throne name was known for Kashta, but at this period there are scarabs with the name Ra·nefer·nub (25·2·2, 3). By his titles on these he was king of Upper and Lower Egypt; the ram-head of the scarab is of the Ethiopian dynasty. The work during that dynasty shows continuous decline; and the work of this scarab is better than that of Shabaka, and therefore presumably of one of his predecessors. These facts make it probable that Nefer·nub·ra was the throne name of Kashta.

Pl. lii. Of Amenardas, scarabs are very rare; the pieces here are a foundation plaque, an *uzat* eye, and part of an inlay of lazuli. Shabaka adopted the familiar cartouche of Neferkara, and formerly many of his objects were wrongly attributed to the earlier kings of that name. On the contrary, some scarabs are at present attributed to Shabaka which may belong to earlier kings (Brit. Mus. *Cat.* 2486); so far as I have seen Shabaka, Shabataka, and later kings, do not use the *ka* sign with loops for hands, and this may serve to discriminate the earlier objects.

The fresh style coming in with the Ethiopians is very marked. The work is much better than anything since Sety I or Ramessu II. The scarab frequently has a ram's head (25·3·19; 25·5·4) or the ram on the back (25·3·3). Another feature is the kingly sphinx holding a *hes* vase (25·3·1, 19; 25·5·3, 4). The large coarse beads of glazed pottery are an innovation (25·3·15, 16; 25·4·5, 6). Little cartouches of glazed pottery are frequent (25·3·8–13).

64. We now reach the age of vassal kings, which continued to the dodecarchy. From the records of Pankhy and Esarhaddon, we see how numerous were the petty chiefs, eighteen or twenty, and the tale of the breast-plate names twenty-three chiefs. Several of these can be identified on scarabs; and these lists can by no means sum up every chief who ruled during sixty years of such divisions. It is therefore only natural to find many personages named on scarabs and small objects, who have not been embalmed in history.

Menkara appears to have been a vassal of Shabaka; on the cylinder (25·3·20) we read Ra·men·ka along with Ra·nefer·ka (Shabaka). On 25·3·22, 23, 24, he calls himself the Horus Menkara, not taking the *nesut bat* or *sa ra* titles of a king. He honours Bastet (23, 24), and was therefore probably a ruler of Bubastis. There are many of this ruler in the British Museum (*Cat.* 27–32, 34–42, all of the same style).

A son of this later Menkara, or Menkaura, is named in a piece of a late Book of the Dead in the Parma Museum. This was written for the "scribe of the divine offerings Zesef·em·hăă, son of the *nesut deshert* Ra·men·kau." This form of the royal title shows that he was a Delta king, and there can be no question left as to this late recurrence of the name.

The group of late re-issues of early kings found at Saqqara (QUIBELL, *Excavations at Saqqara*, 1905–6, p. 31, pl. xxxvii) of which the sketches are here given, show the style of late issues. They are entirely different to the contemporary issues of those kings.

65. To Pankhy II a scarab in the British Museum is assigned; another is in Cairo (sketched here), which has been hitherto overlooked. Associated with his son Taharqa, as regent of Egypt, his name is on a scarab in the Ward Collection; and associated with his daughter Shepenapt, on a scarab at Munich (*Frazer*, 363).

Taharqa is fairly common, and nearly half of all the examples are here. They are coarser than the work of his predecessors. The later Ethiopian Asperuta, who reigned during the earlier half of the xxvith dynasty, is placed here at the close of the Ethiopian series. His name is only known on stone inscriptions, beside this pendant.

Pl. liii. Of all the vassal chiefs Men·her·ra has left most remains; but he always took a subordinate place in relation to Men·kheper·ra Khmeny. The latter king is well authenticated by the stele of him and his daughter (*Student's History*, iii, 293); and the indications point to his having ruled in Upper Egypt, probably at Hermopolis. Thus the way would be clear for Men·her·ra to be a Delta vassal, and both of them to be under the overlordship of the Ethiopians. (For Men·her·ra in British Museum, see *Cat.* 1418, 1419, 1421; for Men·kheper·ra, *Cat.* 1420, 1422, 1423). There is a very curious expression on 25·c, ·22, 23, "Thou becomest with a cartouche," suggesting that he was then aspiring to take a cartouche like a full king; and on his other scarabs the name is in a cartouche. He appears with full royal titles on a plaque of this age in the British Museum (*Cat.* 1484). Men·ab·ra was another of these vassal kings of this period.

Pl. liv. Several other obscure names appear, which may perhaps be some day put in their true place and connection. The historical link is re-established in Baknerenf, of whom two objects are given here (24·2·1, 2), and one in the British Museum (*Cat.* 233).

66. Nekau I, the father of Psemthek I, has hitherto been very obscure. His remains are cleared up by the statuette of Horus, dedicated by "the king Ra·men·kheper, son of Ra, Nekau, the Horus, given life by Neit lady of Sais." This Men·kheper·ra name of Nekau I is confirmed by a scarab in the British Museum, with the conjoined cartouches (*Cat.* 2529, see also No. 1484). A scarab with Men·kheper·ra and the Theban ram of this age (25·5·2) is probably of this king, but may be of Menkheperra Khmeny. Another scarab (25·5·3) is very interesting; it is headed by the sun and lion which belong to Psemthek I, and then has Psemthek as king of Upper and Lower Egypt, kneeling and adoring the name of his father Men·kheper·ra Nekau.

Pl. lv. Psemthek appears to have taken the Ra and lion as his badge, as it here heads a large scarab bearing his falcon name and personal name (26·1·1). The allusion of the lion seems to be to the origin of his name "the lion's son," the word *zam* or *them* for a lion occurring in both Upper and Lower Egypt (see DE ROUGÉ, *Geog.* 99), and in Libyan *izem*. On 26·1·2 the lion is accompanied with *Psem* or *Pthem*; and the other Ra and lion scarabs (3 to 10) are all of this period. The sphinx and *hes* vase of the Ethiopians was continued on 26·1·17. There is a very unusual scarab of massive silver (No. 45) with the names and titles of Psemthek and his Theban consort Shepenapt.

There seems to have been a vassal ruler named Kheper·măot-ra, of whom three amulets are here; one, with the cartouche of Psemthek on the reverse, dates the group.

67. Pl. lvi. The objects of Nekau II are not common, the majority of those known being here. The fine scarab 26·2·1 is the best work known after the xixth dynasty. The *menat* with a private dedication on the back (26·2·4) is extremely unusual, if not unique. The scarabs of Psemthek II are rather common, and they seem to have been made by Greeks for trading purposes. The scarabs of Men·ab·ra (pl. liii) must not be confounded with these, as is done in some collections.

The scarab of Onkh·nes·ra·nefer·ab is rather suspicious in the colour and appearance; but a forger might have more exactly copied the cartouche, which is here bungled. The bronze stamp (26·3·10) is unquestionable, as also the sealing of her minister Sheshenq. No other small objects of this queen are known. Apries (Hoo·ab·ra, Hophra) having the same throne name as Psemthek I, it is very likely that some of the scarabs with that name belong to the later king, especially those made at

Naukratis. Against this is to be set the absence of any scarabs with his personal name, and the large number with the name Psemthek.

Under Aohmes II appears the last signet cylinder of Egypt, 26·5·3. His scarabs are very rare, and foundation plaques, *menats*, and sealings are the usual objects. Of Psemthek III no objects are known, except the scarab 26·6; this appears to give his name, Onkh·ka·ne·ra, abbreviated as Onkh·ne·ra.

68. Pl. lvii. Rare as scarabs became under the xxvith dynasty, they disappear entirely under the Persians, and only *menats* and seals are known. This is an evidence of the essentially religious character still attached to the scarab amulet; for were it only a seal, it would be as likely to be made under the Persians or Ptolemies as under the Saites or Mendesian kings. The sling bullet of Khabbash, 28·1, is the only object of this king. One scarab appears under Naifourud (29·1); this is not likely to be of Merneptah, as the earlier king always uses the figure of Ra and not only the sign, and he never follows the natural order by placing the *Ba* first. The work is delicate, but has none of the virility of the xixth dynasty. Of Haker only one object is known, the sealing here.

69. A few scarabs of the xxxth dynasty are known. By the evidence of building at Khargeh Nekht·neb·f preceded Nekht·her·heb, and is therefore so placed here. The scarab 30·1·1 is certainly very late, by the uraei proceeding from the sides of the *kheper*, and cannot be of the xiith dynasty. Zeher is only known, in small objects, by the piece of a splendid blue bowl, found in the palace at Memphis (30·2·). Nekht·her·heb is only represented by seals and foundation deposits, and no scarabs are known.

Of the second Persian rule there are no remains, large or small, except the jar lid here, with a rude cartouche of Arsess, the Arsēs of Greek history. The colour and style of this glazed pottery is between that of the xxxth and Ptolemaic periods, exactly what would be expected of the xxxist dynasty.

70. Alexander's conquest is represented by a single bronze stamp in the British Museum. The onyx here ascribed to Ptolemy I is certainly of Greek period; it represents an Egyptian king in native head-dress, and the full jaw and straight nose well accord with the coins of Ptolemy Soter in his earlier days. As it is much less likely that later Ptolemies would appear in Egyptian style, this may be ascribed to Soter. Of Ptolemy III there are two well-made foundation plaques; the second has on the reverse the same cartouche as the first. A stout seal of bronze, formerly gilt, bears a bearded head of a king, closely like Ptolemy IV, and no other attribution seems possible. Of later Ptolemies, the British Museum has stamps and foundation deposits of vii and xiii.

The Roman period has left no objects with emperors' names except the large white marble scarab in Paris, with the wings inscribed for Antoninus; and the gold ring shown here, with an impression, probably the official signet of the prefect of Egypt. The prefect was usually a knight—the lowest class that might legally use a gold ring—so for official purposes of a royal signet, gold would be restricted to the use of the prefect.

71. The private scarabs and seals which belong to the xxvith to xxxth dynasties are placed at the end. Three are of viziers; the vizier Khet (30·C.) is unknown otherwise; the scarab is of soft brown steatite, and the style of it suggests the xxvth dynasty. It can hardly be earlier, from the agate beads found with it, when the tomb at Abusir was robbed by natives in 1904. Her·să·ast (30·D.) has a variant title *mer nuti* (in place of *nut*) which is very unusual. But he may well be the prophet of Amen, *mer nut*, vizier, Her·să·ast, whose coffin is at Cairo; from his genealogy he was about the xxist, and certainly before the xxvith dynasty. Tehuti (30·E) might possibly be the vizier Tehuti·em·nefa·baka; he lived under Ptolemy Soter, as his grandfather was named Nekht·her·heb. This amulet with the baboon does not however seem to be nearly as late as that, and might even go back to the xixth dynasty.

The scarabs with private names are placed in alphabetic order; and after them are the seals and impressions, likewise. They belong to the official world of the latest dynasties. The only peculiar title is "servant of Neit at the stele" (A.D.), and "the stele of the water" (B.R.).

CONTENTS OF PLATES IN HISTORICAL ORDER

PERSONS not of the royal families are indexed alphabetically in the subsequent list.

The number before a name is the king's number in the dynasty. Where a letter precedes the name the order in the dynasty is unknown. Following the name is the total number of scarabs, cylinders, amulets, etc., which are published. The numbers in each separate collection follow in columns. The names in the families of the kings are slightly set back. The plate numbers are put at the right-hand edge. This list is not exhaustive, but will show the minimum of what is published.

	Total.	Univ. C.	B.M.	Cairo.	Paris.	Turin.	Munich.	Aberdeen.	Golenishef.		Plate.
DYNASTY I											
1 MENA	3	2	—	—	1	—	—	—	—		VIII
2 AHA	1	1									
5 HESEPTI	2	2									
DYNASTY II											
4 PERABSEN	1	1									
6 KARA	1	—	—	—	—	—	—	—	—	Oxford	
9 KHOSEKHEMUI	1	1									
DYNASTY III											
1 NEBKARA	13	4	3	—	3	—	1	—	—	Sayce, Price	
? KHOBAU	1	1									
9 SNEFERU	5	3	1	1							
DYNASTY IV											
2 KHUFU	22	7	6	1	1	1	2	4	—		
KHNEM·KHUF	1	1									
3 KHOFRA	26	11	11	—	—	—	1	2	1		
4 MENKAURA	10	2	2	1	—	—	1	3	1		IX
5 ZEDEFRA	2	2 ?									
6 SHEPSESKAF	1	1									
Private	1	1									
DYNASTY V											
1 USERKAF	1	—	1								
2 SAHURA	7	4	2	—	—	—	1				
3 NEFERARKARA	4	—	1	—	—	—	2	—	—	Ward	
4 SHEPSESKARA	1	—	—	—	—	—	—	1			
6 NEUSERRA	3	2	1								
7 MENKAUHER	1	—	1								
8 ZEDKARA	6	4	—	—	—	—	—	1	—	Price	
9 UNAS	29	6	14	2	1	—	3	2	1		
DYNASTY VI											X
1 TETA	1	—	1								
3 PEPY I	20	6	7	—	—	3	—	2	—	Murch. Price	
4 MERENRA	1	1									
5 PEPY II	1	1									
? NEFER·SA	1	1									

	Total.	Univ. C.	B.M.	Cairo.	Paris.	Turin.	Munich.	Aberdeen.	Golenishef.		Plate.
DYNASTIES VII–VIII											
2 NEFERKARA . . .	5	2	1	—	—	—	1	1			
9 NEKARA . . .	2	2									
10 TERERU . . .	1	1									
? SNEFER·ONKH·RA . .	1	1									
DYNASTIES IX–X											
1 KHETY I . . .	3	1	—	—	2						
2 KHETY II . . .	1	1									
? KA·MERY·RA . .	1	—	—	—	1						
? SHENES . . .	2	—	1	—	—	—	—	1			
Private ix–xi . .	25	25	—	—	—	—	—	—	—		XI
DYNASTY XI											
ANENTUF	2	—	—	—	—	—	1	1			
MENTUHETEP II . .	13	4	4	1	2	—	1	1			
ANTEF V	14	8	3	—	2	—	—	—	—	Price	
NUB·SESHES·RA. . .	1	1									
DADAMES . . .	1	1									
MENTUEMSAF . . .	2	1	1								
NEBHAPRA . . .	2	—	1	—	1						
OASHET	1	—	1								
SONKH·KARA . . .	2	1	1								
DYNASTY XII											XII
1 AMENEMHOT I . .	13	6	3	—	2	—	1	—	1		
2 SENUSERT I . . .	67	35	12	2	6	—	4	4	2	Price 2	
3 AMENEMHOT II . .	40	16	8	3	6	1	1	4	1		XIII
4 SENUSERT II. . .	28	10	9	3	—	1	2	—	2	Oxford	
HATHER·SAT . .	1	—	—	1							
MERRYT . . .	5	—	—	5							
5 SENUSERT III . .	57	21	18	3	9	2	3	1			
6 AMENEMHOT III . .	64	24	28	5	—	1	5	—	—	Brocklehurst	XIV
7 SEBEKNEFRU . .	2	—	1	—	—	—	—	1			
8 AMENEMHOT IV . .	4	1	1	—	2						
Private xii–xiii . .	517	168	100 ?	14	21	11	48	15	30	110 others	XV
ERDANEPTAH . .	1	—	—	—	—	—	—	—	—	Brocklehurst	XVIII
KHENSU . . .	1	—	—	—	1						
SENBHENOS . .	2	—	1	1							
UAZET . . .	1	1									
NUBEMTHA . .	1	1									
RESUNEFER . .	1	—	1								
SAT·SEBEK . .	1	—	—	—	—	—	—	—	—	Davis	
DYNASTY XIII											
? HER·TEP·TAUI . .	1	—	—	—	—	—	—	—	—	March	
2 SEKHEM·KA·RA . .	1	1									
? ONKH·NEFERU·UAH·RA .	1	1									
? NEFER·ONKH·RA . .	5	3	—	—	—	—	2				
6 SONKH·AB·RA . .	1	1									
8 SEHETEP·AB·RA . .	1	1									
9 SESHESH·KA·RA . .	1	—	—	—	—	—	—	—	—	Amherst	
11 RA·SEBEK·HETEP . .	4	1	—	—	2	—	—	—	—	Price	
15 SEBEK·HETEP I . .	13	4	4	—	—	—	2	2	—	Murch	
? HETEP·KA·RA . .	1	1									
SE·BEKA·KA·RA . .	2	2									
20 SEBEK·HETEP II . .	10	2	1	2	1	—	—	—	3	Palin	
HA·ONKH·TEF . .	1	1									
KEMA . . .	1	1									

DYNASTY XIII (*Contd.*)	Total.	Univ.C.	B.M.	Cairo.	Paris.	Turin.	Munich.	Aberdeen.	Golenishef.		Plate.
21 NEFER·HETEP	20	6	5	1	2	1	3	—	1	Stuttgart	
22 SEBEK·HETEP III	86	23	28	6	6	—	6	4	5	8 others	XIX
? KHO·KA·RA	1	1									
24 SEBEK·HETEP IV	4	2	?	1	1						
25 AOAB	2	1	—	—	—	—	—	1			
26 AY	23	5	5	4	2	—	2	1	1	3 others	
27 ANA	1	—	—	—	1						
ANA	8	3	1	—	1	—	1	—	1	Thilenius	
36 MER·KHEPER·RA	1	—	1								
41 ABA	2	1	1								
53 NEHESI·RA	2	1	—	—	—	—	—	—	—	Amherst	
A·SAT·HATHER	2	1	—	—	1						
ATHA	1	—	—	—	—	—	—	—	1		
NUB·EM·ANT	1	—	—	—	—	—	1				
KHOT·KA·KAU	1	—	—	—	1						
NEB·TEP·AHIU	1	—	1								
SAKETSA	1	—	1								
B ANTEF	1	1									
C, D NEHESI	3	2	—	—	—	—	1				
E QEPUPEN	2	1	—	—	1						
F SEPED·NEB	1	1									
G–J APEQ	12	3	3	—	—	—	3	1	—	Pr. MacGr.	
K NEFERT·ONQET·UBU	3	1	—	—	—	—	2				
L TUR	1	1									
AOH·TAU·THA	2	—	1	—	—	—	—	—	—	Davis	
REN·SENB	1	—	1								
NEB·NETERU	1	—	1								
? UAZED	3	—	1	1	—	—	—	1			
? SMEN·ABT·RA	1	—	—	—	—	—	1				

DYNASTY XIV	Total.	Univ.C.	B.M.	Cairo.	Paris.	Turin.	Munich.	Aberdeen.	Golenishef.		Plate.
69 SUAZENRA	10	5	2	—	1	—	—	—	—	Alnwick, Sayce	
76 NEFER·AB·RA	1	1									
? SEBEK·EM·SAF	2	—	1	—	—	—	—	—	—	Price	
M KHENZER	4	2	1	—	—	—	1				
N KHONDY	2	1	—	—	—	—	—	—	—	Blanchard	
O SEKHEM·ZET·ONKH·RA	1	1	—	—	—	—	—	—	—		XX
P PEMAOT·RA	1	1									
Q, R SMA·KA·RA	2	2									
S–AC NEFER·RA	11	11									
AD NEFERUI RA	1	1									
AE NEFERU RA	1	1									
Names ?	4	4									
AK UAZ·KA·RA	5	1	4								
AL NE·KA·RA	17	4	4	—	3	—	3	1	—	Ward. Leiden	
Names ?	11	11									
BA KA·ZED·UAH·RA·UAZ·RA	1	1									

DYNASTY XV	Total.	Univ.C.	B.M.	Cairo.	Paris.	Turin.	Munich.	Aberdeen.	Golenishef.		Plate.
1 ONTHA	2	1	—	—	—	—	1	—	—		XXI
2 SEMKEN	1	—	—	—	—	—	1				
3 KHYAN	17	1	3	1	—	—	3	—	—	4 Murch, 5 others	
4 YAQEB·ORH	9	—	2	1	1	—	1	1	—	2 Murch, Price	
5 APEPA I	35	19	6	—	1	—	2	1	—	6 others	
APEPA	1	—	—	—	—	—	—	—	—	Oxford	

DYNASTY XVI		Total	Univ. C.	B.M.	Cairo.	Paris.	Turin.	Munich.	Aberdeen.	Golenishef.		Plate.
A	OA·NEB·RA	3	3									
	SEKTI	1	—	1								
B	MAOTABRA	54	9	21	7	3	1	3	2	2	6 others	
C	PEPA	63	16	14	4	5	1	5	4	2	12 others	
D	NEFER·GER	1	1	—	—	—	—	—	—	—		XXII
E	KHO·USER·RA	7	2	—	1	—	—	—	2	—	Brux. Oxford	
F	SE·KHO·NE·RA	27	8	6	1	3	1	2	3	—	3 others	
G	NEB·UAH·AB.	2	1	—	1							
H	YEKEB·BOR	6	5	—	—	—	—	—	1			
J	OA·HETEP·RA	5	2	1	—	—	—	1	—	—	Davis	
	QAR	2	—	—	—	—	—	—	2			
K	KHO·RA	2	2									
L	OA	8	4	—	1	—	—	—	—	—	3 others	
	NUBY·RA	1	—	1								
M	MAOT·RA	1	1									

DYNASTY XVII		Total	Univ. C.	B.M.	Cairo.	Paris.	Turin.	Munich.	Aberdeen.	Golenishef.		Plate.
A	APEPA III	3	1	1	—	—	—	—	—	—	Alnwick	
B	NUB·ONKH·RA	1	1									
C	NEB·DAT·RA	1	1									
D	NEB·NEFERUI·RA	1	1									
E	NUB·SMA·RA	1	1									
F	NUB·PEH·RA	1	1									
G	NUB·HETEP·RA	5	3	—	—	—	—	2				
H	RA·HETEP	10	6	—	—	1	—	3	—	—		XXIII
J	MEN·HETEP·RA	1	?	—	—	—	—	—	1			
K	KHNEM·TAUI·RA	1	1									
L	KHU·UAZ	1	1									
M	NEB·KA·RA	2	1	—	1							
N	SEQENEN·RA I	1	1									
O	KAMES	4	2	2 ?								

DYNASTY XVIII		Total	Univ. C.	B.M.	Cairo.	Paris.	Turin.	Munich.	Aberdeen.	Golenishef.		Plate.
1	AOHMES I	51	12	15	2	2	3	4	3	2	8 others	
	NEFERTARI	68	17	29	5	2	3	2	1	2	7 others	
2	AMENHETEP I	179	43	81	11	6	8	6	3	3	18 others	XXIV
	AOH·HETEP	11	3	4	1	2	—	1				
	NEBTA	2	1	—	—	—	—	—	—	—	Mather	
	MERYT·AMEN	7	2	2	1	—	—	—	1	—	Ward	
	SAT·AMEN	4	1	2	—	1						
	MES·AMEN	1	1									
	KA·MES	1	1									
	ONKHET·TAUI	1	1									
	SAT·AOH	3	2	—	1							
	TURSI	1	—	—	—	—	—	—	—	—	Diospolis	
	BEKT	1	—	1								
	MER·NUBTI	1	—	1								
	TEMT	1	—	1								
3	TEHUTMES I	86	21	29	8	5	2	3	3	4	11 others	XXV
	Private	3	3									
4	TEHUTMES II	19	7	5	1	—	—	2	1	—	3 others	
5	HOTSHEPSUT	149	35	65	3	11	4	5	1	—	25 others	XXVI
	NEFRURA	16	8	4	—	4						
6	TEHUTMES III	1791	146	1068	106	14 +	27 +	27	14 +	22	367 others	XXVII
	HOTSHEPSI	1	1									
	Private	19	18	—	—	—	—	—	—	—	Murch	
7	AMENHETEP II	195	41	91	5	7	6	6	2	6	31 others	XXX
	ARAT	1	—	—	—	—	—	1				
8	TEHUTMES IV	67	12	29	3	6	2	4	2	—	9 others	
	NEFERTARTI	1	1									

DYNASTY XVIII (*Contd.*)	Total.	Univ. C.	B.M.	Cairo.	Paris.	Turin.	Munich.	Aberdeen.	Golenishef.		Plate.
9 AMENHETEP III	624	131	220	28	48	21	14	14	8	140 others	XXXI
TAIY	113	37	34	2	5	3	3	5	4	20 others	XXXV
HENT·TA·NEB	1	1									
10 AMENHETEP IV	11	9	2								
AKHENATEN	98	26	33	3	2	1	5	1	—	27 others	XXXVI
NEFERYTAI	14	7	2	—	1	—	1	—	—	3 others	
THE ATEN	11	9	—	—	—	—	1	—	—	Price	
MERTATEN	2	2									
ONKHSNEPA·ATEN	2	1	1	—	—	—	—	—	—		XXXVII
11 SMENKH·KA·ATEN	24	11	7	—	—	—	2	—	—	4 others	
MERT·ATEN	1	1									
12 TUT·ONKH·AMEN	86	31	16	—	2	1	6	1	—	29 others	
AMEN·ONKHS	6	3	1	—	—	—	2				
13 AY	25	10	7	—	1	—	2	—	—	5 others	
14 HEREMHEB	86	27	20	1	7	3	4	1	—	23 others	XXXVIII
NEZEM·MUT	3	2	—	—	—	—	—	—	—	Berlin	
3 Private	3	3									
DYNASTY XIX											
1 RAMESSU I	40	11	15	1	3	1	2	4	—	3 others	
2 SETY I.	147	43	45	6	12	7	4	2	—	28 others	XXXIX
TUA	3	1	2								
3 RAMESSU II	510	148	183	28	39	23	7	12	4	66 others	XL
NEFERTARI	22	7	9	1	3	—	—	—	—	Ward, Price	
MAOT·NEFRU·RA	2	—	2								
KHOEMUAS	2	1	—	—	—	—	—	—	1		XLIII
18 Private	21	19	1	—	—	1					
4 MERNEPTAH	31	14	4	—	2	2	2	1	—	6 others	XLIV
5 AMENMESES	5	1	4								
6 SAPTAH (462)*	6	4	1	—	—	—	1				
BAY (78)*	4	3	—	—	—	—	1				
7 TAUSERT (551)*	13	6	1	—	—	—	1	—	—	5 others	
8 SETY II	95	33	24	2	6	2	1	4	2	21 others	XLV
9 SAPTAH II	2	2									
10 SET·NEKHT	10	1	6	1	—	—	1	—	—	Alnwick	
DYNASTY XX											
1 RAMESSU III	88	26	39	—	5	1	6	—	—	11 others	
2 RAMESSU IV	49	12	20	1	2	—	2	2	—	10 others	
3 RAMESSU V	23	17	5	—	—	—	—	—	—	Ward 2	XLVI
4 RAMESSU VI	17	8	4	1	2	—	—	—	—	2 others	
5 RAMESSU VII	3	1	—	—	1	1					
6 RAMESSU VIII	4	2	2								
8 RAMESSU X	9	7	—	—	1	—	—	1			
9 RAMESSU XI	7	4	1	—	—	1	1				
10 RAMESSU XII	6	4	1	—	1						
Uncertain	7	4	3								
Heart scarabs	29	29	—	—	—	—	—	—	—		XLVII
DYNASTY XXI											
1 NESI·BA·NEB·ZEDU	1	1									
THENT·AMEN	1	1	—	—	—	—	—	—	—		XLIX
2 PA·SEB·KHONUT I.	8	3	2	—	—	—	—	—	—	3 others	
5 SA·AMEN	33	11	13	1	1	—	1	2	1	3 others	
6 PA·SEB·KHONUT II	1	1									
THEBAN XXI											
3 PAINEZEM I	12	4	—	—	6	2					
4 MEN·KHEPER·RA				} 1							
AST·EM·KHEBT	1	—	—								

* Total numbers in foundation deposits (*Six Temples at Thebes*).

DYNASTY XXII

	Total.	Univ. C.	B.M.	Cairo.	Paris.	Turin.	Munich.	Aberdeen.	Golenishef.		Plate.
1 SHESHENQ I . . .	88	14	32	4	7	5	3	4	1	18 others	
2 USARKEN I . . .	18	7	1	—	—	1	—	—	—	9 others	
3 TAKERAT I . . .	10	7	2	—	1	—	—	—	—		L
KAROMOA . . .	1	—	—	—	—	—	—	—	—	Ready	
4 USARKEN II . . .	40 ?	8	20 ?	1 ?	1	1	3	—	—	6 others	
KAROMO . . .		} 1									
5 SHESHENQ II . .	1	}									
6 TAKERAT II . . .	2	1	1								
7 SHESHENQ III . .	12	8	—	1	1	—	—	-	—	2 others	
MEN·NEH·RA . .	1	1									
8 PAMAY . . .	8	6	—	—	—	—	—	1	1		
9 SHESHENQ IV . .	39	17	7	—	1	1	5	4	—	4 others	

DYNASTY XXIII

	Total.	Univ. C.	B.M.	Cairo.	Paris.	Turin.	Munich.	Aberdeen.	Golenishef.		Plate.
1 PEDA·SA·BASTET . .	2	1	1	—	—	—	—	—	—		LI
2 USARKEN III. . .	27	15	6	—	1	—	5	—	—	Alnwick	
? KHEPER·NEB·RA . .	4	3	—	—	—	—	—				
? SHESHENQ V . .	1	1									
RUDAMEN . . .	1	—	—	—	1						
PEMA	5	1	—	—	—	—	3	—	—	MacGr.	
ONKH·HER . . .	1	1									
PTAH·NEFER. . .	1	1									
Private . . .	3	3									

DYNASTY XXV

	Total.	Univ. C.	B.M.	Cairo.	Paris.	Turin.	Munich.	Aberdeen.	Golenishef.		Plate.
1 PANKHY I . . .	1	1									
2 KASHTA . . .	9	3	1	2	—	—	1	—	—	Price, Leiden	
AMENARDAS . .	9	3	2	2	—	—	—	—	—	Alnwick 2	LII
3 SHABAKA . . .	65	17	16	2	4	3	5	2	1	15 others	
A MENKARA . . .	27	5	17	1	—	—	2	—	1	Price	
4 SHABATAKA . . .	14	6	1	1	1	1	1	—	1	2 others	
PANKHY II . . .	2	—	1	1							
5 TAHARQA . . .	20	8	3	2	1	—	1	—	1	4 others	
ASPERUTA . . .	1	1									
ADILENERS . . .	1	—	—	—	1						
B MEN·HER·RA . .	27	20	—	—	—	3	2	2	—		LIII
With next . . .	10	6	—	—	—	1	3				
C MEN·KHEPER·RA . .	25	17	(2383)	6	—	1					
D MEN·AB·RA . . .	22	15	5	—	—	—	2				
E AB·MAOT·RA . .	2	2	—	—	—	—	—	—	—		LIV
F NUB·AB·RA . . .	2	1	1								
G KHEPER·AB·RA . .	2	2									
H AR·AB·RA . . .	3	1	1	—	1						
J MEN·NEFER·AB . .	1	1									
Names ? . . .	9	9									
K NUB·MAOT·RA . .	2	2									
L MAOT·HETHES·RA . .	8	8									
Names ? . . .	7	7									

SAITES
DYNASTY XXIV

	Total.	Univ. C.	B.M.	Cairo.	Paris.	Turin.	Munich.	Aberdeen.	Golenishef.		Plate.
2 BAKNERANF . . .	6	2	1	—	1	—	1	—	—	Davis	

DYNASTY XXV

	Total.	Univ. C.	B.M.	Cairo.	Paris.	Turin.	Munich.	Aberdeen.	Golenishef.		Plate.
5 NEKAU I . . .	5	3	1	1							

	Total.	Univ. C.	B.M.	Cairo.	Paris.	Turin.	Munich.	Aberdeen.	Golenishef.		Plate.
DYNASTY XXVI											
1 PSEMTHEK I	101	42	29	7	2	2	2	3	1	13 others	LV
SHEPENAPT	7	2	2	—	2	—	—	—	—	Hood	
A·KHEPER·MAOT·RA	5	3	2								
2 NEKAU II	14	8	5	1	—	—	—	—	—		LVI
NEITAQERT	2	—	1	—	1						
3 PSEMTHEK II	21	8	2	—	2	2	1	—	—	6 others	
ONKH·NES·RA·NEFER·AB	2	2									
Private	1	1									
4 HOO·AB·RA	21	4	5	1	3	1	2	3	—	2 Berlin	
5 AOHMES II	39	7	8	3	7	1	5	—	—	8 others	
6 PSEMTHEK III	1	1									
DYNASTY XXVII											
2 DARIUS	8	2	1	1	2	—	—	—	—	2 others	LVII
DYNASTY XXVIII											
1 KHABBASH	1	1									
DYNASTY XXIX											
1 NAIFOURUD	3	1	1	—	—	—	—	—	—	Petrograd	
2 HAKER	1	1									
3 PSAMUT	1										
DYNASTY XXX											
1 NEKHT·NEBEF	12	5	1	—	2	—	1	—	—	3 others	
2 ZEHER	1	1									
3 NEKHT·HER·HEB	6	2	2	1	—	—	1	—	—		
DYNASTY XXXI											
2 ARSES	1	1									
GREEK											
ALEXANDER	1	—	1								
PTOLEMY I	1	1									
PTOLEMY III	4	2	1	—	1						
PTOLEMY IV	1	1									
PTOLEMY VII	3	—	3								
PTOLEMY XIII	1	—	1								
ROMAN											
ANTONINUS	2	1	—	—	1						
Private scarabs and seals	65	65	—	—	—	—	—	—	—		LVIII

SUMMARY

We can now make a census of published scarabs, cylinders, and sealings which shows a minimum amount, but which would not probably be increased by more than a sixth or an eighth if completed, apart from the enormous number of Tehutmes III. The numbers in collections are:

	Kings.	Tehut. III.	Private.	Total.	Royal persons.	Early cylinders.
University College .	1648	146	334	2128	240	69
British Museum	1545	1068	101?	2713	149	
Cairo Museum	218	106	14	338	72	
Paris .	318	14+	21	353	90	
Turin .	133	27+	12	172	46	
Munich .	235	27	48	310	94	
Aberdeen .	143	14+	15	172	61	
Golenisheff .	69	22	30	121	34	
Others .	725	367	111	1203	—	107
Totals .	5034	1791	686	7510	297	176

Taking the number of examples in each dynasty, as showing the fluctuations in time, there are in the 7510

ist Dyn.	(6)	ivth .	64	viith–viiith	9
iind .	3	vth .	51	ixth–xth .	7
iiird .	19	vith .	24	xith .	63

xiith .	289	xixth .	942	xxvith .	214
Private .	517	xxth .	214	xxviith .	8
xiiith .	231	xxist .	44	xxviiith .	1
xivth .	74	xxist .	13	xxixth .	4
xvth .	65	xxiind .	220	xxxth .	19
xvith .	183	xxiiird .	45	Private .	65
xviith .	33	xxivth .	269	xxxist .	1
xviiith	1999	xxivth .	6	Ptolem. .	11
Tehut. III,	1791	xxvth .	5	Roman .	2

Regarding individual rulers the names most often occurring are, Tehutmes III, 1791 (probably 5 to 10,000 in all); Amenhetep III, 624 (perhaps 800–1000 in all); Ramessu II, 510 (say 700); Amenhetep II, 195; Amenhetep I, 179; Hatshepsut, 149; Sety I, 147; Taiy, 113; Akhenaten, 109; Psemthek, 101. It is remarkable that the Hyksos kings Maot·ab·ra and Pepa are as often met with as the great kings of the xiith dynasty.

In the above census the hundreds of jar sealings, mostly of the ist dynasty, are not included; they are of a very different class to the scarabs and seal rings, and would unduly swell the list, especially at University College. About fifty more common scarabs of kings are not included above, as they are in the College series of local groups, which are kept apart to illustrate the style of different regions. They will be published with the remainder of the scarabs.

WORKS BY W. M. FLINDERS PETRIE

THE PYRAMIDS AND TEMPLES OF GIZEH. (Out of print.)*
TANIS I. 19 pl., 25*s.* *Quaritch.* TANIS II. Nebesheh and Defenneh. 64 pl., 25*s.* *Quaritch.*
NAUKRATIS I. 45 pl., 25*s.* *Quaritch.*
HAWARA, BIAHMU, AND ARSINOE. (Out of print.)
KAHUN, GUROB, AND HAWARA. (Out of print.)*
ILLAHUN, KAHUN, AND GUROB. 33 pl., 16*s.* (Out of print.)*
MEDUM. 36 pl. (Out of print.)
TELL EL AMARNA. (Out of print.)
KOPTOS. 28 pl., 10*s.* *Quaritch.*
A STUDENT'S HISTORY OF EGYPT. Part I., down to the XVIth Dynasty. 5th ed. 1903. Part II., XVIIth and XVIIIth Dynasties. Part III., XIXth to XXXth Dynasties. 6*s.* each. *Methuen.*
TRANSLATIONS OF EGYPTIAN TALES. With illustrations by Tristram Ellis. 2 vols., 3*s.* 6*d.* each. *Methuen.*
DECORATIVE ART IN EGYPT. 3*s.* 6*d.* *Methuen.*
NAQADA AND BALLAS. 86 pl., 25*s.* *Quaritch.*
SIX TEMPLES AT THEBES. 26 pl., 10*s.* *Quaritch.*
DESHASHEH. 37 pl., 25*s.* *Quaritch.*
RELIGION AND CONSCIENCE IN EGYPT. 2*s.* 6*d.* *Methuen.*
SYRIA AND EGYPT. 2*s.* 6*d.* *Methuen.*
DENDEREH. 38 pl., 25*s.*; 40 additional plates, 10*s.* *Quaritch.*
ROYAL TOMBS OF FIRST DYNASTY. 68 pl., 25*s.* *Quaritch.*
DIOSPOLIS PARVA. 48 pl. (Out of print.)
ROYAL TOMBS OF EARLIEST DYNASTIES. 63 pl., 25*s.*; 35 additional plates, 10*s.* *Quaritch.*
ABYDOS. Part I. 81 pl., 25*s.* *Quaritch.*
ABYDOS. Part II. 64 pl., 25*s.* *Quaritch.*
METHODS AND AIMS IN ARCHAEOLOGY. 66 blocks, 6*s.* *Macmillan.*
EHNASYA. 25*s.* *Quaritch.* ROMAN EHNASYA. 10*s.* *Quaritch.*
RESEARCHES IN SINAI. 186 illustrations and 4 plans, 21*s.* *John Murray.*
MIGRATIONS. Huxley Lecture, 1906. 11 pl., 2*s.* 6*d.* *Anthropological Institute.*
HYKSOS AND ISRAELITE CITIES. 40 pl., 25*s.* *Quaritch.* (With 48 extra plates, 45*s.*, out of print.)
RELIGION OF ANCIENT EGYPT. 1*s.* *Constable.*
GIZEH AND RIFEH. 40 pl., 25*s.* *Quaritch.* (With 69 extra plates, 50*s.*, out of print.)
ATHRIBIS. 43 pl., 25*s.* *Quaritch.* (Out of print.)
PERSONAL RELIGION IN EGYPT BEFORE CHRISTIANITY. 2*s.* 6*d.*; *in leather*, 3*s.* 6*d.* *Harper.*
MEMPHIS I. 54 pl., 25*s.* *Quaritch.*
QURNEH. 56 pl., 25*s.* *Quaritch.* (Out of print.)
THE PALACE OF APRIES (MEMPHIS II). 35 pl., 25*s.* *Quaritch.*
ARTS AND CRAFTS IN ANCIENT EGYPT. 45 pl., 5*s.* *Foulis.*
THE GROWTH OF THE GOSPELS. 2*s.* 6*d.* *Murray.*
MEYDUM AND MEMPHIS III. 47 pl., 25*s.* *Quaritch.*
EGYPT AND ISRAEL. 54 figs. 2*s.* 6*d.* *S.P.C.K.*
HISTORICAL STUDIES. 25 pl., 25*s.* *Quaritch.*
REVOLUTIONS OF CIVILISATION. 57 figs. 2*s.* 6*d.* *Harper.*
THE FORMATION OF THE ALPHABET. 9 pl., 5*s.* *Quaritch.*
ROMAN PORTRAITS (MEMPHIS IV). 32 pl., 25*s.* *Quaritch.*
THE LABYRINTH AND GERZEH. 52 pl., 25*s.* *Quaritch.*
PORTFOLIO OF HAWARA PORTRAITS. 24 col. pl., 50*s.* *Quaritch.*
TARKHAN I AND MEMPHIS V. 81 pl., 25*s.* *Quaritch.*
HELIOPOLIS I, KAFR AMMAR, AND SHURAFEH. 58 pl., 25*s.* *Quaritch.*
TARKHAN II. 72 pl., 25*s.* *Quaritch.*
RIQQEH AND MEMPHIS VI. 62 pl., 25*s.* *Quaritch.*
AMULETS. *Constable.* 53 pl., 21s.
SCARABS. 73 pls., 32*s.* *Quaritch* (*ready soon*).
TOOLS AND WEAPONS. 80 pls. (*in preparation*).

Of works marked * a few copies can be had on application to the Author, University College, London.

INDEX

For royal personages in historical order see the preceding list.
For private persons and titles see the following alphabetical lists lithographed.

INDEX OF PRIVATE NAMES A—M.

INDEX OF PRIVATE NAMES M–S.

INDEX OF PRIVATE NAMES S–Z.

ALL KINGS AND MEMBERS OF THE ROYAL FAMILIES ARE PLACED IN THEIR HISTORICAL ORDER IN THE PREVIOUS LIST.

INDEX OF TITLES A–H.

INDEX OF TITLES H–Z.

CATALOGUE OF SCARABS, CYLINDERS, ETC., BEARING NAMES

EARLY CYLINDERS

All black steatite unless otherwise stated

SEATED FIGURES

No.	Inscription	Translation	Ref.	Collection
1	DA ZEFĂ ER TETY, DA ZEFĂ, DA ZEFĂ, DA.	*Give food to Tety, give food, give food, give* (table of offerings)		U.C.
2	NET AT THETH, NER-HER.	*Like to Neit* (and her) *father, Ner-her.* (Ner-hor, see Nera-ra, name)	A·E·39.	Newberry
3	RY, RY.	*Ry*	A·E·12	Strassburg
4	EM HEH, DA DA HEH.	*In eternity gifted with eternity.* (Seated figure and *aakhet* combined.)		Murch
5	BA, NET,K,RENEN RENEN RENEN.	*Ba and Neit (give) thee youth* (?)		U.C.
6	NETER NET, BA NETER ZEFA.	*The god Neit and the god Ba (give) food*		
7	NET KHET, HATHOR KHET ZEDED.	*Follower of Neit, follower of Hathor, Zeded* (det., a cake)	A·E·6	MacGregor
8	SEN NE ONZ BA.	*Conformed to the Osiris ram*	A·E·5	MacGregor
9	THETH NE OA BA, THETH NET.	*Like to the great Ba, like to Neit*	A·E·36	U.C.
10	THETH ĂHAT, THETH AOH NE BEB.	*Like to Ahat, like to the circulating moon*	A·E·82	Blanchard
11	THETH BA TET, SEKHMET THETH.	*Like to Ba the generator, like to Sekhmet*	A·E·43	MacGregor
12	SEKHENTET HES.	*Cause to repose, Hes*		Murch
13	NET HEN, UAZET HEN NET (HEN).	*Priest of Neit, priest of Uazet*	A·E·8	MacGregor
14	AUOT-S NET S.	*Her inheritance is Neit*	A·E·80	Blanchard
15	NET HEN THETH.	*Like Neit and Hen*	A·E·78	Blanchard
16	(Much worn)			MacGregor
17	KA NEB NET KA NEB.	*Neit is mistress of the Ka*	A·E·79	Blanchard
18	NET KHET HEP (?).	*Neit . . . . . .*	Edwards	U.C.
19	SE KHA-S UAZET, UAZ NET KHA.	*Remember her Uazet . . . . .*	A·E·9	U.C.
20	KAT-S SUN-S.	*May her ka cause her to exist*	S.D·81	Naga ed Deir
21	UAZET SENT SENT SENT-S.	*Uazet conform her*	A·E·10	Murch
22	DET SEN SEN (repeated).	*Gifted with union*		MacGregor
23	THETH NETERU SEKHER NAS (repeated).	*Like to the gods, cause pleasing by invocation* (?)	A·E·42	U.C.
24	UAZET SA SA SA			Blanchard
25	THETH HAIT, SEN SEN HAIT-S.	*Like to Hait, she is united to Hait* (Hait, "shiners," sun and moon)	A·E·44	U.C
26	NET SENSENT.	*United with Neit*	A·E·3	U.C

EARLY CYLINDERS. SEATED FIGURE AND OFFERINGS

I

1 

2 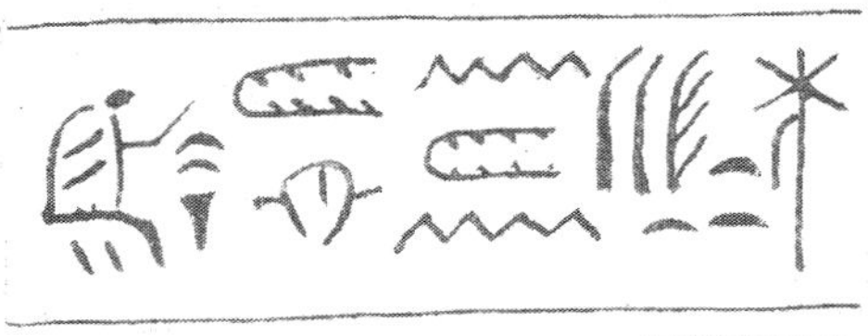

3 

4 

5 

6 

7 

8 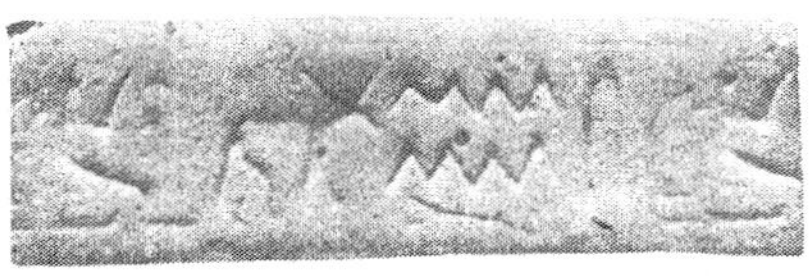

9 

10 

11 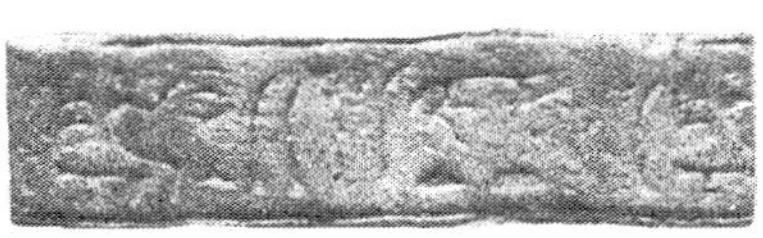

12 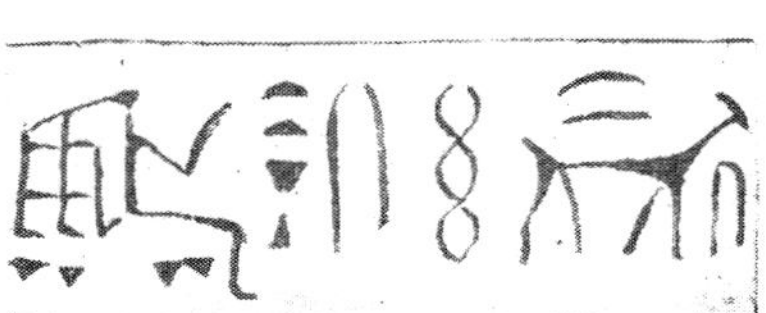

13 

14 

15 

16 

17 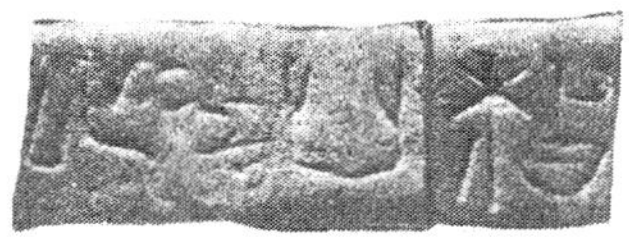

18 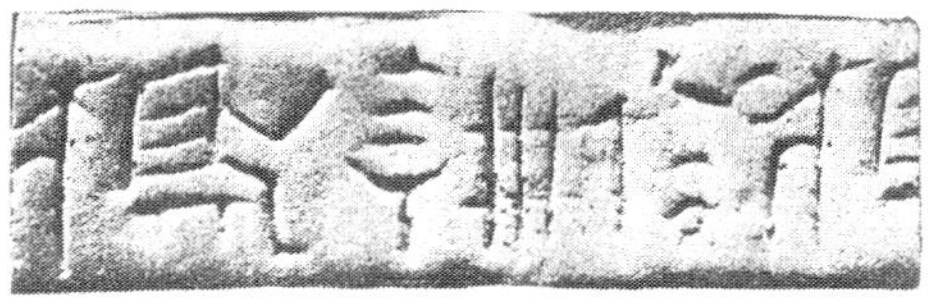

19 

20 

21 

22 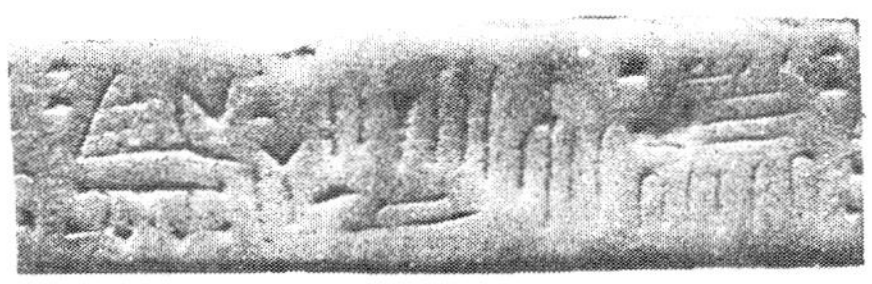

23 

24 

25 

26 

27

28

29

30

31

32

33

34

35

36

37

38

39

40

41

42

43

44

45

46

47
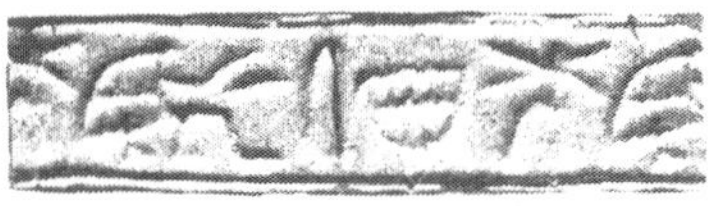

48

49
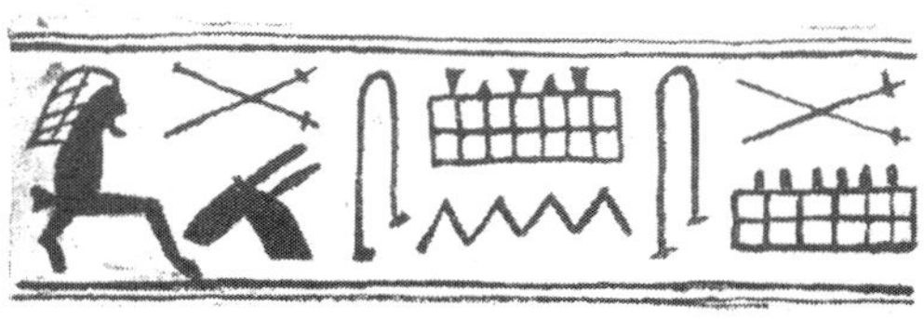

50

51
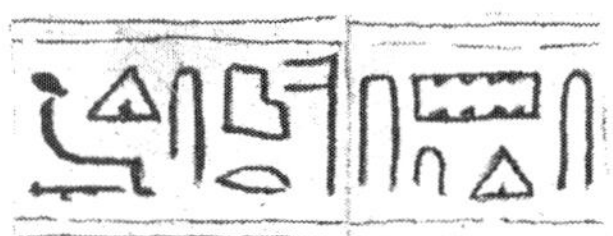

52

53

54

55

56

SEATED FIGURES (*continued*)

No.	Reading	Translation	Ref.	Collection
27	SEMERT THETH, MER-S THETH NET, DA-NEIT.	*Causing love like, she loves like, Neit. Da-neit* (name)	A·E·41	Amherst
28	HĂ BA, HĂ-S.	*Ba is behind* (protects), *behind her*	A·E·4	U.C.
29	THETH NET, UAZET THE, THETH UAZET; M,.	*Like to Neit, like to Uazet, M* (or Ma, name)	A·E·37	U.C.
30	NET THETHET, HEN THETH.	*Like to Neit, like to Hen.*	A·E·38	U.C.
31	NET THETHET, NER.	*Like to Neit, Ner* (name).	A·E·33	U.C.
32	HER PER NET KA, HER ER SENTHI PER KA, KA NET.	*Over the temple of the ka of Neit, over the surveys of the temple, Ka-neit.*	A·E·62	Naga ed Deir
33	HER PER SENTHI NET PER KA, HER PER-S.	*Over the surveys of the temple of the ka of Neit, over her temple*	A·E·63	Naga ed Deir
34	HER(?) SENTHI AN, KAHERS, PER AS, KAHERS.	*Over the surveys of the valley cemetery, and office of plans, Ka-her-s*	A·E·64	Naga ed Deir
35	NET PER KA, HER SENTHI AS. S.D. 81, also 32–34	*Temple of ka of Neit, over the surveys and plans.*	A·E·61	Naga ed Deir
36	KA-S ONZ SHEPSES.	*May her ka be safe and glorious*		Newberry
37	THETHET NET, SHU THETHET.	*Like to Neit, like to Shu*	A·E·35	Murch
38	SHU TET, TET NET.	*Like to Shu, like to Neit*		
39	SHEDET NE DESHET.	*Food for Deshet* ("Rhodopis," *r* omitted as in *deshet* = Mars)	A·E·46	U.C.
40	NET HĂ.	*Neit is behind* (protects)	A·E·7	MacGregor
41	NET THE.			Murch
42	THETHET NET, PA-KA-ASHED.	*Like to Neit, Pa-ka-ashed* ("This ka of the Persea")	A·E·87	Blanchard
43	PA-KHET-NET.	*Pa-khet-neit* ("This offering to Neit")	A·E·81	Blanchard
44	HEP SEN·S HEP		Edwards	U.C.
45	MEMU or MUI.	*Memu* or *Mui* (*name*)		Lady Smyth
46	HETEP HETEP.	*Hetep* (name)		U.C.
47	NET NEB-S.	*Neit is her mistress*, or name ?	A·E·76	Blanchard
48	NET THE, HEKASEN.	*Like to Neit, Hekasen*	A·E·77	Blanchard
48A	NET HENT, BA HENT (see pl. lxxii).	*Priestess of Neit, priestess of Ba* (*Ab.* ii, xii)		Abydos
49	NET MEN-S, MEN-S NET.	*Net establish her* S.D. 81	A·E·2	Naga ed Deir
50	DY HEH.	*Gifted with eternity*	A·E·84	Blanchard
51	SE DA, SHESES ASAR, SEDA.	*Seda, scribe of Osiris, Seda* (see Sedat wife of Khufu)		Robertson
52	SENT MUT, DA-S SEN.	*United to Mut, grant her union*	A·E·85	Blanchard
53	THETH. *Theth*	Beside these names, the signs by the figure are similar in these two	Frazer 2	Munich
54	AH. *Ah* ("rejoice")	(as 53)	A·E·1	U.C.
55	URP SHEPS (?)			U.C.

56 Fragment dated to S.D. 78–80, beginning of ist dynasty, *El Amrah*, pl. vi

PHRASES

No.	Inscription	Translation	Reference	Collection
57	NEH, NEH (inverted).	*Protect, protect*		U.C.
58	?			U.C.
59	NETER SEKER SEZEF.	*The god Sokar nourish* (the dead)	Edwards	U.C.
60	RESHEF FĂOĂ.	*May He rejoice, Faoa* (name) ?		U.C.
61	KA SHEPS, KA SHEPS.	*The glorious ka*		U.C.
62	MER ZEFA (repeated).	*Loving food*	Edwards	U.C.
63	Fragment with double animal.			U.C.
64	Two figures of goats, signs reversed and confused.			U.C.
65	AS UNUT NET.	*Place of the hour-priest of Neit*	A·E·65	Amherst
66	AS REST UNUT NET.	*Place of watching of the hour-priest of Neit*	A·E·66	Naga ed Deir
67	Too much worn to read clearly		5034	Brussels
68	HEN SETI, ANPU, NET.	*Priest of Sati Anpu and Neit*	2865	Brussels
69	?		A·E·102	Blanchard
70	?			U.C.
71	S-KHENT NEN NE KA-S.	*Establish the form of her ka*	A·E·29	Naga ed Deir
72	S-KHENT ZED-S KA-S.	*Establish the words of her ka*	A·E·30	Naga ed Deir
73	Similar, but confused.			
74	?		Brown stone	
75	SEHES-S SAHU NETER-S.	*She causes the praises of Sahu her god.*		Naga ed Deir
76	S·AUN, S·UN, SEN NET (repeated).	*Cause union, cause existence conformed to Neit*	A·E·24	Athens
77	NEZEM SEN NEZEM-S UAZET-NES.	*Sweetness conformed to her sweetness, Nes-uazet*	A·E·57	MacGregor
78	Fragment			Naga ed Deir
79	SEN-S, SEN-S, SEN-S			Blanchard
80	ANPU SEN-S, KAT SENSEN-S, SENKA. (name)	*Anpu conform her, the ka be united to her. Senka*	A·E·31	MacGregor
81	SEN SEN SĂ, TET.	*United to the god Sa, Tet* (name)	A·E·94	Blanchard
82	Fragment.		S.D. 65–76	Ivory, *Diospolis* pl. x
83	?			U.C.
84	A MET MET (?)			U.C.

57
58
59
60
61
62
63
64
65
66
67
68
69
70
71
72
73
74
75
76
77
78
79
80
81
82
83
84

85 

86 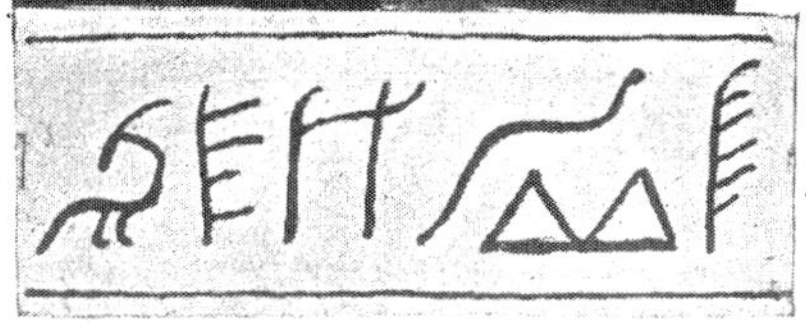

87 

88 

89 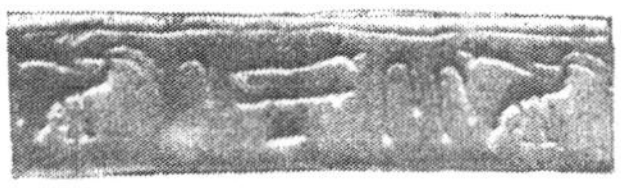

90 

91 

92 

93 

94 

95 

96 

97 

98 

99 

100 

101 

102 

103 

104 

105 

106 

107 

108 

109 

110 

111 

112 

113 

114 

AĂKHU BIRDS

No.	Inscription	Translation	Source	Reg.	Collection
85	AB, AĂBA.	*Aaba* (name)		A·E·88	Blanchard
86	AZU . . . . (Signs not clear)			Frazer 5	Munich
87	TEKHA . . . . TEKHA.	*Tekha* (name, "belonging to Tehuti")	Plain of Sharon		Herbert Clarke
88	THETH KA, THETH KA.	*Like to the ka*	Edwards	A·E·15	U.C.
89	S-SEF OĂT-S.	*Cause purity in her dwelling*		A·E·21	MacGregor
90	THETHET MAFDET, AT THETHET.	*Like to Mafdet, like to the father*		A·E·14	U.C.
91	SEKHMET MĂ, SEKHEM-S MĂOT.	*Beholding Sekhmet, truly she rules*		A·E·18	
92	S·SEKH MĂO, SEKHEM-S MĂOT (repeated).	*Truly making to abound, truly she rules*		A·E·19	
93	REKA (repeated).	*Reka* (name)		A·E·16	U.C.
94	KA-F SEMES KA-S.	*His ka causes to be born her ka*		A·E·22	MacGregor
95	ATHET REKHES HU, TEPA.	*Of King Athet (Zet), carver of food, Tepa* (see L.D. ii 35, *Rekhes*)		5035	Brussels
96			S.D. 81	A·E·20	Naga ed Deir
97	KA-NE-HER.	*Kanehor* (name)			Robertson
98	S-MEN-S ANPU, SET.	*Anpu make her enduring, Set* (name)	S.D. 81	A·E·17	Naga ed Deir
99	SES, HEN BA, SES BA.	*Priest of Ba, Ses* (name, see Sesa usual in Old Kingdom)		Frazer 3	Munich
100				A·E·89	Blanchard
101	SEKHMET THETHET PEKA.	*Like to Sekhmet, Peka*	Edwards	A·E·13	U.C.

TITLES AND PHRASES

No.	Inscription	Translation	Source	Reg.	Collection
102	SEM KHNEM, PE HES HETEP.	*Sem Priest of Khnum, Peheshotep*			
103	PER NET PE, NER PE PER NET.	*This temple of Neit, Guardian of this temple of Neit*		A.E·90	Blanchard
104	KA ANTI AM NETER.	*May the ka return among the gods* (?)			Blanchard
105	HEN B RY, NEFER UZ MĂO RY.	*Ry, truly excellent in command Ry.*		A·E·55	U.C.
106	TET NE NET, NET-MEST-ONKH.	*Like unto Neit, Neit-mest-onkh* (name)		A·E·47	U.C.
107	?				U.C.
108	. . . . SEKHEN KA F.	*May the sunboat morn and even contain his ka.*			U.C.
108A	(pl. lxxii) RE NE NETER AM SERQET PER NETER.	*Mouth of god who is in the temple of Selqet*			Blanchard
109	. . . . . . HER UASEB ?	*The lands of Horus* (the king) *in Oxyrhynkhos*	Edwards	A·E·67	U.C.
110	HENT BA NEB HER-MER-SHE, HEN BA, HEN NET.	*Priest of Ba lord of Hormershe, priest of Ba, priest of Neit*		A·E·23	U.C.
111	PEKH DENA UP OĂ.	*Cutter of dykes, opener of canal banks*		A·E·69	U.C.
112	UP OĂ NENA.	*Opener of canal banks Nena*		A·E·100	Blanchard
113	BENERT NEF NE DUAT.	*Sweetness of breath for Dua* (name)		A·E·59	MacGregor
114	. . . . DEN (UDYMU).	(DEN name joined with Aăkhu)			MacGregor

PHRASES (*continued*)

115	NETER SHED, NETER SHEDET.	*God save, God nourish thee*	A·E·27	U.C.
116	NETER HEMT, SHEDET.	*Wife of the god, Shedet*	A·E·96	Blanchard
117	DA NE SEBEK, NEFER-HETEM.	*Gift of Sebek, Nefer-hetem* ("Excellence of fulfilment")	A·E·91	Blanchard
118	SETEM NET, SEBA.	*Neit makes perfect Seba* (crocodile as Neit)	A·E·92	Blanchard
119	HEN RĂ UN.	*Let pleasing speech be*	A·E·58	MacGregor
120	UNENKA.	*Unenka* (name)	A·E·101	Blanchard
121	HEMT-F TEMKA.	*His wife Temka*	A·E·56	U.C.
122	APT PERT NEFER.	*The woman's house, the house of beauty*	A·E·68	U.C.
123	NETERU AĂKHU ONKH, DADA ONKH.	*Gods of the living spirits give life*	A·E·95	Blanchard
124	. . . . ERDANEFER.	. . . . . . *Erda nefer* (name, as Eudōros)	A·E·99	Blanchard
125	KA-S SENEN BAT.	*Her ka is united to the king.*	A·E·93	Blanchard
126	PER-S SEN NE KHENT, SHA.	*May she go forth conformed from the Khent hall, Sha*	A·E·98	Blanchard
127	?			U.C.
128	AM KA, AM KA, ZET AM.	*Be with the ka, be with the ka, forever with it*	Frazer 4	Munich

COLUMNAR INSCRIPTIONS

These continue into the Old Kingdom, and are later than most other cylinders: the style of them is mostly very corrupt

129	NESUT HEN NEFER HETEP, AHU.	*Royal servant of Nefer-hetep* (Khonsu of Thebes) *Ahu.*		U.C.
130	NETER NEFER AR KHET HATHER NETER HEN, NEBT AM DUAT.	*Good god of action, priest of Hathor, mistress in the palace hall*	A·E·105	Blanchard
131	SEHEZ . . . . . . SENSHE.	*Interpreter* (of an office) *at Senshe* (a place)	Wood	Murch
132	NEFER PERT RA NEB, TET NE MERUT NEKHEBT, HER-NESA.	*A good going forth every day, like Nekhebt for love, Nesa-hor*	A·E·52	U.C.
133	NETER NEFER SE UN NE NEFER-NI-ONKHTI.	*Good God cause existence for Nefer-ni-onkhti*	A·E·25	U.C.
134	ZEFA SHEMU AĂKHET, REN	*Food in harvest and inundation for Ren . . . .*		U.C.
135	?			U.C.
136	REN NEFER.	*Good name*		U.C.
137	REN SHESET (?)		Edwards	U.C.
138	?			MacGregor
139	Debased imitation of inscription			U.C.

115

116

117

118

119

120
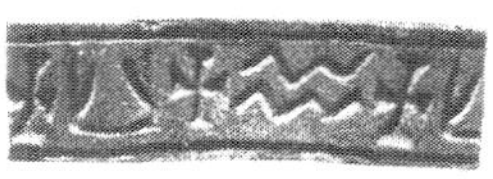

121

122

123

124

125

126

127

128
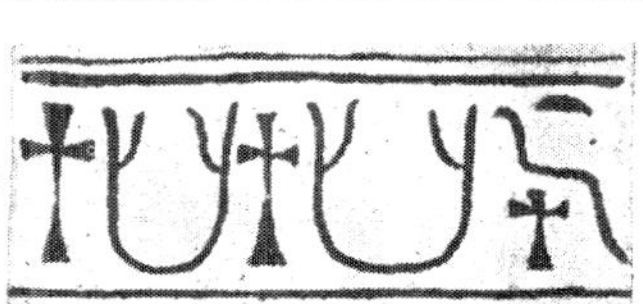

129

130

131

132

133

134

135

136

137

138

139

FIGURES

140 

141 

142 

143 

144 

145 

146 

147 

TITULAR INSCRIPTIONS

148 

149 

150 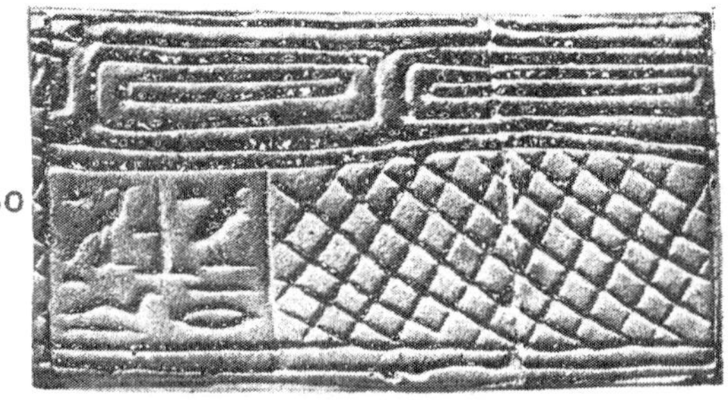

151 

152 

153 

154 

155 

FIGURES

No.	Description	Material	Owner
140	Two men facing, carrying a triple bunch; couchant lion and hippopotamus; two human figures combined	Red limestone	U.C.
141	Man marching, two lizards, two scarabs, Taurt and man	Yellow steatite	Murch
142	Man marching with staff, crocodile, seated man (inverted)	Limestone	U.C.
143	Three men marching, one kneeling (captive ?), wavy lines interlaced and loop patterns	Limestone	U.C.
144	RA NEFER . . . . . Man dancing, two fishes	Limestone	U.C.
145	Man marching with ibex, circles and barred pattern	Brown steatite	U.C.
146	Ram, cow, and ibex, with plants		MacGregor
147	Men dancing, somersaulting and running, two royal hornets, two scarabs, dog ? and monkey ?	Black steatite	U.C.

TITULAR INSCRIPTIONS

No.	Inscription	Translation	Material / Ref.	Owner
148	QĂ OĂ KA NETER HER QA, KAT.	*Lifter of the door of the ka of divine Horus statue, Kat.*	Wood	U.C.
149	NESUT MERERT REP NEFER, HER·NESAT.	*Whom the king loves increases excellently, Nesat hor*	A·E·60	MacGregor
150	TU NER UZAT ZETTA.	*Thou art tended and preserved for ever*	Bone A·E·26	U.C.
151	ZESTA HEB NEFERT RENNUT, NEFERTU.	*Sealer of cultivation, excellent of crops, Nefertu*	A·E·72	MacGregor
152	KHENT KHERP, TEHUTI HEN, BA HEN ANPU HEN, TEHUTI BA HEN.	*Leader of the Khent hall, priest of Tehuti, Ba, and Anpu*	A·E·97	Blanchard
153	O KHETMI SHEPSESH.	*Caravan (imports) sealer, Shepsesh* (Shepses ?)	A·E·86	Blanchard
154	HER KHETM SESH NEB, SEZA.	*Over the sealing of all secrets, Seza*	A·E·103	Blanchard
155	King walking with *sag* animal and birds; in a foreign style different to others		A·E·104	Blanchard

ROYAL AND PRIVATE CYLINDERS

156 NESUT BAT, King seated ?, Crocodile, HER MER TAUI (?). If this be read so, it is of Pepy I Limestone U.C.

157 HER NET HO (?), HER PA KHRED, ..., KHER HEB MER·NE·HEZ (crown ?) MacGregor

158 ? Black steatite Murch

159 EMTRE NESUT SEN-MUT NEBT MERT. *Royal overseer, Sen-mut, loved by her mistress* Berlin

160 NESUT SĂT, MEHEN-PET-TA. *Royal daughter, Mehen-pet-ta* Carnelian Munich

161 KHERP MĂOT, ONKH-NEKHT, OĂT NEFER MER, ONKH-NEKHT. *True ruler, keeper of the excellent gems* (?) *Onkh-nekht* Limestone U.C.

162 HETEP UR HER ONKHFNEKHT. *Great peace be upon Onkhefnekht* Clay incised wet U.C.

162A (pl. lxxii) ONKH·NE·SET. *Onkh-ne-set* (name, see Onkhneptah, Onkhneamen) Blanchard

163 KHETM UZAU PERZET SHENUT . . . . *Seal of stores of the estate, the granary of barley and speit,*
DEB MĂ SHE, *at the lake of the hippopotamus and lion,*
MESAH SĂ SĂT-EM-SELQET. *Mesah son of Sat-em-selqet* Limestone A·E·75 U.C.

164 ? A·E·54 Macgregor

165 S·UAZ NE NESUT, TET NE NEFER HAIT, *Caused to flourish because of the king, like to the excellence of Hait,*
MART TET NE NEKHEBT MERU, PER-SEN (?) *similarly like to Nekhebt loving, Per-sen* A·E·53 Goodison

166–170 NETER HEN HATHER TET NE MERU NEKHEBT — *Prophet of Hathor, like Nekhebt for love* (This phrase seems to mean that the person has been assimilated to the goddess Nekhebt by the love of the goddess, or of the person.) A·E·48, 50, 49, 51 U.C.

171 HATHER TET NE, SET, NET, HER, UN (NEFER). *Like to Hathor, Set, Neit, Horus and Unnefer* A·E·45 U.C.

172 HATHER DUAT, MERA. *The adorer of Hathor, Mera* A·E·28 U.C.

173 HATHER NETER HEN, HEB NEHAT, NEFER. *Prophet of Hathor lady of the Sycomore, Nefer* (name) U.C.

174 Onkh between two falcons, and emblem of Hathor, are evidently copied and debased from the button seals. This cylinder must therefore belong to the vith or viith dynasty U.C.

156

157

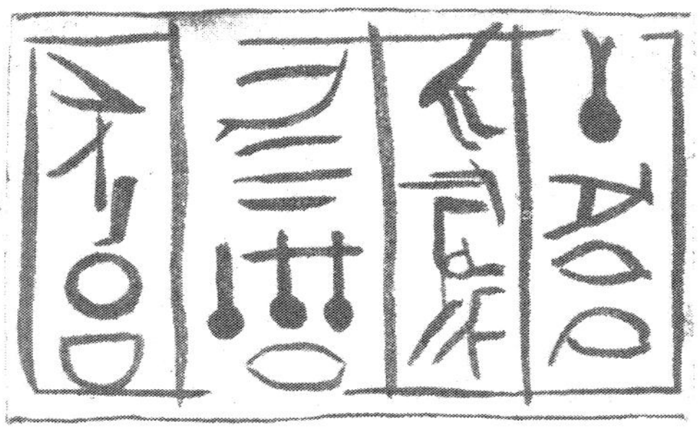
158

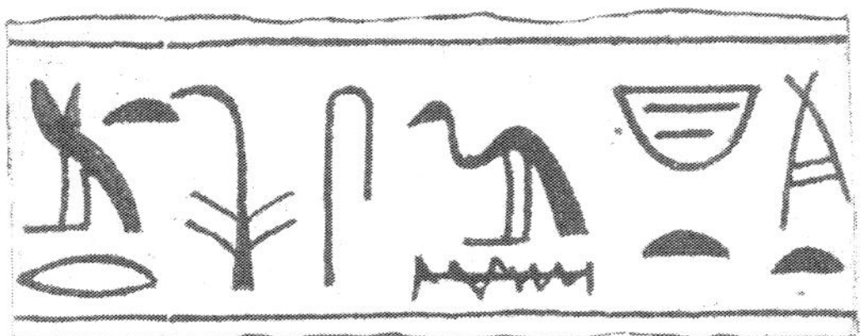
159

160

161

162

163

164

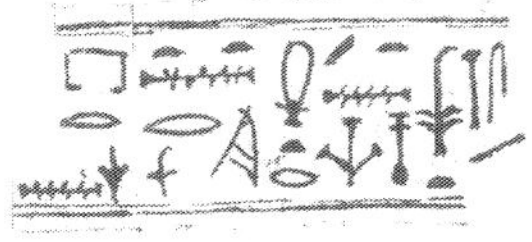
165

166

167

168

169

170

171

172

173

174

DYNASTY I MENA 1 2

1.2 AHA

1.5 HESEPTI 1 2

DYNASTY II 2.4 PERABSEN 2.6 KARA

2.9 KHO. SEKHEMUI

2 ? KHO. BAU

DYNASTY III 3.1. NEB. KA. RA 1 2 3 4

3.9 SENEFERU 1 2 3 A

DYNASTY IV 4.2 KHUFU 1 2 3 4

5 6 7

KHNEM-KHUF

4.3 KHOFRA 1 2 3 4 5 6 7 8

9 10 11 12

SCARABS, CYLINDERS, ETC., IN UNIVERSITY COLLEGE

1·1 — *Ist DYNASTY.* 1. MENA

No.	Inscription	Material	Ref.
1	RA MENAS (Of late date, possibly commemorating Mena)	Glaze gone white	N. 18
2	RA MENAS " " " " "	Gone grey	K. 74

1·2 — 1·2. AHA (TETA)

No.	Inscription	Material	Ref.
	HER AHA. Ka name	Abydos, Crystal	Vase

1·5 — 1·5. SEMTI (HESEPTI)

No.	Inscription	Material	Ref.
1	HESEPTI MĂOT KHERU. (Of late date, perhaps modern)	Pottery, green glazed	L. 92
2	" " " "	Blue green glaze	C. 12

2·4 — *IInd DYNASTY.* 4. PERABSEN

No.	Inscription	Material	Ref.
	RES KHETM O NEB, HER SEKHEM-AB PERABSEN. *South sealer of every document of Perabsen*	Clay seal	

2·9 — 2·9. KHO-SEKHEMUI

No.	Inscription	Material	Ref.
	HER, KHOSEKHEM (UI); SET, NETERUI AM-F (HETEP). *Khasekhemui, in him the two deities are in peace*	Abydos. Diorite	Bowl

2 ? — 2 ? KHO-BAU

No.	Inscription	Material	Ref.
	HER, KHO·BAU; HER NUBTI, ART·ZEDF	Clay sealing	

3·1 — *IIIrd DYNASTY.* 3·1. NEBKARA

No.	Inscription	Material	Ref.
1	RA-NEB-KA	Bright greenish-blue glaze	L. 24
2	"	Bright light blue glaze	K. 30
3	"	Pottery, Blue-green glaze	L. 83
4	RA-NEB-KA, RA-NEFER. (Date uncertain)	Steatite. Glaze gone	H. 40

3·9 — 3·9. SENEFRU

No.	Inscription	Material	Ref.
1	SNEFER	Gone brown	Q. 73
2	SNEFER	Gone white	Q. 73
3	. . . NEFERU	Gizeh Diorite	Bowl
A	UR HEMU KHET. *Great worker of things*. Perhaps early form of *Ur kherp hemut*, high priest of Memphis.	Bright light blue	J. 91

4·2 — *IVth DYNASTY.* 4·2. KHUFU

No.	Inscription	Material	Ref.
1	MEZERU. Ka name of Khufu	Diorite	Bowl
2	KHUF. (Beak of chick slightly open)	Gone brown	T. 57
3	KHUF	Pottery green	T. 64
4	KHUF. Reverse; king seated before table of offerings, winged sun above	Steatite. Opaque light blue.	Plaque
5	NETER NEFER, NEB TAUI, KHUFU, NETER OĂ, HER NUBTI, AĂKHET TA. *Good god, lord of both lands, Khufu, Great God, Triumphant Horus, of the Glorious Horizon Pyramid.*	Great Pyramid Seal. Basalt.	Cylinder
6	KHUFU, king seated	Koptos. Alabaster.	Vase
7	KHUF, Reverse uncertain figures	Gizeh. Plummet. Hard yellow limestone	

4·2·A — 4·2·A. KHNEM-KHUF (co-regent of Khufu, see *Memphis* iii, 43)

No.	Inscription	Material	Ref.
	HER NEB . . . . KHNEM-KHU(F) KHUFU	Clay sealing	

4·3 — 4·3. KHOFRA IV·3

No.	Inscription	Material	Ref.
1	RA·KHO·F DA NESUT NEFER NEFER. *Khofra, may the king give good things*	Ochre-red. Glaze gone	L. 30
2	RA·KHO·F	Pottery. Light blue	G. 72
3	"	Grey steatite	L. 71
4	"	Blue paste	L. 54
5	" (Exchanged away)	Green glaze	
6	"	Steatite, gone white	L. 18
7	"	Pottery, green glaze	Z. 40
8	"	Pottery, green glaze	N. 98
9	RA·NE·KHO·F NETERU MERY. *Khofra beloved by the gods*	Steatite, pale green	Cylinder
10	RA·KHO·F, HATHER DUA MERY NETER. *Khofra, adoring Hathor loved by the god*	Steatite, green-grey	Cylinder
11	HER USER AB, NESUT BATI RA (KHOF). Temple of Second Pyramid.	Magnesite.	Part of mace head
12	HER USER AB, NESUT BATI RAKHOF PERT NE PER DUAT. *Office of the inner cabinet*	Clay sealing from a cylinder	

4·4

4·4. MENKAURA

1 RA·MEN·KAU, HATHER ZED MEDU UAB ? RA·MEN·KAU NETERU REN MERY
Menkaura, Hathor speaking pure words, Menkaura beloved child of the gods Black steatite. Cylinder

2 RA·MEN·KAU, NETER NEFER, HATHER MERY, RA·MEN·KAU NETER (NEFER) NEB KHO TAUI
Menkaura good god loved by Hathor, Menkaura good god, Lord of glory of both lands Black steatite. Cylinder
(See Menkara, vassal of Shabaka, xxvth dynasty)

4·5

4·5. ZEDEFRA

1 RA·ZEDEF. Probably modern Blue green J. 60
2 RA·ZED. From similarity to back of Nebkara 3·1·1, it appears to be early Gone grey W. 30

4·6

4·6. SHEPSESKAF

RA·SHEPSES·KA·F. (Very perfect work of head and back) Gone light brown F. 81

4·A
HETEP·HER·S. Private scarab, name only known in ivth and vth dynasties Gone white G. 42

Vth DYNASTY

5·2

5·2. SAHURA

1 NEB·KHO·RA (throne name, see Sect. 25) Grass green. Head broken, back H. 22

2 EM KHET KHENNUT, HER NEB KHOU . . . *in affairs of the cabinet of Horus Neb Khou*
From a papyrus, clay sealing

3 RA SAHU NETERU MERER, HATHER NETER HEN NET MER.
Sahura whom the gods love, prophet of Hathor, loved by Neit Abutig. Green steatite. Cylinder

SAB HER UDEB SMĂO . . . HER, PET KHOU.
Judge, over the dykes, making justice, Horus Pet Khou (unknown king) From papyrus, clay sealing

5·6

5·6. NEUSERRA

1 HER SĂ UPUAT, AST AB TAUI RA·NE·USER, HER NUBTI NETER, RA·NE (USER) Limestone. Cylinder
Horus son of Upuati (Osiris of Siut) Ast ab taui Neuser ra, Triumphant Horus the god.

2 RA SĂ AN. *Son of Ra, An* (name of Neuserra). Pottery. Blue green N. 64

5·8

5·8. ZEDKARA

1 RA·ZED·KA, SEMAUTI, BA S AST AB EM UPT MĂOT.
Zedkara Lord of Hierakonpolis and Buto (title)
HER NUBTI ZED RA·ZED·KA, UAZET NEBT MERY
Horus Victor, enduring, Zedkara, loved by the lady Uazet
SEMAUTI ZED EM SEKHEMTI KHER HOT.
Lord of Hierakonpolis and Buto (title)
NESUT BATI RA·ZED·KA, NESUT NETER OĂ
King of Upper and Lower Egypt, Z, King, Great God
HER, ZED KHOU
Horus, Zed khou (title)
HER SMA TAUI, ZED KHOU
Horus uniter of both lands, Zed khou
HER ZED KHOU
Horus zed khou
HER SMA TAUI ZED KHOU
Horus Uniter of both lands, Zed khou Cast metal. Cylinder
UZ KHERI-O
Decree of the assistant
UZ NETER SMĂOTI
Decree of the Sacred Rector
UZ HAT
Decree of the Palace
(Cylinder seen by Wiedemann at Luqsor, then lost, and later bought in Cairo.)

2 ATY HER ZED KHOU, NET NETER HEN, HAT HER NETER HEN.
Horus Prince Zed khou, priest of Neit and Hathor. Edwards. Steatite. Cylinder

3 NESUT BATI RA·ZED·KA, ONKH ZETTA, *King U. and L., Zed ka ra, living eternally.* Chert ink slab

4 RA·ZED·KA in spirals Gone red H. 66

5·9

5·9. UNAS

1 NETER NEFER NEB TAUI UNAS HETEP. *Good god, lord of both lands, Unas, satisfied* Gone red W. 12
2 ASUN. Name of Unas reversed, "Behold the being" Grey steatite L. 26
3 UNAS Dull green Z. 95
4 UNAS Gone brown H. 44
5 UNAS Gone brown G. 78
6 UNAS Gone brown E. 62

(Objects of Userkaf, Neferarkara, Shepseskara, and Menkauher are added from other collections.)

DYNASTIES IV AND V

4.4 MENKAURA

1 

2 

3

4.5 ZEDEFRA

1

2

4.6 SHEPSESKAF

HETEP-HERS

DYNASTY V

5.1 USERKAF

5.2 SAHURA

1

2

3

4

5.3 NEFER.AR.KA.RA

5.4 SHEPSES.KA.RA

5.6 NE.USER.RA

1

2

5.7 MENKAUHER

5.8 ZED.KA.RA

1

2

3

4

5.9 UNAS

1

2

3

4

5

6

DYNASTIES VI TO IX

DYNASTY VI

6.1 TETA

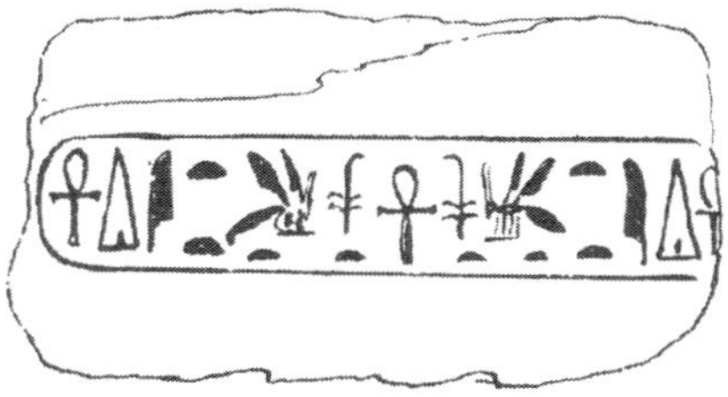

6.3 MERY. RA PEPY

1

2

3

4

5

6

6.4 MERENRA

NEFER SǍ

6.5 PEPY II

DYNASTY VII

7.2, 4 or 6, NEFER. KA. RA

1

2

7.9 NE. KA. RA

1

1

7.10 TERERU

2

SNEFER. ONKH. RA
PEPY

DYNASTY IX

PEPENOSS

1

2

9.1 KHETY I

PARIS

9.2 KHETY II

SHENES

VIth DYNASTY

6·3 — 6·3. PEPY I

1 RA·MERY — Gone brown N. 76
2 RA·MERY — Pottery, glaze gone W. 64
3 RA·MERY, MIN MERY. *Ramery beloved by Min.* Foundation plaque — Pottery. Blue-green. Flat
4 KHER HEB AR ER UZET NEB·F HER MERY TAUI
The reciter, officiating by command of his lord, the Horus Mery·taui — Black steatite. Cylinder
5 HER DESHERT (of North) MERY TAUI, NESUT BAT PEPY HETHER MERY — Hard blue paste. Cylinder
NESUT SHEPS, SEHEZ PER, MERER NEBEF RA NEB, HER SHUTI (of Edfu), MERY TAUI
NESUT SHEPS AR ER HESSET NEBET HER HEZ (of South) MERY TAUI
NESUT SHEPS HEZ PER AR ER HESSET NETER ASTEF
Horus of the north Merytaui, king of south and north, Pepy, loved by Hathor.
Royal noble, overseer of the palace loved by his lord every day, by Horus of Edfu, Merytaui.
Royal noble, officiating by favour of his lord, Horus of the South, Merytaui.
Royal noble, overseer of the palace, officiating by favour of his lord in his divine dwelling.
6 [NESUT BAT PEPY of some god beloved, ONKH] ZETTA — Piece of hard blue paste. Cylinder
[NESUT TEP KHER, ... AN] EK MUT, HER SHUTI, MERY TAUI
NESUT TEP KHER, SEHEZ AST MER ER NEBEF, [HER HEZ MERY TAUI]
NESUT TEP KHER, HER SESHTA . . . . REF.
King Pepy loved by (some god) *living for ever.*
Chief under the king . . . . Anmutek, Horus of Edfu Merytaui.
Chief under the king, overseer of the palace, loved by his lord the Horus of the south, Merytaui.
Chief under the king, over the secrets . . . .

6·4 — 6·4. MERENRA

RA·NE·MER — Pottery. Peacock blue Y. 85

6·5 — 6·5. PEPY II

ONKH HER, NETER KHOU, RA·NEFER·KA, ONKH ZETTA. — Alabaster. Lid

HER NEFER·SĂ on thick piece of broken alabaster. See Cairo Papyrus 8, *Recueil.* xx, 72.

7·2 — 7·2, 4 or 6. NEFERKARA

1 RA·NEFER·KA — Gone brown-nacreous L. 79
1 RA·NEFER·KA. Reverse same — Full blue-green. Cartouche

7·9 — 7·9. NE·KA·RA

1 RA·NE·KA, RA·NUB·NEB. *Ne·ka·ra, Nub·neb·ra* — Pottery. Blue Cartouche
2 RA·R·KA·NEN between uraei. *Ne·ka·ra* ? — Gone white Z. 55

7·10 — 7·10. NEFER·KA·RA TERERRU

TERURU, NEFER·KA, HĂ NEB. *Teruru, Neferka(ra) Lord of the North* — Gone grey. Handle

7 — 7·A. SENEFERONKH·RA PEPY

A RA·SENEFER·ONKH PEPY. *Seneferonkhra Pepy* — Gone grey T. 94

B PEPENOSS. *Pepenoss* (name " Apep summons her ") — Nubt. Pottery. Deep blue T. 69
C PENOSS — Pottery. Deep blue T. 71

IXth DYNASTY

9·1 — 9·1. KHETY I

RA·AB·MER — Gone buff M. 56

9·2 — 9·2. KHETY II

NESUT BAT, KHETY NEB KAU, ONKH ZETTA — Tell Retabeh. Weight. Red jasper

Xth–XIth DYNASTY

PRIVATE SCARABS. HARD STONE

A	UORT DENAT (?).	*Marshal of the dykes*	Black jasper	H. 80
B	NESUT KHETM MER-MERTO.	*Royal sealer, Mer-merto.* (Merto goddess of inundation)	Brown calcite	T. 61
C	UZU NEHA.	*The commander, Neha.* (*Lieb. Dict.* 201, early xiith)	Dark green jasper	K. 68
D	RE NEKHTET ? TEHUTI·HETEP.	*Strong of speech ? Tehuti·hetep*	Amethyst	J. 48
E	. . . . UAH NE . . .		Amethyst	C. 40
F	AKH ASTHAR.	*Akh-asthar.* (" Praise Astarte " ?)	White quartz	L. 76
G	UAHEM SEZEM QAMU.	*Deputy hearer, Qamu* (*Lieb. Dict.* 259, xith dyn.)	Green-grey jasper	C. 20
H	ATF NETER ATMU-HETEP.	*Divine Father, Atmu-hotep*	Grey quartz	Y. 90
J	KHENTI-KHATI-SĂ.	*Să-khentĭ-khati*	Quartz and pink felspar	Z. 88
K	MER NETER HENU, ANTEF.	*Overseer of priests, Antef*	Lazuli	K. 76
L	MER HOU NEFER, ANTEF.	*Overseer of transport boats, Antef*	Green felspar and quartz	C. 4
M	SHEMSU ONKHU SĂ MENTUEMHO.	*Follower, Onkhu son of Mentuemho*	Green jasper	E. 87

(See stele of Antef-aqer-onkhu son of Mentuemhot, Brit. Mus. 563.)

KA NEFER UAH SERIES

N	KHET-PE-ONKH, KA NEFER UAH.	*Khetponkh, the good ka is established*	Green-grey steatite	Z. 90
O	KA NEFER UAH, KHETY.	*Khety, the good ka is established*	Dark green jasper	H. 80
P	KA NEFER, SĂ-SETEM.	*Să-setem, the good ka is established*	Dark green jasper	C. 7
Q	. . . KANEFER, ... U . . . . S.	(*Mentu nes* ?)	Grey jasper	W. 30
R	MER PER (?), NEFER KA NE UAH.		Green jasper	H. 96
S	BEBA ATHY, KA NEFER UAH.	*Beba, Athy* (*Lieb. Dict.* 61, names viith dyn.)	Brown shelly marble	C. 4
T	NEBT PER NEBHAT-NEFER-KA MER NET.	*Lady Nebhat-nefer-ka, loved by Neit*	Amethyst	D. 4
U	ANTEF SĂT SEHEB, KA NEFER UAH.	*Antef daughter of Seheb*	Amethyst	C. 8
V	MENTUHETEP SĂ AMENY, KA NEFER UAH.	*Mentu-hotep son of Ameny*	Dark green jasper	C. 20
W	KA NEFER HETI-MER.	*Heti-mer* (" loved by the heart ")	Limestone.	Stamp
X	KA NEFER UAH, MER.	*Mer* (name in vith and xiiith dynasties)	Blue-green glaze	C. 70
Y	MER PER MENTU-USER, UAH KA NEFER.	*Keeper of the house, Mentu-user*	Gone light brown	M. 88
Z	ARI OT RAN·EF·ONKH, KA NEFER UAH.	*Store-keeper Ranefonkh*	Blue-green glaze	D. 88

11·5 *XIth DYNASTY.* 11·5. MENTUHETEP II

1	BAT RA-NEB-TAUI.	*King Neb-taui-ra,* Mentuhotep II	Gone grey	K. 58
2	RA-NEB-TAUI.	*Nebtaui-ra*	Gone grey	J. 85
3	ORYT MERT, RA·NEB·TAUI.	*Loved by* (*Hathor of*) *Oryt, Nebtauira*	Grey green	Z. 92
4	,, ,, ,, ,,	,, ,, ,, ,,	Gone white	Prism

11·A

RA KHEPER. Guarded by Sebek and Ra	Purple-brown	J. 26

11·7 11·7. ANTEF V

1	RA·KHEPER·NUB. Guarded by winged figures. Delicate work on both sides	Peacock-blue on white quartz	E. 89
2	,, between uraei	Edwards. Full green glaze	K. 46
3	RA·NUB·KHEPER NESUT NEFER. *Gracious king*	Full green	J. 30
4	NESUT BAT RA·KHEPER·NUB, NEFER	Peacock blue	J. 28
5	RA·KHEPER·NUB, ONKH NEFERUI	Green gone ruby brown, head broken	D.
6	RA·KHEPER·NUB, KA ZED. Uraeus, *Uzat, hot,* and red crown at sides	Gone white	D. 40
7	UAH, RA·KHEPER·NUB; *Her, uzat, onkh* at sides	Gone white	M. 92
8	NEFER KHEPERUI NUB, uraei	Green	J. 40

11·B 11 ?. NUB·SESHESHT·RA

RA·NUB·SESHESHT, hawk with *skhent* crown on each side. (See names of Antef I and III)	Peacock blue	J. 40

11·C

UAZ·KHEPER·UAH, uraei, *onkh, ka, neb* at sides (evidently of same period as above)	Peacock blue	J. 40

11·D 11 ?. DA·DA·MES

RA·NEFER·ZED, between four uraei	Green-blue	M. 52

11·E 11 ?. MENTU·EM·SAF

NETER NEFER RA·ZEDUI·ONKH, in a border of circular spirals	Gone white	C. 75

11·9. SONKH·KA·RA

RA·SONKH·KA. Delicate work	Gone white	K. 60

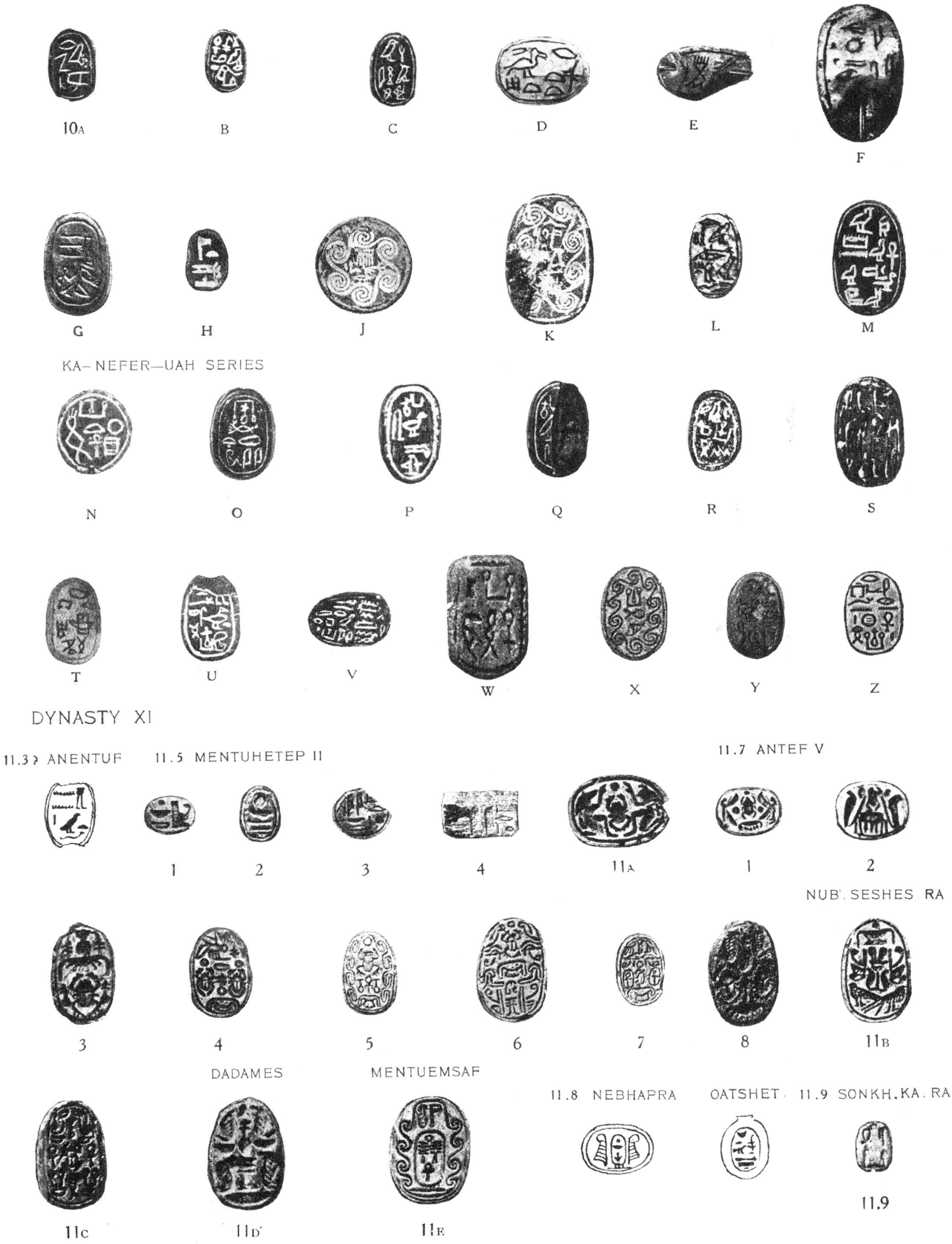

10A B C D E F

G H J K L M

KA–NEFER—UAH SERIES

N O P Q R S

T U V W X Y Z

DYNASTY XI

11.3? ANENTUF 11.5 MENTUHETEP II 11.7 ANTEF V

1 2 3 4 11A 1 2

NUB. SESHES. RA

3 4 5 6 7 8 11B

DADAMES MENTUEMSAF 11.8 NEBHAPRA OATSHET 11.9 SONKH.KA.RA

11C 11D 11E 11.9

12.1 AMENEMHOT I

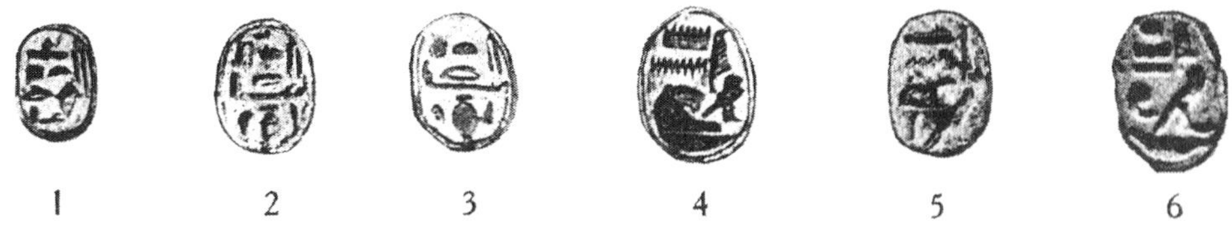

12.2 SENUSERT I

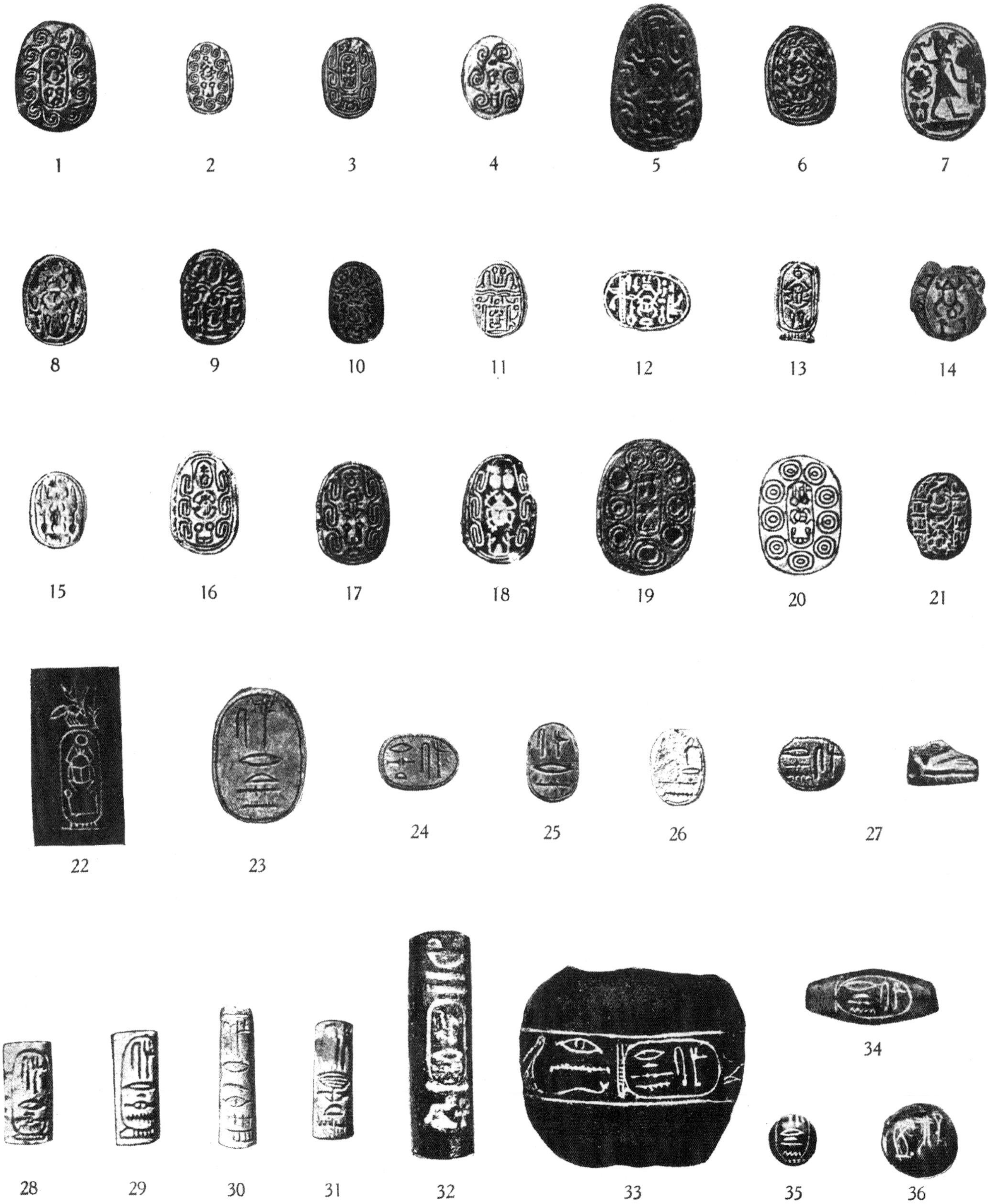

XIIth DYNASTY

12·1

12·1. AMENEMHOT I

1 SEHETEP·AB·RA (Throne name as pronounced, without inversion of writing) Brown E. 22
2, 3 SEHETEP·RA·AB (Partly inverted) Edwards, Pottery, gone white, F 25A. Brown E. 22
4 AMEN·EM·HOT NEB Gone buff H. 20
5 AMEN·EM·HOT (Delicate work of early xiith dynasty) Brown M. 46
6 AMEN·RA·EM·HOT NEB (Probably of xxiind–xxvth dynasties) Pottery. Green K. 48

12·2

12·2. SENUSERT I

1 RA·KHEPER·KA. Fine circular spirals around Full peacock blue J. 19
2 ,, Finest form of circular spirals Blue D. 8
3 ONKH NEFERUI (= RA ?) RA·KHEPER·KA, NUB. Oval spirals around Blue D. 38
4 RA·KHEPER·KA. Rough scrolls Gone brown H. 8
5 NETER NEFER, RA·KHEPER·KA. *The good god Kheperkara.* Very rare in wood. Nubt. Wood C. 16
6 RA·KHEPER·KA. Twisted border Peacock blue D. 86
7 ,, King marching with shield and falchion Peacock blue J. 29
8 ,, NEFER ONKH on each side Peacock blue J. 34
9 KA·RA·KHEPER. Uraeus, *uzat*, and *bati* crown on each side. Peacock blue M. 50
10 ,, Uraeus, *uzat*, *onkh* and *uaz* on each side, NUB below Green ? D. 38
11 KA·RA·NE·KHEPER. Lotus, *uzat*, and *bati* crown on each side Brilliant sky blue V. 60
12 KA·RA·KHEPER. *Nesut*, *onkh*, *bati* crown, *nefer*, on each side Peacock green V. 43
13 RA·KHEPER·KA. Reverse, same Gone white. Cartouche
14 KHEPER·RA·KA. Flat back, two thread holes Kahun. Sky blue. Pendant
15 RA·KHEPER·KA·NUB, NESUT·NEFER on each side Edwards. Gone white X. 90

There has long been a surmise that two *nefers* were used in place of *Ra*. The following scarabs strongly support this view, as they agree in style with those of Senusert I. In 16 the *nefer* is in an elongated *Ra*; in 17 the *nefer* has a circular body like *Ra*, and very short stem; in 18–20 the two *nefers* are used.

16 RA(NEFER)·KHEPER·KA Gone white D. 18
17 NEFER·KHEPER·KA·KHO Gone brown D. 40
18 NEFERUI·KHEPER·KA Gone brown W. 6
19 ,, Surrounded by circles. Probably of XVIIIth dynasty Gone light brown X. 20
20 ,, ,, ,, ,, ,, ,, Dark green X. 20
21 RA·KHEPERU and 8 KA. Probably of xviiith dynasty Grey schist X. 80
22 NESUT BAT, RA·KHEPER·KA. Imitation lazuli cylinder for furniture, 2·3 in. long, 2·5 in. wide. Blue stoneware
23 USERTSEN Peacock blue J. 65
24 USERSET. Very finely cut, though blundered Gone white D. 28
25 USERS. Very finely cut, though blundered Peacock blue H. 72
26 USERTESEN Gone white Z. 95
27 USERSEN. Duck on back Quft (Koptos xxiv. 2). Gone white. Duck
28 USERTSEN Edwards. Gone white. Cylinder
29 USERTSEN SEBEK NEB SMENNU MERY. *By Sebek lord of Smennu beloved.* Edwards. Light blue. Cylinder
30 USERTSEN Gone white. Cylinder
31 NETER NEFER, NEB TAUI, DA ONKH USER-NEB-SETEN (blundered) Gone white. Cylinder
32 (NEB AR) KHET, NEB TAUI USERSET ONKH ZETTA. Half-round rod of inlay. Pottery. Brown. Flat
33 SĂRA USERTESEN AR NEF EM . . . *Son of Ra Senusert, made by him in. . . .* Half-ring of black obsidian.
34 USERTESEN Amethyst Bead
35 ,, Carnelian Bead
36 NESUT HEMT KHNUM NEFER HEZ. *Royal wife united to the white crown.* (See *Dachour* xix. 37). Early xiith dynasty. Carnelian Bead

12·3.

12·3. AMENEMHOT II

1 HER, HEKEN·EM·MĂOT. *Horus, adoring the truth* (Ka name) Slate slip for inlay. Flat
2, 3 NESUT BAT, NUB·RA·KA Edwards. Gone brown. Peacock blue. G. 10, L. 76
4 RA·NUB·KA. Contemporary, because material as the next Light blue paste L. 76
5 NUB·KA·RA, SEN·USER. Throne name Am. II with personal name Sen. II. Both names in spoken form Light blue paste N. 60
6 RA·NUB·KA Pottery. Bright green. Cartouche. Flat
7 ,, UZAT eye at side Fibrous green-grey steatite. Traces of glaze gone brown. Bead
8 RA·NUB·KAU Dark brown limestone. Beard
9 RA·NUB·KAU SEBEK NEB SMENNU. *Sebek lord of Smennu* = Khnoubis opp. Latopolis. Grass green. Cylinder
10, 11 RA·NUB·KAU SEBEK NEB SMENNU MERY. *Loved by Sebek Lord of Smennu.* Edwards. Green, Cylinder, Kahun. Dull green. Cylinder
12, 13, 14 RA·NUB·KAU. Blue green. Cylinder. Gone white. Cylinder. Bead
15 (RA·NUB)KAU. Reverse same Kahun. Full blue. Prism
16 AMENEMHOT. SEBEK NEB AUT-NEFERU MERY. *By Sebek lord of Edfu beloved* Edwards. Green, gone buff. Cylinder
17 AMEN(EMHOT) KHNUMT . . . . (Not figured here) Kahun. Blue-green. Cylinder

12·4.

12·4. SENUSERT II

1 HER, SESHEM·TAUI. *Horus, traversing both lands* (Ka name) Blue paste G.30
2 KHO-KHEPER·NEFERUI. Name in spoken form, with *neferui* used for *Ra.* Blue D. 32
3 NESUT BAT RA·KHO·KHEPER, ONKH each side White W. 90
4 KHO KHEPER, uraeus and crocodile. Perhaps the uraeus = *Ra.* Work like Sen. I. Green-blue W. 90
5 USER SENT blundered Kahun. Blue. Half prism
6 NETER NEFER NEBT TAUIT (*sic*) RA·KHO·KHEPER Edwards. Kahun. Blue-green. Cylinder
7 RA·KHO·KHEPER Edwards. Kahun. Green-blue. Cylinder
8 RA·KHO·KHEPER. SENUSERT Kahun. Grey steatite. Cylinder
9 SA RA USERTESEN Kahun. Two of a group of four cylinders, split in half. Green-blue
10–14 Fragments of blue glazed cylinders, Kahun.
15 HAT·SENUSERT·HETEP, HOT NETER HAT NEFER, MER . . . PEPY-ONKH Kahun, clay sealing from papyrus *In Senusert's town of the Hetep pyramid, Prince of the excellent temple, Keeper of the . . . . Pepyonkh*

12·5.

12·5. SENUSERT III

1 RA·KHO·KAU Glaze lost. Grey steatite Y. 35
2 ,, Green glaze L. 4
3 RA·KHO·KA BATI crown at each side Blue V. 43
4 ,, winged sun and uraeus at sides Black steatite G. 10
5, 6 ,, in rope border Grass green. Gone white. W. 90, D. 36
7 ,, in scroll border degraded Green D. 44
8, 9 ,, Gone brown. Gone white. G. 32, N. 4
10 ,, or RA·RES·KA, a king of later date, XXV ? Pottery. Green N. 60
11 ,, in scrolls Pottery. Blue-green burnt red Q. 68
12 NESUTI KA·KHO. NESUTI used perhaps for RA, like NEFERUI. Work as of Sen. I Peacock blue J. 24
13 RA·KHO·KAU Peacock blue Frog
14 RA·KHO·KAU·KA (found with next) Kahun. Blue-green. Cylinder
15 RA·KHO·KA·KA, NETER NEFER, NEB TAUI, ONKH DA Kahun. Blue-green. Cylinder
16 . . . . KAU,. . NE·MĂOT. Co-regency of Senusert III and Amenemhot III Broken. Bright blue. Cylinder
17 KHO·RA·KA·MEN Stamp of wood Handle
18 RA·KAU Stamp of limestone
19 NEFERUI (?) KHO·KA, MĂOT feathers on either side. Two cartouches of MEN·KHEPER·RA on back. xviiith dyn. Z. 95
20 RA·KHO·KA between royal uraei. Reverse, *uzat* on *nub* Gone white. Uzat
21 HER·ZED·UAS, RA·KHO·KA, winged sun above. Horus, son of Upuati-Osiris. Reverse: Uzat eyes. xxvth dyn. ? Gone white. Uzat

12·6

12·6. AMENEMHOT III

1 HER RA OĂ BAU. *Horus-Ra, Great of Spirits* (*Ka* name) Pottery. Gone white G. 78
2 RA·NE·MĂOT in rectangle, uraei at sides Gone white. Broken
3, 4, 5, 6, 7, 8 RA·NE·MĂOT. Green-blue. Gone brown. Gone whitey-brown. Blue. Blue-green. Green. H. 16, L. 86, G. 8, hedgehog. K. 18, W. 40

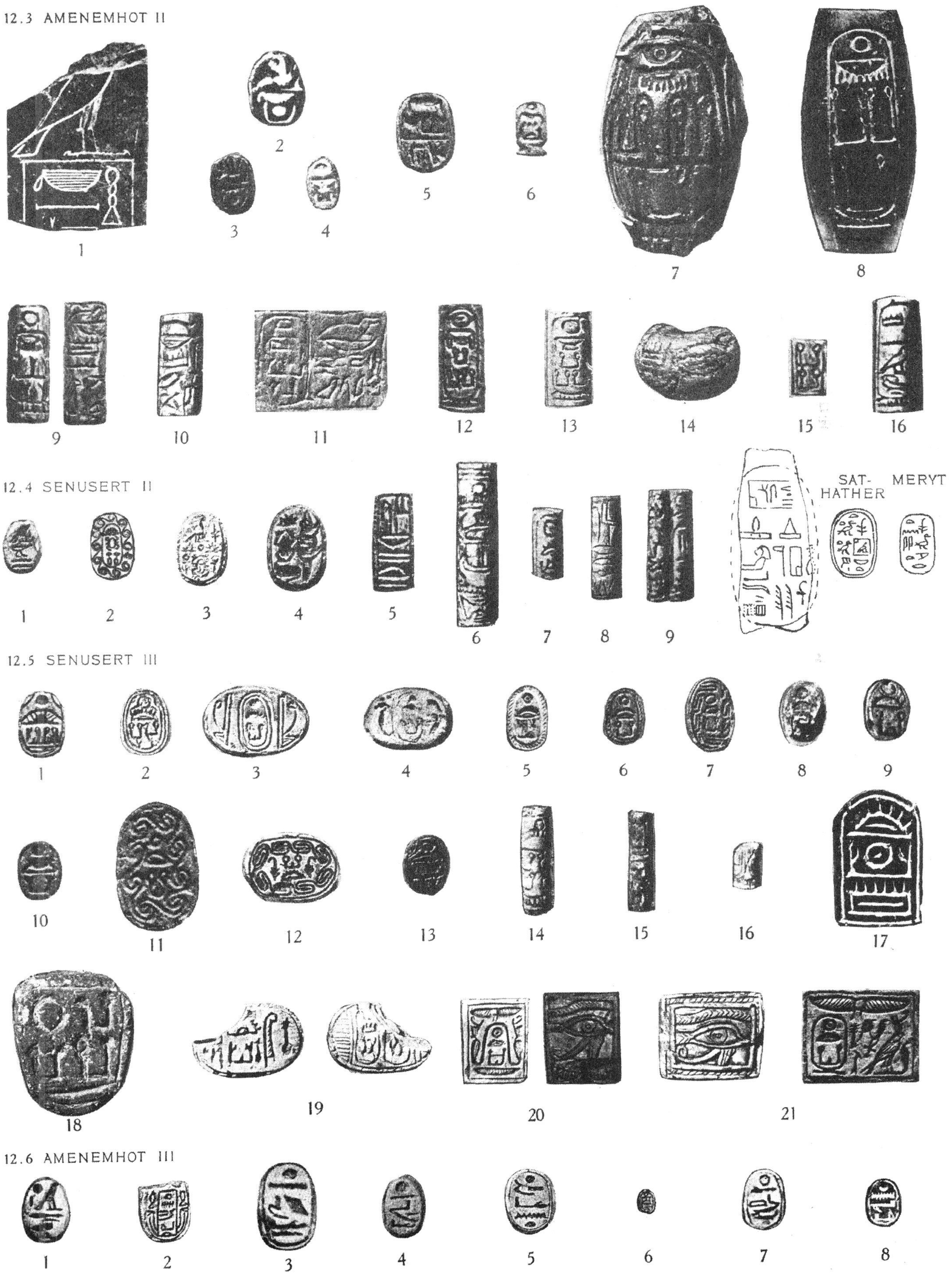

12.3 AMENEMHOT II 1–16

12.4 SENUSERT II 1–9

12.5 SENUSERT III 1–21

12.6 AMENEMHOT III 1–8

12.6 AMENEMHOT III

10 11 12 13 14

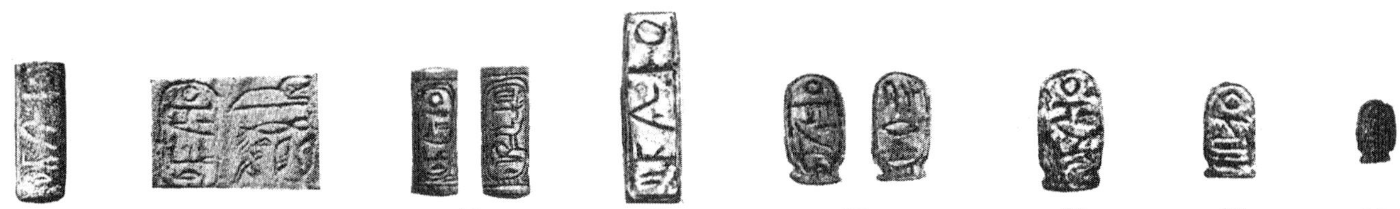

15 16 17 20 21 22 23 24

26 27 28

SEBEKNEFERU

12.7 AMENEMHOT IV

12. PRIVATE SCARABS.

A B C D E F G

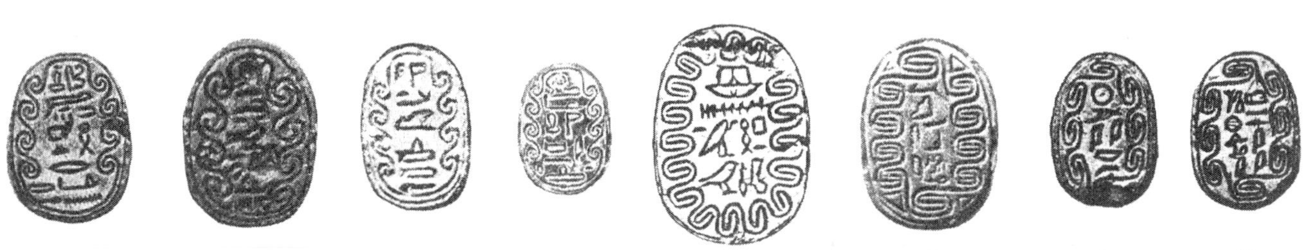

H J K L M N O P

Q R S T U V W

12·6.

12·6. AMENEMHOT III (*continued*)

No.	Inscription	Notes	Material	Form
9	NETER NEFER NEB TAUI DA ONKH, SĂ RA AMEN·EM·HOT, NESUT BATI RA·NE·MĂOT		Gone buff.	Cylinder
10	NETER NEFER ONKH, NEB TAUI ONKH ZETTA, RA·NE·MĂOT	*Koptos* xxiv 1.	Gone brown.	Cylinder
11	NETER NEFER NEB TAUI ONKH DA, AMEN·EM·HO		Green.	Cylinder
12	NETER NEFER NEB TAUI ZETTA, RA·NE·MĂOT		Green.	Cylinder
13	RA·NE·MĂOT, SEBEK SHEDTI MERY. *By Sebek of the Fayum city beloved.*	Edwards. Tell Yehudiyeh.	Gone buff.	Cylinder
14	,, ,, *By Sebek of the Fayum city beloved.*		Gone yellow.	Cylinder
15	,, ,, ,, ,, ,,		Gone brown.	Cylinder
16	,, ,, ,, ,, ,,		Gone white.	Cylinder
17	RA·NE·MĂOT, repeated, AMEN·EM·HOT		Perfect greenish-blue.	Cylinder
18	NETER NEFER NEB TAUI AMEN, NESUT BATI RA·NE . . . (Fragment, not figured)	Kahun.	Greenish-blue.	Cylinder
19	NETER NEFER RA·NE . . . (Fragment, not figured)	Kahun.	Light blue.	Cylinder
20	RA·NE·MĂOT, repeated on back	Quft.	Gone white.	Prism
21	,, USERTESEN (Senusert III and Amenemhot III)		Gone buff.	Cartouche
22	,, repeated on back	Kahun.	Strong blue.	Cartouche
23	,, ,, ,,		Gone grey.	Cartouche
24	,, ,, ,,	Kahun.	Light blue.	Cartouche
25	RA·NE . . . . (not figured)	Half cartouche. Kahun.	Blue.	Cartouche
26	RA·NE·MĂOT	Wire-work soldered on to electrum.		Shell
27	. . . RA·NE·MĂOT DA ONKH ZETTA	On base of hawk.	Gone buff.	Hawk
28	NETER·NEFER, NEB TAUI, AMENEMHOT.	On base of fore part of crocodile, of fine work.	Gone white.	

12·7.

12·7. AMENEMHOT IV

NETER·NEFER, NEB TAUI, RA·NE·MĂOT ; SĂRA NE KHETF, AMENEMHOT ; HER KHEPERU.
Ka name of Am. IV between the cartouches of Am. III, during co-regency.
Pierced with three holes, end to end. Gone white Q. 10

12

XII. PRIVATE SCARABS

Round spirals continuous.

	Inscription	Translation	Material	No.
A	MER MET, KHENSU-SĂ.	*Overseer of organizing, Sakhonsu*	Peacock blue	D. 20
B	SESHI NE KHENERT UR, SEBEK-SĂ.	*Scribe of the great prison, Sasebek*	Gone white	M. 16
C	NEFER KA HATHOR PERT, AMENY M·K·.	*(Title) of Hathor temple, Ameny, justified*	Clear blue	S. 10
D	. . . NEFKAU		Clay sealing	
E	ONKH NE NUT, SEBEK-NEKHT.	*Citizen, Sebeknekht.* Base of seated figure, now lost	Peacock blue	figure

Round spirals at sides.

	Inscription	Translation	Material	No.
F	UR RES MOBĂ, ONKH·TEFI.	*Chief of Nubia* (?) *Onkhtefi*	Peacock blue	S. 50
G	MER AST NE HO, KA·AB·SĂT.	*Overseer of place of the tomb, Kaabsat*	Dark green	S. 10
H	BATI KHETM, MER DENAT, PTAHERDUEN, M·K·	*Royal sealer, overseer of dykes, Ptaherdun*	Peacock blue	C. 65
J	SESHI NE KHENERT URT, ZATIEN NEB AMĂKH.	*Scribe of the great prison, Zatien, devoted*	White	Q. 62
K	NETER ATEF, SEBEKHETEP·M·K.	*Divine father Sebekhotep, justified*	Peacock blue	S. 10
L	HO, NETER KHETM, AMENHETEP.	*Prince, Sealer of the god, Amenhotep*	Peacock blue	S. 10

Oval scrolls continuous.

	Inscription	Translation	Material	No.
M	KHER HEB NE PTAH MUT, UAHEM·NEFER·UR.	*Reciter of Ptah and Mut, Uahem-nefer-ur*	Rich clear blue	C. 60
N	MER AST, SENBA, M·K·.	*Overseer of the residence, Senba, justified* Hard paste.	Dull green	H. 48
O	RA·MERY, NEB AMAKH.	*Meryra, devoted to his lord.* (*Illahun* viii 40) Kahun.	Peacock blue	C. 60
P	SESHI NE SEKH, AY.	*Scribe of punishment* (fist determinative) *Ay*	Blue green	S. 25
Q	ARI OT HEBT NEB AMĂKH.	*Guard of the store, Hebt, devoted to his lord*	Green blue	C. 32
R	KA·NEFER·KHRED.	*Ka-nefer-khred* Hard paste.	Dull green	N. 38
S	MENAKHEP (or SEP).	*Menakhep*	Gone white	L. 26

Oval scrolls at sides.

	Inscription	Translation	Material	No.
T	NESUT KHEKER, MU-AB.	*Royal adornment, Muab* Nubt.	Amethyst and gold plate	J. 70
U	HER NE TEM, SETMES.	*Chief of the sledges, Set mes.*	Peacock blue	S. 20
V	MER SHENO NEB, SENU.	*Overseer of all granaries, Senu.* Harageh 308. Hard paste.	Blue green	C. 24
W	THA, KHER NE SAHU, AKH.	*Vizier, proclaimer of the treasury, Akh* Harageh 275.	Bright green	S. 10
X	SESH MEDU, RASENB (not figured here).	*Scribe of speech* (reporter) *Rasenb.* Kahun	Clay sealing	

12. XII. PRIVATE (*continued*)

Y UR RES MOBĂ, AMENY M·K· *Chief of Nubia* (?). *Ameny, justified* Peacock blue S. 10
Z UR RES MOBĂ, PTAH-ZEDA M·K· (Lieb. Dict. 1088) *Chief of Nubia* (?). *Zeda-ptah, justified.* Gone brown D. 74
AA ARI OUT, HETEP, NEB AMĂKH. *Guard of the flocks, Hetep.* Rich clear blue S. 25
AB NEBT PER SEBEK-HETEP. . . . . *Lady of the house Sebekhetep. . . . .* Peacock blue S. 10
AC ARI OĂMU, SHET MET, USER-KHEPESH. *Guard of the Amu* 110 *Userkhepesh* Gone white D. 18
AD MER PER NE SHENUT, AUFSENB. *Overseer of the house of the granary, Aufsenb.* Schist in gold band S. 10
AE SEHEZ SHEMSU-U MENY. *Interpreter of the followers, Mery.* Brown jasper in gold mount H. 82
AF AMEN beneath flying hawk. (For persons with god's names see Amen, Aset, Hor, etc., *Lieb. Dict.*) Brown limestone J. 36
AG UORTU NE HEQ UZHU, AOH-SĂ. *Marshal of the prince's table, Sa-aoh* Brown jasper H. 30
AH ,, ,, SEBEK-EM-HO. *Marshal of the prince's table, Sebek-em-ho* Peacock blue S. 10
AJ UORTU OĂ NE NUT SENOO-AB. *Chief Marshal of the city, Senooab.* Tell Yehudiyeh Peacock blue S. 10
AK HO, SEKHRU-AB. *Prince, Sekhru-ab.* ("Scheme of the heart") Gone white S. 10
AL UN NE SEBĂ, PTAH-MEN. *Opener of the door, Ptah men* Nubt. Peacock blue D. 74
AM SHEMSU NOI TEP TA, AU-AB (see Frazer, 107). *Follower, travelling over the land Auab* Peacock blue S. 25
AN SEMSU HĂYT, AUFEN, UAHEM ONKH. *Elder of the temple, Aufen, again living* Peacock blue S. 10
AO SĂB ARI NEKHEN, AUQEP. *Judge of Hierakonpolis, Auqep* Green blue S. 10
AP HO, MER HAT NETER AMEN, SENBY-NEFER-HAT-NETER. *Prince, overseer of the temple of Amen, Senby-nefer-hat-neter* Green H. 90
AQ NUBY, NEBPU, UAHEM ONKH. *Goldsmith, Nebpu, again living* Gone white, red in hollows S. 10
AR NEBT PER, HENTPU. *Lady of the house, Hentpu* Hard paste. Blue green S. 45
AS ARI KHETM OPER, BOĂ. *Keeper of contracts of supply, Boa* Gone white D. 76
AT THAY NE SESH HEZ SHENU, NEFER ATMU. *Porter of the Scribe of white funeral bread, Neferatmu* Hard blue paste N. 28
AU ARI OT NE PER NE QED, SENB. *Guard of the house of workmen, Senb.* Hard blue paste J. 24
AV SENES, NEFER·HER M·K. (Title on Louvre stele). *Nefer her, justified.* Blue gone white S. 70
AW SESH NE ZĂZĂT, OĂM MES NE THATH. *Scribe of the College, Am born of Thath.* Hard grey paste, green face N. 26
AX NEBT PER, YAB. *Lady of the house, Yab* Hard green paste S. 80
AY ,, ,, ,, ,, Hard grey paste H. 8
AZ SEHEZ SHEMSUI, NETER-HETEP. *Interpreter of followers, Neter hotep* (*Koptos* xxiv, 6) Blue green S. 10
BA ARI PEZET, SENB·F M·K· *Guard of the bows, Senbf, justified* Obsidian J. 10
BB METI NE SA, KA-EM-HETEP. *Organiser of the priests, Ka-em-hotep* Obsidian J. 13
BC NESUT PATIU, SĂTU. *Royal Caterer, Satu* Obsidian J. 10
BD KHETM SAB ARI NEKHEN, HER-HETEP. *Sealer, Judge of Hierakonpolis, Horhotep* Obsidian J. 12
BE KHETM, NEFER-HES-UAH. *Sealer, Nefer-hes-uah* Obsidian J. 13
BF . . . . . URT, HER. *Great . . . . . Hor* Obsidian J. 13
BG UORTU NETERU, RENEFSENB. *Marshal of the gods, Renefsenb* Edwards. Obsidian J. 10
BH BATI KHETM, MER PER DENAT, HER, M.K. *Royal sealer, keeper of the office of dykes, Hor. justified* Peacock blue J. 19?
BJ MER OKHENUTI, MER MEH, PUSENBA. *Keeper of the cabinet, keeper of the crown, Pusenba.* Gone brown S. 50
BK Hard brown stone C. 44
BL Black steatite C. 85
BM Limestone, yellowed S. 80
BN, BO Black steatite, M. 81, N. 60
BP Bare schist V. 13
BQ MER PER, NEFER-HETEP. *Keeper of the house, Neferhetep* (3 holes from end to end, see 12·7) Orange-buff H. 9
BR SESHESHTI, ABT, NEFER ONKH. *Priestess, Abt, of good life* Edwards. Blue gone ruby red S. 60
BS SĂ HA NEFERUI Green Y. 50

Side ovals not continuous.

BT MER KHOU, SPERNEF. *Keeper of the crown, Spernef* Dark green S. 10
BU BATI KHETM, MER KHETM, HĂR. *Royal sealer, over the sealers, Har.* (3 holes end to end) Green-blue J. 17
BV RUDU, KHENAMSU. *Inspector, Khenamsu* (= Khenuahemsu of XII) Green S. 25

12. Y—BV. PRIVATE SCARABS, SCROLLS

Y Z AA AB AC AD AE

AF AG AH AJ AK AL

AM AN AO AP AQ AR AS

AT AU AV AW AX AY AZ

BA BB BC BD BE BF BG

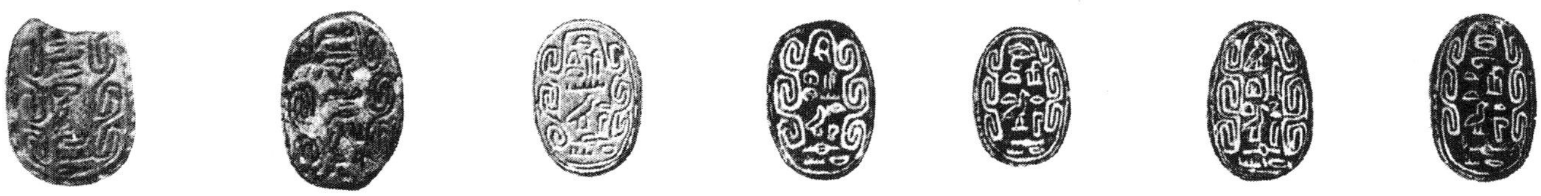

BH BJ BK BL BM BN BO

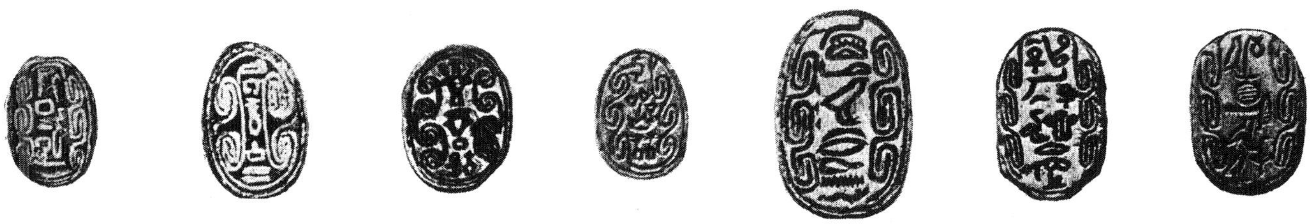

BP BQ BR BS BT BU BV

13. A–AV. PRIVATE SCARABS. NO SCROLLS

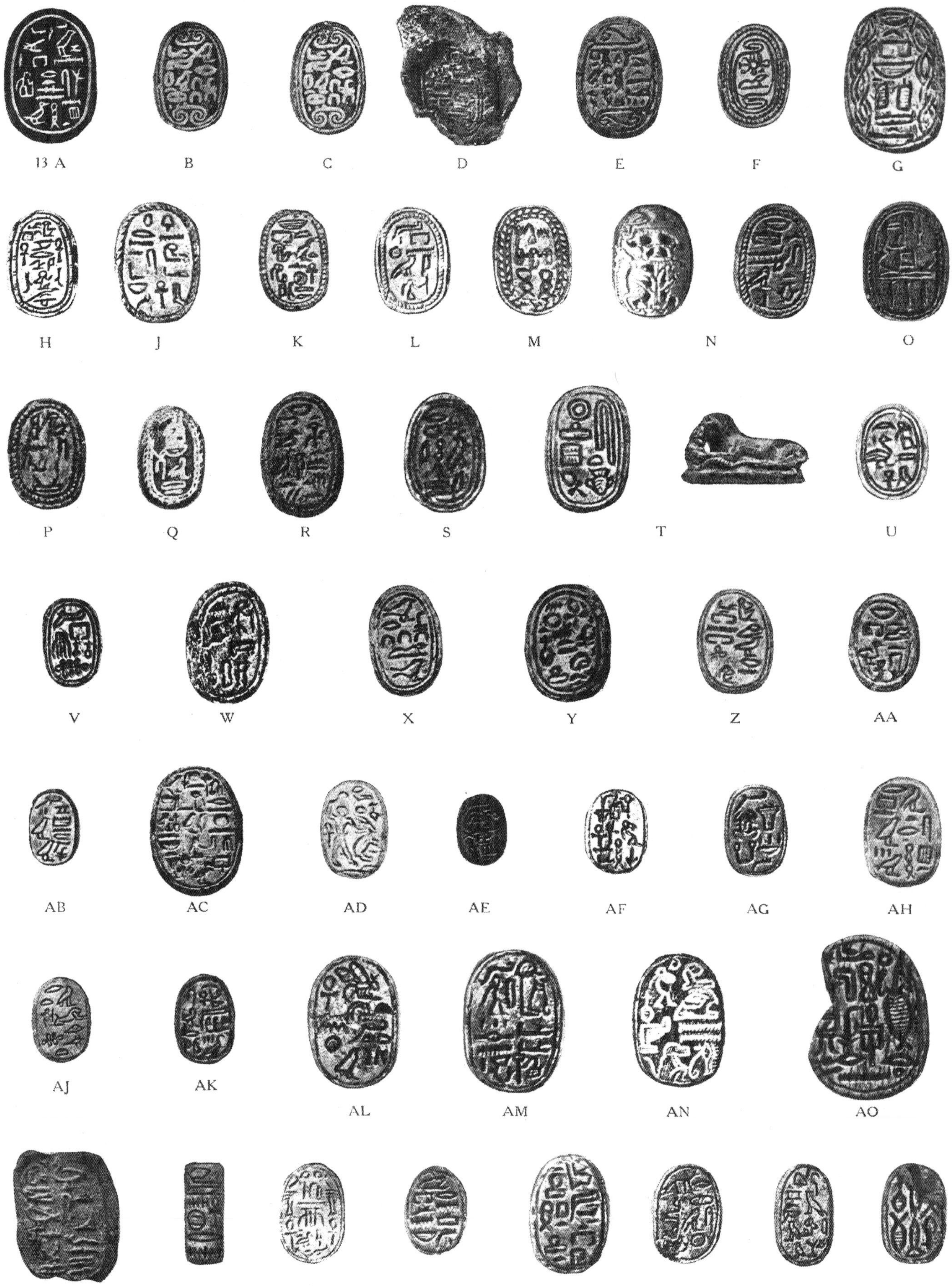

13 A B C D E F G

H J K L M N O

P Q R S T U

V W X Y Z AA

AB AC AD AE AF AG AH

AJ AK AL AM AN AO

AP AQ AR AS AT AU AV

13. XIII. PRIVATE NAMES

A MER OT U NE HEB, USERTESEN (SĂ) NE PTAH-SĂ. *Overseer of the office of the district for agriculture Senusert son of Saptah* Obsidian C. 4

B UR RES MOBĂ, OKUT. *Chief of Nubia (?). Okut* Gone grey S. 75

C NEBT PER, SOPDU-SĂT, M·K. *Lady of the house, Sat-sopdu, justified* Edwards. Gone grey C. 8

D UBU NE OTU, TENNU, NEB AMĂKH. *Controller of store houses, Tennu* Clay sealing

E MER AST NE HOU, HEPT-PU-UAHI. *Keeper of the place of rejoicings, Hept-pu-uahi* Peacock blue S. 30

F SESHESHTI SEBEK. *Priestess of Sebek* Green J. 63

G NEBT PER, NEBTANTA, M·K· (border, Ward 224, Fraser 83). *Lady of the house, Nebtanta justified.* (Hathor) Green gone white S. 10

H ARI OT MERA, ONKH UAHEM ZETTĂ. *Guard of the store, Mera, living again eternally* Gone white D. 28

J MENKH NE HO REN-SENB, UAHEM ONKH, NEB AMĂKH. *Carpenter of the prince, Ren-senb, living again* Gone light brown J. 99

K NEBT PER, MUT-ONKH-THA, M·K· *Lady of the house Mut-onkh-tha, justified* Gone white S. 25

L MER PER NE AKHM, SEMSU. *Keeper of the house of enemies, Semsu.* Harageh 37. Nacreous white S. 55

M SESH NE KHENT, HEH. *Scribe of the Khent hall, Heh* Harageh 291. Hard green paste J. 62

N NEBT PER, STEM-AB. Taurts on back. *Lady of the house Stemab* ("making perfect the heart") Peacock blue

O KHERP OHO OHOU. *Commander of the palace boats* Gone brown S. 30

P ARI PEZET, SENB. *Guard of the bows, Senb* Gone nacreous white S. 65

Q . . . . SHE, KEMS M·K· *. . . . . . of the Fayum, Kems, justified* Grey brown S. 40

R NEBT PER, UAZET-HETEP, MEST NE SĂT-NEMTI. Koptos xxiv 4. *Lady of the house Uazet-hotep, born of Sat-nemti* Blue-green S. 10

S NESUT REKH, NEHY, M·K· *Royal friend, Nehy, justified.* Edwards. Nacreous white S. 50

T RA-SEHETEP-AB-ONKH. *Sehotep-ab-ra-onkh* Cat and kitten on back. Peacock blue Cat

U SEMSU HĂYT, AOH-SĂ, UAHEM ONKH. *Elder of the temple, Sa-aoh, again living* Greenish-blue M. 42

V MER PER NEFERUI, KHENTY-SĂ. *Keeper of the house of . . . . . Khenty (khety em) sa* Peacock blue S. 95

W SEMSU HAYT, ANTEF, M·K· *Elder of the temple, Antef, justified* Gone white S. 10

X UR RES MOBĂ, SEBEK-UR. *Chief of Nubia (?) Sebek-ur* Peacock blue J. 63

Y ONKH NE NUT, NESUT TA TEP, NEFERHETEP. *Citizen, over Royal land (?), Neferhotep* Gone white J. 63

Z ARI OT NE PER HEZ, SEBEK·UR·NE. *Guard of the Treasury, Urnesebek* Gone dark brown S. 70

AA NEBT PER, SEBEK-SĂT, UAHEM ONKH. *Lady of the house, Sat-sebek, again living* Peacock blue N. 8

AB MER U, MENTUNESU. *Overseer of the district, Mentu-nesu.* Kahun (Illahun viii, 41) Full blue D. 66

AC SESHI, KHENSU, ARI NE UAB NE AMEN KHENSU-NEFER, MES NE NEBT PER BĂBĂ. *Scribe, Khensu, son of the priest of Amen Khensunefer, born of the lady of the house Baba* Gone grey F. 3

AD HO NEFER-RA. Prince slaying gazelle, behind ONKH. *Prince Nefer-ra* Blue gone white S. 10

AE MER NUB, SĂ-PTAH. *Overseer of gold, Saptah* Light blue M. 86

AF SESH NESUT SEN, USER·ONKH·HENO. *Scribe of royal (brothers ?) User·onkh·heno* Blue-green J. 97

AG MER BESU, KHEPER-RA, NEB AMAKH. *Keeper of the unguents, Kheper-ra* Gone white nacreous C. 40

AH MER PER NE SETRU, PTAH·UR. *Overseer of the house of bandages, Ptahur* Gone grey M. 66

AJ MER ARUT, SEMSU, ARI KHETY SĂ. *Keeper of the store, Semsu born of (Khenty)-khety·să.* Kahun. Intense blue L. 95

AK BATI KHETM, MER SEKHTIU, SURTHA. *Royal sealer, overseer of peasants, Surtha* Blue green T. 9

AL BATI KHETM, MER TĂU, ONKHU. *Royal sealer, overseer of lards, Onkhu* Blue green D. 60

AM MER MESHOU PTAH, SENOO-AB. *General of the army of Ptah, Senoo-ab* Peacock green C. 4 ?

AN HO ZAMU (NE) UNNEFER, AOH-TEHUTI. *Leader of the youths of Unnefer, Aoh-tehuti* Gone white D. 56

AO RA-NEFER, NETER HEN NET NE RES, SERQ NE AĂBT. *Ra·nefer, prophet of Neit of the South and Selq of the East* Grey green T. 3

AP SESH NE KHENERT UR SENB-HETEP SĂ SENBEFNE, M·K· *Scribe of great prison, Senbhetep son of Senbefne* Clay sealing

AQ HO ONKHREN. *Prince Onkhren* Grey-green. Cylinder

AR SESH NE KHENT SEKHEM-TEHUTI, ONKH ZED ONKH NEFER at sides. *Scribe of the Khent hall, Sekhem-tehuti* Harageh 275. White S. 30

AS KHET NE SEBEK PER, REN-HETEP NEB AMĂKH. *Attached to the temple of Sebek, Ren-hetep* Gone nacreous white D. 95

AT BATI KHETM MER KHENERT PTAH-HETEP. *Royal sealer, keeper of the prison, Ptah-hetep* Green, burnt red M. 96

AU SAB ARI NEKHEN, SEMEKH. *Judge of Hierakonpolis, Semekh* ("the careless") Blue J. 62

AV HER SHĂT, KEMMAU, UAZ, NEFER, UAH on back. *Prince of the Lake* (Fayum) *Kemmau* Gone white

13.

AW UORTU HEQ UZHU SEBEK·HETEP — *Marshal of the prince's table, Sebek·hotep,* — Gone white — S. 30

AX SĂ NE UORTU HEQ UZHU MENTUHETEP. — *Son of the Marshal of the prince's table Mentu·hotep* — Grey-green gone brown — S. 90

AY HO, SEBEK·DA. — *Prince, Da-sebek* — Gold plate on quartz crystal — N. 90

AZ SEBEK·HETEP·SĂ (and another similar). — *Sa-sebekhetep.* — Grey, broken back. Gone buff — E. 70

BA SEMSU SEBEK. — *The elder, Sebek* — Blue — D. 12

BB SESH NE KHENERT UR, SESA. — *Scribe of the great prison, Sesa* — Peacock blue — M. 72

BC SESH NE KHENERT, SESA. — *Scribe of the prison, Sesa* — Grey green — M. 48

BD SESH UR NE MER KHETM, NEHES. — *Great scribe of the keeper of the seal, Nehes* — Gone brown — J. 63

BE BATI KHETM, MER MESHOU, SĂNEB. — *Royal sealer, general, Saneb* — Green blue — S. 25

BF SESH SEPT, SĂURT. — *Scribe of the nome, Saurt* — Gone buff — M. 68

BG BATI KHETM, SEMER UATI, MER KHETM, NEB·RĂ·SEHUI.
Royal sealer, companion, keeper of the seal, Nebra sehui. ("Lord of words in Councils") — Gone brown — T. 30

BH SEMSU HĂYT, PTAH·SĂ, NEB AMĂKH. — *Elder of the temple, Sa-ptah* — Green — M. 48

BJ NESUT QEB, AMENY. — *Royal purser* (?) *Ameny.* — Gone white — J. 62

BK ,, ,, ,, — ,, ,, ,, — Gone white — J. 62

BL MER SHENT, NEB-TĂ-HĂ (Fraser 82). — *Overseer of the rolls, Nebtaha.* (Pierret 589–90) — Peacock blue — N. 93

BM NESUT REKH HEM·EM·HĂ. — *Royal friend, Hem·em·ha* — Blue-green — M. 12

BN MER KHETM ER·DA·HĂ. — *Keeper of the seal, Erdaha* — Blue-green — T. 35

BO MER QERSTIU, SENBTEFI. — *Overseer of embalmers, Senbtefi* — Gone buff — M. 42

BP QERSTI, ONKH·NEB·EM·SENEFER. — *Embalmer, Onkh-neb-em-senefer* — Grey limestone. Human face

BQ BATI KHETM, MER DENAT PER, SEBEK·NEB·KA.
Royal sealer, keeper of office of dykes, Sebek-neb-ka — Intense light blue — K. 24

BR BATI KHETM, SEMER UATI, MER KHETM, SENBSUMA.
Royal sealer, companion, keeper of the seal, Senbsuma, Kahun (*Illahun* viii, 42) — Intense light blue — S. 50

BS Same — Edwards, gone dark grey — S. 70

BT BATI KHETM, SEMER UATI, MER KHETM, HĂAR. (Same titles) *Haar* — Green — J. 29

BU BATI KHETM, MER KHETM, HĂAR. — *Royal sealer, keeper of the seal, Haar.* — Nacreous blue-green — T. 33

BV ,, ,, ,, ,, — ,, ,, ,, — Greyish-blue green — J. 33

BW, BX, BY, BZ BATI KHETM, MER KHETM, HĂCR. — ,, ,, ,,
Dull blue, gone white, blue, burnt red. — T. 9, U. 30, T. 63, T. 9

CA BATI KHETM, MER KHETM, HĂAR. — *Royal sealer, keeper of the seal, Haar*
Well-cut legs, nacreous blue-green — J. 29

CB ,, ,, ,, — ,, *keeper of the seal, Haar* — Gone brown — T. 41

CC, CD, CE BATI KHETM, MER KHETM, HAAR. — ,, ,, ,,
Edwards. Gone white. — T. 37, U. 30, T. 33

CF BATI KHETM, MER KHETM, SEZEM, HER·ER·DA·OSHĂU. *Royal sealer . . . . Her·er·da·oshau.*
Blue-green, white nacreous — J. 6

CG HO, MER UAZ, MENTUHETEP. — *Prince, overseer of transports, Mentuhetep.* Pottery. Light green — Q. 70

CH BATI KHETM, SEMER UATI, MER KHETM, PTAH·ER·DAEN.
Royal sealer companion, keeper of the seal, Ptaherdaen — Gone brown — J. 63

CJ SESH NESUT OT . . . HERAB. — *Scribe of royal house . . . Herab* — Light blue — J. 63

CK NESUT HETEP DA SEBEK NEB SUNU, NE KA NE BATI KHETM, MER KHETM, SEMER UATI, SENBEFTI — Brown — N. 28
Royal offering to Sebek lord of Syene, for ka of royal sealer, keeper of seal, companion, Senbefti.

CL BATI KHETM, MER KHETM, SEN-HEB-ONKHU. *Royal sealer, keeper of the seal, Senhebonkhu.*
Peacock blue — L. 84

CM ,, ,, AMENHETEP. — ,, ,, ,, *Amenhetep* — Greenish-blue — M. 72

CN SESH NE KHENERT URT, NEB·ONKH. — *Scribe of the great prison, Nebonkh* — Dark blue-green — M. 30

CO MER KHETM ERDAHĂ. — *Keeper of the seal, Erdaha* — Blue-green — T. 43

CP MER KHETM, PER·EM·UAH. — ,, ,, *Peremuah* — Dull blue-green — T. 42

CQ BATI KHETM, SEMER UATI, MER KHETM, PER·EM·UAH. *Royal sealer, companion, keeper of seal, Peremuah* — White — T. 42

CR MER KHETM NEB, PER·EM·UAH. — *Keeper of the general seal, Peremuah* — Gone brown — U. 25

CS — Gone brown

CT MER HEZT, HERAKA. — *Overseer of interpreters, Heraka* — Gone brown — U. 50

CU BATI KHETM, SEMER BATI. — *Royal sealer, royal companion.* Tell Yehudiyeh Peacock green — U. 20

CV MER KHETM, QEBU. — *Keeper of the seal, Qebu.* (Name with Ameny, *Lieb.* p. 479) — Gone white — T. 88

CW KHEN·MEN·EM·HOT. — *Khent·men·em·hot.* (Khent·men, a jackal god) — Pottery green — W. 53

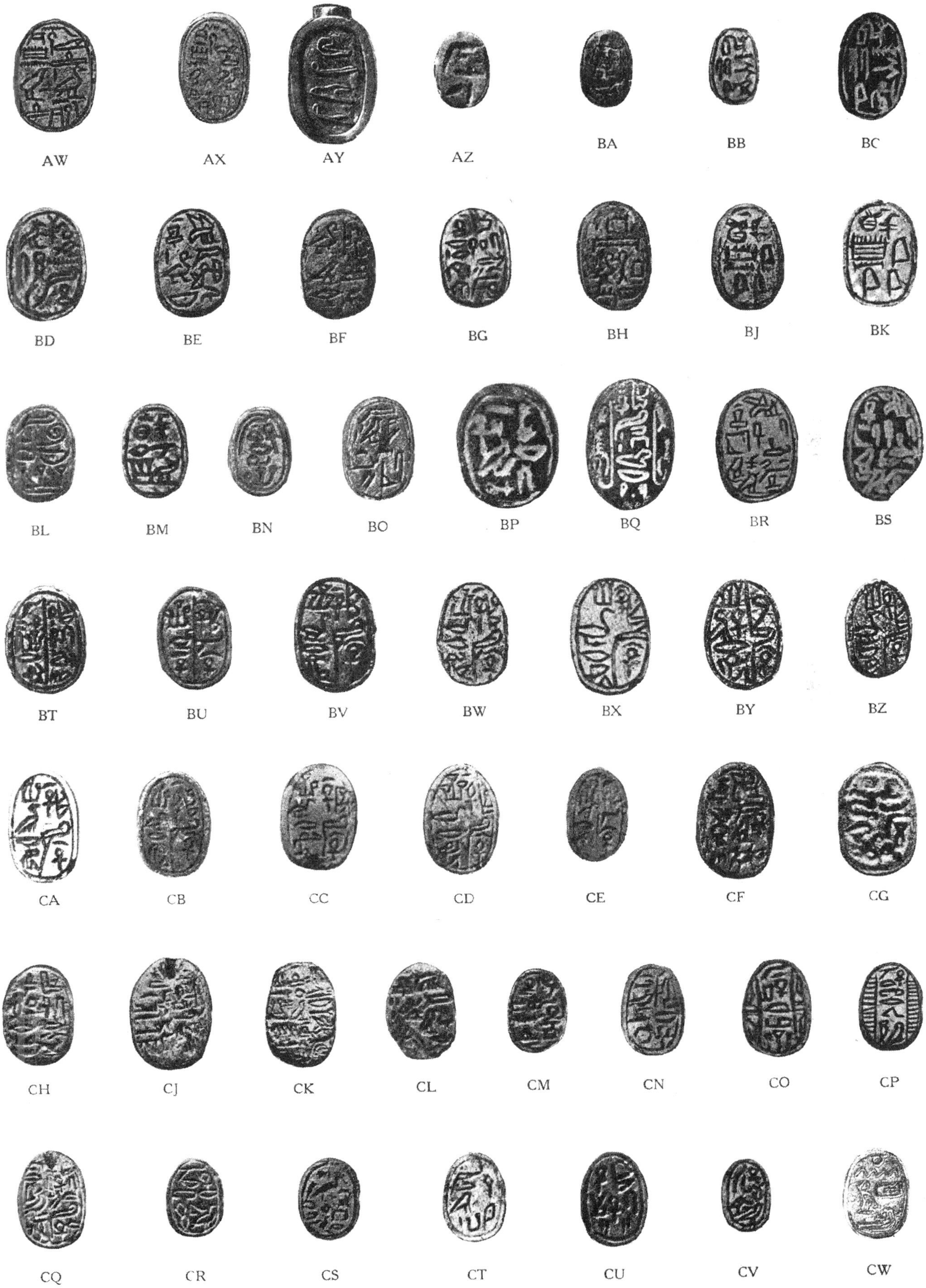
AW AX AY AZ BA BB BC
BD BE BF BG BH BJ BK
BL BM BN BO BP BQ BR BS
BT BU BV BW BX BY BZ
CA CB CC CD CE CF CG
CH CJ CK CL CM CN CO CP
CQ CR CS CT CU CV CW

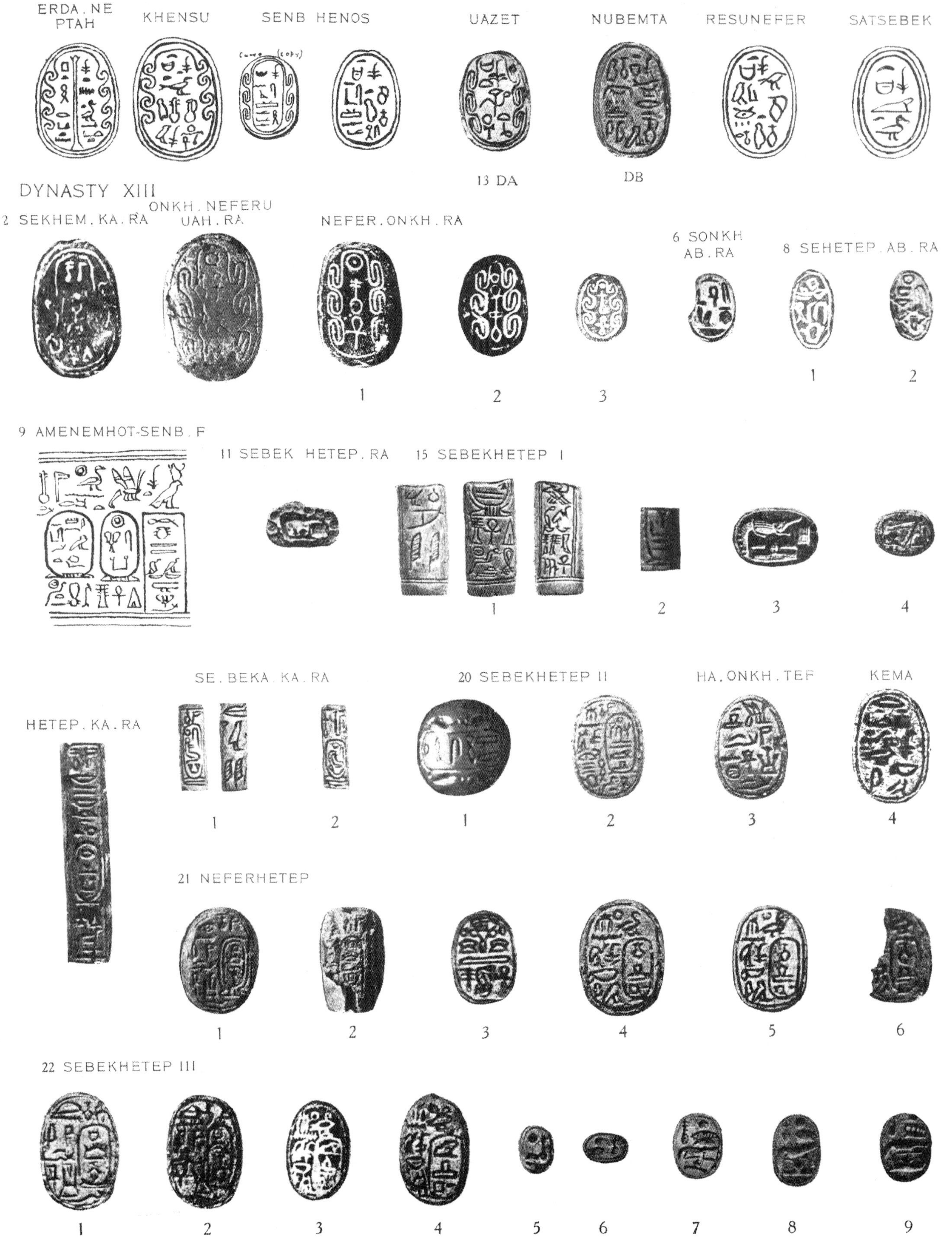
ERDA.NE PTAH
KHENSU
SENB HENOS
UAZET
NUBEMTA
RESUNEFER
SATSEBEK
13 DA
DB
DYNASTY XIII
2 SEKHEM.KA.RA
ONKH.NEFERU UAH.RA
NEFER.ONKH.RA
1 2 3
6 SONKH AB.RA
8 SEHETEP.AB.RA
1 2
9 AMENEMHOT-SENB.F
11 SEBEK HETEP.RA
15 SEBEKHETEP I
1 2 3 4
HETEP.KA.RA
SE.BEKA.KA.RA
1 2
20 SEBEKHETEP II
1 2
HA.ONKH.TEF
3
KEMA
4
21 NEFERHETEP
1 2 3 4 5 6
22 SEBEKHETEP III
1 2 3 4 5 6 7 8 9

13. QUEENS OF DYNASTIES XII OR XIII

DA NESUT HEMT UAZET, UAHEM ONKH *Royal wife Uazet, again living.* Gone white D. 74
DB NESUT HEMT URT, KHNEM NEFER, NUBTI·HETEP·TA.
Great royal wife, united to the crown, Nubti·hetep·ta Intense light blue S. 30

XIIIth DYNASTY. 13·2. SEKHEM·KA·RA

NETER NEFER, RA·SEKHEM·KA, DA ONKH. *Good god Sekhem·ka·ra, giving life* Dark brown limestone K. 26

13·DC. 13 ? DC. ONKH·NEFERU·UAH·RA
RA·ONKH·NEFERU·UAH. *Ra·onkh·neferu·uah* Pottery. Blue-green M. 94

13·DD. 13 ? DD. NEFER·ONKH·RA.
1, 2 RA·NEFER·ONKH. *Nefer·onkh·ra* Obsidian L. 37, N. 28
3 ,, *Nefer·onkh·ra* (Head finely worked) Hard brown limestone F. 49

13·6. 13·6. SEONKH·AB·RA
RA·SEONKH·AB NEB. *Seonkhabra, lord.* Full green F. 42

13·8 13·8. SEHETEP·AB·RA
1, 2 RA·SEHETEP·AB blundered. *Sehetepabra* Both gone light brown Z. 76

13·11 13·11. SEBEK·HETEP·RA
RA·SEBEK·HETEP. *Sebekhetepra* Gone browny white G. 52

13·15 13·15. SEBEKHETEP I
1 (HER KHO) BAU, NEBTI, UAHEM ONKH ZEDUI RENPITU (RA·SEKHEM)·KHU·TAUI, DA ONKH ZED MA RA ZETTA } Titles of Sebekhotep I
(SEBEK NEB SMEN·)NU MERY. *Beloved of Sebek lord of Smennu* Greenish-blue. Cylinder
2 (RA)·SEKHEM·KHU·TAUI, (SEBEK NEB . . .) AU MERY. *Beloved of Sebek lord of . . . . . au*
Edwards. Grey-blue. Cylinder
3 SEBEKT·HETEP. *Sebekthetep* (similar Golenisheff) Gone brown H. 50
4 HES HER SEBEKHETEP. *Praise to Horus Sebekhetep* Gone drab J. 34

13·DE. 13 ? DE. HETEP·KA·RA
NETER NEFER, NEB TAUI, NEB ARKHET, RA·HETEP·KA, DA ONKH ZETTA.
Good god, lord of both lands, lord of action, Hetepkara, giving life eternally Light brown. Cylinder

13·DF. 13 ? DF. SEBEKA·KA·RA
NETER NEFER, RA·SE·BEKA·KA, SEBEK NEB SUUAZ MERY. *Good god, Sebekakara, loved by Sebek lord of Suuaz* Light blue. Cylinder

13·20. 13·20. SEBEKHETEP II
1 RA·SEKHEM·SEUAZ·TAUI, SEBEKHETEP, between uraei Hollow gold ball
2 NETER NEFER, RA·SEKHEM·SEUAZ·TAUI, SEBEKHETEP ONKH ZETTA, MES NE NESUT MUT AUH·ABU. Kuft White M. 58
Good god, Sekhem·seuaz·taui·ra, Sebekhetep, living eternally, born of the royal mother Auh·abu.
3 BATI KHETM, NETERATEF, HĂONKHTEF } parents of next kings *Royal sealer, divine father, Haonkhtef* Peacock blue S. 10
4 REPOTET, NESUT SĂT, KEMA } *Princess, Royal daughter Kema* Gone white S. 10

13·21. 13·21. NEFERHETEP
1 NETER NEFER, RA·KHO·SESHESH, AR NE NETER ATF HĂONKHEF.
Good god, Kho-seshesh-ra, born of the divine father Haonkhtef Kahun. Full blue S. 30
2 NETER NEFER, RA·KHO·SESHESH, SEBEK·RA NEB SU·UAZ MERY. *Loved by Sebek lord of Suuaz* Full blue Bead
3 RA·KHO·SESHESH, ONKH ZED. *Kho·seshesh·ra, life enduring.* Uraeus. Peacock blue, gone brown Q. 92
4 } SĂ RA NEFER·HETEP, MES NE NESUT MUT KEMA. } Gone light brown S. 30
5, 6 } *Son of Ra, Neferhotep, born of the royal mother, Kema* } Deep blue J. 50

13·23. 13·23. SEBEKHETEP III
1, 2 NETER NEFER, RA·KHO·NEFER, AR NE NETER ATEF HĂ·ONKHF.
Good god Kho·neferra, born of the divine father Haonkhef. Grass green Peacock blue S. 30 T. 30
3 Same (not figured) Gone white T. 30
4 SĂ RA SEBEKHETEP MES NE NESUT MUT KEMA.
Son of Ra Sebek hetep, born of the royal mother, Kema Gone brown T. 30
5, 6 RA·KHO·NEFER Dull green. Wood brown. T. 68, G. 14
7, 8, 9 RA·KHO·NEFER, SEBEKHETEP Gone white, wood brown, wood brown, L. 46, W. 10, H. 94

13·23. SEBEKHETEP III (*continued*)

10 RA·KHO·NEFER, SEBEKHETEP Coarse. C type feather sides. Yellow-brown Y. 25
11, 12, 13 Same Buff. Wood brown. Pottery, olive. F. 71, G. 8, S. 30
14, 15, 16 Same Edwards, wood brown. Yellow brown. Gone white. J. 74, F. 26, E. 74
17 KHO NEFER, SEBEKHETEP Gone white G.
18 KHO NEFERUI (= RA NEFER) SEBEKHETEP Edwards. Light brown. Broken
19, 20, 21, 22, 23 SEBEKHETEP (probably of xxvith dyn.)
Green limestone, green, yellow paste, gone white, blue paste. E. 29, P. 5, W. 60, K. 24, W. 60

13 ? DG. KHO·KA·RA

RA·KHO·KA Green Z. 70

13·24. SEBEKHETEP IV

1 RA·KHO·HETEP Gone yellow-brown M. 94
2 RA·KHO·HETEP SĂ RA SEBEKHETEP Clay sealing

13·25. AO·AB

RA·UĂH·AB, NETER NEFER Gone yellow U. 5

13·26. AY

1, 2 NETER NEFER, RA·MER·NEFER Gone white. Bare steatite. M. 48 Worn
3, 4 ,, ,, Blue. Gone white. T. 30, T. 30
5 RA·MER·NEFER Uraeus Blue-green, gone white L. 51

13·DH. QUEEN ANA

1 NESUT HEMT URT, KHNUMT NEFER, ANA. *Great royal wife, united to the crown, Ana.* Clear light blue M. 38
2, 3 ,, ,, ,, ,, ,, ,,
Gone white. Blue. M. 44, M. 38

13·41. ABA

RA·NEB·MĂOT (Too rough to be of xviiith dynasty) Black steatite Lion

13·53. NEHESI-RA

SĂ RA NEHESI, DA ONKH. *Son of Ra, Nehesi, giving life* Gone white D. 84

14. *XIIIth–XIVth DYNASTIES.* ROYAL FAMILIES

A NESUT HEMT SĂT-HATHER. *Royal wife, Sat-hathor* Gone white J. 62
B NESUT SĂ ANTEF (Form of back of Sebekhetep III to Ay). *Royal son, Antef* Dull green M. 12
C NESUT SĂ NEHESI. *Royal son, Nehesi* Gone white U. 55
D ,, ,, ,, ,, Gone yellow U. 55
E NESUT SĂ SEMSU, QEPUPEN. *Royal son, eldest, Qepupen* Gone white J. 29
F NESUT SĂ, MER SEK, SEPED·NEB. *Royal son, over the guides, Sopedneb* ("All ready") Gone buff T. 48
G, H, J NESUT SĂ APEQ *Royal son, Apeq.* Edwards. Gone white, Gone grey, Gone white T. 40, T. 40, P. 40
K REPOTI, NESUT SĂT NEFERT-ONQET·UBEN. *Princess, royal daughter, Nefert-onqet·uben*
(Fraser, 75, 76) Gone yellow-brown M. 72
L NESUT SĂ TUR. *Royal son, Tur* Blue-green, burnt red L. 65

14·69. ·69. SEUAZNERA

1 RA·SE·UAZ·NE Pottery. Full blue N. 2
2, 3, 4, 5 ,, Pottery, grey-blue, dirty grey-blue, blue gone white M. 80, N. 2

14·76. ·76. NEFER·AB·RA

RA·NEFER·AB·RA, NEFER BATI at each side Dirty green-blue T. 75

UNPLACED KINGS

14·M. KHENZER

1, 2 KHENZER Buff limestone. Slate. T. 87, L. 94

KHONDY

14·N.
NE·ONKH, KHONDY before king in Egyptian dress, giving ONKH, *Life,* to an Asiatic subject; beyond, an Egyptian subject, HEN *servant,* holding a papyrus plant with a bird upon it. Column of five ibexes; guilloche pattern. Syro-Mesopotamian work. Greenish-black jasper. Cylinder

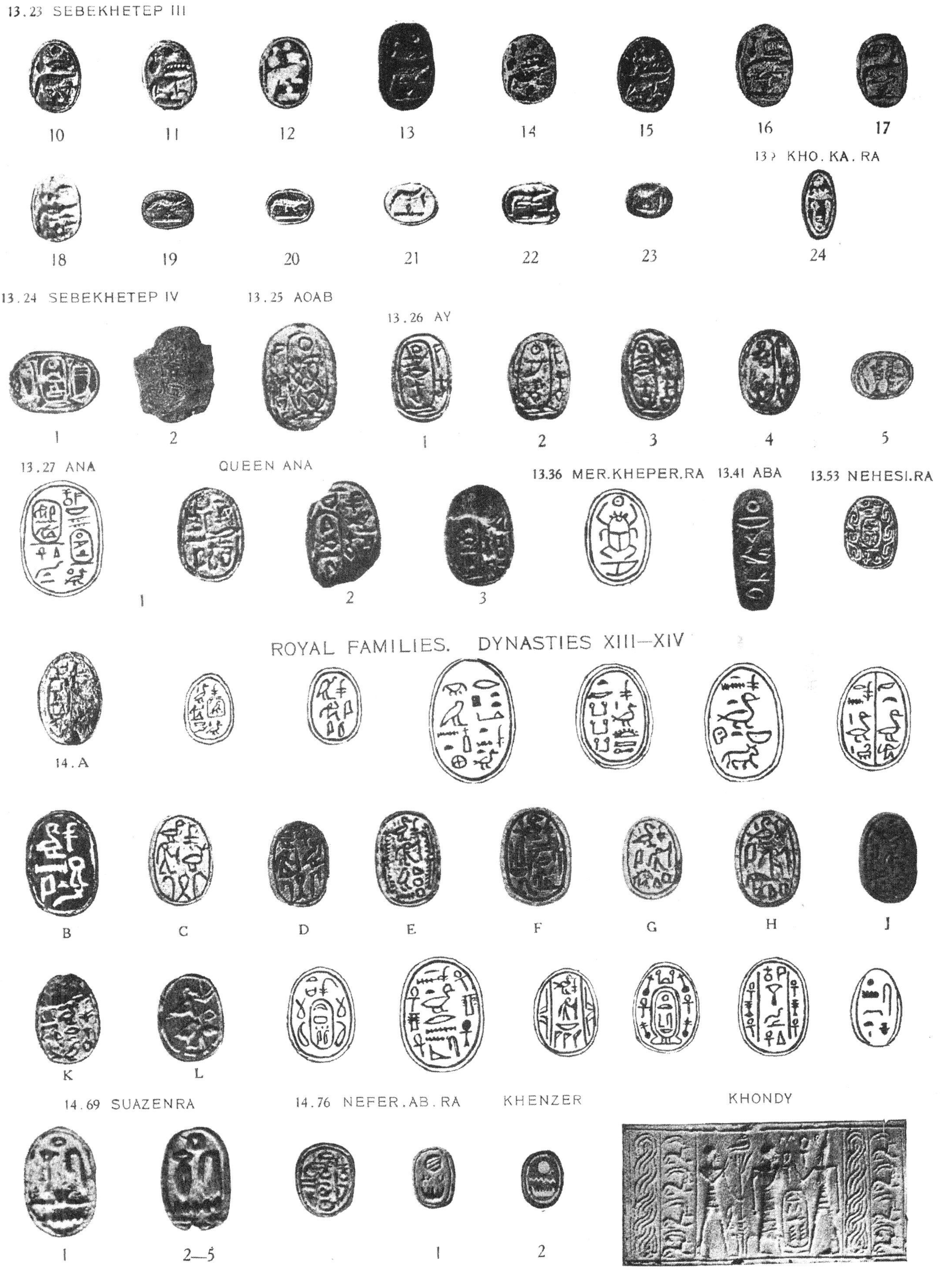
13.23 SEBEKHETEP III
10 11 12 13 14 15 16 17
13.? KHO.KA.RA
18 19 20 21 22 23 24
13.24 SEBEKHETEP IV
13.25 AOAB
13.26 AY
1 2 1 2 3 4 5
13.27 ANA
QUEEN ANA
13.36 MER.KHEPER.RA
13.41 ABA
13.53 NEHESI.RA
1 2 3
ROYAL FAMILIES. DYNASTIES XIII—XIV
14.A
B C D E F G H J
K L
14.69 SUAZENRA
14.76 NEFER.AB.RA
KHENZER
KHONDY
1 2—5 1 2

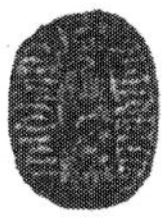

14.0

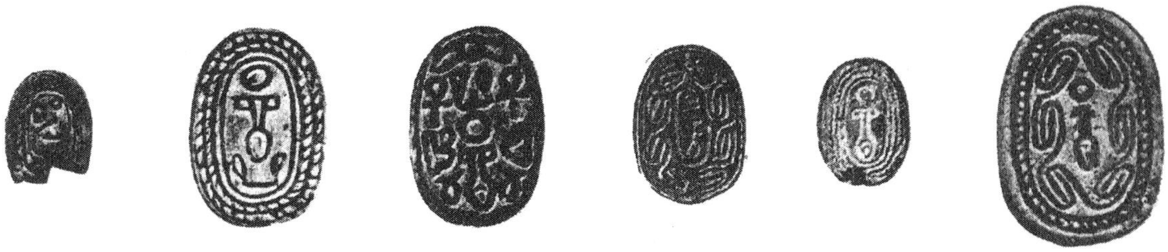

P Q R S T U

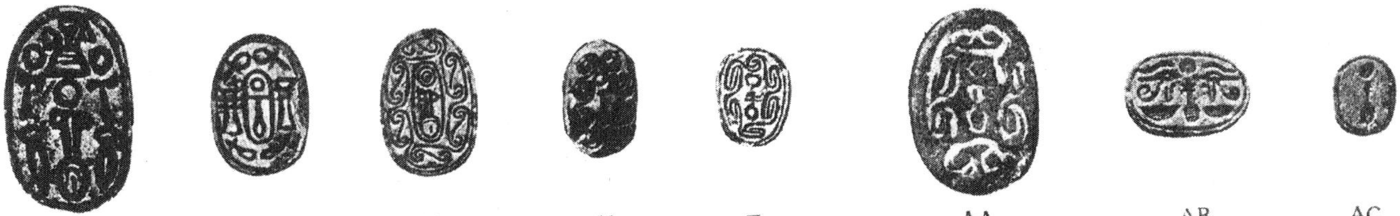

V W X Y Z AA AB AC

AD AE AF AG AH AJ AK

AL AM AN AO AP AQ

AR AS AT AU AV AW

AX AY AZ

KA.ZED UAH RA AND UAZ.RA

BA

14.

SEKHEM·ZET·ONKH·RA or SEKHEM·RA

O	RA·SEKHEM·ZET·ONKH, border of REN REN at each side	Gone wood brown	T. 82

PE·MĂOT·RA

P	RA·PE·MĂOT in rope border	Green-blue	M. 72

SMA·KA·RA

Q	RA·SMA·KA in rope border	Green	S. 30
R	,, ONKH, DESHERT, UAZ each side, winged sun above	Green	S. 70

NEFER·RA

S	RA·NEFER in rope border	Grey steatite	M. 38
T	RA·N·NEFER	Green gone brown	T. 49
U	RA·NEFER in scrolls and rope border	Blue-green	D. 98
V	RA·NEFER; HĂ, NEFER, UAZ around	Green	S. 5
W	RA·NEFER; ONKH, ZED, NEFER at each side	Green	S. 55
X	RA·NEFER, in good scroll border	Gone grey	D. 74
Y	RA·NEFER, in round spiral border	Edwards. Gone buff	D. 80
Z	RA·NEFER in irregular scrolls border	Blue-green	T. 44
AA	RA·NEFER in rude scroll border	Grey steatite	M. 42
AB	RA·NEFER, UZAT NEB at each side	Gone white	W. 90
AC	RA·NEFER	Pottery, green-grey	N. 72

NEFERUI·RA

AD	RA·NEFERUI TEP QEBTI (?). *Neferui·ra, chief of Koptos (?)*	Blue	T. 88

NEFERU·RA

AE	RA·NEFERU, R·N·O·border	Peacock-green	T. 32
AF	KHEPER·NEB·KA; UAZ ONKH HER UZAT KA NEB NEFERUI NUB at sides	Edwards. Grey	D. 52
AG	KHO·KHEPER·KA·R; BATI, ZU REN RON at sides	Edwards. White	D. 92
AH	KHOT·KHEPER·KA·KHEPER; NEFER·ZED BATI at sides	Light green	J. 89
AJ	KHO·KA·KHO; UZAT ONKH NEFER at sides	Edwards. Blue-green	D. 92
AK	RA·UAZ·KA; NEB NEFER at sides	Edwards. Blue-green	J. 45

NE·KA·RA, Etc.

AL	RA·NE·KA; three BATI crowns, NEB	Buff	Z. 30
AM	RA·KA	Brown	Z. 30
AN	RA·KA, uraeus and falcon at sides. Period of Apepa I, see 15.5.12.	Buff	Z. 30
AO	RA·NE·KA, feathers over cartouche and ONKH, scrolls around	White	D. 36
AP	NEFER in RA·KA	White	L. 76
AQ	HETEP KA NEFER	Dull blue	D. 88
AR	RA·NEFER, UAZ HER UZAT KA at sides	Gone white	T. 28
AS	RA·NEFER, uraeus R KA R at sides	Gone grey	T. 66
AT	ONKH·ET·KA, uraeus, ONKH NEFER at sides	Gone white	W. 73
AU	RA·ER·KHEPER	Blue-green	D. 70
AV	RA·NUB·ER·KA	Gone white	J. 72
AW	KA BAT	Blue-green	J. 33
AX	RA·KHENTI·KHERUI, NESUT KA NEB below	Gone white	X. 10
AY	RA·KHEPER·NEB in scroll border	Gone wood-brown	Z. 10
AZ	UAZ·KHO·NEFERUI; HO UZAT ONKH at sides	Pottery. Green	M. 88

14

14·BA. KA·ZED·UAH·RA and vassal UAZ·RA (NEFERUI = RA)

BA KA·ONKH·ER·NEFER·KHO, personal name. NEFERUI (= RA)·KA·ZED·UAH, throne name, standing, taking lotus from vassal Uaz·ra, with his son and daughter kneeling. The vassal holding palm branch, standing, before him BAT NUB, NEFERUI (= RA) UAZ, UR, *King, victor, Uazra the great.*
Below his wife (?) kneeling, priestess (?) of Hathor, offering palm to the suzerain KA·ONKH·ER·NEFER·KHO — Gone white. Cylinder

These two halves of the cylinder are engraved base to base, in one length.

15·1. *XVth DYNASTY.* 15·1. ONTHA

HEQ SEMTU, HERYT, ONTHA; NEFERT NO KHO NEFER at sides.
Prince of the Desert, the Terror, Ontha Greenish-blue. C sides Q. 20

15·3 15·3. KHYAN

HEQ SEMTU KHYĂN, ONKH NEFER at sides. *Prince of the Desert, Khyan* Gone white T. 53

15·5. 15·5. APEPA I

1 APEPA, between UAZ, NEFER, and human headed uraeus Gone brown, back lost
2 AP (EPA) (RA)-O-SEUSER; good scroll and entwined pattern Gone light brown D. 80
3 RA·O·SEUSER; twists at sides Peacock blue D. 90
4 RA·O·SEUSER, NUB above, twist at side Blue T. 66
5 RA·O·SEUSER in rope border Gone light brown M. 74
6 ,, NUB above, uraeus at side Gone yellow T. 55
7 ,, ,, ,, Dull green T. 44
8 ,, UAZ NEFER at each side *Koptos* xxiv 8. Gone wood-brown T. 44
9 NESUT BAT, RA·O·SEUSER, DESHERT Gone white T. 44
10 RA·O·SEUSER Gone white L. 9
11 RA·O·S; NESUT each side, plants of south and north below Gone buff T 26
12 RA·O·SEUSER, uraeus and falcon on each side, NUB below Dull green Z. 30
13 RA·O·SEUSER Grey steatite Z. 30
14, 15, 16, 17, 18, 19 RA·O·SEUSER, partly blundered Pottery. Dull blue, burnt brown T. 75
All pottery, green-blue, light blue, gone yellow, clear blue, blue. Four of T. 89, T. 98

16·A. *XVIth DYNASTY.* A. NOA·NEB·RA

1 RA·NOĂ·NEB, NEFER uraeus and UZAT at sides Gone white J. 15
2 ,, uraeus at each side Green Z. 30
3 ,, Pottery. Blue-green T. 61

16·B. 16·B. MĂOT·AB·RA

1 NETER NEFER, RA·MĂOT·AB, ONKH DA. *The good god, Maotabra, given life.* Edwards. Blue-green J. 29
2 ,, ,, ,, Scrolls at sides. Green, gone brown T. 43
3 NETER NEFER, RA·MĂOT·AB, ONKH DA. ONKH UAZ at sides. *The good god, Maotabra,* Green T. 33
4 NETER NEFER, RA·MĂOT·AB, ONKH DA. NESUT NEB NEFER at sides Gone brown T. 42
5 NETER NEFER, RA·MĂOT·AB, ONKH DA. NESUT NEB NEFER at sides Edwards. Light green-blue T. 42
6 NETER NEFER, RA·MĂOT·AB, ONKH DA. NETER ONKH at sides Edwards. Gone white T. 33
7 NETER NEFER, RA·MĂOT·AB, ONKH DA. NETER NETER at sides Edwards. Gone white T. 43
8 NETER NEFER, RA·MĂOT·AB, ONKH DA. NETER ONKH at sides Gone brown T. 41
9 NETER NEFER, RA·MĂOT·AB, ONKH DA. HEN repeated at sides Dark blue-green T. 41

16·C. 16·C. PEPA

As the scarab of best work, No. 1, has clearly PEPA, that reading must be preferred to SHESHA.

1 NETER NEFER, PEPA, DA ONKH. P with vertical bars. *Good god, Pepa, given life*
Edwards. Rich green-blue T. 5
2 SĂ RA PEPA, ONKH ZETTA. Between scrolls. *Son of Ra Pepa, living eternally* Gone light brown T. 38
3 ,, ,, ,, ,, ,, ,, ,, ,, Gone white J. 89
4 ,, ,, ,, ,, ,, ,, ,, ,, Gone brown T. 33
5 ,, ,, ,, ,, ,, ,, ,, ,, Gone white T. 33
6 ,, ,, ,, In rows of rings. *Son of Ra Pepa, living eternally* Blue-green T. 79
7 ,, ,, ,, ONKH ONKHET NEFER at sides. *Son of Ra Pepa, living eternally* Gone drab J. 29
8 ,, ,, ,, UAHU NEFER at sides. *Son of Ra Pepa, living eternally* Gone drab T. 50
9 ,, ,, ,, ONKH NEFER at sides. *Son of Ra Pepa, living eternally* Green T. 42
10, 11, 12 SĂ RA PEPA, ONKH ZETTA. NETER ONKH at sides. *Son of Ra Pepa, living eternally*
Gone white, gone brown, blue-green T. 41, 49, 20
13, 14 SĂ RA PEPA, ONKH DA. NETER NETER at sides. *Son of Ra Pepa, given life* Gone brown T. 37, L. 11
15 ,, ,, ONKH NETER DA degraded NETER, bars. *Son of Ra Pepa, given divine life*
Gone yellow U. 30
16 ,, ,, ONKH ZETTA in rope border (or perhaps APEP). *Son of Ra Pepa, living eternally* Gone white T. 50

1 ONTHA 2 SEMQEN 3 KHYAN 4 YAQEB. ORH 5 APEPA I

1 2 3

4 5 6 7 8 9 10 11

12 13 14 15 16 17 18 19

PRINCE APEPA DYNASTY XVI A. OANEBRA SEKTI B. MĂOTABRA

1 2 3 1 2

3 4 5 6 7 8 9

C. PEPA

1 2 3 4 5 6 7 8

9 10 11 12 13 14 15 16

DYNASTIES XVI, XVII

XXII

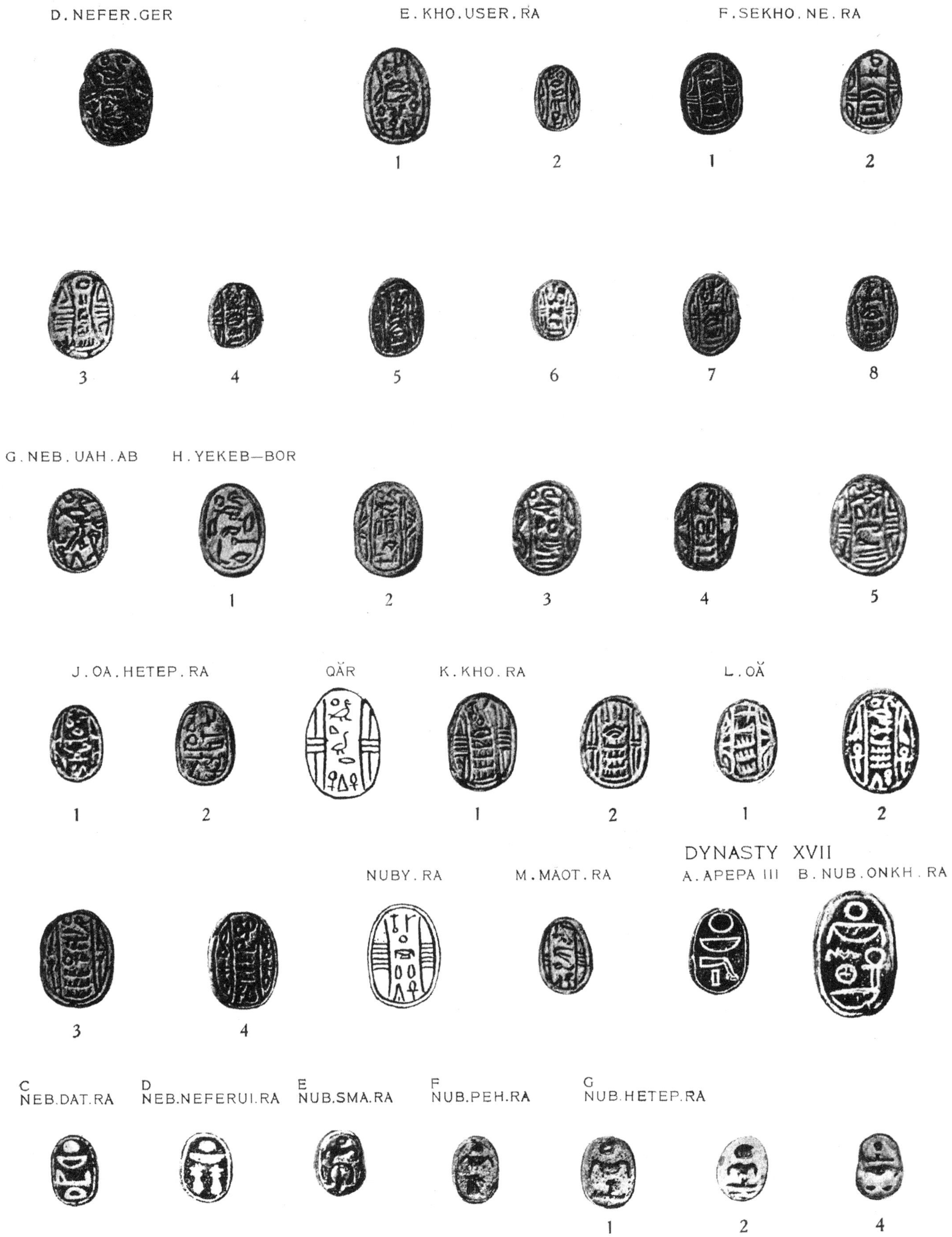

XVIth DYNASTY (*continued*). D. NEFER-GER

SĂ RA NEFER-GER MU, DA ONKH; NETER ONKH at sides. *Son of Ra, Nefer-ger, given life* Gone flesh red T. 28

16·E. E. KHO·USER·RA

1 NETER NEFER RA·KHO·USER, DA ONKH, NETER ONKH at sides. *The good god Khouser·ra, given life* Gone white T. 28
2 NETER NEFER RA·KHO·USER, DA ONKH, loops at sides Gone white T. 41

16·F. F. SE·KHO·NE·RA

1, 2 RA·SE·KHO·NE, degraded NETERS at sides Gone brown, gone buff T. 33, T. 43
3 ,, same reduced to bars Gone white T. 33
4, 5, 6, 7, 8 NETER NEFER, RA·SE·KHO·NE Gone white, light green-blue, light blue, gone white, blue-green L. 9, 76, 12. U. 70, 55

16·G. G. NEB·UĂH·ĂB

SĂ RA NEB·UĂH·ĂB, DA ONKH. *Son of Ra, Nebuahab, given life* Green U. 50

16·H. H. YEKEB-BOR (YAKUB·BAAL)

1 SĂ RA YEKEB (B) OR. *Son of Ra, Yekeb-baal* Green-blue U. 50
2 SĂ RA YEKEB S(?), degraded NETERS at sides Gone light brown T. 40
3 SĂ RA YEKEB MU, degraded NETERS at sides Gone red U. 50
4 YEKEB MU, degraded NETERS at sides Blue-green U. 35
5 SĂ RA YEKEB MU, degraded NETERS at sides Blue-green T. 33

16·J. J. OĂ·HETEP·RA

1 NETER NEFER, RA·OĂ·HETEP, DA ONKH. *Good god Oahetepra, given life* Blue-green T. 41
2 ,, ,, ,, ,, ,, ,, Gone brown H. 70

16·K. K. KHO·RA

1 NETER NEFER, RA·KHO, MU, degraded NETERS. *Good god Khora* Gone white U. 60
2 ,, ,, ,, ,, ,, Gone white T. 50

16·L. L. OĂ(MU)

1 OĂ MU degraded NETERS at sides Gone brown T. 49
2 SĂ RA OĂ MU DA ONKH, NETER ONKH at sides. *Son of Ra, Oa(mu), given life* Green-blue T. 38
3 SĂ RA OĂ MU, NETERS at sides Gone grey T. 50
4 NETER NEFER OĂ MU DA ONKH, UAZ NEFER at sides Gone grey T. 33

16·M. M. MĂOT·RA

NETER NEFER RA·MĂOT, ONKH DA. *Good God Maotra given life* Gone white T. 47

17·A. *XVIIth DYNASTY.* A. APEPA III

RA·NEB·KHEPESH Hard green paste N. 30

17·B. B. NUB·ONKH·RA

RA·NUB·ONKH NEB. Deep lumpy back Gone brown N. 44

17·C. C. NEB·DAT·RA

RA·NEB·DA·T Green-blue T. 9

17·D. D. NEB·NEFERUI·RA

RA·NEB·NEFERUI Pottery. Gone brown V. 57

17·E. E. NUB·SMA·RA

RA·NUB·SMA and plants of south and north Pottery. Light green N. 60

17·F. F. NUB·PEH·RA

RA·NUB·PEH Pottery. Gone white N. 60

17·G. G. NUB·HETEP·RA

1 RA·NUB·HETEP Pottery. Green N. 60
2 ,, Pottery. Gone white K. 56
3 ,, (not figured) Pottery. Green L. 95
4 RA·HETEP·NUB Pottery. Gone white K.

17·H. *XVIIth DYNASTY.* 17·H. RAHETEP

1 RA·HETEP — Gone red-brown H. 94
2, 3 ,, — Pottery, green faded. Light blue paste. K. 92, Z. 97
4 ,, spelt out — Light green T. 58
5, 6 ,, — Pottery green. Hard light blue paste. N. 60, Z. 97

17·J. 17·J. MEN·HETEP·RA (successor of Rahetep)

RA·MEN (HETEP ?) SĂ, NUB, and crowned uraeus (as Brit. Mus. *Cat.* 602) — Gone brown. Back lost

17·K. 17·K. KHNEMU·TAUI·RA

RA·KHNEMU·TAUI NUB — Green H. 14

17·L. 17·L. KHU·UĂZ

KHU·UĂZ — Gone drab N. 68

17·M. 17·M. NEB·KA·RA

RA·NEB·KA, reverse ONKH NEFER (see Cartouche in Cairo Catalogue v, 37082) — Gone brown Flat

17·N. 17·N. SEQENENRA I

SĂRA TAOĂ, DA ONKH. *Son of Ra Taoa given life.* Probably from royal jewellery. Gold shell.

17·O. 17·O. KAMES

1 RA·UAZ·KHEPER, double feathers at top, NETER NEFER DA ONKH at sides. In gold mount — Green-blue M. 6
2 RA·UAZ·KHEPER, reverse PA HEQ OĂ. *The great prince.* Rope pattern on edge — Dark blue paste

XVIIIth DYNASTY

18·I 18·I. AOHMES I

1 RA·NEB·PEHTI in oval scrolls — Pottery. Blue-green Q. 65
2 RA·NEB·PEHTI ONKH, NEFER scratched in front — Black steatite K. 88
3 RA·NEB·PEH — Pottery gone drab N. 82
4 RA·PEH·NEB. RA with uraei — Gone wood-brown H. 60
5 ,, ,, — Edwards. Gone light-brown L. 49
6 ,, ,, — Gone white J. 59
7 RA·PEH·NEB; reverse, hedgehog — Green. Hedgehog
8 ,, — Light wood-brown N. 76
9 ,, — Gone white T. 25
10 RA·PEH·NEB MĂO — Gone white G. 50
11 ,, ,, — Edwards. Gone white L. 70
12 RA·NEB·PEH, NEBTI ONKH; reverse DESHERT and falcon head — Hard paste. Dull green Flat

QUEEN ĂOHMES NEFERTARI

13 NESUT HEMT ĂOHMES. *Royal wife Aohmes* — Slate L. 98
14 ,, ,, — Pottery. Gone white M. 22
15 ĂOHMES NEFERTARI — Gone white H. 10
16 NETER HEMT NEFERTARI, AMEN MERYT. *Divine wife Nefertari, beloved by Amen* — Gone yellow Uzat
17, 18 NETER HEMT NEFERTARI — Both Edwards, green, green-blue. H. 10, L. 52
19 ,, ,, — Blue-green T. 67
20, 21 ,, ,, — Green. Gone white. L. 14, L. 28
22 NESUT HEMT NEFER — Green Flat
23 NEFER TAI (*sic*) — Gone white L. 52
24 NEFERTARI, reverse lotus plant — Light green. Flat
25 KHNUMT NEFERT NEFERTARI. *United to the white crown, Nefertari* — Green Bead
26 NESUT SĂT, NETER HEMT, NESUT SENT, NEFERTARI. *Royal daughter, divine wife, royal sister, Nefertari* — Gone white Bead
27 NETER HEMT ĂOHMES . . . reverse same. Piece of *menat* — Blue Flat
28 ,, ,, ,, ,, — Blue. Flat
29 ĂOHMES NEFERTARI DA ONKH — Pottery. Blue and black. Flat

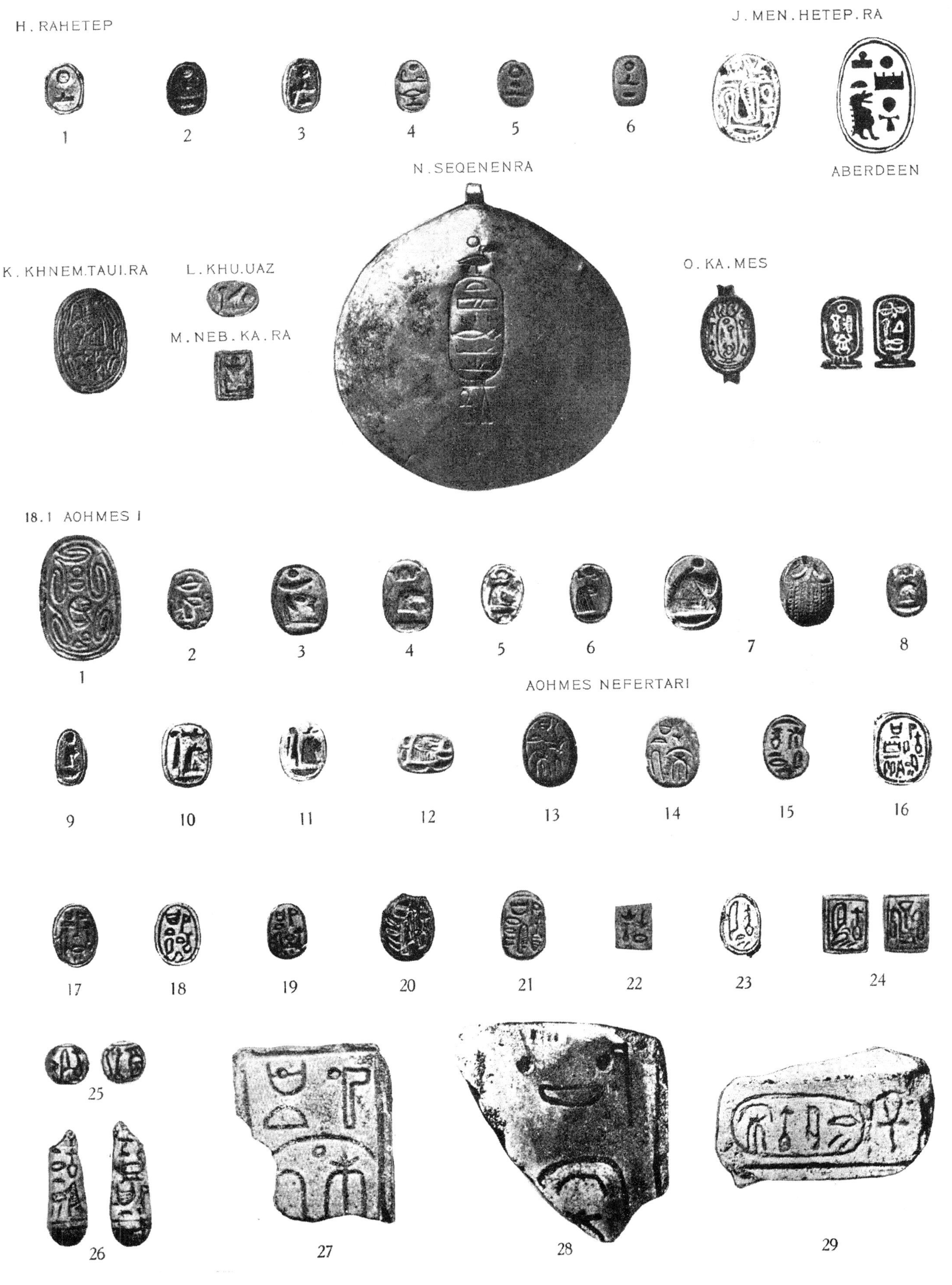
H. RAHETEP
1 2 3 4 5 6
J. MEN. HETEP. RA
ABERDEEN
N. SEQENENRA
K. KHNEM.TAUI.RA
L. KHU.UAZ
M. NEB. KA. RA
O. KA. MES
18. 1 AOHMES I
1 2 3 4 5 6 7 8
AOHMES NEFERTARI
9 10 11 12 13 14 15 16
17 18 19 20 21 22 23 24
25
26 27 28 29

18.2 AMENHETEP I

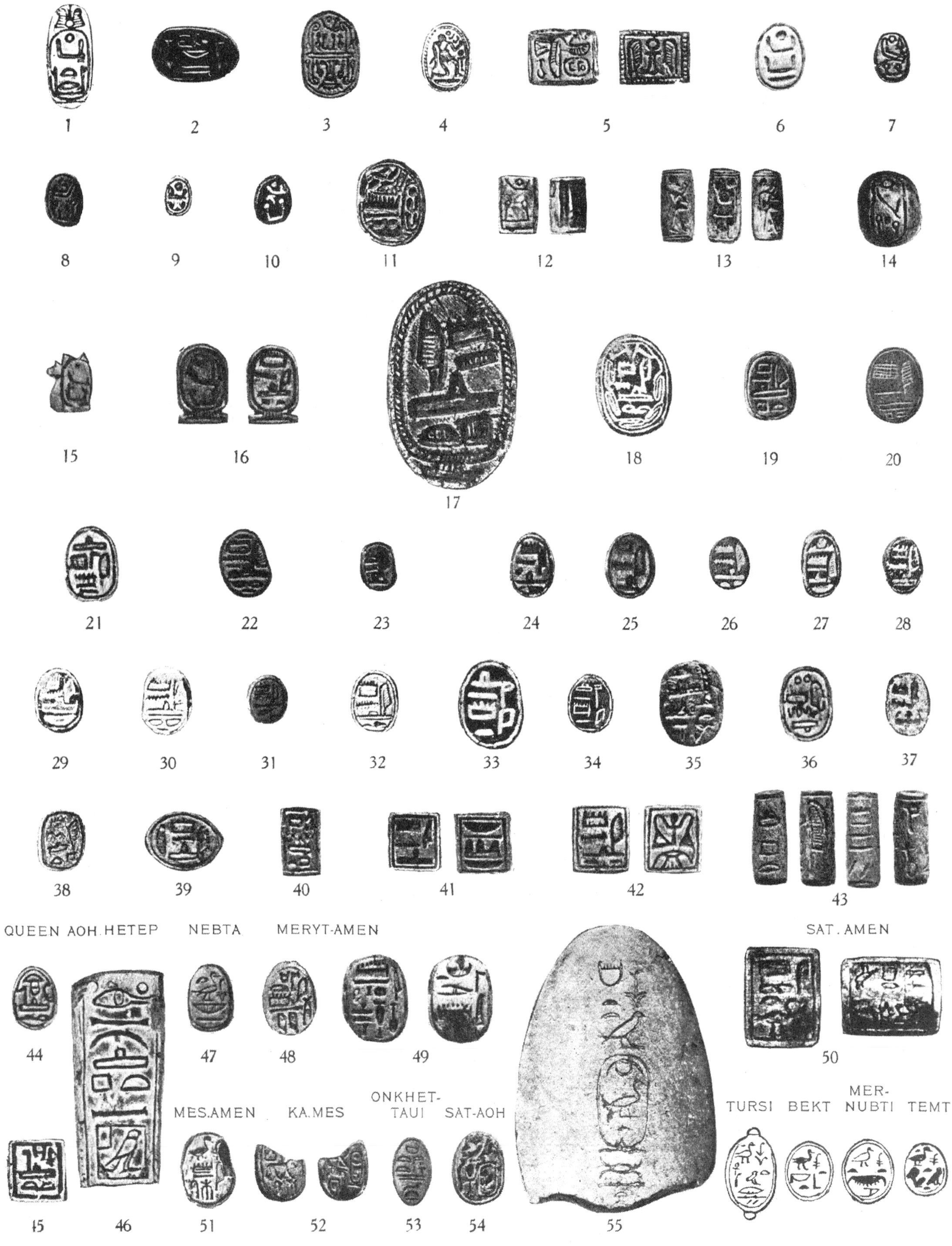

XVIIIth DYNASTY

18·2.

18·2. AMENHETEP I

No.	Inscription	Material	Ref.
1	RA·ZESERT·KA. Gold finger ring. Bought 12 April 1914, from Thebes	Gold.	Ring.
2	NETER NEFER, NEB TAUI, RA·ZESER·KA. *Good god, lord of both lands, Zeserkara*	Dark green jasper	L. 94
3	RA·ZESER·KA, NEFERS, HA NUB	Green	W. 57
4	RA·ZESER·KA ONKH. Kneeling man	Edwards. Green	L. 66
5	RA·ZESER·KA NEFER, Falcon. Reverse, ONKH and two reed leaves	Blue.	Flat
6	RA·ZESER·KA NEB	Pottery. Blue	L. 46
7	RA·ZESER·KA. Hollowed out, legs separate	Dull blue-green	K. 62
8, 9, 10	RA·ZESER·KA	Light green. Gone white. Flesh-coloured limestone	L. 58, 58, 11
11	RA·ZESER KA BAT MEN . . .	Gone yellow	G. 20
12	RA·ZESER·KA; ONKH NEFER repeated on back	Turquoise blue	Prism
13	RA·ZESER·KA NETER NEFER. Two figures of the king	Gone white	Cylinder
14	RA·ZESER·KA	Blue	Bead
15	,,	Turquoise blue glass	Uzat
16	,, Reverse AMENHETEP	Cartouche. Dull green	Flat
17	AMENHETEP	Stamp with handle. Green.	Handle
18	,, in scrolls border	Hard green paste	W. 90
19	,,	Green	L. 20
20	,,	Slate	L. 28
21	,,	Gone brown	K. 2
22, 23, 24, 25	AMENHETEP	Gone white. Dull blue. Green-blue. Green.	N. 88, T. 92, Y. 20, L. 95
26	AMENHETEP	Pottery. Dirty olive	L. 76
27	,, RA·AKHTI above, NEB below	Gone brown	H. 78
28	,,	Red limestone	L. 18
29	,,	Gone grey	L. 22
30	,,	Edwards. Gone white	L. 52
31	,,	Blue paste	N. 22
32	,,	Edwards. Blue-green burnt red	L. 16
33	NETER HETEP AMEN	Green	H. 12
34	,, ,,	Slate	H. 62
35, 36, 37, 38	AMENHETEP blundered	Green. Blue. Gone grey. Gone white.	N. 51, H. 38, E. 74, Uzat
39	AMENHETEP NEB	Green	Z. 84
40	,, zigzag lines on cylindrical back	Green, hemi-cylinder	
41	AMENHETEP; reverse NEB TA SEMT NEB. *Lord of plain and mountain all*	Blue-green	Flat
42	AMENHETEP; lotus flowers over NUB	Blue-green	Flat
43	AMEN TAUI NETER NEFER HETEP blundered	Buff	Cylinder

FAMILY OF AMENHETEP I

No.	Inscription	Translation	Material	Ref.
44	NESUT HEMT NETER ĂOH-HETEP.	*Royal and Divine wife Aoh-hetep*	Green	L. 18
45	NESUT HEMT NETER HETEP; reverse HES, NEFER, HES on facets		Blue-green	Prism
46	AR NE ĂOH·HETEP NE HATHER.	*Made by Aoh-hetep for Hathor.* Upper half of *menat*	Green	Flat
47	NESUT SĂT NEBTA.	*Royal daughter Nebta*	Green	H. 78
48	NETER HEMT AMEN·MERYT.	*Divine wife Merytamen*	Gone white	L. 26
49	NETER HEMT MERT·AMEN; rev. AMEN RA ear, NEFER HES HETEPT	*Divine wife Mertamen. Amen Ra listen well to praise and offering*	Pottery. Blue-green	Flat
50	AMEN SĂT, MER PER ĂO-NE-BAU.	*(Princess) Satamen. Steward Aonebau*	Green	Curved
51	NESUT SĂ AMEN·MES.	*Royal son Mesamen*	Gone white	L. 26
52	. . . . . KAMES; rev. RA·NEB·PEHTI.	King seated. Prince Kames and Aahmes I	Pottery. Green-blue	Flat
53	NETER HEMT ONKHET·TAUI·ZETTA.	*Divine wife Onkhet'taui·zetta*	Green	Fish
54	NESUT·HEMT URT, ĂOH·SĂT ONKH THA.	*Great royal wife, Sataoh, the living*	Gone white	J. 46
55	NESUT'HEMT URT, ĂOH·SĂT, NET (MERYT).	*Great royal wife, Sataoh, beloved by Neit*	Pink limestone	ovoid

18·3.

18·3. TEHUTMES I

1 NEKHEB NEB, UAZET NEB, NESRET OĂ PEHTI. *Lord of Nekhen and Buto, A flame great and mighty* Green L. 31
2 RA·OĂ·KHEPER·KA; reverse, UAZET KHOU. *Flourishing in epiphanies* Hard black limestone. Flat
3 RA·OĂ·KHEPER·KA SĂ AMEN. *Son of Amen* Green M. 70
4 RA·OĂ·KHEPER·KA, sphinx seated; reverse Syrian captive kneeling Gone grey
5 ,, falcon Gone white L. 26
6 ,, two falcons Gone brown F. 48
7 ,, bud and scroll Hard blue paste L. 52
8, 9 ,, NEB below Pottery. Gone brown. Olive-green G. 16
10 ,, between uraei, NEB above and below Gone white L. 60
11 ,, Gone white L. 56
12 ,, NETER NEFER at sides Gone brown J. 74
13 ,, the *ka* hands turned outward Gone brown E. 47
14 ,, HES Gone white G. 74
15 RA·OĂ·KHEPER·KA, OĂ MER AMEN } The style of these scarabs, and the lack of any such { Gone white L. 80
16 ,, ,, } name with *nefer*, obliges us to read *oa* here { Steatite Worn
17, 18 ,, Gone brown. Full blue. Z. 70, Z. 70
19 OĂ-KHEPER·KA Gone white P. 86
20 RA-OĂ-KHEPER Gurob. Edwards. Hard green paste N. 44
21 NETER NEFER, NEB TAUI, RA-OĂ·KHEPER, TEHUTI·MES. Throne and personal name. Gone light brown F. 34

PRIVATE NAMES

22 ĂOHMES. Draughtsman Pottery. Faded green
23 . . . AR AR NE AS SESH SEBEK·HENO. . . . *made for the Osirian, Scribe, Sebekheno* Pendant. Slate. Flat
24 SESH SEN·NEFER. *Scribe Sen·nefer.* Top of scribe's palette. Schist. Green. Flat
25 AMEN NE NETER HEN, TEHUTI. *Prophet of Amen, Tehuti* Edwards. Green. H. 20

18·4.

18·4. TEHUTMES II

1 HER USER PEHTI. Falcon name Hard paste. Brilliant light blue G. 68
2 HER NUB, SEKHEM KHEPERU Green E. 46
3 NETER NEFER NEB TAUI, RA·OĂ·KHEPER·NE, RA MER. *Beloved by Ra* Gone white Z. 25
4 RA·OĂ·KHEPER·NE. Lion and NEB Hard green paste L. 6
5, 6 RA·OĂ·KHEPER·NE Both green paste. G. 94, M. 26
7 ,, reverse TEHUTI·MES Pottery. Blue-green. Flat

18·5.

18·5. HOTSHEPSUT

1 USERT KAU, RA·MĂOT·KA. (Falcon name) Greyish-blue Flat
2 HER NUB, UĂZ-RENPETU. (Nekheb and Uazet name) Gone brown M. 34
3 RA·MĂOT-KA, UĂZ·RENPET. (Nekheb and Uazet name) Gone white L. 40
4 NETER RA KHO, RA·MĂOT·KA. (Falcon on *nub*, Horus Victor, name) Gone brown J. 80
5, 6 RA·MĂOT-KA, AMEN RA EM UĂZET PER. *Amen ra in the temple of Uazet* Pottery. Gone white. Blue. Flat
7 RA·MĂOT·KA, MEN MENNU. *Setting up monuments* Gone brown F. 78
8 RA·MĂOT·KA, MER MĂOT, ONKH THA. *Beloved of Maot* Green F. 61
9 NETER NEFER, NEB TAUI, RA·MĂOT·KA Gone white H. or J.
10 NETER NEFER, RA·MĂOT·KA Carnelian Z. 74
11 RA·MĂOT·KA, TAT·RA. *Substance of Ra* Gone light brown L. 7
12 KA·MĂOT·RA, DA ONKH, supported by kneeling figure. NETER NEFER, NEBTAUI Hollowed out. Gone white H. 71
13 KA·MĂOT·RA. Kneeling winged figure Gone brown Uzat
14 KA·MĂOT·RA, TAT AMEN. *Substance of Amen* Gone light drab F. 26
15 RA·MĂOT·KA, MĂOT at sides Gone white H. 26
16 ,, MĂOT and UĂST at sides Dark green E. 58
17 RA·MĂOT·KA, NEFERT Gone brown H. 26
18 ,, surrounded by two linked lines of scrolls. Gold mount, silver ring broken away. Blue-green V. 35

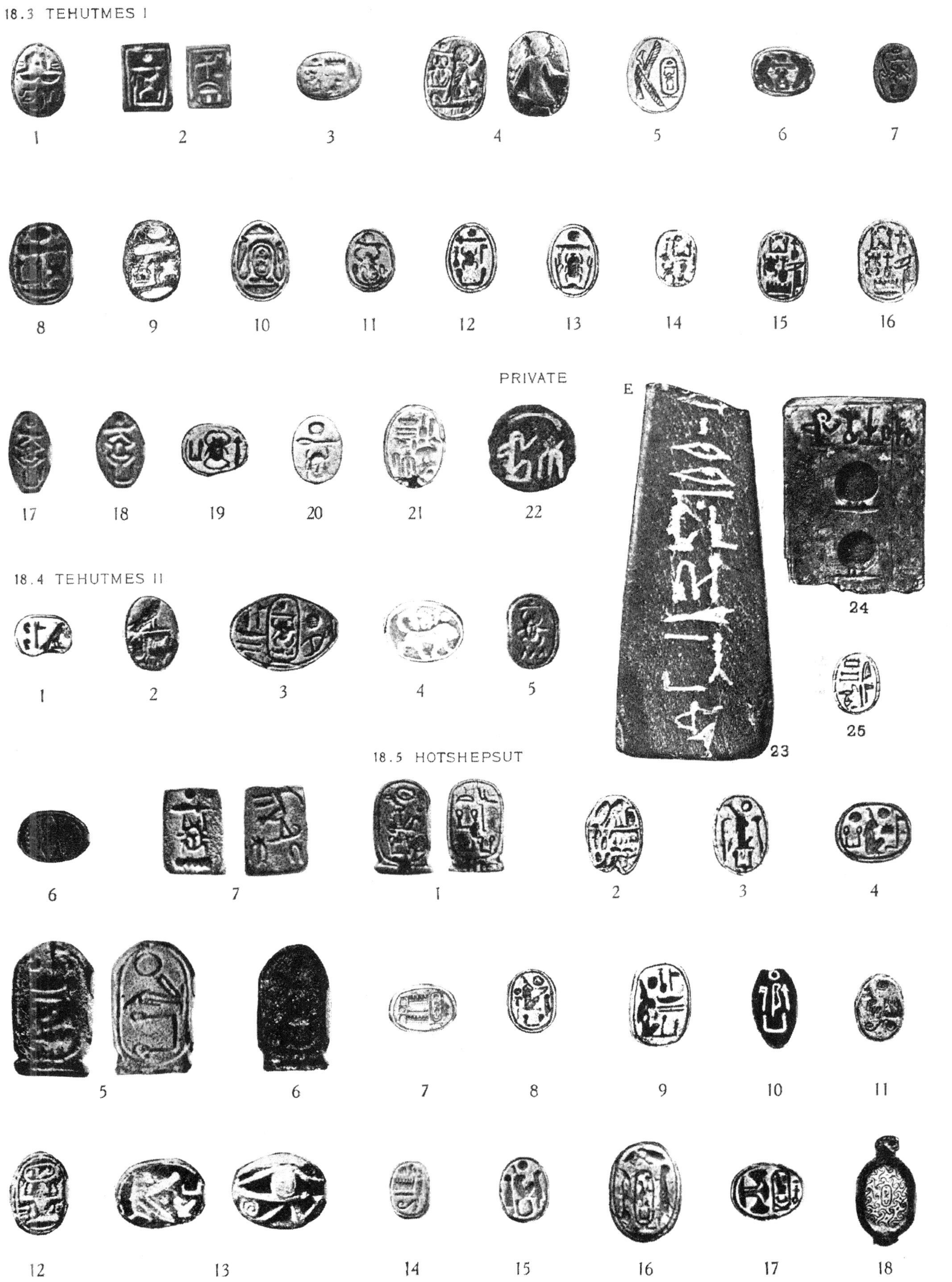

18.3 TEHUTMES I — 1–22; PRIVATE — 23 (E), 24, 25

18.4 TEHUTMES II — 1–7

18.5 HOTSHEPSUT — 1–18

18.5 HOTSHEPSUT *(continued)*

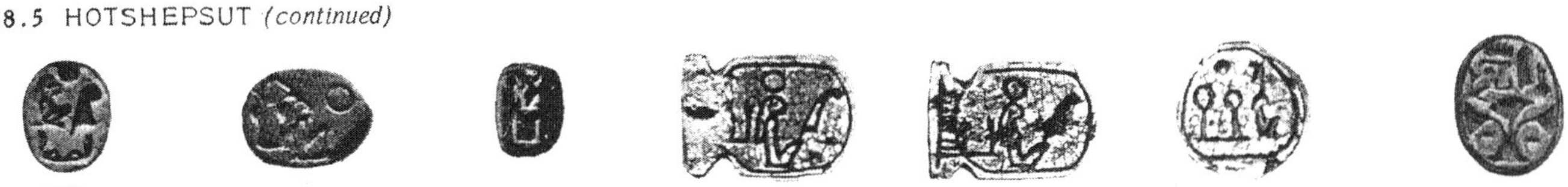

19 20 21 22 23 24

25 26 27 28 29 30 31

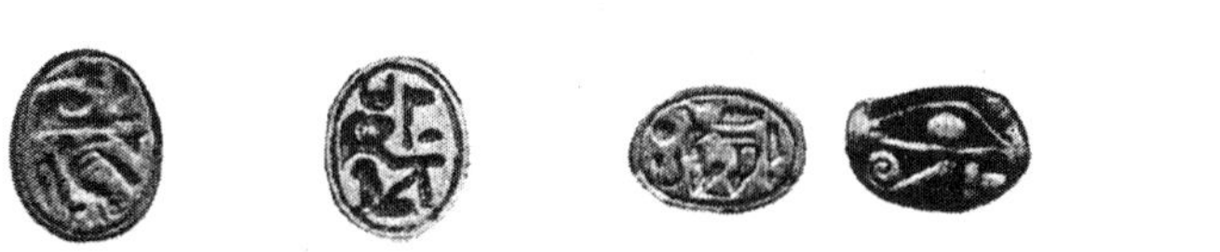

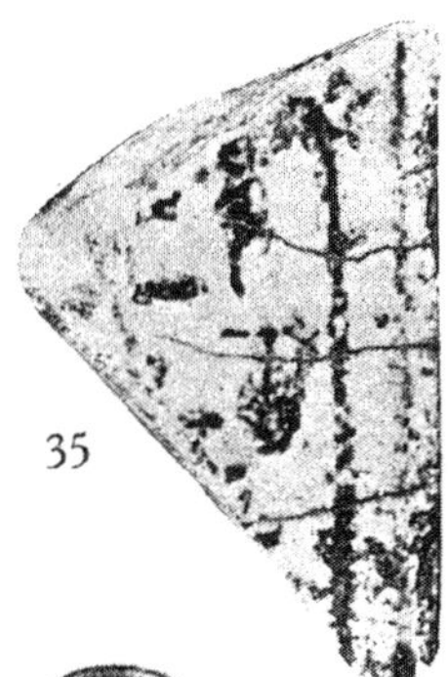

32 33 34 35 36 37

NEFRURA

38 39 40 41 42 43 44

18.6 TEHUTMES III

1 2 3 4 5 6 7 45

8 9 10 11 12

13 14 15 16 17 18 19 20

18·5.

18·5. HOTSHEPSUT (*continued*)

No.	Inscription	Material	Ref.
19, 20	RA·MĂOT·KA	Pottery, green-blue. Soft blue paste. Both	M. 26
21	,, Hă plant on back	Dark brown limestone	Flat
22, 23	,,	Blue, blue-green. Flat	Z. 60
24	KHNEMT·AMEN RA·KA·MĂOT. Hă plant. *United with Amen*	Green-blue	L. 7
25	AMEN·KHNEMT HOT-SHEPSET on bronze ring. ,, ,,	Dark green	H. 20
26	AMEN·KHNEMT RA·MĂOT. ,, ,,	Edwards. Gone white	E. 93?
27, 28, 29	AMEN·EM·KHNEMT, RA·MĂOT NEB. ,, ,,	Gone grey, broken. Gone grey. Green gone light brown	E. 55, 55
30	NETER HEMT, ONKH THA, HOT-SHEPSUT. *Divine wife, the living*	Gone light brown	E. 47
31	NEFER HEMT HOT·SHEPSUT ONKH. ,, ,,	Gone brown	Z. 30
32	AMEN·KHNEMT, HOT·SHEPS	Gone light brown	L. 47
33	NETER HEMT HOT·SHEPS	Green	L. 31
34	AMEN KHNEMT, RA·MĂOT·KA	Green	Uzat
35	AMEN KHNEMT . . . ., reverse . . . . MĂOT·KA Piece of *menat*.	Blue pottery, purple signs	Flat
36	RA·MĂOT·KA, reverse HO·SHEPS	Pottery. Dark brown	Flat
37	NETER NEFER, NEB TAUI. Of this period by the pattern, see 39	Dark green	Y. 5

NEFERU-RA

No.	Inscription	Material	Ref.
38	NESUT SĂT, NESUT SENT, RA·NEFERU. *Royal daughter, royal sister, Neferura*	Dark green	F. 5
39	RA·NEFERU, ONKHTI. Hollowed, legs pierced through	Green	F. 6
40	RA·NEFERU, NUB	Gone white	E. 10
41	RA·NEFERU NEB	Burnt jasper	H. 26
42	,,	Pottery. Gone brown	V. 90
43	,,	Blue-green	Broken
44	RA·NEB·NEFER, BAT each side	Dull green-blue	Y. 40
45	NETER HEMT, RA·NEFERU, MĂOT KHERU KHER ASAR. *Justified from Osiris*	Alabaster	Flat

18·6.

18·6. TEHUTMES III

No.	Inscription	Material	Ref.
1	HER KHO·EM·AĂKHUT (new falcon name, probably of Tehutmes III)	Blue-green	C. 28
2	RA·MEN·KHEPER UAH NESUT(Y). (Nekheb and Uazet name)	Grey-green	F. 61
3	NESUT BAT, ONKH NEFER, KHO·NE·SHEPS, *manifestation of ancestors* NEB TAUI RA·MEN·KHEPER NETER NEFER, NEB TAUI, ONKH NEFER, NEFERU, NEFER ONKH	Gone white	F. 20
4	NETER NEFER, NEB TAUI, RA·MEN·KHEPER. King shooting, protected by falcon. Legs pierced	Gone brown	F. 72
5	(NESUT) BAT, (RA)MEN(KHEPER) fragment	Green	F. ?
6	NETER NEFER RA·MEN·KHEPER, AMEN RA MERY. All in one cartouche	Gone white	Bead
7	NETER NEFER, NEB TAUI, RA·MEN·KHEPER, ZETTA	Impressed in violet glass	Bead
8	NETER NEFER RA·MEN·KHEPER, reverse AMEN RA MER. *Beloved by Amen·ra*	Pottery. Olive-green	Flat
9	,, ,, reverse AMEN RA	Pottery. Gone white	Flat
10	NETER NEFER, NEB TAUI, RA·MEN·KHEPER, NEB KHEPESH, KHO SEMTU HEQU, HUT PEZETU. *Lord of might, Rising on the lands of the princes, smiting the nine bows*	Pottery. Light green-blue. Flat.	Broken
11	NETER NEFER, NEB TAUI, RA·MEN·KHEPER KHO NESUT. *Glory of king(s)*	Gone white	F. 72
12	,, ,, ONKH NEB, RA·MEN·KHEPER. King adoring obelisk	Brown quartz	F. 35
13	RA·KHEPER·MEN, MES UAST, AMEN·RA MER. *Born at Thebes, beloved by Amen·ra*	Gurob. Bronze ring	
14	NETER NEFER RA·MEN·KHEPER SEKHER QEDESH. *Overthrowing Qedesh.* Captive bowing.	Green paste	F. 1
15	RA·MEN·KHEPER PET PET QEDESH. *Smiting Qedesh.* Syrian girl crouching, undercut.	Light green	Girl
16	RA·MEN·KHEPER MEN SETA HER HETER SHED KHETU ZET. *Establishing hunting on the horse, carrying off things alive*	Gone brown	H. 2
17	RA·MEN·KHEPER UAH MENNU EM PER AMEN. *Placing monuments in the temple of Amen*	Blue pottery.	F. 72
18	RA·MEN·KHEPER MEN TEKHENUI EM PER AMEN·RA. *Setting up two obelisks in the temple of Amen·ra*	Gone white	F.
19	RA·MEN·KHEPER MEN MENNU. *Setting up monuments*	Green	F. 72
20	,, ,,	Gone white	F. 72

18·6.

18·6. TEHUTMES III (*continued*)

No.	Inscription and description	Source, material, condition	Form
21	HEQ UAST RA·MEN·KHEPER, NEB KHEPESH PEZETU. *Prince of Thebes, R, mighty lord of the 9 bows*	Gone brown	Broken
22	RA·MEN·KHEPER, NESUT HEQU. *King of princes*	Silver mounting. Green	L. 6
23	,, RU HEQU. *Lion of princes*	Gone light brown	E. 58
24	,, HEQ, *the Prince.* RA·MEN·KHEPER AMEN MERY. *Loved by Amen*	Hard green paste	Flat
25	,, HEQ UAST, NEB KHEPESH, NETERU MER. *Prince of Thebes, mighty lord, loved by the gods*	Blue-green	E. 55
26	,, UAST NEB, MENTU MER. *Lord of Thebes, loved by Mentu*	Gone grey	F. 61
27	,, SĂ AMEN. Rev. Sistrum between two cats. *Son of Amen*	Gone white	Flat
28, 29	,, AMEN RA TAT. *Of the substance of Amen·ra*	Gurob. Green burnt red. Blue.	Broken U. 10
30	,, AMEN·TAT MER. *Of the substance of Amen, beloved*	Gone brown	Z. 70
31	,, AMEN MERY. Amen seated. *Loved by Amen*	Gone brown	F. 72
32	,, rev. RA·MEN·KHEPER AMEN MERY. *Loved by Amen.*	Pottery. Gone olive-green	Flat
33	,, TEHUTI, ASET, BENNU SĂ (relief). *Protected by Thoth Isis and Bennu*	Pottery. Green	M. 62
34	,, NETER SĂ. *Divine son*	Benha. Gone brown	H. 7
35	,, NEFER KHEPER (cartouche variant)	Edwards. Hard paste. Gone white	F. 61
36	,, SEBEK NEB SUNU MER. *Beloved by Sebek lord of Syene*	Green	Flat
37	,, NETER SEBEK. *The god Sebek*	Dark green	E. 24
38	,, Sebek crowned.	Blue paste	W. 80
39	,, NETER NEFER. King standing	Pottery. Light green	Broken
40	,, AMEN NEFER NEB. Amen seated. *Amen the Excellent is lord*	Gone light brown	F. 72
41	,, NETER NEFER, ONKH ZED UAST. *Good god living firmly in Thebes* King smiting two enemies, hunting lion below. Goddess Mut behind	Gone white	F. 83
42	,, DA ONKH MA RA. King smiting enemy. *Giving life like Ra*	Gone brown	E. 48
43	,, King in boat	Gone buff	H. 7
44	,, King between crowned uraei. Legs pierced through	Gone grey	F. 90
45	,, King seated	Gurob. Green-blue	Broken
46	,, King seated over uraei, ONKH behind. Rev. Four uraei entwined	Lahun. Green	Flat
47	,, King standing. Rev. Lion trampling on captive, name above	Pottery. Gone olive-brown	Flat
48	,, AMEN TAT. *Of the substance of Amen*	Gurob. Gone white	E. 15
49	,, NETER NEFER NEB TAUI, sphinx. Rev. RA·MEN·KHEPER King seated	Gurob. Pottery. Blue	Flat
50	,, NETER, NEB TAUI, sphinx on a captive. *Divine lord of both lands*	Gone brown	G. 80
51	,, HES NETER NEFER NEB TAUI. *Praise the King, good god lord of both lands*	Gone white	Uzat
52	,, Sphinx over SMĂ TAUI group. *Union of the lands*	Green	F. 72
53	,, Sphinx and falcon. Rev. Entwined uraei in cross pattern	Gone white	Flat
54, 55	,, Sphinx	Ring bezel, blue. Gone white. Ring	F. 99
56	NETER NEFER, NEB TAUI, RA·MEN·KHEPER. Uraeus. Rev. Name between feathers and *neb*	Gurob. Gone white	Flat
57	RA·MEN·KHEPER, AMEN RA TAT. RA·MEN·KHEPER NUB. 3 as I. RA·NEFER AMEN·RA TAT	Gone white	Prism
58	,, RAU·NEFERU. 57 and 58 seem to belong to the marriage of T. III with Raneferu	Bronze	Prism
59	,, ONKH AMEN, NEFER HES AMEN	Bronze	Prism
60	,, repeated	Black steatite	Prism
61	RA·MEN·KHEPER·KA, NEB TAUI	Gone brown	V. 30
62	,, NEFER MĂOT	Gurob. Blue paste	Z. 70
63	RA·MEN·KHEPER. Two kneeling Nile figures holding feathers. Plant below	Edwards. Gone buff	W. 15
64	,, Two figures of Ra	Edwards. Gone brown	F. 87
65	,, Set standing	Gurob. Pottery. Gone white	F. 64
66	,, Baboon of Thoth	Gone white	F. 72
67	NETER NEFER RA·MEN·KHEPER, ONKH DA. *Good god R. giving life.* Rev. Bark of Hathor	Gurob. Limestone	
68	RA·MEN·KHEPER. Ibis	Gone grey	Broken
69	,, RA KHEPER between falcons. Winged sun above	Gone brown	N. 6

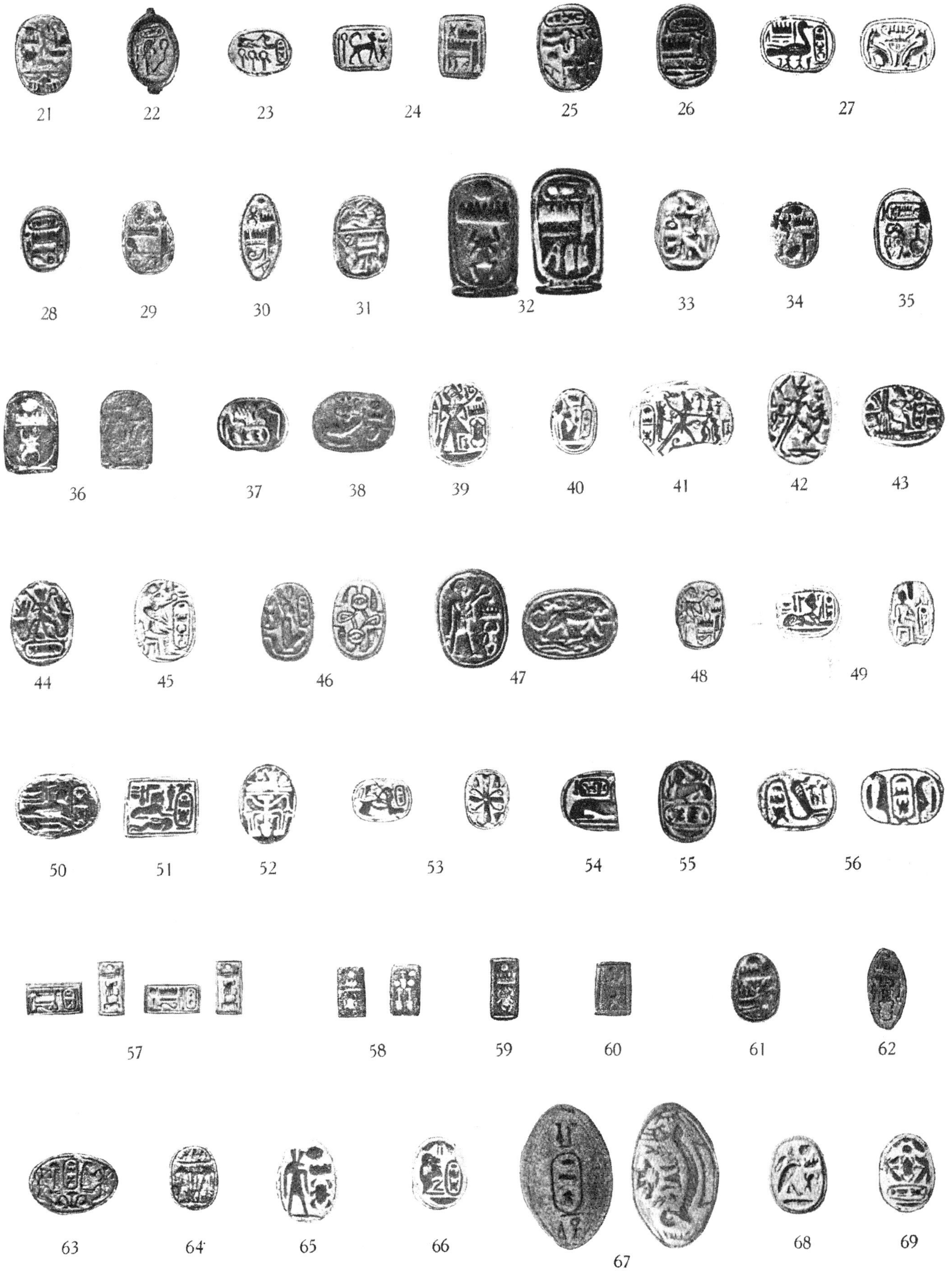
21 22 23 24 25 26 27
28 29 30 31 32 33 34 35
36 37 38 39 40 41 42 43
44 45 46 47 48 49
50 51 52 53 54 55 56
57 58 59 60 61 62
63 64 65 66 67 68 69

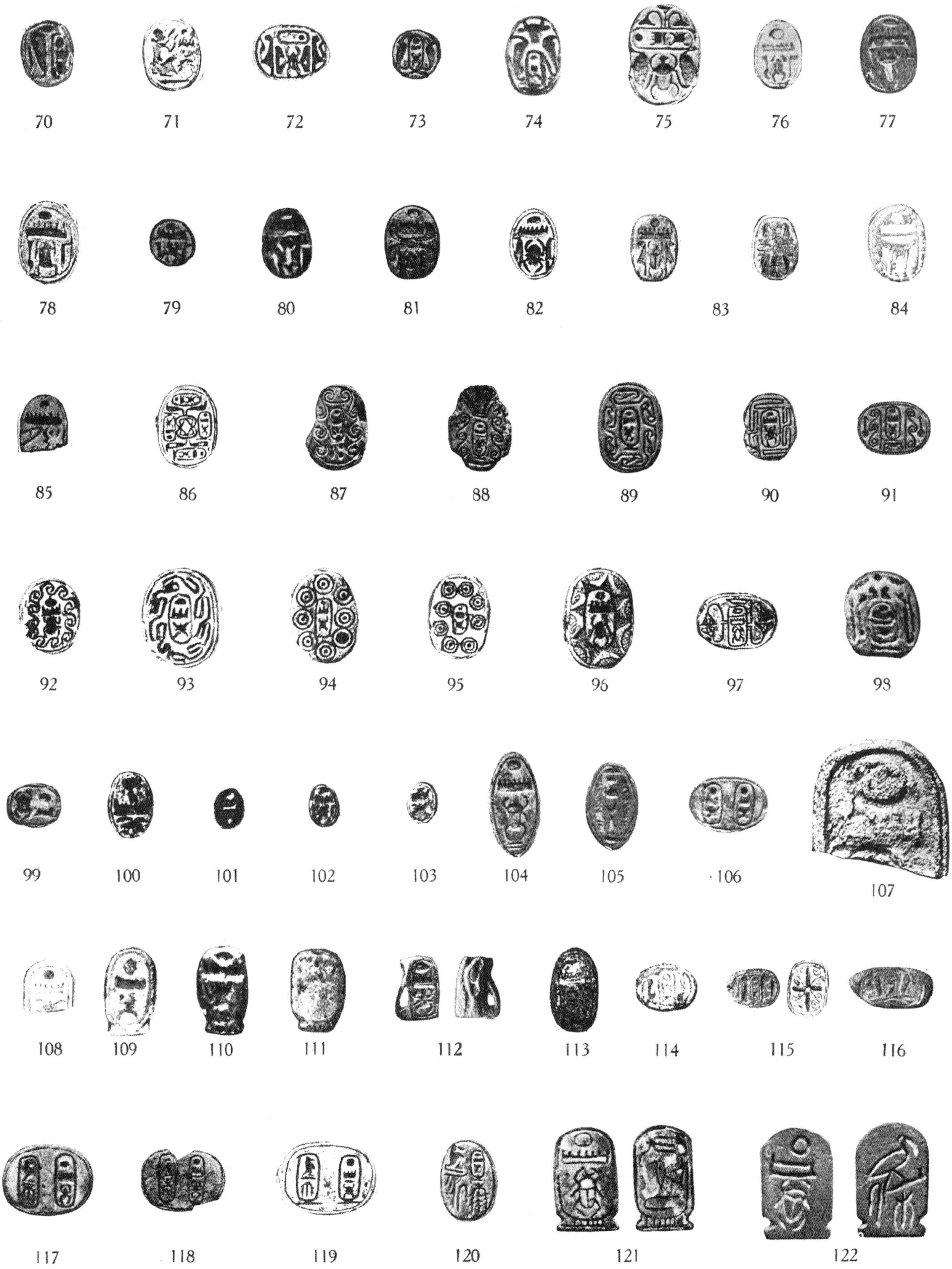
70 71 72 73 74 75 76 77
78 79 80 81 82 83 84
85 86 87 88 89 90 91
92 93 94 95 96 97 98
99 100 101 102 103 104 105 106 107
108 109 110 111 112 113 114 115 116
117 118 119 120 121 122

18·6. 18·6. TEHUTMES III (*continued*)

No.	King	Design	Details	Ref.
70	RA·MEN·KHEPER.	Uraeus	Pottery. Green	N. 22
71	,,	King adoring	Green-blue	G. 54
72	,,	Winged scarab and two feathers	Koptos. Pottery. Gone white	E. 24
73	,,	Between uraei	Gone brown	Z. 92
74	,,	,, bull's head above	Gone brown	E. 74
75	,,	Scarab and uraei below, plant above	Gone buff	T. 60
76	,,	NETER NEFER	Hollow. Pottery. Rich blue	E. 91
77	,,	,,	Gurob. Pottery. Light green	G. 20
78	,,	,,	Pottery. Dirty olive	N. 28
79	,,	,,	Grey-green	Z. 92
80	,,	,,	Lazuli	E. 64
81	,,	MĂOT feathers. Branching pattern	Gone brown	E. 15
82	,,	,,	Gurob. Edwards. Green	K. 34
83	,,	,, Reverse ZED and uraei repeated	Gurob. Grey paste	Flat
84	,,	,,	Gone brown	F. 24
85	,,	MER . . .	Gurob. Pottery. Grey-blue	G. 20
86	,,	Four cartouches, and four uraei entwined	Blue	F. 1
87	,,	NEFERUI in scrolls. Shallow smooth back	Gone yellow	N. 52
88	,,	Between scrolls, plant above. Shallow smooth back	Light green	M. 54
89	,,	In continuous scrolls	Pottery. Full blue	E. 92
90	,,	In square fret, continuous	Gurob. Light green	V. 66
91	,,	Between scrolls. NEFER at each side, NUB below	Yellow-green	E. 58
92	,,	In continuous spirals	Gone yellow-white	N. 26
93	,,	In continuous fret	Gurob. Gone white	U. 70
94	,,	In row of rings	Gone white. Broken	J. or M.
95	,,	,,	Gone white	N. 84
96	,,	In looped border	Gone grey	C. 36
97	,,	Between four lotus flowers	Gurob. Edwards. Gone red-brown	Y. 55
98	,,	Uraei at sides, winged disc above	Pottery. Light blue	J. 8
99, 100	,,		Gone brown. Gone white.	K. 56, E. 4
101, 102	,,		Both Edwards. Light green. Green.	J. 54, L. 78
103	,,		Gurob. Green.	V. 96
104	,,		Full blue-green	Z. 70
105	,,		Gurob. Blue paste	Z. 80
106	,,	Two cartouches	Gone brown	Z. 94
107	,,	For inlaying	Tell Amarna. Dark grey-violet	Flat
108	,,		Tell Amarna. Bright blue	Flat
109	,,	Reverse NETER NEFER, NEB TAUI	Blue paste	Flat
110	,,		Edwards. Blue.	Flat
111	,,	In relief	Blue	Flat
112	,,		Gurob. Gone drab	Uzat
113	,,	HEQ, MĂOT MER. *Prince, beloved by Maot*	Bronze	Ring
114, 115	,,	Between feathers	Bronze scarab. Reverse as here	
116	,,	Between uraei	Clay sealing	
117	,,	TEHUTI·MES	Gone white	H. 2
118	,,	,,	Gone red-brown	E. 44
119	,,	,,	Gone brown	G. 76
120	,,	,,	Gone light brown	L. 28
121	,,	Reverse TEHUTI·MES	Cartouche. Olive-green	Flat
122	,,	TEHUTI·MES	Cartouche. Pottery. Blue-grey	Flat

18·6. TEHUTMES III (*continued*)

18·6.

No.	Inscription	Material	Ref.
123	RA·MEN·KHEPER between feathers. Rev. RA·KHEPER TEHUTIMES	Pottery. Green	Flat
124	,, ,, Rev. TEHUTIMES between winged scarabs	Gone brown	Flat
125	NEB TAUI MES·TEHUTI in continuous scrolls	Hard paste. Green-blue	K. 38
126	TEHUTI·MES NEB	Gone light brown	P. 88
127	,,	Pottery. Blue-green	T. 81
128	,,	Edwards. Bubastis. Pottery. Burnt brown	T. 76
129	,, AMEN·RA (MERY)	Slip of grey granite	Flat
130	RA·MEN·KHEPER. Bull and falcon	Pottery. Blue-green	W. 96
131	NETER NEFER, NEB TAUI, RA·MEN·KHEPER. Repeated	Gone drab	E. 55
132	RA·MEN·KHEPER TAT RA. *R. of the Substance of Ra.* PTAH and BAT above and below	Gone grey	V. 20
133	,, ,, ,, ,, ,, ,,	Gone grey	V. 87
134	RA·MEN·KHEPER, MĂOT feathers at sides	Pottery. Green	L. 90
135	,, ,, ,, Reverse AMEN·RA blundered	Gurob. Green-blue	Flat
136	,, ,, ,, Rev. NUB AR KA NEFER	Lahun. Bone.	Flat
137	RA·MEN·KHEPER·KA. Ra with uraei	Gurob. Hard blue paste	E. 54
138	,, REN REN MĂOT at sides	Gone brown	Z. 20
139	RA·MEN·KHEPER. Bes and two captives	Gone white	F. 20
140	,, Repeated. Reverse, Bes and two baboons	Edwards. Lahun. Green	Flat
141	,, Reverse same, in row of circles	Green	Flat
142	,, Border of loops	Gone white.	Button
143	,, And reversed	Yellow-green	L. 16
144	,,	Pottery. Dirty blue-green.	Handle
145	,,	Pottery. Blue-green	J. 50
146	,, Repeated. Pyramidal back, pierced	Pottery. Blue-green.	Pyramid
147	,, Reverse, head of Bes	Pottery. Blue-green	Bes
148	,, *Zed* between uraei above ; below *kheper* between *onkhs*	Edwards. Pottery. Blue-green	W. 16
149	(RA)·MEN·KHEPER. On handle of sistrum	Pottery. Blue	

QUEEN HOTSHEPSI

No.	Inscription	Material	Ref.
150	ONKH NETER HEMT NEBT TAUI HOT·SHEPSI AMEN MERY *Living, divine wife, Lady of both lands Hotshepsi beloved of Amen*	Pottery. Dark violet.	Bead

18·6. PRIVATE NAMES

	Inscription	Translation	Material	Ref.
A	MER KHENTISH UR NE AMEN MUT, MER PER URT NE NESUT TAUI SEN·MUT	*Keeper of the great garden of Amen and Mut, keeper of the palace of the king of both lands, Sen mut*	Grey-green.	Cylinder
B	MER NUT, THĂT, TETANEFER.	*Mayor, Vizier, Tetanefer*	Dark brown jasper	Z. 80
C	MER PER, ASI.	*Keeper of the palace, Asi*	Black jasper	H. 18
D	THĂT, IMHETEP.	*Vizier Imhetep*, under Tahutmes I	Gone white.	Broken
E	SESH NESUT, AMEN·HETEP.	*Scribe of the king, Amenhetep*	Blue-green	E. 15
F	,, ,, ,,	,, ,,	Green	K. 8
G	SĂB, RY (fine work).	*Judge, Ry*	Ivory, stained green	V. 3
H	HATHER·HETEP.	*Hathor-hotep*	Gone white	J. 65
J	MER AHU NE AMEN, SEN·NEFERU.	*Keeper of the cattle of Amen, Senneferu*	Nubt. Hard black limestone	H. 80
K	KHNEMU·HOTEP·NEFERA, AMĂKH·AB, SĂB EM SAHU.	*Khnumu·hotep·nefera, devoted in heart, judge in the treasury*	Gone buff	L. 99
L	HER·ARI·HO.	*Her·ar·ho* (name, " Horus creates the body ")	Gone grey	K. 70
M	MEN·ZEFĂ.	*Men·zefa*	Gone brown	K. 84
N	SAB, AMENHETEP.	*Judge, Amenhetep*	Gone white	F. 72
O	,,	,,	Gone white	F. 72
P	,,	,,	Gone buff	F. 72
Q	,,	,,	Gone white	Z. 97
R	,,	,,	Pottery. Blue-green.	Broken
S	ASAR MEN·NEKHT MĂOT·KHERU.	*The Osiris Min·nekht, justified*	Seal. Gone white	Handle

123 124 125 126 127 128 129

PROBABLY LATER

130 131 132 133 134 135 136

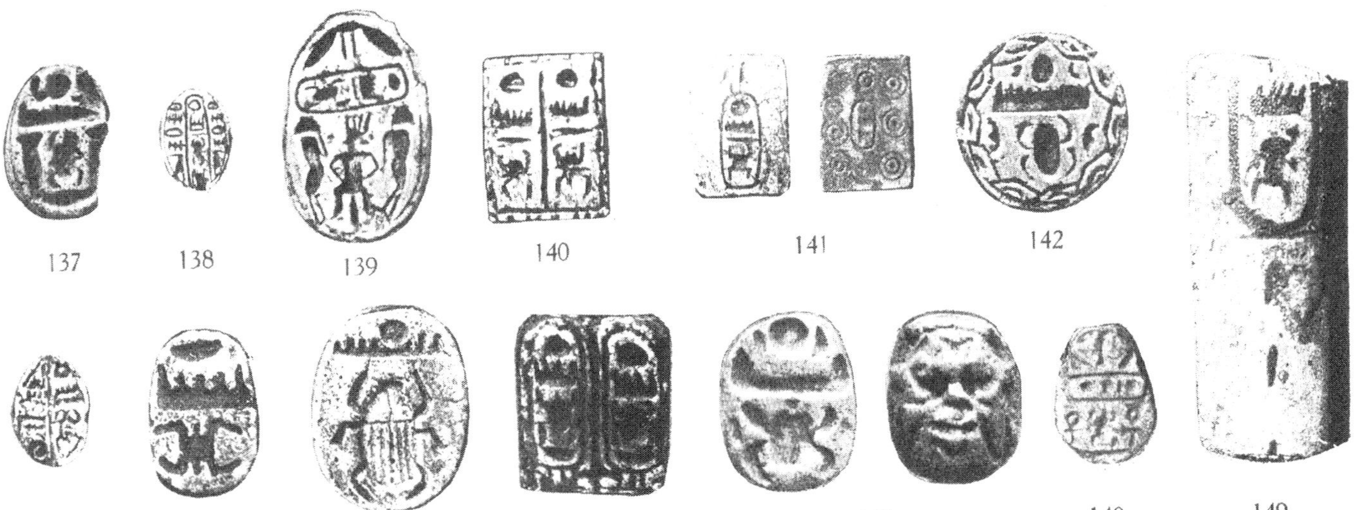

137 138 139 140 141 142

143 144 145 146 147 148 149

HOTSHEPSI PRIVATE NAMES

150 A B C D

E F G H J K L

M N O P Q R S

18.7 AMENHETEP II

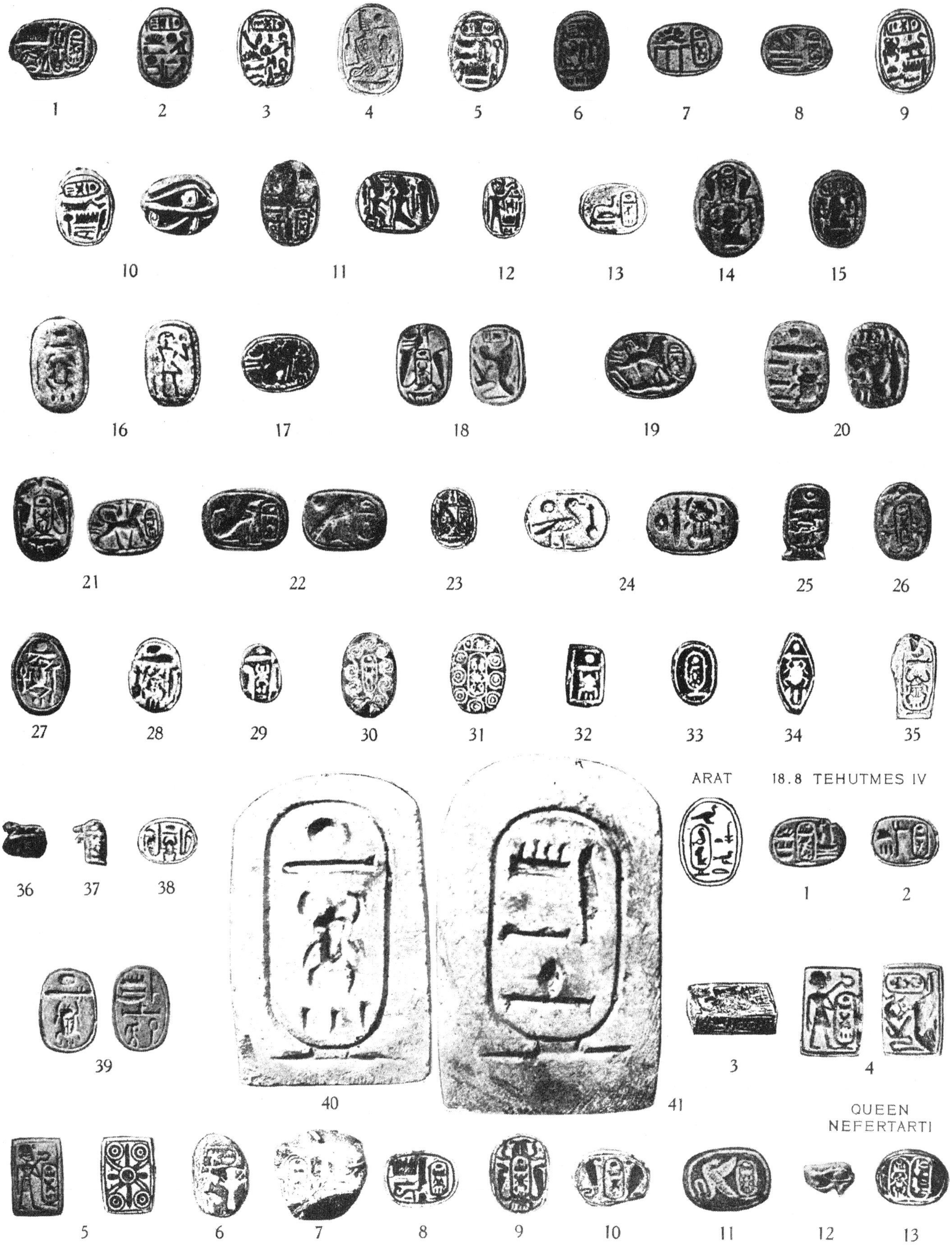

18·7.

18·7. AMENHETEP II

1 RA·OĂ·KHEPERU, MES MEN·NEFER. *Amenhetep II, born at Memphis* Gone brown F. 24

2 ,, SĂ RA KHO EM AST RA. *A. son of Ra, rising in (Hat)ast·ra* (vith nome Delta) Green F. 62

3 RA·OĂ·KHEPERU, RA TAT EM UAST ZESER KHO. *A. of the being of Ra in Thebes gloriously appearing* Kahun. Green F. 62

4 RA·OĂ·KHEPERU, MER (RENNUT) NEFERT, KA(U) NEB. *A. loved by Rannut the good, mistress of food* Gone white F. 90

5 ,, HEQ UAST, NEB KHEPESH, AMEN MER. *A. prince of Thebes, mighty Lord, loved by Amen* Gurob. Green F. 61

6 ,, HEQ UAST HUA PEZETU IX. *A. prince of Thebes, beating the 9 bows* Green F. 37

7 ,, KHO NETERU. *A. manifestation of the gods* Gone white E. 71

8 ,, HEQ TAUI. *A. prince of both lands* Gone white F. 85

9 ,, SĂ AMEN KHEPER TEF. *A. son of Amen who became his father* Gurob. Green F. 94

10 ,, NEB KHEPESH HEZ, AMEN MER. *A. lord mighty and brilliant, loved by Amen* Blue-green Uzat

11 . . . . . . ATMU (NE) ANU RA·OĂ·KHEPERU, KHEPER NE AMEN ZET NESUT HEQ(U) *. . . . . by Atmu of Heliopolis; A. created by Amen, living, king of princes.* Amen·ra, king, and goddess Green Flat

12 RA·OĂ·KHEPERU AMEN TAT. Rev. 4 entwined uraei. *A. of the substance of Amen* Gone brown Flat

13 ,, ZETTA. *A. Eternal* Gone white F. 19

14 ,, NETER NEFER HEH RENPETU. *A. good god, of ages* Bare steatite F. 90

15 ,, HEH RENPETU ONKH, NUB. *A. ages of life* Green E. 48

16 ,, Reverse, standing figure adoring White limestone Flat

17 ,, NETER NEFER NEB TAUI. Sphinx. Reverse, name, *zed* with uraei Green Flat

18 NETER NEFER NEB TAUI RA·OĂ·KHEPERU, uraei, NUB. Rev. name, sphinx and winged uraeus Gone brown Flat

19 NETER NEFER NEB TAUI RA·OĂ·KHEPERU, sphinx trampling on enemy Gone drab F. 62

20 RA·OĂ·KHEPERU. Reverse, name, NETER NEFER NEB TA. Sphinx on NEB. Blue-green, burnt red-brown Flat

21 ,, Uraei and NUB. Rev. name NEFER NEB TA. Sphinx walking Green Flat

22 ,, Lion. Rev. name, falcon of RA Blue-green, gone grey Flat

23 NETER NEFER, MER TEHUTI, RA·OĂ·KHEPERU. *A. good god, loved by Thoth* Gone white F. 61

24 NEFER SĂ RA. Reverse, RA·OĂ·KHEPERU Gone white Flat

25 RA·OĂ·KHEPERU. Reverse AMEN MER. *A. loved by Amen* Green Flat

26 ,, Four uraei Green Worn

27 ,, NETER ONKH. *A. the living god* Durite H. 92

28 ,, NETER NEFER. *A. the good god* Pottery. Full blue G. 36

29, 30 ,, between feathers; 30, in scrolls Pottery, dull blue; steatite V. 13; X. 50

31 ,, NEFERUI KHEPER KA in row of circles (*Senusert I*) Steatite X. 40

32 ,, Reverse, AMEN RA Pottery. Dirty olive Flat

33, 34, 35, 36, 37 RA·OĂ·KHEPERU Dark blue glass. Black limestone. Gone brown. Pottery, Blue. Pottery, Blue. H. 98; Z. 74; Uzat; Rana; Uzat

38 RA·OĂ·KHEPERU between uraei Gone white H. 84

39 ,, Reverse, AMENHETEP HEQ UAST. *A. prince of Thebes* Gone white Flat

40 ,, Foundation deposit from temple of Amenhetep II at Thebes Limestone Flat

41 AMENHETEP. Foundation deposit from temple of Amenhetep II at Thebes Limestone Flat

18·8.

18·8. TEHUTMES IV

1 NETER NEFER, NEB TAUI, RA·MEN·KHEPERU, KHO SEMT NEB. *T. shining on every land* Gone white E. 89

2 RA·MEN·KHEPERU USER KHOU. *T. mighty in manifestations* Green M. 84

3 ,, AMEN MER, Amen seated on each side. ZED ONKH on other edge. *Firm and living* Gone white Flat

4 ,, King standing. Reverse, name, sphinx and winged uraeus Green Flat

5 ,, King standing. Reverse, cross pattern and circles Gone white Flat

6 ,, HATHER PEHTI. *Hathor the mighty* Dull green F. 62

7 ,, NEB KHEPESH AMEN MER. *T. Lord of might, loved by Amen* Clay impression

8 ,, AMEN TAT. *T. of the being of Amen* Gone brown F. 62

9, 10 ,, crowned with feathers and uraei, uraei at sides, NUB below. Name between uraei Gone brown F. 85, 62

11, 12 ,, with winged uraeus Pottery Blue Silver Uzat, Ring

13 ,, NEFERTARTI, with a queen Nefertarti, otherwise unknown Edwards. Obsidian H. 76

18·9. AMENHETEP III.

Lion hunt scarabs. "Live the Horus, the strong bull, uprising in Truth, Lord of the Double Crown, establishing laws, making ready both plains. Horus on Nubti, great and mighty, smiting the Setiu, King of Upper and Lower Egypt, RA·NEB·MĂOT, son of Ra, AMENHETEP HEQ UAST, granted life, and the royal wife TAIY who liveth. Reckoning of lions brought by His Majesty in his shooting by himself, beginning in the first year up to the tenth year, lions, terrible, 102." Single line between elytra.

18·9.

1		Edwards.	Blue-green	F. 14
2			Green	F. 14
3			Gone white.	Broken
4			Blue-green.	Broken

Marriage scarabs. "Live the Horus, the strong bull, uprising in Truth, Lord of the Double Crown, establishing laws, making ready both plains, Horus on Nubti, great and mighty, smiting the Setiu, King of Upper and Lower Egypt, RA·NEB·MĂOT, son of Ra, AMENHETEP HEQ UAST, granted life eternally, and the great royal wife TAIY who liveth. The name of her father YUA, the name of her mother THUAĂ, this who is the wife of a king strong and famous, his southern boundary as far as the land of Kary, the northern as far as the lands of Nehărină." Double or triple lines between elytra.

5	Under the legs, right NESUT RA·NEB·MĂOT; left, HEMT TAIY	Edwards.	Rich blue	F. 11
6		(Hilton Price 1209)	Green	F. 11
7			Gone white	F.
8	*Tank inscription.* A fragment with parts of 4th to 9th lines, agreeing with the spacing of the Vatican example.		Green	
9	Back of a scarab with RA·NEB·MĂOT under the legs on each side. (Not figured)		Gone white	G 24
10	RA·MĂOT·NEB, KA NEKHT.	*The strong bull* (Falcon name)	Gone white	F. 12
11	,, HEQ HEQU.	*Prince of Princes* (Falcon name)	Bright blue.	Broken
12	,, KHO EM MĂOT.	*Uprising in Truth* (Falcon name)	Gone white	F. 70
13	,, MES NETERU NEBU.	*Born of all the gods* (Falcon name)	Gone white	F. 79

1

2

3

4

5

6

7

8

10

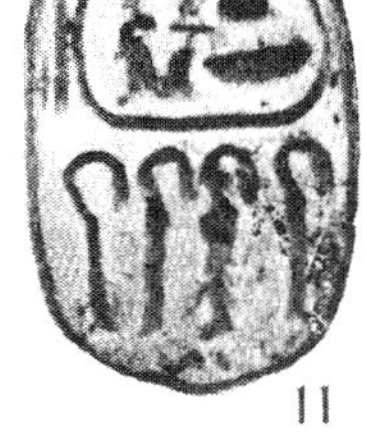
11

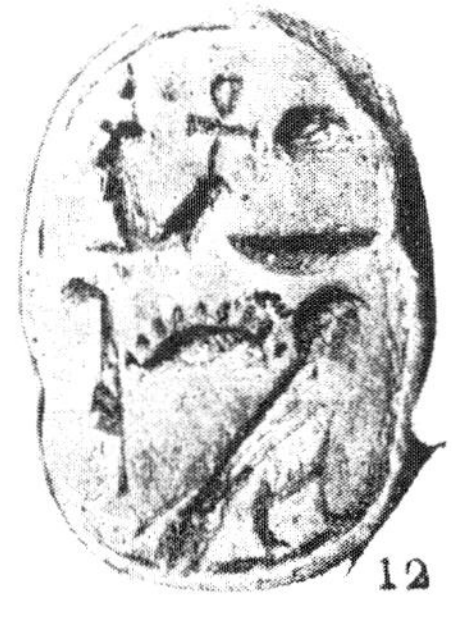
12

13

14 15 16 17 18

19 20 21 22 23

24 25 26 27 28

29 30 31 32 33

34 35 36 37 38

18·9.

18·9. AMENHETEP III (*continued*)

No.	Name		Translation	Material	Colour	Ref.
14	RA·MĂOT·NEB,	SMEN HE(P)U.	*A. Establishing laws.* (Nekheb and Uazet name)	Pottery.	Gone white	F. 16
15	,,	AR HEPU.	*A. Making laws*	Pottery.	Green.	K. 40
16	,,	MES UAST.	*A. Born at Thebes*		Gone brown	K. 40
17	,,	HĂQ SANUGER.	*A. Seizing Singar*		Full blue	E. 18
18	,,	GERG ANU.	*A. Establishing Anu*		Blue	F. 15B
19	,,	SNEZ EF EM TAU.	*A. The fear of him is in the lands*		Green-blue	F. 15
20	,,	KHO RA MA.	*A. Rising like the sun*		Gone white	K. 40
21	,,	KHESEF HEH.	*A. Repelling millions*		Gone brown	J. 51
22	,,	USER KHEPESH.	*A. Powerful and strong*		Green	F. 15
23	,,	HEQ UAST.	*A. Prince of Thebes*		Green	E. 21
24	,,	NETERU NEBU HET OĂT MER.	*A. By all the gods of the palace, beloved*	Gurob.	Pale green	F. 36
25	,,	PTAH HEQ PĂUT NETERU NEB MER.	*A. By Ptah prince of the mass of all the gods, beloved*		Grey-blue	F. 15
26	,,	AMEN·RA MER.	*A. By Amen·ra, beloved*		Green	F. 56
27	,,	AMEN HEQ UAST MER.	*A. By Amen prince of Thebes, beloved*		Gone brown	F. 55
28	,,	SNEKHT NE AMEN·RA.	*A. Strengthened by Amen·ra*		Gone white	Broken
29	,,	AMEN AĂBT MER.	*A. By Amen of the East, beloved*		Gone black	E. 67
30	NESUT BAT RA·MĂOT·NEB AMEN·RA MER.		*King A. by Amen·ra beloved*	Pottery.	Dark blue	M. 20
31	RA·MĂOT·NEB.	AMEN TAT.	*A. of the substance of Amen*		Gone white	F. 79
32	,,	BĂU PE MER.	*A. By the Spirits of Buto, beloved*		Gone white	F. 15
33	,,	URT·HEKAU MER.	*A. By Urt·hekau (Isis) beloved*		Gone brown	E. 33
34	,,	BASTET MERY.	*A. By Bastet beloved*		Gone white and grey	E. 18
35	,,	MUT NEBT PET MER.	*A. By Mut mistress of heaven, beloved*		Gone white	K. 86
36	,,	MENTU NEB UAST MER.	*A. By Mentu Lord of Thebes, beloved*	Edwards.	Green-blue	F. 79
37	,,	NEKHEBT MERY.	*A. By Nekhebt beloved*		Gone grey	E. 33
38	,,	RA TAT.	*A. Of the substance of Ra*		Gone white	F. 15

18·9.

18·9. AMENHETEP III (*continued*)

No.	Name	Inscription	Translation	Material	Ref.
39	RA·NEB·MĂOT	HATHER NEBT HETEPT MER.	*A. By Hathor mistress of Hetept, beloved* (The above is a blunder for the following type)	Gone light brown	J. 51
40	,,	HATHER NEBT HETEP HEMT MERY.	*A. By Hathor mistress of Belbeys, beloved*	Green	F. 13
41	,,	KHENSU MERY.	*A. By Khonsu beloved*	Gone light brown	J. 51
42	,,	KHENSU TEHUTI MER.	*A. By Khonsu and Tahuti, beloved*	Green	F. 18
43	,,	SEKHMET NEBT MĂOT MER.	*A. By Sekhmet mistress of truth, beloved*	Blue-green	E. 19
44	,,	DUĂ HER KEMT.	*A. The morning star rising on Egypt*	Gone grey	E. 33
45	,,	MEH SHENUT EM PER ATEF AMEN.	*A. Filling the granaries in the house of his father Amen*	Clay impression	
46	RA·MĂOT·NEB	NEB AR KHET.	*A. Lord of action*	Blue-green	E. 33
47	,,	,, ,,	,, ,,	Gone white	E. 12
48	,,			Pottery. Green	E. 33
49	,,			Pottery. Dark violet	E. 32
50	,,			Pottery. Green	E. 32
51	,,			Edwards. Pottery. Blue-green	K. 40
52	,,			Pottery. Gone white	K. 40
53	RA·MĂOT NEB,	NEB SED HEB.	*A. Lord of the Sed festival*	Gone brown	E. 90
54	NETER NEFER, NEB TAUI, RA·MĂOT·NEB, KHO NEFERUI.		*Good God, Lord of both lands, Amenhetep, appearing very excellently*	Pottery. Grey	G. 16
55	RA·MĂOT·NEB,	NEB KHOU.	*A. Lord of epiphanies*	Grey-blue	Broken
56	,,	,,	,, ,,	Blue, burnt red	E. 92
57	,,	PET PET SEMTU.	*A. Subduing countries*	Gone buff	F. 24
58	,,	RU HEQU.	*A. Lion of princes*	Gone white	F. 94
59	AMENHETEP MĂOT in cartouche.	King on throne carried by four men trampling on two captives		Gone white	V. 12
60	RA·NEB·MĂOT,	AMEN MERY.	*A. beloved by Amen*	Green	E. 42
61	,,	AMEN MEN RA MER.	*A. beloved by Amen* blundered	Gone brown	E. 75
62	NESUT BAT RA·MĂOT·NEB AMEN·RA SETEP NE.		*King A. approved by Amen*	Gone brown	E. 26
63	RA·MĂOT·NEB	AMEN TAT.	*A. of the substance of Amen*	Gone brown	G. 36
64	,,	RA TAT.	*A. of the substance of Ra*	Green	E. 71
65	,,	Anher standing		Gone grey	G. 6
66	,,	PTAH MER.	*A. Loved by Ptah*	Gurob, with 18·10·5 Silver	Ring
67	,,	KHEPER NUB, between four winged genii. Legs pierced through.		Pottery. Gone brown	F. 23
68	,,	between feathers and uraei		Edwards. Green	X 60
69	,,		Stitch holes for sewing on royal garment (?)	Gold	Sheet
70	,,			Bezel of bronze	Ring
71	,,			Green	F. 61
72	,,			Gone white	Y. 30
73	,,			Pottery. Gone brown	F. 72
74	,,			Steatite	Broken

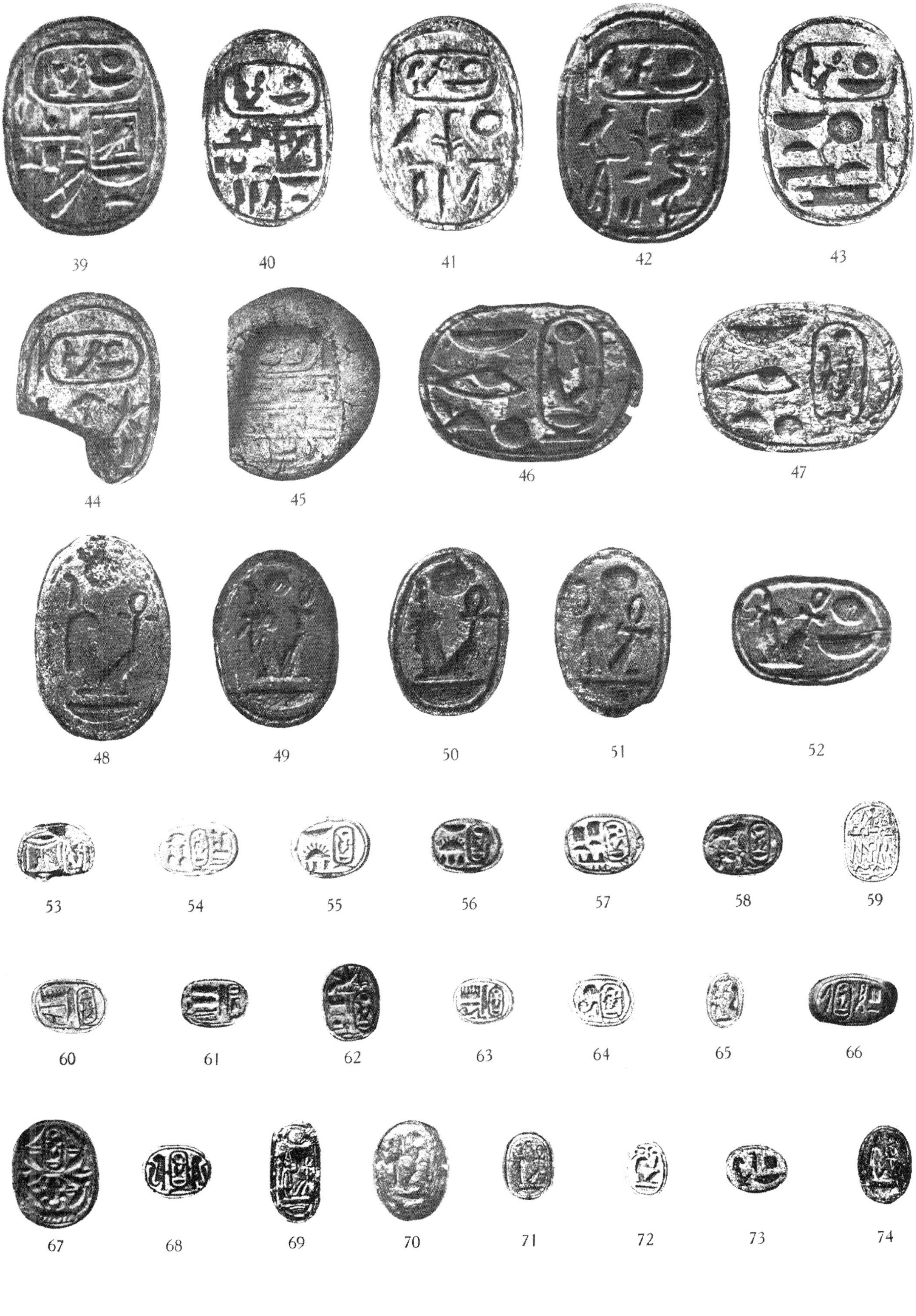

39 40 41 42 43

44 45 46 47

48 49 50 51 52

53 54 55 56 57 58 59

60 61 62 63 64 65 66

67 68 69 70 71 72 73 74

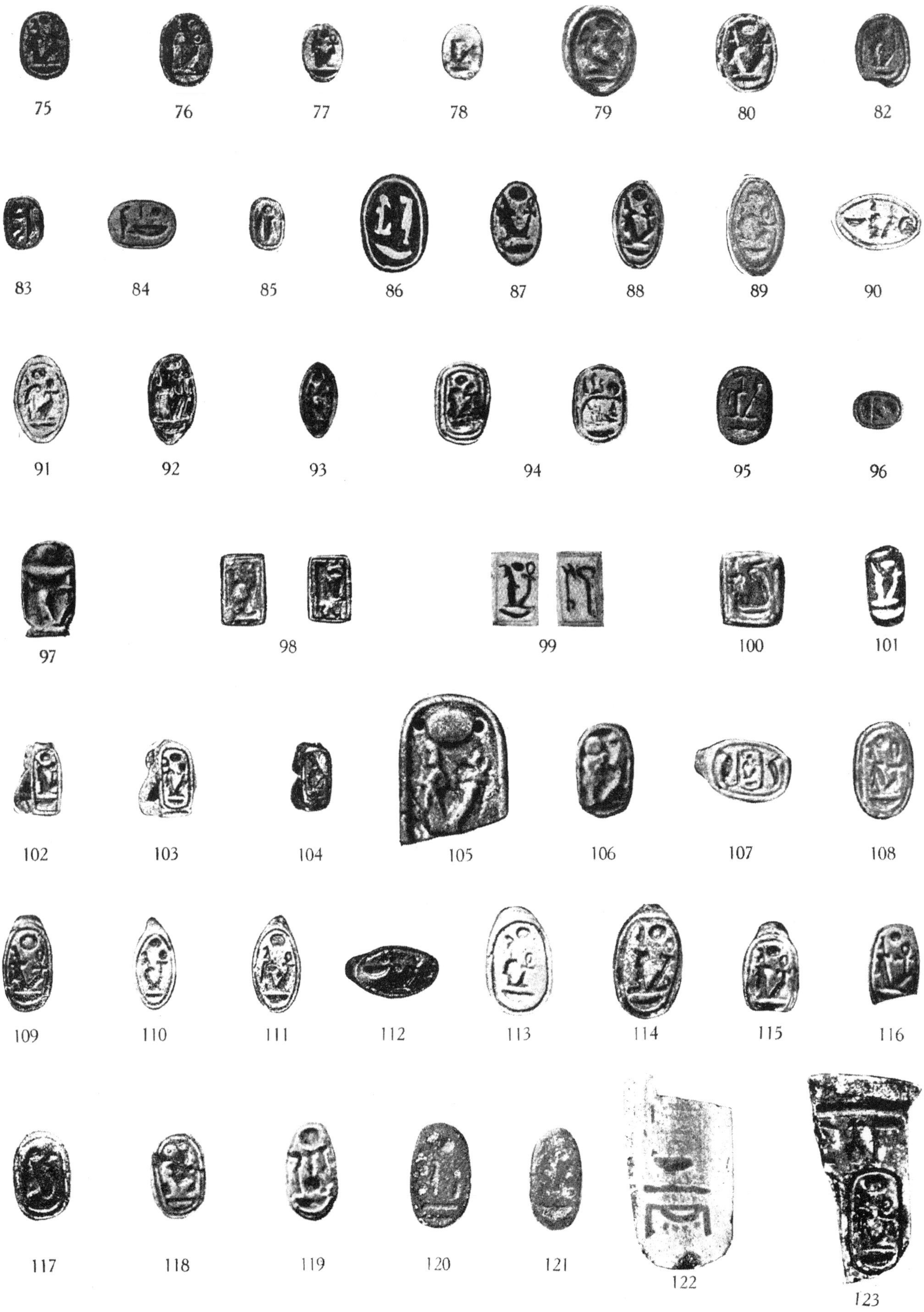
75 76 77 78 79 80 82
83 84 85 86 87 88 89 90
91 92 93 94 95 96
97 98 99 100 101
102 103 104 105 106 107 108
109 110 111 112 113 114 115 116
117 118 119 120 121 122 123

18·9. 18·9. AMENHETEP III (*continued*)

75	RA·MĂOT·NEB		Gone brown	F. 37
76	,,		Gone brown	F. 95
77	,,		Edwards. Dark green	Worn
78	,,		Fayum. Green felspar	H. 94
79	,,		Pottery. Olive	G. 20
80	,,		Pottery. Light-blue	G. 20
81	,,	(and half of a similar)	Pottery. Blue-grey	G. 20
82	,,		Tell Amarna. Pottery. Rough blue	K. 71
83	RA·NEB·MĂOTI		Dark green	F. 26
84	RA·NEB·MĂOT		Blue-green	H. 20
85	,,		Benha. Pottery. Rough dull blue	N. 34
86	MĂOT·PTAH·NEB		Blue glass	Broken
87	RA·MĂOT·NEB		Grey-blue	Z. 20
88	,,		Rich violet	Z. 20
89	,,		Dull blue-green	Z. 70
90	,,		Gone white	Z. 70
91	,,		Green-blue	Z. 20
92	NETER NEFER RA·MĂOT·NEB		Gone white	Z. 20
93	RA·MĂOT·NEB		Pottery. Blue	Z. 20
94	,,	Reverse, ONKH NEB, Hawk-head of Ra	Pottery. Lilac	Flat
95	,,		Blue paste	Z. 94
96	,,		Bought at Jerusalem. Pottery. Olive	Z. 97
97	RA·NEB·MĂOT	(in relief)	Pottery. Green-blue	Flat
98	RA·MĂOT·NEB.	Reverse, Taurt	Green	Flat
99	,,	Reverse, HEQ UAST. *Prince of Thebes*	Blue glass	Flat
100	,,	Ra written as a uraeus	Gurob. Pottery. Deep blue	Curved
101	,,		Edwards. Sard.	Cylinder
102	,,		Blue	Uzat
103	,,		Green-blue	Uzat
104	,,		Green	Uzat
105	,,	(in relief)	With stitch-holes to fix on dress. Pottery. Dark violet	Flat
106	,,	(in relief)	Pottery. Brown-violet	Ring
107	,,	with uraei	Gurob. Pottery. Light blue	Ring
108	,,		Pottery. Dark violet	Ring
109–10	,,		Pottery. Violet	Rings
111	,,		Pottery. Yellow	Ring
112	,,		Pottery. Green	Ring
113	,,		Pottery. Violet	Ring
114	,,		Pottery. Light blue	Ring
115	,,		Found under threshold, chapel of Uazmes, Thebes. Pottery. Dark blue	Ring
116	,,		Tell Amarna. Pottery. Blue	Ring
117	,,	Ra as a uraeus	Pottery. Apple-green	Ring
118	,,	openwork	Edwards. Pottery. Blue	Ring
119	,,	HEQ MĂOT. *Prince of Truth*	Gurob. Pottery. Light blue	Ring
120	,,		Bronze	Ring
121	,,		Bronze	Ring
122	,,	NUB. Top of *zed* ?	Pottery. Full blue	
123	NETER NEFER RA·MĂOT·NEB		Tell Amarna. Part of bowl. Blue paste	

18·9.

18·9. AMENHETEP III (*continued*)

124	NETER NEFER RA·MĂOT·(NEB) SĂ RA AMENHETEP HEQ UAST. *The Good God Maot nebra, son of Ra Amenhetep Prince of Thebes*		Stoneware. Violet	Knob
125	RA·MĂOT·NEB. Reverse AMENHETEP		Gone buff	Flat
126	AMENHETEP HEQ UAST.	*Amenhetep Prince of Thebes*	Pottery. Gone grey	E. 9
127	,, ,, Worn away.	Reverse ONKH ZED, *Firm of life.* Ptah standing.	Steatite	Z. 67
128	,, NETER HEQ UAST.	*Amenhetep, divine prince of Thebes*	Steatite	P. 80
129	,, USER HEQ.	*A. mighty one of princes.* Legs pierced through	Gone brown	F. 92
130	,, HEQ UAST.	*A. Prince of Thebes*	Green	F. 85
131	,, ,,	,,	Gone brown	E. 75
132	,, ,,	,,	Dark green	E. 10
133	,, ,,	,,	Glass. Light blue	Z. 94
134	,, ,,	,,	Paste. Dark blue	G. 40
135	,, ,,	,,	Pottery. Light blue	N. 30
136	,, ,,	,,	Pottery. Light green	K. 98
137	,, ,,	Reverse, uraeus and NEFER, winged sun above	Edwards. Dark green	Flat
138	,, ,,	*A. Prince of Thebes*	Lazuli	Flat
139	,, ,,	,,	Edwards. Blue-green	Uzat
140	AMENHETEP HEQ UAST HER MERY.	*A. Prince of Thebes, loved by Horus* Handle.	Amarna. Violet glass	
141	AMENHETEP SETEP NE RA.	*A. approved by Ra*	Gone white	E. worn
142	AMEN·RA·(HETEP ?) MES MĂOT.	*A born of Maot*	Pottery. Light green	G. 20
143	AMEN·RA·HETEP, MĂOT USER. Barque	Pierced, hollow inside.	Gone brown	Broken
144	AMEN·HETEP		Pottery. Green-blue	E. 74
145	,, SĂRA.	*A. Son of Ra*	Gone white	K. 80
146	,,		Gone brown	H. 34
147	,, ...	Pottery. Green.	Gone brown	Flat
148	AMEN·RA·HETEP MĂOT		Silver	Ring

QUEEN TAIY WITH AMENHETEP III

149	NETER NEFER RA·MĂOT·NEB, NESUT HEMT TAIY, ONKH DA RA MA *Good God, Maot·neb·ra, Royal wife Taiy, granted life like Ra*		Light green	E. 12
150	Similar, but ending ONKH DA ZETTA.	*Granted life eternally*	Gone white	Broken
151	Similar, but no lower line		Pottery. Light green	K. 40
152	RA·MĂOT·NEB incised. Reverse, TAIY in relief		Pottery. Apple-green	Flat
153	RA·MĂOT·NEB NEB NEF NEZEM, Rev. NESUT HEMT TAIY.	*A. Lord of the sweet wind*	Gone white	Flat
154	AMENHETEP HEQ UAST, NESUT HEMT TAIY.	*A. prince of Thebes. Royal wife Taiy*	Full blue	Flat

QUEEN TAIY ALONE

155, 156	NESUT HEMT URT, TAIY.	*Royal wife, Great one, Taiy*	Gone white	E. 43, F. 60
157	NESUT HEMT TAIY ONKH TAT.	*Royal wife, Taiy, the living*	Pottery. Dark blue	K. 28
158	,, ,, ,,	,, ,, ,,	Pottery. Full blue	Z. 70
159	NESUT HEMT TAIY.	*Royal wife Taiy*	Pottery. Blue faded	K. 40
160	,, ,,	,,	Dark green	Z. 80
161	,, ,,	,,	Edwards. Dark green	Z. 80
162	,, ,,	,,	Gone brown	Z. 80
163	,, ,,		Gone white	Z. 92
164	TAIY		Tell Amarna. Pottery. Violet	Ring
165	,,		Pottery. Green	Ring
166	,,		Calcite	Bead
167	,,		Brown shelly limestone	Bead
168	HENT·TA·NEB. Princess Hent·ta·neb	From a kohl tube.	Light blue on dark violet	

124
125
126
127
128
129
130
131
132
133
134
135
136
137
138
139
140
141
142
143
144
145
146
147
148
QUEEN TAIY
149
150
151
152
153
154
155
156
157
158
159
160
161
162
163
164
165
166
167
168

18.10 AMENHETEP IV=AKHENATEN

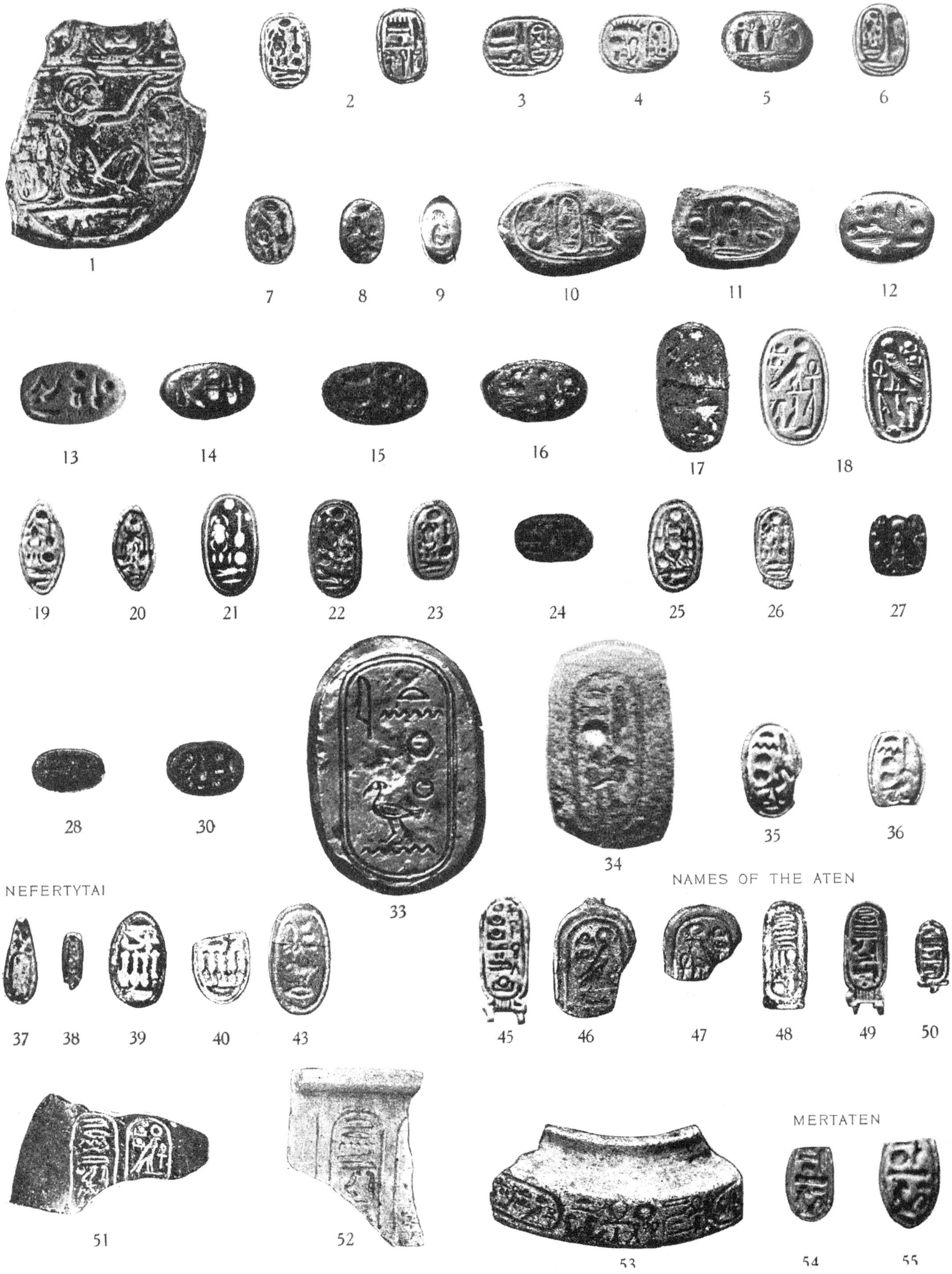

1 2 3 4 5 6 7 8 9 10 11 12 13 14 15 16 17 18 19 20 21 22 23 24 25 26 27 28 30 33 34 35 36

NEFERTYTAI

37 38 39 40 43

NAMES OF THE ATEN

45 46 47 48 49 50 51 52 53

MERTATEN

54 55

18·10.

18·10. AMENHETEP IV (AKHENATEN)

1 RA·NEFER·KHEPERU, UO·NE·RA; AMEN·HETEP NETER HEQ UAST. Traces of Aten names above.
Amenhotep kneeling upholding the Aten names. Most natural head to scarab — Gone white — G. 26
2 RA·NEFER·KHEPERU, UO·NE·RA; AMENHETEP NETER HEQ UAST.
Nefer·kheperu·ra Uo·ne·ra. Amenhotep divine prince of Thebes — Gone white — Flat
3 Same AMEN SETEP NE. — *A. The chosen of Amen* — Tell Amarna. Gone brown — F. 62
4 Same KHO·MA·RA. — *A. Uprising like Ra* — Blue — E. 16
5 Amenhotep seated before Măot and Ra. Found with silver ring 18·9·66, at Gurob — Silver — Ring
6 RA·NEFER·KHEPERU, UO·NE·RA, MĂOT — Tell Amarna. Blue — F. 41
7 RA·NEFER·KHEPERU — Blue-green — F. 72
8 ,, — Tell Amarna. Pottery. Turquoise-blue — L. 40
9 Amenhotep seated as youthful prince — Gold — Ring

AKHENATEN after Conversion (RA·NEFER·KHEPERU, UO·NE·ATEN termed *name* below)

10 *Name.* . . . BEN ONKHU UO·NE·RA. . . . *Glory of the living.* Akhenaten seated before the Aten — Clay sealing
11 *Name.* UR OQU EM PER ATEN. *Chief of the offerings in the temple of Aten* (an official) — Clay sealing
12 KHEPER NEB ONKH, ATEN MER. — *Creator lord of life, beloved by Aten* — Base gold — Ring
13 *Name.* ATEN NE REKHYT NEB. — *Sun of all mankind* — Bronze — Ring
14 *Name.* Winged uraeus — Tell Amarna. Bronze — Ring
15 *Name.* NEF NEB. — *Breath of all* — Bronze — Ring
16 *Name.* KHEN, NEB, gazelle — Bronze — Ring
17 RA with two uraei, Falcon, Bull, NEB, at side MĂOT MER — Bronze — Ring
18 ONKH HER AĂKHUTI MERT MĂOT. *Lives the Horus of the horizons, loved by Maot* — Base gold — Ring
19, 20 *Name* — Pottery. Dark blue. Edwards. Pale blue — Z. 70, Z. 40
21, 22 *Name* — Violet glass. Pottery; apple-green — Rings
23 *Name* — Tell Amarna. Edwards. Pottery. Dark violet — Ring
24, 25, 26, 27, 28 *Name* Tell Amarna. Pottery. Dark violet. Ring.—3 Bronze Rings.
Tell Amarna. Pottery. Light blue — Flat
29 *Name* (no figure) — Very minute, part of bezel. Blue — Flat
30 *Name*, between uraei — Gurob. Pendant. Full blue — Flat
31 *Name*, part of wand — (no figure) — Pottery. Apple-green — Curved
32 *Names*, fragment of glazed work — (no figure) — Blue — Flat
33 ATEN·AKHEN. Tell Amarna. Body scarab from the mummy. Silver plate on brown quartz — K. 86
34 ,, — Knob from box. Pottery. Gone olive-grey
35, 36 ,, — Pottery, violet. Pottery, blue — Rings

QUEEN NEFERYTAI

37 NESUT HEMT, ATEN·NEFER·NEFERU, NEFERTYTAI. *Royal wife Nefertytai*
Pottery pendant. Full blue — Flat
38 ATEN·NEFER·NEFERU — Pottery. Dark blue — Flat
39 . . . . . NEFERTYTAI — Pottery. Yellow — Ring
40-41 ATEN·NEFER·NEFERU NEB — Pottery. Yellow. Red and white — Rings
42 (NEFERTY)TAI, ONKH·ZETTA·MA·RA. — *Living eternally like the sun* — Pottery. Blue-green — Flat
43 NESUT HEMT UR(T) (Dated by colour). — *Great royal wife* — Pottery. Violet — Ring
44 . . . . . . NEFERT(Y) TA(I) — Edwards. Pottery. Violet inlay in white — From vase

NAMES OF THE ATEN

45, 46, 47 ONKH HEQ AĂKHUTI HOI EM AĂKHUT — Pottery. Full blue. Green. Red — Flat
Lives the prince of the two horizons, rejoicing in the horizon.
48, 49, 50 EM RENEF EM SHU ENTI EM ATEN — Bronze. Pottery. Full blue. Bright yellow — Flat
In his name of Heat which is in the Aten.
51, 52 The above names — Tell Amarna. Parts of vases. Blue glass. Alabaster
53 ATEN HEH ONKH TET REMTU (name of the Aten) . . . . (NEFERT)YTAI ONKHET ZETTA — Alabaster base
Aten the vast, living, father of mankind, the Aten, ... N. living eternally.

PRINCESS MERTATEN

54, 55 ATEN MERT — Pottery. Blue — Rings

PRINCESS ONKHS·NE·PA·ATEN

56, 57, 58	ONKHS·NE·PA·ATEN		Tell Amarna. Pottery. Violet, green, yellow	Rings

18·11.

18·11. SMENKH·KA·KHEPERU·ATEN

1, 2, 3	ATEN·ONKH·KHEPERU MER ATEN·NEFER·KHEPERU.	*Beloved by Akhenaten*	Pottery. Blue (2), Red	Rings
4, 5	ATEN·ONKH·KHEPERU MER UO·NE·RA.	*Beloved by Akhenaten*	Pottery. Blue. Apple-green	Rings
6, 7, 8	ATEN·ONKH·KHEPERU		Pottery. Blue	Rings
9	PET·ATEN·ONKH·KHEPERU, ATEN·SMENKH·KA·KHEPERU		Clay sealing	
10, 11	ATEN·SMENKH·KA·KHEPERU.	*Aten causes to be made the ka of created things*	Pottery. Blue	Rings

QUEEN MERTATEN

12	ATEN·MERT (Determined by the heiress-queen with dou ble feathers)		Pottery. Grey-blue	Ring

18·12.

18·12. TUT·ONKH·ATEN (changed to AMEN)

1	ATEN·KHEPERU·NEB,	between uraei of Upper and Lower Egypt		Part of wand. Pottery. Violet	Curved
2	,,	,, ,,		Knob handle of box. Pottery. Green	in violet
3, 4, 5, 6	,,			Pottery. Gone white. Full blue. Faded blue. Yellow	Flat
7	,,			Gurob. Glass. Violet	Ring
8	,,	between uraei		Pottery. Blue	Ring
9	,,	HEQ MĂOT.	*Prince of Truth*	Pottery. Blue	Ring
10	,,	NETER NEFER.	*The good God*	Edwards. Pottery. Blue	Ring
11, 12	,,	Kheper winged		Pottery. Dark violet. Bronze	Ring
13, 14	,,	in relief		Pottery. Rich dark blue. Full blue	Ring
15, 16, 17	,,	incised		Pottery. Full blue. Grey-blue. Red	Ring
18	ATEN·NEB·KHEPER			Pottery. Blue	Ring
19	ATEN·KHEPERU·NEB			Terracotta mould	

TUT·ONKH·AMEN after Conversion

20	RA·KHEPERU·NEB HEQ MĂOT.	*Prince of Truth*	Gone white	F. 25
21	RA·KHEPERU·NEB, RE·F·SE·HER·KHET·NETERU·F *His speech causes to feel awe of the things of his gods*		Pottery. Gone white	Ring
22	RA·NEB·KHEPERU TAT RA.	*Of the substance of Ra*	Pottery. Full blue	Ring
23, 24	RA·NEB·KHEPERU AMEN TAT.	*Of the substance of Amen*	Pottery. Blue. Yellow-green	Ring
25	AMEN·RA·KHEPERU·NEB		Pottery. Blue	Ring
26	RA·NEB·KHEPERU, MER PTAH NEB MĂOT.	*Beloved of Ptah lord of truth*	Bronze	Ring
27, 28, 29	AMEN·ONKH·TUT HEQ AN NESUT.	*Prince of Heliopolis, King*	Pottery. Violet. Blue (2)	Ring
30	,, ,,		Terracotta mould	
31	,, ,,	Feathers above, NUB below.	Knob handle. Stoneware. Violet	

QUEEN AMEN·ONKHS (Formerly Princess Onkhsnepaaten)

32, 33	AMEN·ONKHS	Pottery. Olive-green. Blue-green	E. 75, L. 44
34, 35	AMEN·ONKHS·NE	Pottery. Full blue. Fragment apple-green	Ring

18·13.

18·13. AY

1	RA·KHEPER·KHEPERU AR MĂOT AMEN MER.	*Beloved by Amen*	Green	G. 38
2	,, ,, ,, between uraei		Gone white	E. 75
3	,, ,, ,, NETER NEFER.	*The good God*	Green	F. 73
4	,, ,, HEQ.	*The Prince*	Pottery. Dull green	Broken
5	,, ,, uraeus		Blue-green	W. 37
6, 7	,, ,, AR·MĂOT		Pottery. Blue	Ring
8	RA·KHEPER·KHEPERU·AMEN.		Stamp on pottery jar handle	
9	NETER ATEF, AY, NETER AR MĂOT.	*Divine father Ay, the God making truth*	Gurob. Pottery. Blue	Ring
10	NETER ATEF, AY, NETER HEQ UAST.	*The god, prince of Thebes*	Pottery. Dull blue	Ring

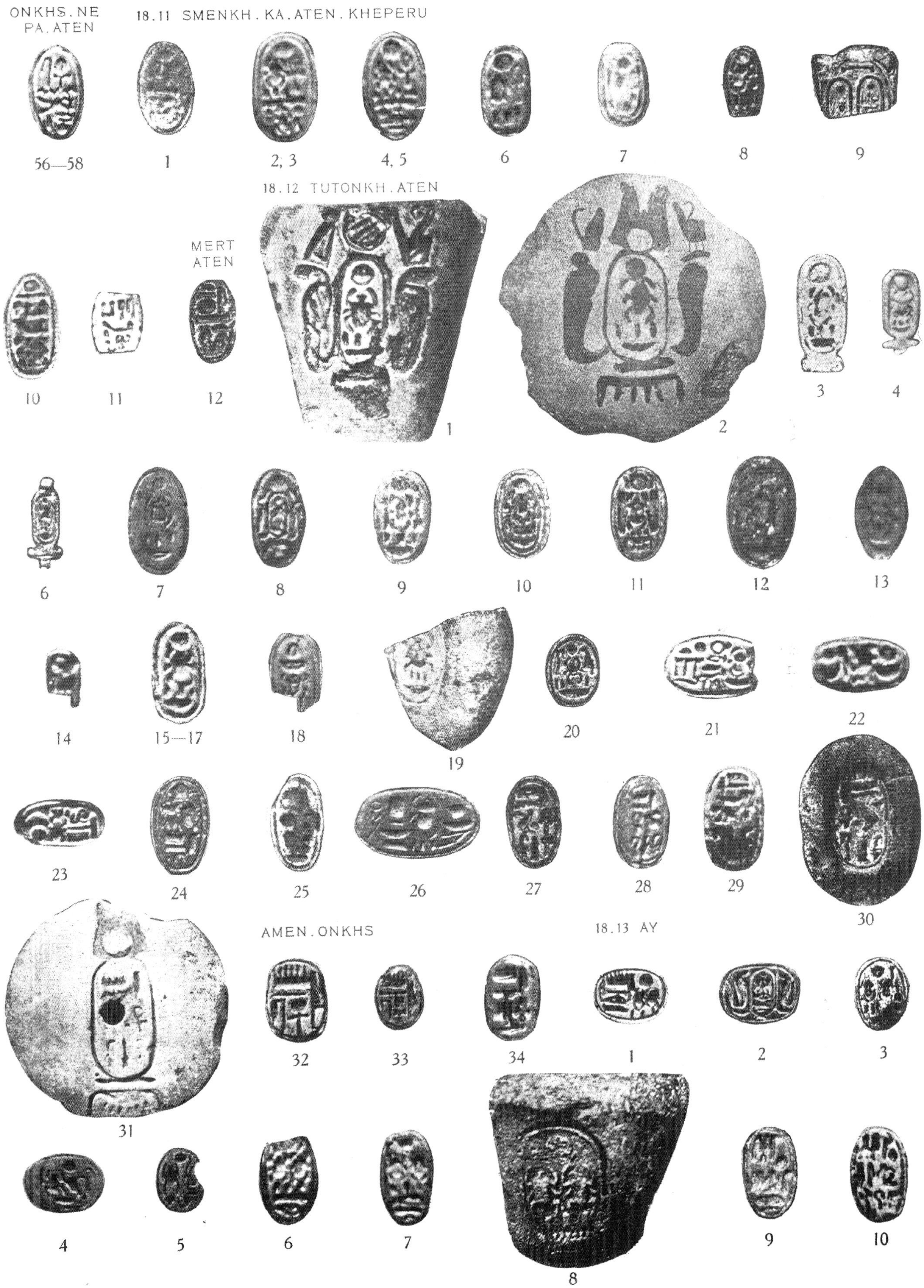
ONKHS.NE PA.ATEN
18.11 SMENKH.KA.ATEN.KHEPERU
56—58
1
2, 3
4, 5
6
7
8
9
18.12 TUTONKH.ATEN
MERT ATEN
10
11
12
1
2
3
4
6
7
8
9
10
11
12
13
14
15—17
18
19
20
21
22
23
24
25
26
27
28
29
30
AMEN.ONKHS
18.13 AY
31
32
33
34
1
2
3
4
5
6
7
8
9
10

18.14 HEREMHEB

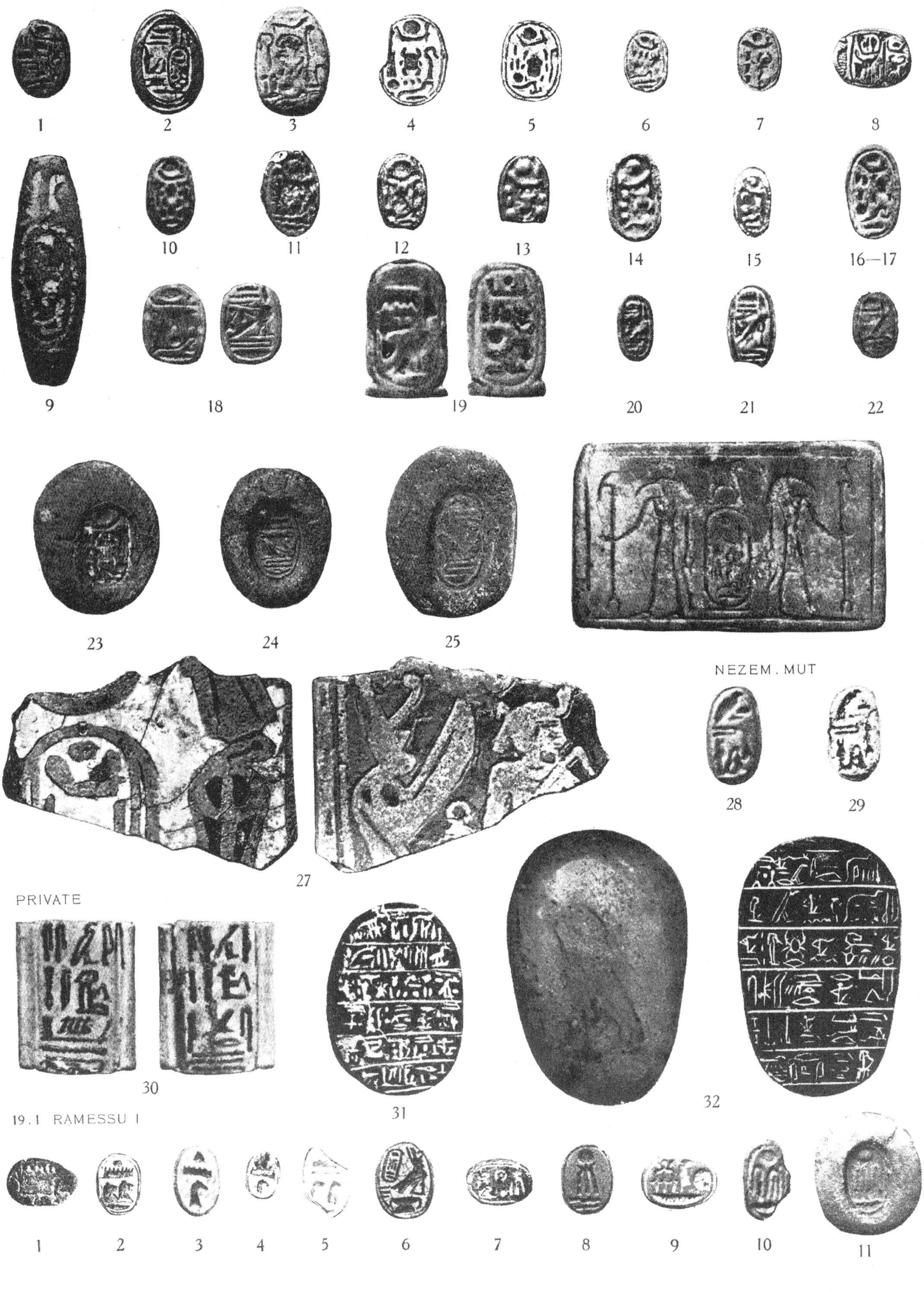

1 2 3 4 5 6 7 8

9 10 11 12 13 14 15 16—17 18 19 20 21 22

23 24 25 26

27

NEZEM. MUT

28 29

PRIVATE

30 31 32

19.1 RAMESSU I

1 2 3 4 5 6 7 8 9 10 11

18·14.

18·14. HEREMHEB

1 RA·ZESER·KHEPERU, SETEP·NE·RA, AMEN TEKHENUI MEN PER. *H. Approved by Ra, Erecting obelisks in the temple of Amen* — Gone buff — E. 74
2 NETER NEFER NEB TAUI, RA·ZESER·KHEPERU, SETEP·NE·RA, MĂOT MER. *Beloved by Măot.* — In gold mount Blue — F. 65
3 *Name*, SETEP·NE·RA. HEQ MĂOT, NETER NEFER, NEB TAUI. *Prince of Truth* — Bare grey — Y. 65
4 ,, ,, HEQ MĂOT. *Prince of Truth* — Gone drab — F. 8
5 ,, ,, NETER. *The god* — Edwards. Blue-green — E. 74
6 ,, ,, — Green-blue — E. 71
7 ,, — Gone white — H. 71
8 ,, RA·OĂ·KHEPER (Amenhetep II ?) — Gone grey — X. 30
9 ,, SETEP·NE·RA — Pottery. Light green in violet — Bead
10 ,, HEQ MĂOT — Pottery. Dull blue — Ring
11 ,, ,, in relief — Pottery. Violet — Ring
12 ,, ,, — Pottery. Dull blue — Ring
13, 14, 15 *Name*, SETEP·NE·RA in relief — Pottery. Blue. Green. Green — Ring
16 *Name* ,, — Edwards. Pottery. Green-blue — Ring
17 ,, ,, — Pottery. Blue — Ring
18 ,, ,, HEQ MĂOT; AMEN·MER·NE, HER·EM·HEB. *Approved of Ra, Prince of Truth, Beloved by Amen, Heremheb* — Pottery. Green — Flat
19 *Name*, SETEP·NE·RA; AMEN·MER, HER·HEB — Pottery. Light blue — Flat
20, 21, 22 AMEN·MER·NE, HER·EM·HEB — Pottery. In relief, green. Dull blue (2) — Ring
23 RA·ZESER·KHEPER, SETEP·NE·RA — Terracotta mould
24, 25 AMEN·MER·NE, HER·EM·HEB — Terracotta mould
26 RA·ZESER·KHEPERU, SETEP·NE·RA, between two figures of Tehuti — Alabaster tablet, pectoral? — Flat
27 ,, yellow and red inlay in white. Reverse, king and uraei — Pottery. White in faded purple

QUEEN NEZEMT-MUT

28–29 MUT·NEZEM, queen seated — Pottery. Green. Gone white — Ring

PRIVATE NAMES

30 AY MĂOT·KHERU, SESHEP EN(T)EK. . . . *Ay justified, receive thou. . . . .* From strip on a mummy. AY SURA. Reverse, *Ay, drink. . . .* AM on top, NEFER on base edge Pottery. Black on blue
31 ZED MEDU ASAR MER AHU ZEHUTI·MES and abbreviated heart chapter. *Speech of the Osiris, keeper of the cattle, Tehutmes . . . . .* — Lazuli — K. 82
32 BENNU SĂ NE RA. The Bennu drawn in black, inside hollow crystal cover. *Bennu son of Ra.* ZED MEDU NE ASAR AUF·NE·REM·NEHEH. Name *Aufnerem·neheh,* and abbreviated chapter, opaque violet glass plate. The crystal was lined with gold foil, resin, and plaster; with the plate below, it formed a heart in a pectoral. — Gurob

19·1. *XIXth DYNASTY*

19·1. RAMESSU I

1 RA·MEN·PEHT, AMEN·RA·MER — Blue paste — V. 75
2 RA·MEN·PEHTI NEB — Gone buff — F. 89
3 RA·MEN·PEH — Green — Z. 94
4 ,, — Gone white — F. 78
5 RA·MEN·PEHTI — Edwards. Gurob. Pottery. Blue — Ring
6 The Falcon on NUB, RA·MES·SES — Green — F. 28
7 MES·RA. Baboon — Green — N. 14
8 RA·MES·SES — Gurob. Green — F. 93
9 RA·MES, MĂOT NEB — Edwards. Blue paste — F. 26
10 RA·MES·NEB — Pottery. Dull green — Ring
11 RA·MES·ES — Terracotta mould

19·2.

19·2. SETY I

No.	Inscription	Translation / Notes	Material	Form
1	ONKH NETER NEFER, NEB TAUI, RA·MĂOT·MEN, PTAH NEB MĂOT MER, SĂ RA NEB KHOU, SETY	*Live the Good God, Lord of both lands, Men·maotra, by Ptah lord of truth loved, Son of Ra, Lord of epiphanies, Sety.*	Gone white.	Cylinder
2	NETER HET SETY PTAH·MER·NE·PTAH OĂKHET EM PER. Smooth ovoid back, for deposit or inlay.	*Temple of Sety Merneptah, named "Ptah glorious in the temple"*	Pottery. Green inlay in purple	Curved
3	ONKH NETER NEFER, NEB TAUI, RA·MĂOT·MEN, NEFER NEB. Rannut uraeus. NETER NEFER, NEB TAUI. Royal sphinx		Blue	Flat
4	(NEB) TAUI RA·MEN·MĂOT	Piece of vase. Lahun.	Pottery. Blue	
5	NETER NEFER, NEB TAUI, RA·MĂOT·MEN ONKH DA	Pendant. Gurob.	Pottery. Blue	Flat
6	RA·MĂOT·MEN, HEQ UAST.	*Prince of Thebes*	Gone white	Worn
7	RA·MEN·MĂOT, SETEP NE (RA), NEB		Bare steatite	G. 4
8	RA·MĂOT·MEN, NUB. Two feathers		Pottery. Gone brown	E. 52
9	RA·MEN·MĂOT. Two feathers and uraei		Gone white	Z. 74
10	,, Uraeus		Gone white	F. 88
11	,, NEFER		Pottery. Gone brown	N. 14
12	RA·MĂOT·MEN, PTAH MER.	*Beloved by Ptah*	Gone white	G. 22
13	RA·MEN·MĂOT, RA NEB		Gone white	J. 22
14	RA·MĂOT·MEN		Gone white	G. 68
15	MEN·MĂOT·RA		Gone white	N. 14
16	RA·MEN·MĂOT	Gurob.	Gone white	N. 34
17	,, Reverse, NESUT·KHET·NE.	*Property of the King.* xxvth dynasty?	Apple-green	
18	,, between crowns	Gurob.	Dark green	T. 74
19	RA·MĂOT·MEN between crowned uraei with ONKH	Knob handle.	Stoneware. Violet glaze	Knob
20	,,	Pendant.	Pottery. Blue	Flat
21	RA·MEN·MĂOT, HEQ MĂOT		Pottery. Light blue	Ring
22	RA·MĂOT·MEN		Pottery. Blue	Ring
23	,,		Pottery. Blue	Ring
24	,,		Pottery. Blue	Ring
25	PTAH MER SETY, MĂOT HEQ. Scarab head to foot of inscription		Pottery. Blue	F. 24
26	RA·MĂOT·MEN, PTAH MER SETY.	*Beloved of Ptah Sety*	Pottery. Violet	Flat
27	,, ,,	,,	Pottery. Violet	Flat
28	SETY MER·NE·PTAH		Pottery. Blue-green	F. 93
29	SETY MER PTAH		Pottery. Blue-black	Flat
30	SĂ RA, AMEN MER, SETY.	*Son of Ra, beloved by Amen, Sety*	Pottery. Violet in blue base	Bead
31	PTAH MER SETY	Edwards.	Pottery. Blue	Ring
32	PTAH SETY MER	Edwards. Gurob.	Pottery. Blue	Ring
33	PTAH MER SETY NE		Pottery. Blue	Flat
34	SETY NETER.	*Sety the God*	Pottery. Blue	Ring

Re-issue of TEHUTMES III

No.	Inscription	Notes	Material	Form
35	RA·MEN MĂOT KHEPER. Double reading. T. III and Sety I.		Blue-green	W. 83
36	RA·MEN·MĂOT, RA·MEN·KHEPER		Gone white	E. 96
37	RA·MEN·KHEPER; RA·MĂOT·MEN, SETEP·NE·RA		Gone white	G. 12
38	,, ,, ,, very coarse		Gone white	E. 3
39, 40	,, ,, ,,	Edwards.	Gone drab. Gone red-brown.	N. 78, M. 14

Probably later issues of Sety I

No.	Inscription	Notes	Material	Form
41	RA·MEN·MĂOT. Bes between baboons		Gone yellow	F. 21
42	RA·MEN·MĂOT, HER MĂOT.	*The true Horus*	Gone brown	Fish
43	MEN·MĂOT·RA Sphinx. Reverse, RA·KHEPER·MĂOT		Pottery. Blue.	Flat

QUEEN TUA

No.	Inscription	Material	Form
44	RA TUA	Gone white	L. 30

DYNASTY XIX. SETY I

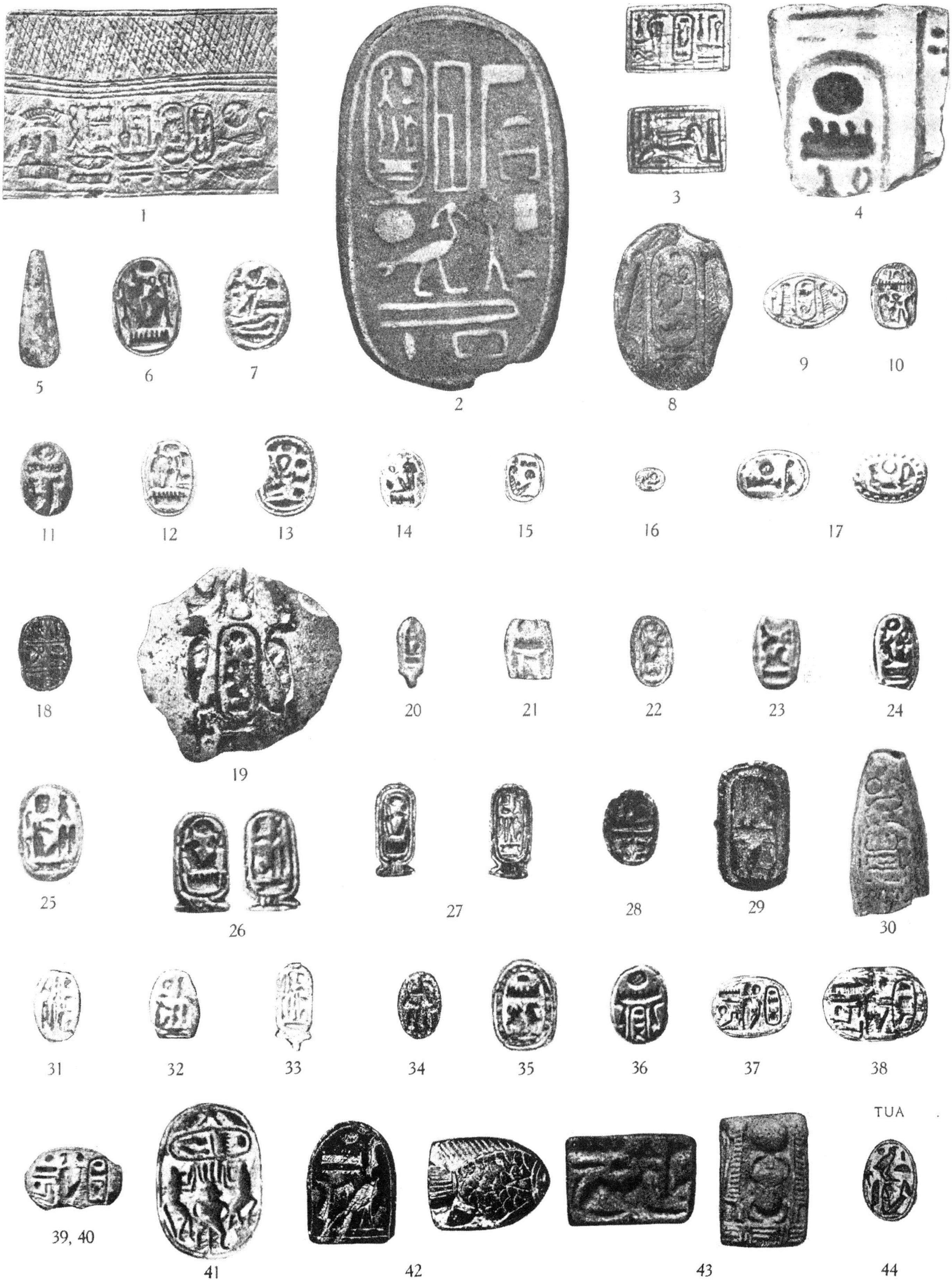

1 2 3 4 5 6 7 8 9 10 11 12 13 14 15 16 17 18 19 20 21 22 23 24 25 26 27 28 29 30 31 32 33 34 35 36 37 38 39, 40 41 42 43 TUA 44

SETY I AND RAMESSU II

45 46 47 48 50 51 52 53

19.3 RAMESSU II

54 1 2 3 4

5 6 7 8 9 10

11 12 13 14 15 16 17 18

19 20 21 22 23 24 25

26 27 28 29 30 31

19·2. 19·2. SETY I and RAMESSU II. 19·3.

45 RA·USER·MĂOT SETEP·NE·RA, RA·MĂOT·MEN Red jasper Ring
46, 47, 48 RA·USER—MEN—MĂOT, SETEP·NE·RA Gone white (2). Gone buff. F. 42, G. 76, G. 74
49 ,, ,, Reverse, KHEPER between feathers in rope border Gone brown Flat
50 ,, ,, Edwards. Gone brown Z. 95
51 USER·MĂOT·MEN·RA Pottery. Gone white N. 22
52 RA·USER·MĂOT, RA·MEN·MĂOT SETEP·NE·RA Gone brown Uzat
53 RA·USER—MEN—MĂOT, SETEP Gone brown Fish
54 RA·USER·MĂOT, SETEP·NE·RA, Ra standing. Reverse, RA·MEN·KHEPER, Tahutmes III standing Gone white Flat

19·3. 19·3. RAMESSU II

1 The Horus KA NEKHT SEKHEM PEHTI. *Strong bull, powerful and mighty* (Falcon name) Nekhebt and Uazet on plants at sides, sun with uraei in middle Bronze Flat
2 PER·NE·PTAH, RAMESSU MER AMEN. *Temple of Ptah, Ramessu loved by Amen.*
NESUT BAT, RA·USER·MĂOT, SETEP·NE·RA, SĂ RA RAMESSU MER AMEN
ONKH DA RA MA ZETTA. *Given life like Ra eternally* Pottery. Blue-green E. 18
3 NETER NEFER, NEB TAUI, RA·USER·MĂOT, SETEP·NE·RA, PET PET SEMTU.
Smiting lands. Set, Ramessu, Amen, and Ra hand in hand Gone white F. 27
4 RAMESSU MER AMEN PET PET SEMTU NEB. *Smiting all lands* Gone grey F. 65
5 (NETER) NEFER, NEB TAUI, RA·USER·MĂOT, SETEP·NE·RA, PET PET SEMTU Gone white F. 72
6 RA·USER·MĂOT, SETEP·NE·RA, SAR ONKH NE TEM. *Living prince of the perfect* Gone white V. 25
7 ,, ,, NEB NO, P·NETER, NUB MER. *Great Lord, the God, loved by Set* Black steatite E. 7
8 NEB TAUI RA·USER·MĂOT, NEB SED HEB MA TATHNEN. *Lord of the Sed feast like Tanen* Gone white
Reverse, Head of Hathor.
9 RA·USER·MĂOT, SETEP·NE·RA. King before Ra. Sun and uraei above Grey steatite E. 14
10 ,, ,, King offering to ram-headed standard of Amen Gone white F. 95
11 ,, ,, King offering to baboon of Tehuti Gurob. Green-blue F. 95
12 ,, ,, King offering Măot to baboon Gurob. Blue F. 20
13 ,, ,, ,, ,, Gone white E. 88
14 ,, ,, NEFER Baboon seated, *Tehuti* MER *beloved* Gurob. Gone white H. 36
15 NEB KA NEFER. Rennut, and Ptah. (Period of Ramessu II) Gone white F. 24
16 RA·USER·MĂOT, SETEP·NE·RA. King offering to Rennut Gone white F. 32
17 ,, ,, NEFER, Rennut Green F. 32
18 ,, PTAH. Bearded *ba* on *zed*, Ptah and King Gone white F. 27
19 UAS ONKH UAS. King kneeling offering Măot. Falcon behind Tell Yehudiyeh. Gone white F. 72
20 RA·USER·MĂOT, SETEP·NE·RA. King between Ptah and Tehuti Edwards. Gone grey E. 93
21 RA TAUI, RA·USER·MĂOT MER NUB. *Loved by Set* Edwards. Gone brown F. 8
22 MĂOT. King and Ra Gurob. Green-blue W. 86
23 RA·USER·MĂOT, SETEP·NE·RA. Ra-falcon NEB Green-blue V. 10
24 MĂOT. King smiting enemy, lion below, MEN behind Gone brown F. 21
25 RA·USER·MĂOT, King smiting enemy, Ra-falcon behind Gone white E. 57
26 RA·USER·MĂOT, SETEP·NE·RA between feathers. Reverse, king in chariot Gone white Flat
27 . . . NEB TAUI, RA·USER·MĂOT, SETEP·NE·RA NETER NEFER. Sphinx walking Gone grey E. ?
28 RA·USER·MĂOT SETEP·NE·RA repeated. Sphinx couchant, Maot on hand, Falcon behind Gone grey F. 30
29 ,, King adoring Tehuti. Reverse, KHEPESH MAU, crocodile below. *Strong one of lions* Gone white Flat
30 ,, SETEP-NE-RA. King seated Gone buff J. 83
31 ,, ,, King standing Gone white J. 83

19·3. 19·3. RAMESSU II (*continued*)

No.	Name	Description	Material	Form
32	RA·USER·MĂOT, SETEP·NE·RA.	Ra standing. Reverse, Sphinx holding Măot	Green	Flat
33	,, ,,	King standing	Gurob. Gone white	Worn
34	,, ,,	King standing. Reverse, Baboon	Edwards. Green	Broken
35	,, ,,	King standing	Edwards. Gone grey	E. 75
36	,, ,,	AMEN MER. *Loved by Amen*	Gone white	E. ?
37	,, ,,	,, ,,	Jasper in gold ring	H. 42
38	,, ,,	SĂ AST	Gone white	Cylinder
39	,, ,,	Ra standing	Green	P. 50
40	NESUT BAT, RA·USER·MĂOT NEB.	The finest work known so late	Gone white	E. 81
41	NETER NEFER, NEB TAUI, RA·USER·MĂOT SETEP·NE·RA		Green	G. 8
42	,, ,,	,, ,,	Gone white	F. 26
43, 44	RA·USER·MĂOT, SETEP·NE·RA.	(No. 44 since exchanged away)	Carnelian in gold ring	H. 56
45	,, ,,	in scroll border	Gurob. Green-blue	Broken
46, 47, 48	,, ,,	in border of circles	Full blue, blue, green.	W. 86, V. 25, F. 24
49, 50, 51	,, ,,	,,	All gone white.	P. 50 ?, V. 27, K. 16
52	,, ,,	in rope border	Gone white	Y. 10
53	,, ,,	winged scarab	Gone white	R. 48
54	,, ,,	between solar uraei, on back, front broken	Green	K. 16
55	,, ,,	between uraei	Gone brown	F. 67
56, 57, 58	,, ,,		Gone brown (2) Green.	F. 72, G. 76, J. 51
59, 60, 61	,, ,,	All from Gurob, Edwards.	Green. Gone brown. Blue-green, worn (?)	F. 93
62	,, ,,		Gurob. Dark blue glass.	Baboon
63, 64, 65	,, ,,		Brown jasper. Green. Gone brown.	H. 94, V. 63, G. 44
66, 67, 68	,, ,,		All gone buff. Fish.	G. 44, G. 44
69	,, ,,		Gone white	M. 90
70	,, ,,		Pottery. Green	L. 40
71	,, ,,		Gurob. Pottery. Green	L. 40
72	,, ,,		Gurob. Pottery. Green	L. 40
73, 74, 75	,, ,,		Gone grey. Gone white. Green-blue.	Z. 80, Z. 35, Broken
76, 77, 78	,, ,,		All pottery. Blue	Flat
79	,, ,,		Pottery. Green	Flat
80	,, ,,	solar uraei on side edge	Brown limestone	Ring
81	,, ,,	Relief signs	Gurob. Pottery. Blue	Ring
82	,, ,,		Gurob. Pottery. Full blue	Ring
83	,, ,,		Pottery. Full blue	Ring
84	,, ,,		Pottery. Gone white	Ring
85	,, ,,		Pottery. Blue, with purple ring	Ring
86	,, ,,		Knob handle. Pottery. Green in violet gone grey	Knob
87	,, ,,		Green paste	Uzat
88	,, ,,		Terracotta impression	
89	,, ,,		Terracotta mould	
90	RA·USER·MĂOT NEFER NEB.	Ra in barque. Fine work also on back	Gone brown	E. 49
91	,, NEFER		Gone white	F. 80
92	,, MĂOT		Gone brown	Broken
93	,,	Ra with uraei	Pottery. Gone brown	N. 22
94	,,	,,	Edwards. Gone buff	F. 7
95	,, RA		Gone buff	F. 34
96	,, NEFER NEB		Edwards. Gone buff	H. 64

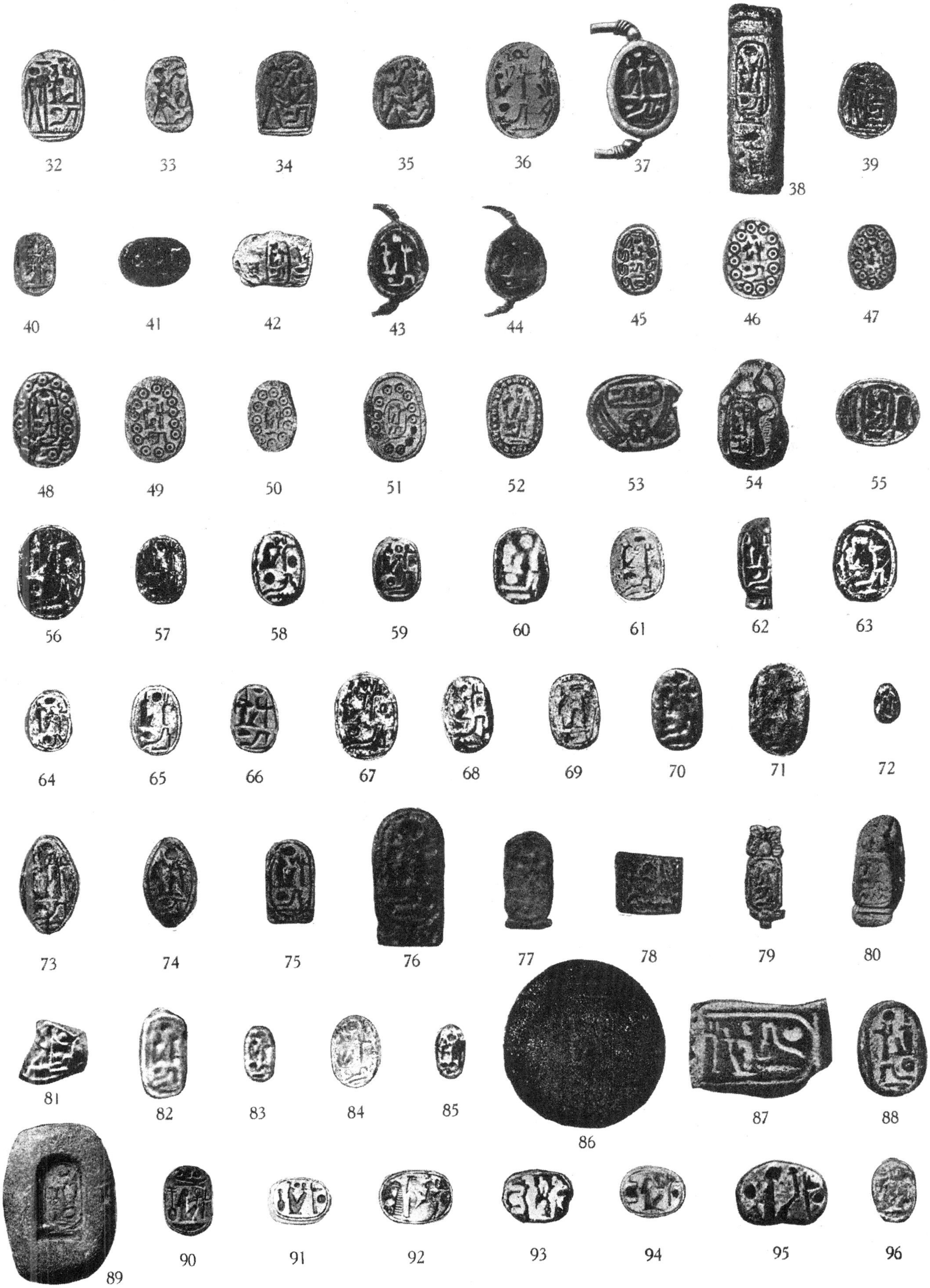
32 33 34 35 36 37 38 39
40 41 42 43 44 45 46 47
48 49 50 51 52 53 54 55
56 57 58 59 60 61 62 63
64 65 66 67 68 69 70 71 72
73 74 75 76 77 78 79 80
81 82 83 84 85 86 87 88
89 90 91 92 93 94 95 96

97 98 99 100 101 102 103 104

105 106 107 108 109 110 111 112

113 114 115 116

117 118 119 120 121

122 123 125 126 127 128 129 130

131 132 133 134 135 136 137 138

NEFERTARI

139 140 141 142 143 144 145 146 147

19·3.

19·3. RAMESSU II (*continued*)

97 RA·USER·MĂOT NEB — Gone buff — N. 20
98 ,, ,, — Blue paste — W. 62
99 ,, between flowers — Green — E. 22
100 ,, ,, finely cut, showing eyes to scarab — Gone white — G. 36
101 ,, — Gone brown — F. 60
102, 103, 104 ,, — All gone white. R. 32, H. 4, E. 6
105 USER·MĂOT·RA in order of pronunciation. Pierced through at sides — Gone grey — G. 92
106 RA·USER·MĂOT — Gone white — G. 62
107 ,, — Edwards. Green — F. 70
108, 109, 110 ,, Pottery, blue; pottery, gone white; Prussian blue glass, H. 32, N. 46 — Broken
111 ,, over NUB — Pottery. Violet — Flat
112 ,, between uraei. Reverse AMEN RA NEFER HES — Grey steatite — Flat
113 ,, on base of hawk — Grey durite
114 ,, SETEP·NE·RA. Sphinx of Mentu — Red jasper

Personal Name

115 NEB KHOU RAMESSU AMEN MER. Royal Sphinx — Lazuli
116 RA·USER·MĂOT, SETEP·NE·RA, MUT MER; RAMESSU, AMEN MER, HERAKHTI MER MA(RA)
Beloved of Mut; Beloved of Amen and Herakhti like Ra — Pale red agate — Flat
117 RA·USER·MĂOT, SETEP·NE·RA, RAMESSU AMEN MER — Red jasper — Ring
118 ,, ,, Reverse ,, ,, — Pottery. Violet — Flat
119 ,, ,, Reverse ,, ,, — Gone white — Flat
120 ,, ,, Reverse ,, ,, — Pottery. Green — Flat
121 ,, ,, ,, ,, two cartouches side by side — Pottery. Blue — Flat
122 ,, ,, ,, ,, ,, ,, — Gurob. Clay impression
123 RAMESSU, AMEN MER — Ramesseum. Obsidian — Broken
124, 125 ,, ,, (124 not figured, similar)
Edwards. Gurob. Pottery. Dark blue. Gurob. Green. G. 12, G. 22
126 ,, ,, — Blue-green — F. 95
127 ,, ,, — Gurob. Pottery. Green-blue — E. 92
128 ,, ,, — Pendant. Pottery. Blue — Flat
129 ,, ,, — Black steatite — Handle
130 ,, ,, KHEPESH foundation deposit — Pottery. Blue — Flat
131 AMEN MER RAMES (·SU) — Pottery. Violet in blue — Bead
132 ,, ,, — Green — F. 61
133 RAMESES MER AMEN — Pottery. Green-brown — N. 54
134 AMEN·RA MER, RAMESSU — Pottery. Blue — Ring
135 ,, ,, ,, — Pottery. Violet — Ring
136 RAMESES. King seated — Gone buff — E. 75
137 RAMESES PA NETER. *Rameses the god* — Gone brown — E. 75
138 RAMESES. Reverse, similar — Pottery. Blue — Flat
139 TU SĂ RA. *Thou art the son of Ra* (probably of this reign) — Gone white — T. 57
140 RA MES (see Kgsb. xxxiii o''' p'''). *Child of Ra.* Very fine work on back,
better than No. 40 — Gone brown — E. 82

QUEEN NEFERTARI

141 MUT NEFERARTI, MERENT. *Nefertari beloved of Mut* — Pottery. Red. — Flat
142 NESUT HEMT NEFERARI. *Royal wife, Neferari* — Gone grey — W. 10
143 ,, ,, ,, ,, — Burnt red — F. 77
144 ,, ,, ,, ,, — Light blue — W. 10
145 ,, ,, ,, ,, — Gone brown — F. 90
146 NETER HEMT NEFERARI. *Divine wife Neferari* — Dull green — K. 64
147 RA NETER HEMT NEFERTARU — Gone white — N. 44

148 ASAR NEB RESTAU. SEM, NESUT SĂ, KHOEMUAS.
To Osiris Lord of Restau, for the High Priest, King's son, Khoemuas Amulet. Black Hornblend Flat

PRIVATE NAMES

149 MER PER APTU, MER NUT, THAT, PASAR.
Keeper of the palace of the harem, Mayor, Vizier, Pasar.
Reverse, Pasar adoring HER·SĂ·AST. Gone white Flat

150 TĂYTI SĂB, MER NUT, THAT, PASAR. *Chief Justice, Mayor, Vizier, Pasar*
A similar bead with ONKH UZAT repeated. Pottery. Black on green Bead

151 . . . . SĂB ER MEHI, NETER HEN MĂOT, MER NUT, THAT, NEFER·RENPET.
. . . *Judge of the North, prophet of Măot, Mayor, Vizier, Nefer·renpet.*
Reverse, RA·MĂOT·USER, SETEP·NE·RA. Nefer·renpet adoring Măot Pottery. Blue-black Flat

152 THĂ KHUT NESUT HER NE AMN ; NESUT SESH SHAT NE NEB TAUI ; MER PER HEN UR NE RES MEHT.
Fan bearer on the right of the king ; Royal scribe of letters of the king ; keeper of the great palaces of the south and north. RAMESES·USER·HER·KHEPESH Gone brown
Reverse, The official with Set over him, adoring the name of RAMESES, Basket-work edge

153 THĂ KHUT HER NESUT AMN ; NESUT SESH MER PER HEN NE NEB TAUI, MEHTI·MES.
Fan bearer on king's right ; royal scribe, keeper of the palace of the king, Mehtimes.
Mehti, two hawks Pottery. Blue Flat
Reverse, NESUT SESH, MER PER HEN, MEHTI·MES (see above)

154 NESUT SESH, MER PER UR, NESUT UPUTI SEMTU NEB, NEZEM, MĂOT-KHERU.
Royal Scribe, keeper of the palace, royal messenger in all lands, Nezem, justified.
Reverse, Nezem adoring Sekhmet Peacock blue Flat

155 NESUT SESH MER PER HER NEB BAK·NE·AMEN. Reverse, B. adoring HER·AĂKHUTI.
Royal Scribe, keeper of the palace of the Lord Horus, (King) Bakneamen Gone white Flat

156 HER NEFER(U) PTAH·NEB·MEN·NEFER·USER. *Over the recruits*
Reverse, RA·USER·MĂOT, SETEP·NE·RA Pottery. Olive-grey R. 45

157 ZED MEDUT AN NESUT SESH PTAHMES(MES) MUTSES. ZED·F AUSEHEZEMSA AR·F SEHEZEMSA.
Say the Speech ; he says, Royal scribe, Ptahmes, born of Mutses ; his name Ausehezemsa born was he of Sehezem(sa ?) Carnelian Serpent

158 ZED MEDUT, ASAR . . . . . . NE SESHU PA-IR. *Of the scribe Pair.* *Thet* tie. Red felspar

159 . . . . ASAR, HER PEZETI, NEKHTA-MIN . . . . *Osiris, over the archers, Nekhtamin.* Red felspar.

160 OĂ NE OT, RA·MES·NEKHT ; ZED NEF RUDNEY·NESUTY (" I have increased the kingdom ")
Chief of the house, Ramesnekht, name of him Rudnynesuty Pottery. Gone yellow

161 MER PER NE AMEN SĂ·RA·NE·AMEN·ER·NEKHT
Keeper of the temple of Amen, Saraneamenernekht Pottery. Blue M. 10

162 ASAR SĂHTU. *The Osirian, Sahtu* Heart pendant. Grey steatite

163 ASAR SĂRY MĂOT-KHERU. *The Osirian Sary, justified* ,, Green jade ?

164 SHEMOYT NE HATHER NEB HETEP·HEMT, NEFER·SHUTI, MĂOT·KHERU.
Chantress of Hathor lady of Hetep-hemt, Nefershuti, justified. Dark green
Reverse, Nefershuti adoring Hather HEMT-HETEP.

165 ZED MEDUT AN AST RY. ZED MEDUT AN ASAR, RY.
Say the speech, she says, the Isis, Ry. Say the speech, she says, the Osirian Ry Thet tie. Red jasper

166 ZED MEDUT NE ASAR SHEMOYT TEHUTI, BAKMUT.
Say the speech, of the Osiris Chantress of Tehuti, Bakmut Name amulet Red agate

167 ASAR NEBT PER, RENPET·NEFER, *The Osiris, lady of the house, Renpet nefer* Serpent. Red glass

148

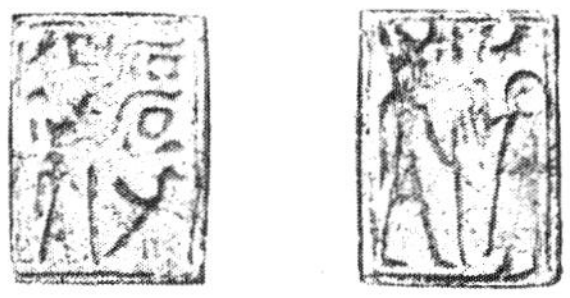
149

150

151

152

153

154

155

156

157

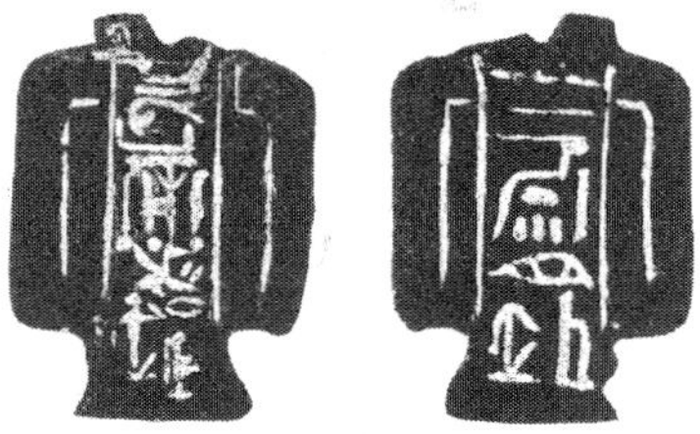
158

159

160

161

162

163

164

165

166

167

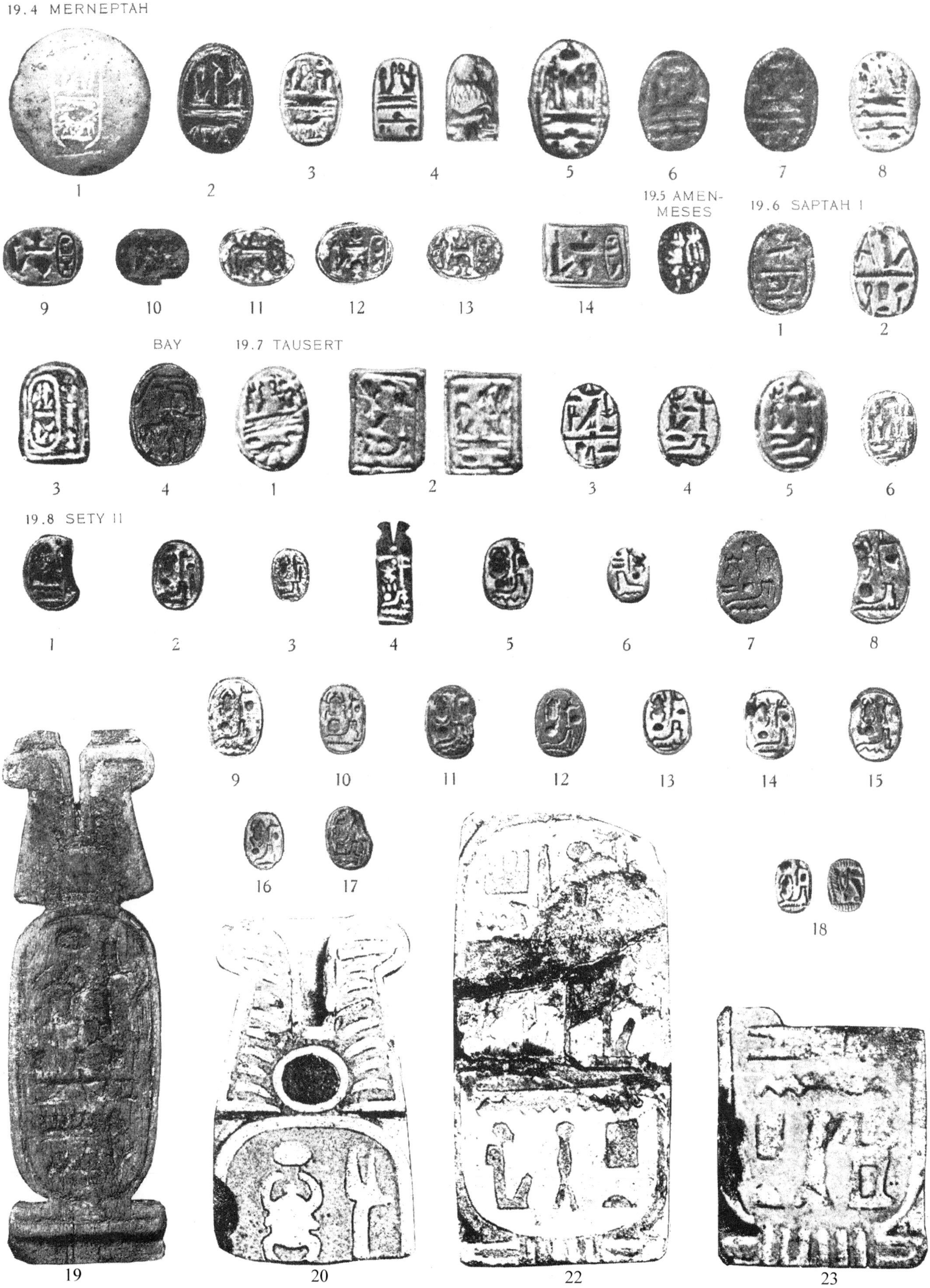
19.4 MERNEPTAH
1 2 3 4 5 6 7 8
9 10 11 12 13 14
19.5 AMEN-MESES
19.6 SAPTAH I
1 2
3
BAY
4
19.7 TAUSERT
1 2 3 4 5 6
19.8 SETY II
1 2 3 4 5 6 7 8
9 10 11 12 13 14 15
16 17
18
19 20 22 23

19·4. MERNEPTAH

19·4.

1 BĂ NE RA, MER AMEN — Glass. Disc for inlaying. Turquoise blue — Rough
2, 3 ,, ,, — Black steatite. Gone salmon-red — H. 92, J. 85
4 MER·NE·PTAH, HETEP·HER·MĂOT. Reverse, Baboon — Green — Baboon
5, 6, 7, 8 ,, ,, — All pottery. Blue, Full blue, Gone olive, Green-blue. — All E. 68

Re-issue of Tahutmes III

9, 10 RA·MEN·KHEPER HETEP·HER·MĂOT — Gone brown. Green. — G. 76, G. 8
11, 12, 13 ,, ,, — Edwards. Gone buff, Gone yellow, Gone brown. — E. 62, E. 70, G. 76
14 ,, ,, Reverse, Fish — Gone brown — Fish

19·5. AMEN MESES

19·5.

AMEN·MES HEQ UAST — Dark blue glass — K. 88

19·6. SĂPTAH I

19·6.

1 AĂKHU·NE·RA, SETEP·NE·RA. From temple of the king, with rings, etc. — Pottery. Blue-green — H. 56
2 PTAH·MER·NE, SĂ·PTAH. Found at Karnak 1887 — Gone white — W. 90
3 ONKH NETER NEFER, MER·NE·PTAH SĂ·PTAH. From temple of king — Pottery. Blue — H. 56 ?
4 MER KHETM BĂY. *Keeper of the seal, Bay* — Gone buff — W. 68
5 MER KHETM TAUI ER ZER·F BĂY. *Keeper of the seal of the land to its limits, Bay* — Pottery. Blue — H. 56
6 MER KHETM BĂY — Pottery. Blue — Ring

19·7. QUEEN TAUSERT

19·7.

1 SĂT RA MER·NE·AMEN — From temple of the queen. Pottery. Full blue — H. 76
2 ,, ,, Reverse TA USERT, SETEP·NE·MUT. From temple of the queen — Pottery. Full blue — Flat
3 NESUT HEMT TAUSERT S . . — Gone white — J. 95
4 TAUSERT, SETEP·NE·MUT — Gurob. Green-blue — H. 8
5 TAUSERT — From temple of queen. Pottery. Full blue — H. 76
6 TAUSERT, SETEP·NE·AMEN — Gone buff — E. 75

19·8. SETY II

19·8.

1 (RA)·USER·KHEPER, AMEN MER — Legs pierced through. Pottery. Olive-green — G. 78
2 RA·USER·KHEPER, SETEP·NE·RA, A(= Amen ?) — Green, gone red-brown — G. 44
3 ,, ,, ,, — Blue — Z. 97
4 RA·USER·KHEPERU, SETEP·NE·RA — Gurob. Red felspar — Ring
5 ,, ,, — Green — G. 44
6 RA·USER—MEN—KHEPER, SETEP·NE·RA, Double reading with Tahutmes III — Legs pierced. Blue paste — N. 80
7 RA·USER·KHEPER, SETEP·NE·RA·BASTET·AMEN — Blue paste — N. 14
8 ,, ,, — Legs pierced through. Gone yellow — G. 44
9 ,, ,, — ,, Gone white — G. 76
10 ,, ,, — Gone white — J. 76
11 ,, ,, — Gone buff — F. 44
12 ,, ,, — Legs pierced through. Gone brown — G. 44
13 ,, ,, — ,, Green — G. 78
14 ,, ,, — Edwards. ,, Gone buff — Broken
15 USER KHEPER, SETEP·NE·RA — ,, ,, Gone white — G. 76
16 RA·USER·KHEPER, ,, — ,, Gone white — G. 44 ?
17 ,, ,, — Gone buff — E. 80
18 ,, ,, Reverse, Uzat eye — Gone brown — Uzat
19 RA·USER·KHEPERU, MER AMEN. Piece of furniture, tenon top and bottom — Wood painted blue — Flat
20 RA·USER·KHEPER . . . . . . Reverse, Uazet serpent and seated female impressed. — Pottery. White in violet, yellow disc
21 ,, (Not figured) — Faded
22 RA·AMEN·MER, SETY MER·NE·PTAH. Reverse, Cross incised — Pottery. Violet in white, faded
23 . . . . ,, ,, ,, — Pottery. White in violet

19·8. SETY II (*continued*)

24 RA·USER·KHEPERU·SETEP·NE·RA, SETY·MER·PTAH on base of sphinx — Blue paste
25 „ MER AMEN. Reverse SETY MER·NE·PTAH — Pottery. Olive-green — Flat
26 „ „ „ „ „ — Pottery. Blue-green — Flat
27 RA with uraei. NEB TAUI, RA·USER·KHEPER, SETEP·NE·RA; NEB KHOU, MER·PTAH·SETY·NE; DA·ONKH·MA·RA — Gone drab — L. 42
28, 29, 30 RA·USER·KHEPER·MER·AMEN; SETY MER·NE·PTAH. Impressed. Pottery. Blue-green. Blue. Gone dark brown. All — F. 22
31 SETY AMEN (abbreviated) — Gone white — H. 88
32 A SET NEB „ — Gone white — F. 90

19·9. 19·9. SĂPTAH II

1 RA·SE·KHO, AMEN·MER — Red felspar — H. 92
2 SĂ·PTAH RAMESSU, MER HATHER NEBT NEHAT. *Beloved of Hathor lady of the sycomore* — Gone yellow — E. 83

19·10. 19·10. SETNEKHT

1 RA·USER·KHEPERU, AMEN(MER), SETEP·NE·RA — Gone buff — F. 77

20·1. *XXth DYNASTY.* 20·1. RAMESSU III

1 RA·USER·MĂOT, MER·AMEN. MEN . . . on each side — Gone buff — F. 90
2 „ „ King seated — Gone white — E. 38
3 „ „ Ptah standing — Gone brown — E. 90
4 „ „ Falcon of Ra — Gone white — E. 90
5 „ „ — Gone white — T. 84
6, 7, 8, 9, 10 „ „ Gone white; Pottery, green; Gone white; Pottery, full blue. 10 as 9 Pottery light blue. M. 82, L. 78, N. 42, F. 86, F. 86
11 „ „ blundered — Pottery. Green — Baboon
12 „ „ Reverse, sphinx, maŏt and uraeus — Gone brown — Flat
13 „ „ blundered. Reverse, Falcon, MĂOT, MEN — Gone white — Flat
14 „ „ Reverse, Standing figure with *uas*, RA, A — Brown limestone — Flat
15 NEB TAUI, RA·USER·MĂOT, MER AMEN (not figured) — Rough, foundation deposit, alabaster plaque — Flat
16 NETER NEFER, NEB TAUI, RA·USER·MĂOT, MER·AMEN, AMEN KHNEM NEHEH. *United to Amen eternally.* Stem of *onkh* — Pottery. Light green — Flat
17 USER·MĂOT, MER·AMEN; RAMESES HEQ AN. Reverse, King standing before criosphinx — Gurob. Dark green — Flat
18 RAMESES, MER·AMEN, NEB SED HEBU MA TANEN. Lord of *sed* feasts like Tanen (Nebti name) — Full blue — F. 77
19 AMEN MER, MES, on back. King seated, shooting, on front — Blue, burnt — V. 45
20 RAMESES HEQ AN. *Prince of Heliopolis* — Foundation deposit. Pottery, green — Flat
21 PER RAMESES HEQ AN. *The palace of Rameses, prince of Heliopolis* — Gone grey — F. 93
22, 23, 24, 25, 26 RAMESES HEQ AN Gone white; Gone brown; Pottery, green; Pottery, green; white steatite G. 4; F. 93; F. 86; F. 86; N. 54

20·2. 20·2. RAMESSU IV

1 RA·HEQ·MĂOT, NEFER KHEPER — Gone white — F. 93
2 „ SETEP·NE·(RA). King standing — Gone brown — F. 90
3 „ Set seated — Green — Uzat
4, 5 „ between four uraei — Black steatite; gone brown; broken — E. 36
6 „ — Pottery. Gone white — F. 37
7, 8 „ (8 not figured) Edwards, Arsinoe, Pottery, burnt brown. Pottery, blue N. 76; E. 42
9 RA·HEQ·MĂOT, RAMESES, AMEN·MER — Gurob. Edwards, Blue-green — M. 82
10 RA·HEQ·MĂOT. Reverse, RA·MES·SES — Pottery, green — Flat
11 „ Reverse, RA·HEQ·MĂOT — Pottery, green — Flat
12 RAMESES — Gone brown — F. 26

DYNASTIES XIX, SETY II TO XX, RAMESSU IV

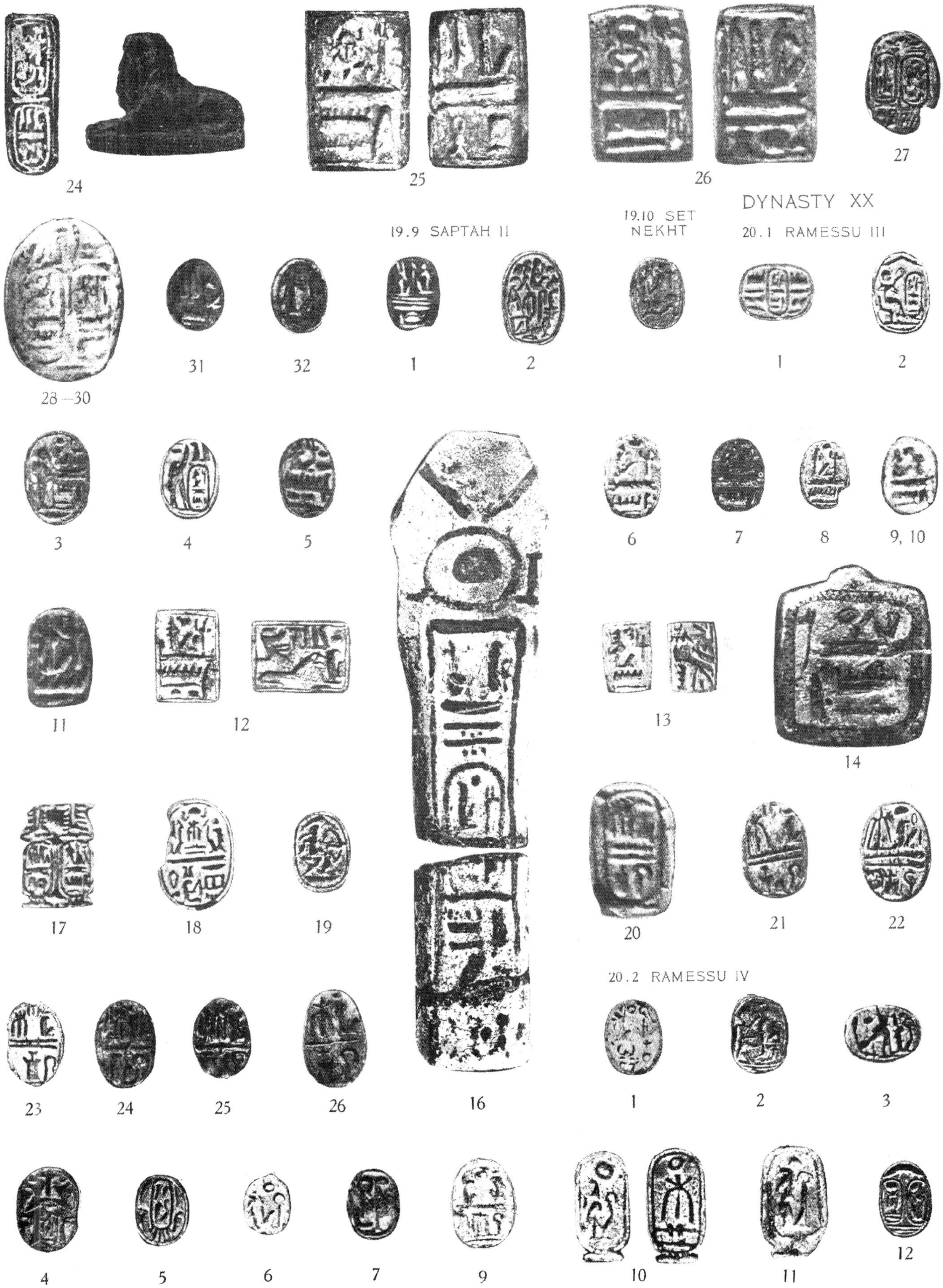

24 25 26 27

28–30 31 32

19.9 SAPTAH II: 1 2

19.10 SET NEKHT

DYNASTY XX

20.1 RAMESSU III: 1 2 3 4 5 6 7 8 9, 10 11 12 13 14 16 17 18 19 20 21 22 23 24 25 26

20.2 RAMESSU IV: 1 2 3 4 5 6 7 9 10 11 12

20.3 RAMESSU V
20.4 RAMESSU VI
20.5 RAMESSU VII
20.6 RAMESSU VIII
20.8 RAMESSU X
20.9 RAMESSU XI
20.10 RAMESSU XII
A
B
C
D

20·3. RAMESSU V

20·3.			
1	RA·USER·MĂOT, SE·KHEPER·NE·RA	Green	F. 30
2	,, ,,	Pottery. Gone white	R. 85
3, 4	,, ,,	Gone white	F. 37
5	,, ,,	Gone white	E. 73
6, 7, 8	,, ,, (8 like 7, not figured)	All pottery. Gone yellow. Gurob; blue	Flat
9	RA·SE·KHEPER·NE. Pendant	Pottery. Blue	Flat
10	RA·USER·MĂOT, RA·SE·KHEPER·NE. Reverse, RA·MESES, AMEN·MER, AMEN·KHEPESH·F	Grey steatite	Flat
11	RA·MESES, AMEN·MER, AMEN·KHEPESH·F	Green	E. 73
12	,, ,, ,,	Foundation deposit tablet. Alabaster	Flat
13	,, ,, ,,	Gone white	E. 74
14, 15, 16	,, ,, ,,	All pottery. Blue. Light blue. Full blue	Flat
17	AMEN·KHEPESH·F. Pendant	Pottery. Blue	Flat

20·4. RAMESSU VI

20·4.			
1	RA·MĂOT·NEB, MER·AMEN between crowned uraei. Stitching groove on back	Brown steatite	Flat
2	,, ,,	Bronze	Ring
3	RA·MĂOT·NEB, AMEN·KHEPESH	Bronze scarab	O. 20
4	RA·NEB AMEN	Pottery. Blue	N. 32
5	RA·NEB·MĂOT, AMEN·KHEPESH·MER. Reverse, RA·MESSU, NETER·HEQ·UAST	Wady Tumilat. Diorite	Flat
6	MĂOT·RA·NEB, MĂOT·USER Set? standing. Reverse, RA·NEB·MĂOT, USER·AMEN	Gone white	Curved
7	AMEN·RA·MESSU, NETER HEQ AN	Gone white	T. 84
8	RA·MESSU, AMEN·USER·MER, NETER·HEQ·AN	Pottery. Gone white	Flat

20·5. RAMESSU VII

20·5.			
1	(RA) MESES A(T·AMEN) NETER HEQ AN. (Only R·VII has A in names)	Gone brown	F. 39

20·6. RAMESSU VIII

20·6.			
1	RAMESSU, AMEN·MER, AĂKHU·NE·RA	Pottery. Gone white	H. 86
2	PA·SAR·OA, RA MESSU, AMEN·MER, AĂKHU·NE·RA. *The great prince Ramessu . . .*	Pottery. Gone yellow	H. 86

(Ramessu Mery-atmu is R·IX; Ramessu Saptah is recognised as Saptah II of xixth dynasty.)

20·8. RAMESSU X

20·8			
1	RA·NEFER·KA, SETEP·NE·RA between crowned uraei; double feathers above, NUB below	Ivory	Knob
2	,, ,,	Pottery gone white	E. 73
3	,, uraeus, NEB	Edwards. Gone brown	E. 40
4	NEFER·KA, uraeus with feathers, NEB	Green	E. 39
5	RA·NEFER·KA, SETEP·NE·RA	Red jasper	Uzat
6	RA·NEFER·KA, uraeus. NEB·KHEPER. Bes. Lion	Gone white	Prism
7	RA·NEFER·KA, SETEP·NE·RA	Pottery. Blue	Ring

20·9. RAMESSU XI

20·9			
1	MĂOT·KHEPER, SETEP·NE	Gone white	W. 3
2	MĂOT·KHEPER, SETEP·NE·RA	Gone brown	G. 46
3	RA·KHEPER·MĂOT, AMEN·MER, SĂ·RA	Green	Broken
4	AMEN·RA·KHEPER, SETEP·NE·RA. Legs pierced through	Gone brown	E. 17

20·10. RAMESSU XII

20·10			
1	RA·MEN·NEIT between uraei	Gone brown	F. 76
2	RA·MEN·NEIT, UAZ NEIT UAZ	Pottery. Green	W. 96
3	RA·MEN·NEIT UAZ KHEPER UAZ	Edwards. Pottery. Gone white	W. 96
4	RA·MEN·NEB·NE·MĂOT, SETEP·NE·RA (Back resembles XX·9, nos. 1 and 2)	Gone white	F. 96

UNCERTAIN RAMESSIDES

20			
A	RA·USER·MĂOT, AMEN KHEPESH, PEHTI. Reverse, hippopotamus couchant	Black steatite	
B	RA·HER(?) MER NEB NETERU EM UAST. Reverse, baboon	Pottery green	
C	RA·USER·MĂOT, SETEP·NE·RA, SĂ·PTAH, MER·NE·TEHUTI	Green	V. 16
D	RA·USER·AMEN, TEHUTI	Green	G. 22

HEART SCARABS, ETC.

Heart scarabs are here divided into classes of styles, approximately dated by the names and quality. The scarab of Apiy from Harageh (*Riqqeh* xvi) shows the rude work done late in the xviiith dynasty, and points to such scarabs having long been usual. The reference to this class is *Ab* and the number.

Ab 1 TETAMES, and chapter of the heart. Name indicates early part of xviiith. Work like next — Durite

Ab 2 SEN·NE·PĂ·NĂY, and chapter of the heart. Name over another erased. Back closely like large scarab of Amenhetep IV (18·10·1), in form of head and legs. Very fine work — Durite

Ab 3 ASAR NEBT PER SHEMOYT, NENĂY. *Osirian, lady of the house, chantress, Nenay.* Chapter of the heart, abbreviated. Limestone, painted yellow and ink-written; back painted green.

Ab 4 NEFERT·HER, standing adoring AST·UR·MUT. *Isis the great mother.* Name early. Pectoral. — Gold

Ab 5 AU AB·K MA RA ASAR, NETER AT·F NE AMEN ZEHUTI·MES; HOTI MA KHEPRA EM AST RA EM KHER·AHA AB·F MA RA. *May thy heart be like Ra, Osirian, Divine father of Amen, Tehutimes.* (*May his*) *heart be like Khepra in the dwelling of Ra in Kher·aha; may his heart be like Ra.* Some clear mistakes, and the freshness of the cutting, make it seem like an old scarab newly engraved; if so, the text is copied from an original. — Edwards. Limestone blackened

Ab 6 ANEK AMAKH OQ EM BAH SOHU·K MA OQ BĂ·K ER RES ATEN SHEP·K TA NE BEDET (?) H(ĂU) HER KHĂUT UN·NEFER AST ATEN AHER. *I am worthy to enter before thy Sahu. I grant to enter thy soul into the guarding by Aten. Receive thou land of wheat belonging upon the altar of Un·nefer in the house of Aten, Aher* (name). This is the only heart scarab of the Aten period, with a formula new to us. The work of the back is very fine, like the best scarabs of Amenhetep III and IV — Edwards. Blue paste

From the fine work of the backs, and early names, the next three seem not later than xviiith dynasty.

Ab 7 TET·BET ("nursing shepherd") Chapter of the heart — Durite

Ab 8 ASAR DADAUT. Chapter of the heart — Durite

Ab 9 Illegible, probably done by an ignorant engraver — Durite

Of late xviiith or early xixth dynasty

Ab 10 ZED MEDU AN ASAR, NEBT PER, SHEMOYT NE ASET HATSHEPS. Chapter of the heart. *Say the words to Osiris, lady of the house, chantress of Isis, Hatsheps.* Flat plate to inlay in pectoral — Limestone, blackened

Ab 11 UOB HUY, *Priest Huy*, chapter of the heart. Only head of scarab — Hard limestone, browned

Ab 12 ASAR, HER MERTU NE MIN, KENURE, chapter of the heart. *Over the serfs of Min. Kenure* — Ekhmim. Limestone, blackened

Ab·13 ASAR TUA·DEB. Chapter of the heart — Black steatite

Ab·14 ZED MEDU AN ASAR HURIA, *Say the words to Osiris, Huria.* Chapter of the heart — Limestone browned

Ab·15 ZED MEDU AN ASAR MĂ·NE·HES. *Say words to Osiris, Manehes.* Chapter of the heart — Black steatite

Ab·16 ASAR HUY. *The Osiris Huy.* Chapter of the heart — Black steatite

Nos. 1, 2, 7, 8, 9, 12, 13, 14, 15, 16 are on a scale of two-thirds; full size copies are already issued in *Amulets*, pls. viii, ix.

1

2

3

4

5

6

7

8

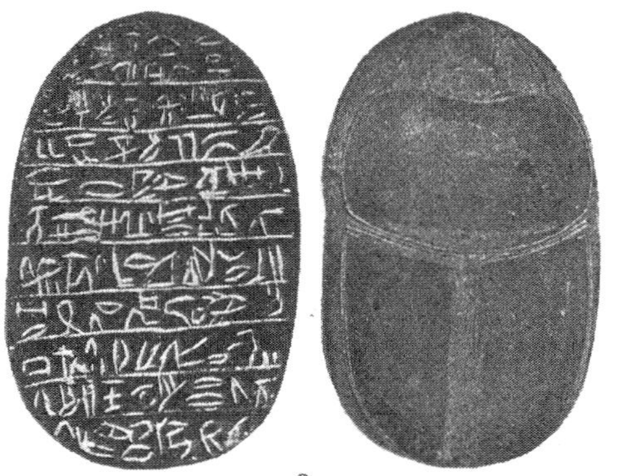
9

10

11

13

14

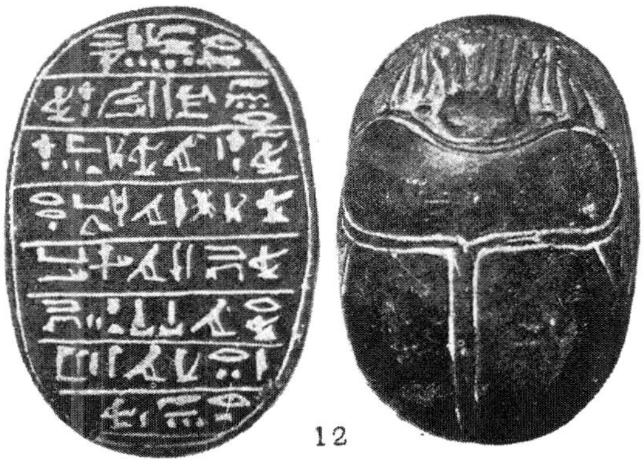
12

15

16

17

18

19

20

21

22

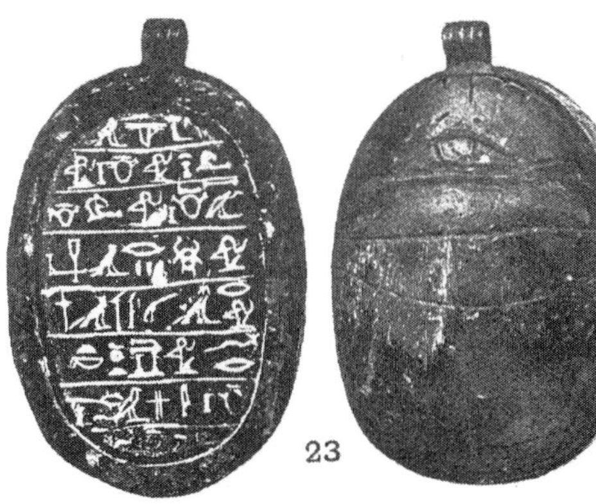
23

24

25

26

27

28

29

HEART SCARABS (*continued*)

Ab 17 NEB TA ZESER, Osiris *Lord of the underworld;* NEB PET Isis *Lady of heaven;* and Nebhat ASAR NEBT PER SHUR(A). *The Osirian, Lady of the house, Shura.* Style as pectoral of Set·ha·em·hapy Amulets 91 b. Black steatite

Ab 18 Phrases from chapter of the heart. AR NE SETMESSU, *made by Setmessu.* Name of xixth dynasty Gone white

Ab 19 ZED MEDU AN ASAR SESH NASHUY. *Say words by the Osirian, Scribe, Nashuy,* and opening of heart chapter Pottery. Green. In copper frame E. 23

Ab 20 ASAR NEBT PER SHEMOYT NE AMEN THENT·EM·MAY (skin det.). Chapter of the heart. *The Osirian, lady of the house, chantress of Amen, Thentem·may.* (Name xviii–xxii) Green jade

Ab 21 ASAR APIY. *Osirian Apiy.* Chapter of the heart. Name late xviiith and early xixth Green jade

The following are of a coarse class of front and back, from xixth to xxiiird dynasties.

Ab 22 A·NEFER. Chapter of the heart. Perhaps before xixth as work is better than the following, and name is early Durite

Ab 23 UOB MIN·EM·HOT. *Priest, Minemhot.* Chapter of the heart In silver frame. Hard yellow limestone

Ab 24 SESH AMEN·MES. *Scribe, Amenmes.* Traces of bennu painted on back. Formerly in a pectoral. Name early xviiith to xxth Durite

Ab 25 ASAR, NEBT PER, SHEMOYT AMEN, SHEBT·MER·NE·AST. Chapter of the heart. *The Osirian, lady of the house, Chantress of Amen, Shebt·mer·ne·ast* Durite

Ab 26 ASAR, UOB OA AMEN, ZED·PTAH·A·ONKH. *The Osirian, chief priest of Amen, Zed·ptah·auf·onkh* Durite

Ab 27 NESUT DA HETEP NE ASAR, DA KHEB NE HETEP THU NE KA NE ASAR HER·SĂ·AST. *Offering given by the king for Osiris, give coolness of peace to him, for the Ka of the Osirian, Hersa·ast* Black steatite

Ab 28 NESUT DA HETEP ASAR . . . . . . (NE KA) NE PETPETUR SĂ . . . . . RUD, AR UABT HER P·H(ĂU) NE·USER·KHO·RA P·ONKH RUD . . . . . *Offering given by the king for Osiris . . . . for the Ka of Petpetur, son of . . . . . . rud, born of the priest of Horus Pahau·neuser khora.* As Userkhora is Setnekht, it appears that the grandfather belonged to that king; hence this scarab is of xxth dynasty. Blue paste

Ab 29 NESUT KHAKER AUUĂAĂ. *The royal adorner Auuăaă* Wooden label, signs painted blue

Two-thirds size, except 17, and the inscriptions of 24, 25, 26, and 28.

XXIst DYNASTY

21·1. 21·1. NESI·BA·NEB·ZEDU (TANITE LINE)

1 RA·KHEPER·HEZ, SETEP·NE·RA. Back and colour as Painezem I, differs from Sheshenq I — Strong green — J. 43

QUEEN THENTAMEN

2 THENTAMEN NEB APT — Gone white — F. 73A

21·2. 21·2. PA·SEB·KHO·NUT I

1, 2 RA·OĂ·KHEPER, SETEP·NE·AMEN. Reverse, AMEN·MER PA·SEB·KHO·NUT. Foundation deposits. Tanis. Pottery. Green — 1 : 2

3 (MER) AMEN·RA·NESUT·NETERU PA·SEB·KHO·NUT — Pottery. Blue-green — Ring

21·5. 21·5. SĂ·AMEN

1 NETER NEFER, NEBTA, RA·NETER·KHEPER, MA AMEN. Sphinx offering Măot to the Ra falcon — Gone yellow — Q. 60

2 RA·NETER·KHEPER, A(MEN), SETEP·NE·RA — Gone brown — F. 72

3 RA·NETER·KHEPER, SETEP·NE·AMEN — Gone white — G. 66

4 NEB TAUI, RA·NETER·KHEPER, AMEN(MER). Foundation deposits Tanis — Copper plate — Flat

5 RA·NETER·KHEPER, NEB (T blundered as Ra) — Pottery. Green — N. 52

6 ,, ,, ,, — Blue paste — V. 93

7 O·HER·NETER·KHEPER AR NEB. Apparently blundered from previous type — Gone white — G. 66

8 RA·NETER·KHEPER, SETEP·NE·RA, NEFER — Gone white — G. 44

9 RA·MEN·NETER·KHEPER, MEN RA. Joint scarab of Menkheperra Theban, and Saamen — Gone white — Broken

10 SĂ·AMEN, MER AMEN — Edwards. Gone yellow — G. 20

11 SĂ·AMEN, MER AMEN. Reverse, RA·MEN·KHEPER, the Theban king — Gone yellow — Curved

21·6. 21·6. PA·SEB·KHO·NUT II

HER PA·SEB·KHO·NUT — Pottery bead, green glaze, black writing. Long groove in back

21·3. 21·3. PAINEZEM I (THEBAN LINE)

1 RA·KHEPER·KHO, SETEP·NE·AMEN; AMEN·MER, PĂI·NEZEM — Ivory knob of walking-stick

2 RA·KHEPER·KHO, AMEN NEB — Bright green — J. 49

3 ,, Nile figure kneeling — Meydum. Gone white — W. 57

4 RA·KHEPER. Nile figure kneeling. Blundered — Gone white — T. 64

21·4. 21·4. MEN·KHEPER·RA

RA·MEN·KHEPER in cartouche. *Menat* from a mummy; stamped white leather, mounted on red leather

22·1. *XXIInd DYNASTY*. 22·1. SHESHENQ I

1 SEKHEM PEH·TI (Horus on Nubti name) — Blue faded — Broken

2, 3 RA·HEZ·KHEPER, SETEP·NE·RA — Pottery, gone white. Gone brown — N. 95, G. 56

4, 5 ,, ,, — Gone white. Edwards. Gone white — F. 72, G. 8

6, 7 ,, ,, — Gone brown. Pottery, Blue faded. — H. 76 — Flat

8 RA·HEZ·KHEPER — Gone brown — K. 50

9, 10 NEB TAUI, AMEN·MER, SHESH; NESUT BAT, RA·HEZ·KHEPER, SETEP·NE·RA, ONKH ONKH NUB.
Lord of both lands, loved by Amen, Sheshenq; King Hez·kheper·ra, approved of Ra
Green. Edwards, pottery blue — F. 19, E. 16

11 RA·HEZ·KHEPER SHE; AMEN SHESH. Legs pierced through — Gone white — E. 82

12 RA·HEZ-SEKHEM-KHEPER, SHESHENK. Joint scarab of Sheshenq I and Usarken I — Pottery. Gone drab — F. 51

13, 14 AMEN·MER, SHESH — Pottery. Green. White limestone. — F. 38, L. 88

22·2. 22·2. USARKEN I

1 RA·SEKHEM·KHEPER, SETEP·NE·RA. — In gold mounting for a ring. Red jasper — L. 38

2, 3 ,, ,, — Both blue paste — K. 50 ?, G. 22

4 AMEN·RA, NEB PET, NESUT NETERU, MER, DA ONKH.
By Amen Ra, lord of heaven, king of the gods, beloved, granted life, over Amen-Min.
NETER NEFER, RA·SEKHEM·KHEPER, SETEP·NE·RA; SĂ RA, AMEN·MER, UASĂRKEN.
To the Good God, Sekhem-kheper-Ra, approved by Ra; son of Ra, loved by Amen Usarken, embracing Amen.
From a burial at the Ramesseum. End of a stole from a mummy. Stamped white leather in red frame.

5 AMEN·RA, NEB PET, MER, DA ONKH over Amen-Min, adored by Usarken. Names as above.
Found at the Ramesseum. Stamped white leather, red leather frame lost.

6 KHENSU EM UAST NEFER HETEP MER. *By Khensu Nefer-hetep in Thebes, beloved*, Khensu standing adored by SĂ·RA, AMEN·MER, UASĂRKEN. Ramesseum. Stamped white leather in red leather frame.

7 NETER NEFER, RA·SEKHEM·KHEPER, SETEP·NE·RA; SĂ·RA, AMEN·MER, UASĂRKEN.
Ramesseum. Menat from mummy. Stamped white leather, in red leather frame.

DYNASTIES XXI, XXII TO USARKEN I

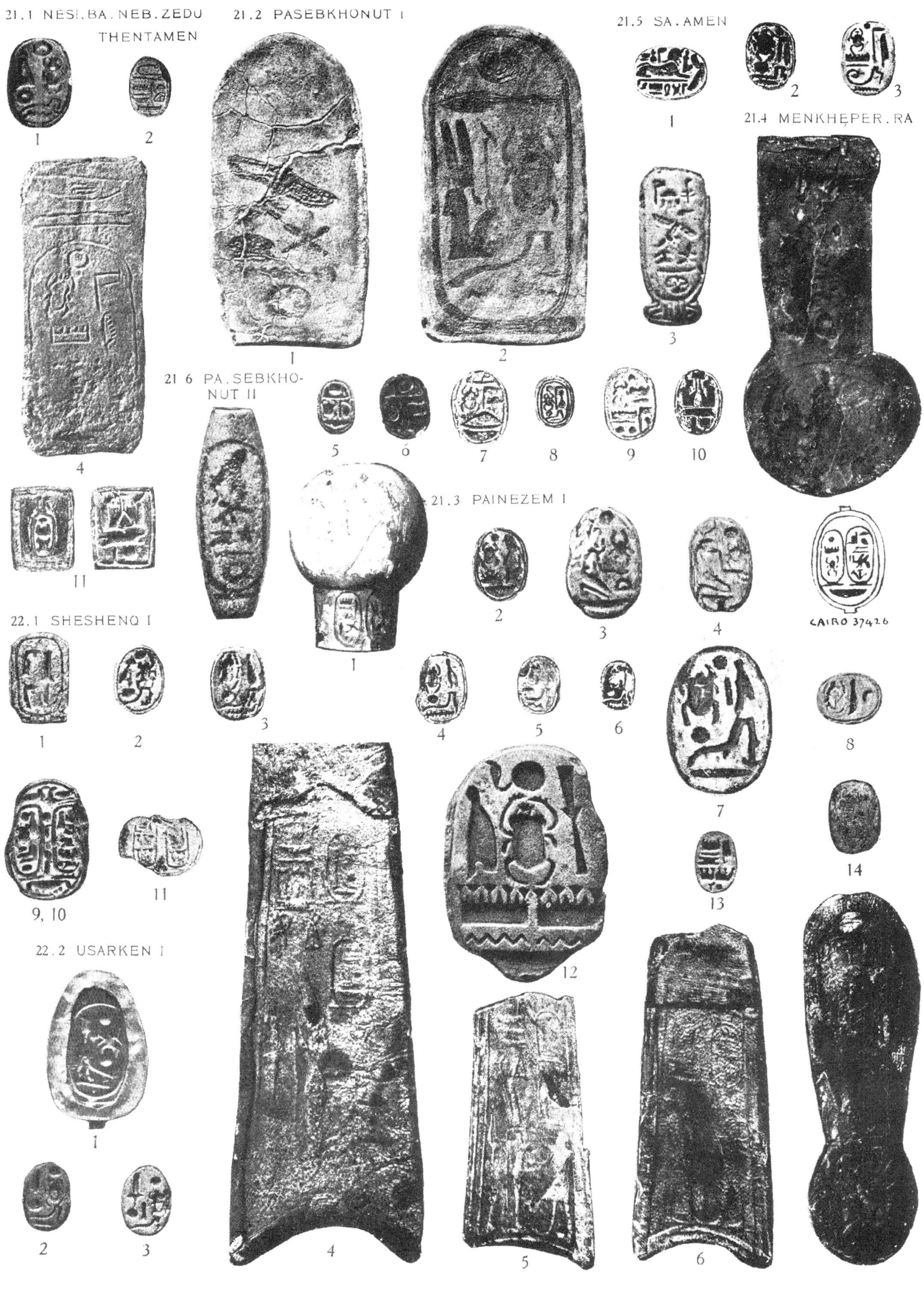

22.3 TAKERAT I

KAROMOA

1 2 3 4 5 6 7

22.4 USARKEN II

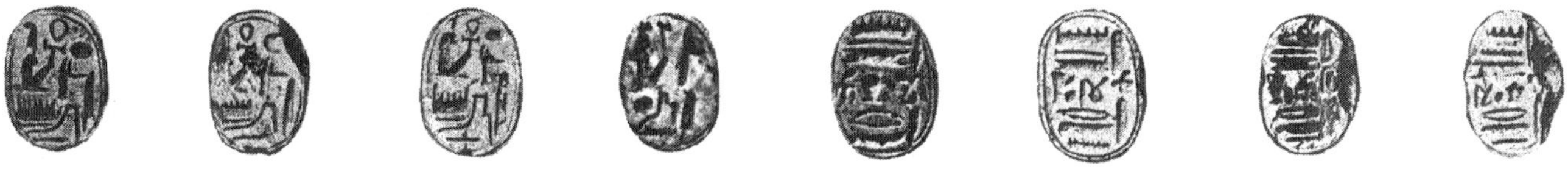

1 2 3 4 5 6 7 8

22.5 SHESHENQ II

22.6 TAKERAT II

22.7 SHESHENQ III

1 2 3 4

5 6 7 8

MEN.NEH.RA

22.8 PAMAY

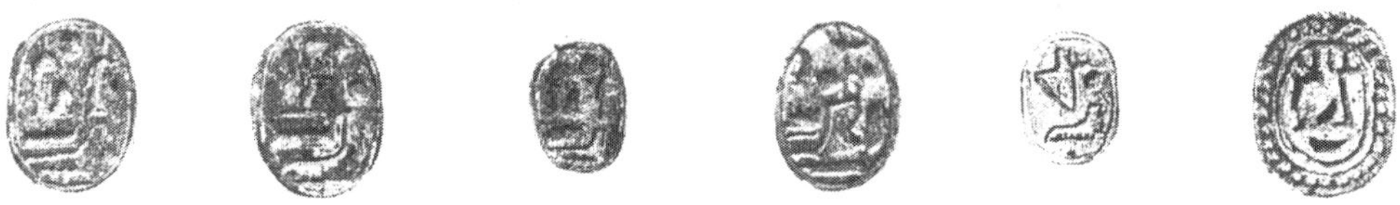

1 2 3 4 5 6

22.9 SHESHENQ IV

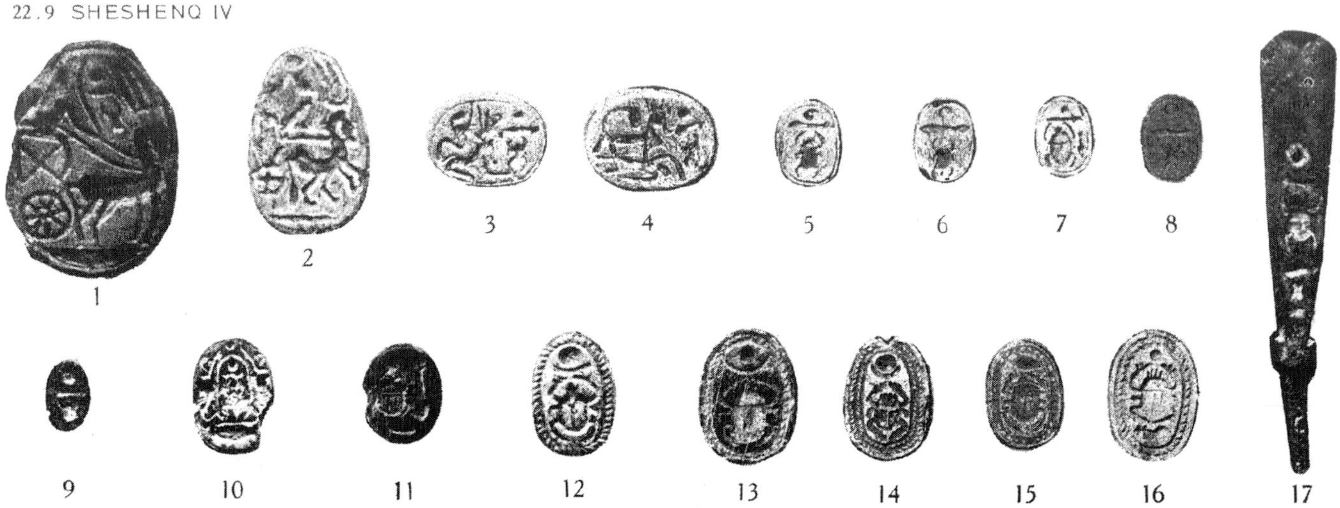

1 2 3 4 5 6 7 8

9 10 11 12 13 14 15 16 17

22·3.

22·3. TAKERAT I

1 RA·USER·MĂOT, AMEN·SETEP·NE — Gone buff F. 63
2, 3 ,, ,, — Gone buff. Gone red-buff F. 76, F. 69
4, 5 ,, ,, — Gone white. Gone brown T. 54, F. 97
6, 7 ,, ,, — Gone brown. Gone white W. 50, F. 74

22·4.

22·4. USARKEN II

1 RA·USER·MĂOT, AMEN·SETEP·NE — Gone brown E. 37
2 ,, ,, — Gone white G. 22
3 ,, ,, — Gone white F. 97
4 ,, ,, blundered — Gone white E. 61
5 AMEN·MER, SĂ·BASTET, UASĂRKEN — Gone grey F. 69
6 ,, ,, ,, — Gone buff E. 72
7 ,, ,, ,, — Gone white F. 63
8 ,, ,, ,, — Gone white F. 96

22·5.

22·5. SHESHENQ II

UPT PTAH RENPET NEFER NE REPOTI SHESHENQ MĂOT KHERU MUT KAROMO.
Open Ptah a year that is good, for the heir Sheshenq, justified, from his mother Karema — Lazuli L. 35
The personal possession of the prince, much worn on the back by use.

22·6.

22·6. TAKERAT II

RA·HEZ·KHEPER, SETEP·NE·RA. By the extreme rudeness, this is after Sheshenq I — Pottery. Dark green F. 98

22·7.

22·7. SHESHENQ III

1, 2, 3 RA·USER·MĂOT, AMEN·SETEP·NE — All gone white G. 68, G. 76, F. 76?
4 ,, ,, — Gone brown V. 77
5 ,, SETEP·NE·RA MĂOT feather. Reverse, Three figures of Bes — Gone grey Flat
6 ,, ,, ,, Reverse, Four uraei, two figures of Măot — Gone dark grey Flat
7 ,, ,, ,, Reverse, King smiting enemy, lion below — Gone white Flat
8 ,, SETEP — Pottery. Olive-green Flat

MEN·NEH·RA

RA·MEN·NEH ("Ra establishes confidence"). MĂOT feather. Reverse, as No. 8 previous. Both sides show this period — Gone white

22·8.

22·8. PAMAY

1, 2, 3 RA·USER·MĂOT, SETEP·NE·(A)MEN — All gone brown. G. 76, G. 60, G. 68
4 ,, SETEP·NE·AMEN — Gone brown (like J. 69) Q. 76
5 ,, SETEP·NE·RA — Gone brown E. 86
6 USER·MĂOT·NEB. By the rope border this is kin to Sheshenq IV — Pottery. Green M. 84

22·9.

22·9. SHESHENQ IV

1 RA·OĂ·KHEPER. King in chariot — Green F. 58
2 King in chariot, of same style as the preceding — Green F. 29
3 RA·OĂ·KHEPER. Sphinx crowned and uraeus — Blue paste F. 46
4 ,, Sphinx trampling on enemy — Blue paste F. 46
5 RA·OĂ·KHEPER — Gone white J. 74
6 ,, bronze pin of a ring through it — Gone white E. 16
7 ,, NEFER — Gone white W. 35
8, 9 ,, — Both gone yellow. W. 33, L. 33
10 ,, between crowned uraei — Grey steatite E. 63
11 ,, OĂ misformed as NEFER — Green K. 96
12, 13, 14, 15 RA·OĂ·KHEPER in rope border, blundered in 13, 14, 15 — 2 gone buff. Gone white. Gone grey. T. 41, T. 40, J. 29, T. 40
16 RA KHEPER·OĂ, misformed as NEFER — Gone white H. 74
12–16 are of the Hyksos type of back; and the rope border is like that of the private scarabs xiii H–P.
17 RA·OĂ·KHEPER — Model oar. Bronze. Flat

XXIIIrd DYNASTY

23·1. 23·1. PEDASĂBASTET

MER KHETM RASEHERAB SA, PSEMTHEK. *Keeper of the seal of Pedasabastet's priesthood, Psamtek* Clay
This impression of a seal shows that this priesthood existed down to the xxvith dynasty.

23·2. 23·2. USARKEN III

1 RA·KHEPER, SETEP·NE·AMEN. The title separates this from Sheshenq IV, and the rude style from Pasebkhonu I Pottery. Blue. Handle
2 NESUT BAT, RA·KHEPER, AMEN MER. This, and others, are dated by the name on No. 1 Gone white, worn. G. 20 ?
3 RA·KHEPER. Ra with uraei as on ring of this king at Leyden Pottery. Blue J. 83
4 RA·KHEPER between crowned uraei, two baboons adoring Ra Gone brown E. 28
5 ,, between spread falcons Pottery. Olive-green N. 36
6, 7 ,, in rope border Gone brown. Pottery, Olive green T. 78, W. 94
8, 9 ,, Pottery, Green-blue. Gone white N. 32, J. 4
10 ,, Lahun. Green T. 64
11 ,, double Lahun. Green L. 40
12 ,, Green N. 42
13 RA·KHEPER·NEB in rope border Grey steatite K. 20
14 Ra with uraei, MEN; RA·KHEPER repeated Gone buff. Sphinx
15 NUB·OĂ·KHEPER (same king ?) Pottery. Green L. 52

23·2. RA·OĂ·KHEPER·NEB. Perhaps of Usarken III

A RA·OĂ·KHEPER·NEB; MĂOT NEB. Reverse, Three standing figures, winged sun and vulture above Gone buff Flat
B RA·KHEPER·NEB; MĂOT MĂOT MER. Back like xxii·9, 3 and 4 Pottery. Green F. 38
C ,, ,, ,, Reverse, RA·MEN·KHEPER. Likexxiii·2·9 Pottery. Blue-green J. 67

23. VASSALS OF PANKHY. SHESHENQ V OF BUSIRIS

D RA·UAS·NETER, SETEP·NE·RA; SHESH AMEN UAS NETER AN Bronze Flat

PEMA of Mendes

E REPOTI HO, NETER HEN ASAR NEB ZEDU, SAR OĂ PEMA.
Hereditary prince, Priest of Osiris lord of Mendes, Great chief, Pema Soft paste. Gone yellow M. 92

ONKH·HER of Hermopolis Parva

F RA·MĂOT·NEB, ONKH HER Gone white. Worn L. 33 ?

NEFER·PTAH

G UZĂT·ER·ZEHUTI NE ATY, HES NETER NEFER, HO HOU, PTAH·NEFER Edwards. Naukratis. Gone white W. 55
(Offerer of) Uzat to Tehuti for the king, by favour of the good god, Prince of Princes Nefer·ptah.

PRIVATE PERSONS

H NETER HEN NE AMEN·RA NESUT NETERU, HER; SĂ NE NETER HEN NE AMEN, NEKHTEF·MUT
Prophet of Amenra, king of the gods, Her; son of the prophet of Amen, Nekhtefmut. Green quartz Z. 94
J AST·MER·NE. *Merneast* Green felspar Z. 97
K ZED MEDU AN ZEHUTI NEB KHEMENU, NETER OĂ, NEB PET; DA ONKH UZA SENB NE SĂ NE NETER HEN TEP NE AMEN UA·SĂK·UASĂ, MĂOT·KHERU; SĂ NE NETER HEN TEP NE AMEN AU·UAR·UATH, MĂOT·KHERU. *Say the words to Tehuti, Lord of Hermopolis, great god, lord of heaven; give life, health and strength for the son of the chief prophet of Amen Uasakuasa, justified; son of the chief prophet of Amen, Au·uar·uath, justified* Electrum. Pectoral

XXVth DYNASTY

25·1. 25·1. PANKHY I

. . . NE ĂU AB NEB NE NESUT BAT RA·USER·MĂOT, SĂ RA. . . . *of all joy for the king Ra·user·maot* Pale-blue-grey. Stoneware
Part of a statuette; by the colour and work close to the xxvith dynasty.

25·2. 25·2. KASHTA

1 NESUT KASHTA; DUĂT NETER AMEN ARDAS. *King Kashta; High priestess Amenardas* Pottery. Blue-green J. 93
2 ? NESUT BAT, DA UAS, RA·NEFER·NUB. Falcon-headed sphinx on southern plant. Set-headed sphinx on northern plant. Reverse, Ram-headed scarab, therefore of Ethiopian dynasty Gone red buff. Broken, as R. 60, 25·3·19
3 ? RA·NUB·NEFER Pottery. Gone brown. Worn N. 22

23.1 PEDA SA BASTET

23.2 USARKEN III

1 2 3 4

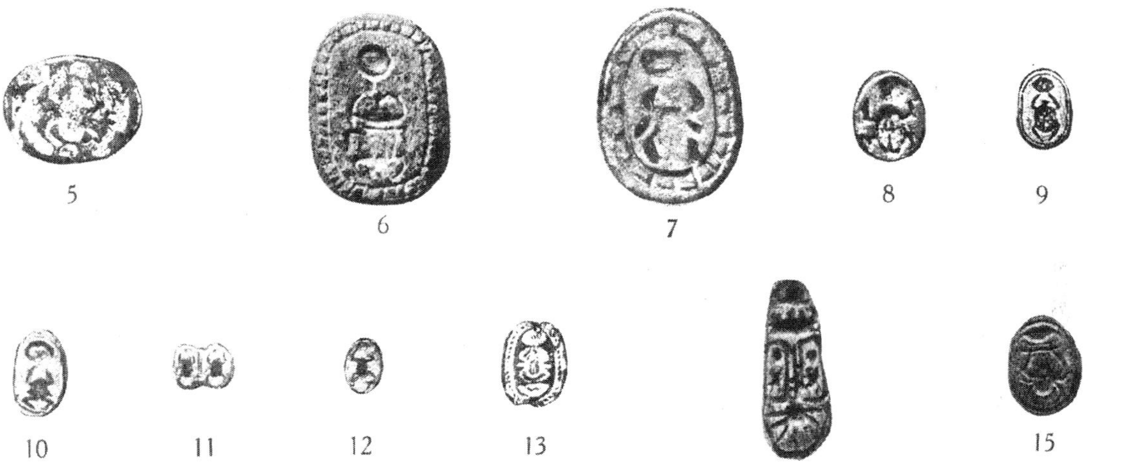

5 6 7 8 9

10 11 12 13 14 15

KHEPER.NEB.RA

A B C

SHESHENQ V

D

PEMA

E

ONKH.HER

F

PTAN.NEFER

G

HER

H

MERNEAST

J

25.1 PANKHY I

UASAKAUASA

K

25.2 KASHTA

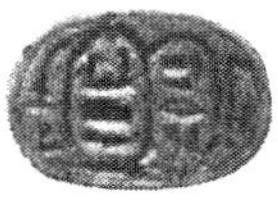

1

NUB.NEFER.RA

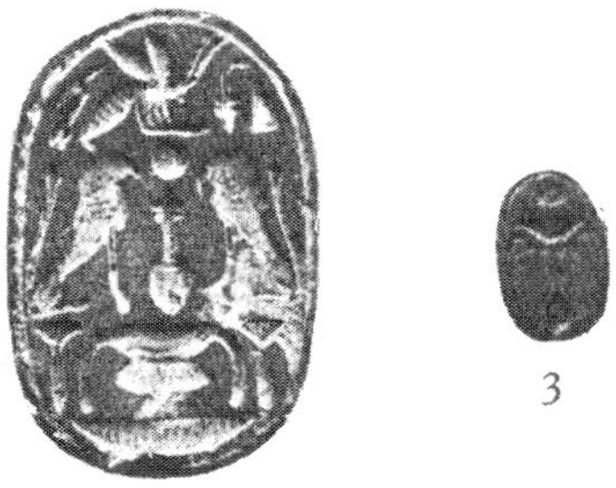

2 3

AMENARDAS
4 5 6 3 4 5 6 7 8
9 10 11 13 14 15 16--18 19
25.3 SHABAKA
1 2
25.4 SHABATAKA
1 2
25 A. MENKARA vassal of SHABAKA
20 21 22 23 24
3 4 5 6
PANKHY II
CAIRO 36608
25.5 TAHARQA
1 2 3
4 5 6 7 8
ASPERUTA

25·2.

25·2. AMENARDAS

4 DUĂT NETER, HEMT NETER, AMENARDAS. *Adorer of the god,* (high priestess), *wife of the god* — Foundation plaque. Pottery. Green and black inlay — Flat
5 DUĂT NETER AMENARDAS — Pottery. Gone brown — Uzat
6 . . . NEB, ĂUT AB NEB, (AMEN)ARDAS. Reverse . . . . NE KHENSU . . . UAST DA
. . . all . . . . . . , all joy, Amenardas. of Khensu . . . . . Thebes, give — Thin plate of lazuli — Flat

25·3.

25·3. SHABAKA

1 HES NEB AMEN·RA NE MER RA·NEFER·KA. *Praise from the king, beloved by Amenra* — Pottery. Gone white — Q. 45
2 Lotus group. RA·NEFER·KA. Spread falcon — Gone white — Q. 40
3 NESUT BAT RA·NEFER·KA. Reverse, Ram of Amen beneath sacred tree, uraeus in front — Gone brown
4 RA·NEFER·KA — Gone grey — J. 58
5 ,, — Green. Rude — F. 53
6 ,, — Pottery. Gone black — E. 73
7 ,, — Pottery. Blue — R. 66
8 ,, vertical hole throughout — Pottery. Green — Flat
9 ,, two cross thread holes — Pottery. Dark blue — Ridge
10 ,, ,, ,, — Pottery. Yellow — Ridge
11 ,, ,, ,, — Pottery. Blue-green — Ridge
12 ,, vertical hole (not figured) — Pottery. Green — Flat
13 ,, uzat above. Two cross holes — Pottery. Gone white — Flat
14 ,, — Lazuli — Bead
15 NESUT BAT, RA·NEFER·KA, ONKH ZETTA. Vertical hole — Pottery. Olive-green — Flat
16, 17, 18 SĂ RA SHABAKA, ONKH ZETTA. Vertical hole — All pottery. 2 green. Gone grey — Flat
19 HES NEB AMEN·RA DA ONKH UAS SHABAKA
Praise from the king to Amen·ra, giving life and power to Shabaka — Gone white. Ram head — R. 60

25·A. MENKARA vassal of Shabaka (of Bubastis ?)

20 HA RA·MEN·KA, RA·NEFER·KA. *Ruler in the north (?) Menkara, Shabaka* — Edwards. Pottery. Gone black. — Cylinder
21 RA·MEN·KA. Sphinx — Pottery. Gone yellow — J. 69
22 RA·MEN·KA. Falcon — Pottery. Olive-green — Z. 97
23 RA·MEN·KA twice, Falcon and Bastet standing — Blue paste — L. 3
24 HER·RA·MEN·KA. Bastet standing — Green glaze. Gone brown — J. 2

25·4.

25·4. SHABATAKA

1 RA·ZED·KA·KA (full name has KAU) — Gone grey — Broken
2 RA·ZED·KA — Pottery. Green — Z. 65
3 RA·ZED·KA — Pottery. Olive-green, red inlay — Flat
4 ,, — Heart. Blue glass — Plain
5 ,, Uzat and name twice repeated — Pottery. Burnt red — Bead
6 ,, ,, ,, — Pottery. Full blue — Bead

25·5.

25·5. TAHARQA

1 RA·NEFER·ATMU·KHU — Pottery. Blue-green — E. 2
2 NESUT BAT, TAHARQA, ONKH ZETTA. *King Taharqa, living eternally* — Gone red and white — M. 24
3 RA NEB TAHARQA. King adoring Ra — Gone white — J. 78
4 HES NEB RA NESUT BAT TAHARQA. *Praise from the king to Ra, king Taharqa* — Gone red and white. Ram head
5 TAHARQA between Măot feathers — Gone grey — J. 78
6 TAHARQA in rope border. Legs pierced through — Pottery. Gone white — F. 4
7 TAHARQA — Pottery. Blue-green — F. 9
8 TAHARQA between uraei — Pottery. Gone brown — F. 9

ASPERUTA

ASPERUTA, between uraei — Pottery. Gone brown — Flat

25·B.

25·B. RA·MEN·HER (vassal of Khmeny)

1, 2, 3 RA·MEN·HER, NETER NEFER — Gone white. Gone brown. Gone light brown. T. 86, Z. 50, F. 93
4 RA·MEN·HER, NETER ONKH. *The living God* — Gone white F. 93
5 RA·MEN·HER S — Pottery. Gone white F. 31
6, 7 RA·MEN·HER — Pottery. Green. Gone brown. G. 58, H. 54
8 RA·MEN·HER NEFER. Ra with uraei — Gone brown P. 82
9, 10 RA·MEN·HER MĂOT MER. *Loved by Maot* — Gone brown. Gone grey. F. 66, P. 15
11, 12 RA·MEN·HER — Both gone grey. Broken K. 42
13 ,, Cross lines at sides — Gone brown P. 10
14 ,, Figures at sides — Edwards. Gone buff P. 84
15 ,, *deshert* crown at sides, uraei becoming square — Gone brown P. 90
16, 17 ,, *deshert* blundered, uraei quite square — Edwards. Gone grey. Gone white. P. 74, P. 84
18, 19 ,, *deshert* and square uraei — Gone brown. Gone grey. P. 86, P. 70
20 NEKHT RA·MEN·HER. Possibly *Nekht* is the personal name, see Tafnekht — Gone brown P. 10

25·C.

25·C. RA·MEN·KHEPER, KHMENY with vassal RA·MEN·HER

1, 2, 3 RA·MEN·KHEPER in cartouche; RA·MEN·HER, never took a cartouche. All gone brown P. 10. P. 84. P. 82
4 ,, ,, ,, Upside down — Gone brown P. 10
5 RA·MEN·KHEPER—NE·HER. Double reading — Gone white P. 78
6 RA·NE·HER, RA·MEN KHEPER at sides. Upside down — Gone brown P. 15

RA·MEN·KHEPER, KHMENY alone (Cairo 36190)

7 RA·MEN·KHEPER, see border of 5, and B·13 — Gone brown P. 84
8 ,, upside down — Gone brown P. 55
9 ,, seated figure of king — Gone brown P. 74
10 ,, vulture of Mut and crocodile — Edwards. Gone brown F. 52
11 ,, HER NEFER. *The good Horus* — Edwards. Gone brown Uzat
12 ,, spread falcon — Edwards. Gone grey T. 61
13 ,, blundered — Edwards. Naukratis. Gone white M. 35
14 MEN·KHEPER. Sphinx and falcon — Edwards. Gone grey G. 22
15 RA·MEN·KHEPER between spread falcons — Gone yellow W. 45
16 RA·MEN·KHEPER, MER·ZED. Reverse, sphinx over the Zed flanked by uraei — Gone buff Flat
17 RA·MEN·KHEPER, SETEP NE (A)MEN — Lahun. Green L. 97
18 RA·MEN·KHEPER, MENY NEFER — Gone buff Cylinder
19 RA, Lion, NE MENKHY, probably blundered — Gone brown E. 40
20, 21 RA·MEN·KHEPER, KHMENY — Gone white. Gone yellow. E. 98, V. 85
22 KHMENY KHEPEREK ER REN. *Thou becomest with a cartouche* (Cairo 36145) — Gone white G. 48
23 ,, ,, ,, with line after KH, reading RA·MEN·KHEPER — Gone buff F. 40

25·D.

25·D. RA·MEN·AB

1 RA·MEN·AB, KHMENY. Khmeny as a vassal of Men·ab·ra. Legs pierced — Blue paste K. 10
2, 3 RA·MEN·AB, NETER DA ER MEN, ONKH HER ONKH. Another blundered.
Gone white. Gone brown. G. 22, G. 80
4 RA·MEN·AB, MĂOT MER. *Beloved by Măot*
5 RA·MEN·AB between uraei crowned — Gone white Broken
6 ,, uraeus — Apple-green N. 70
7, 8 ,, MĂOT NEB — Gone white, Gone grey, both W. 24
9, 10, 11 ,, UAS NEB. *Lord of Thebes*
Pottery; Gone drab. Pottery; Gone white. Gone white. W. 70, W. 70, G. 74
12 RA·AB, UAS NEB — Pottery. Gone white W. 24
13 RA·MEN·AB UAS NEB — Pottery. Green E. 83
14 RA·MEN·AB UAS — Gone brown R. 36
15 RA·MEN·AB ? — Pottery. Olive J. 37

25 B. MEN.HER.RA

25 C. MEN.KHEPER.RA WITH MEN HER RA

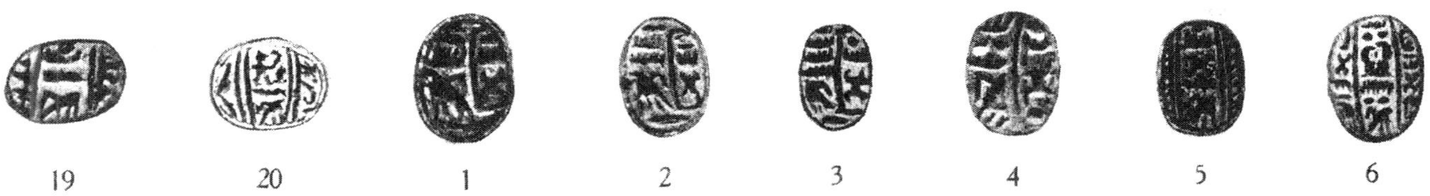

MEN.KHEPER.RA KHMENY

25 D. MEN.AB RA

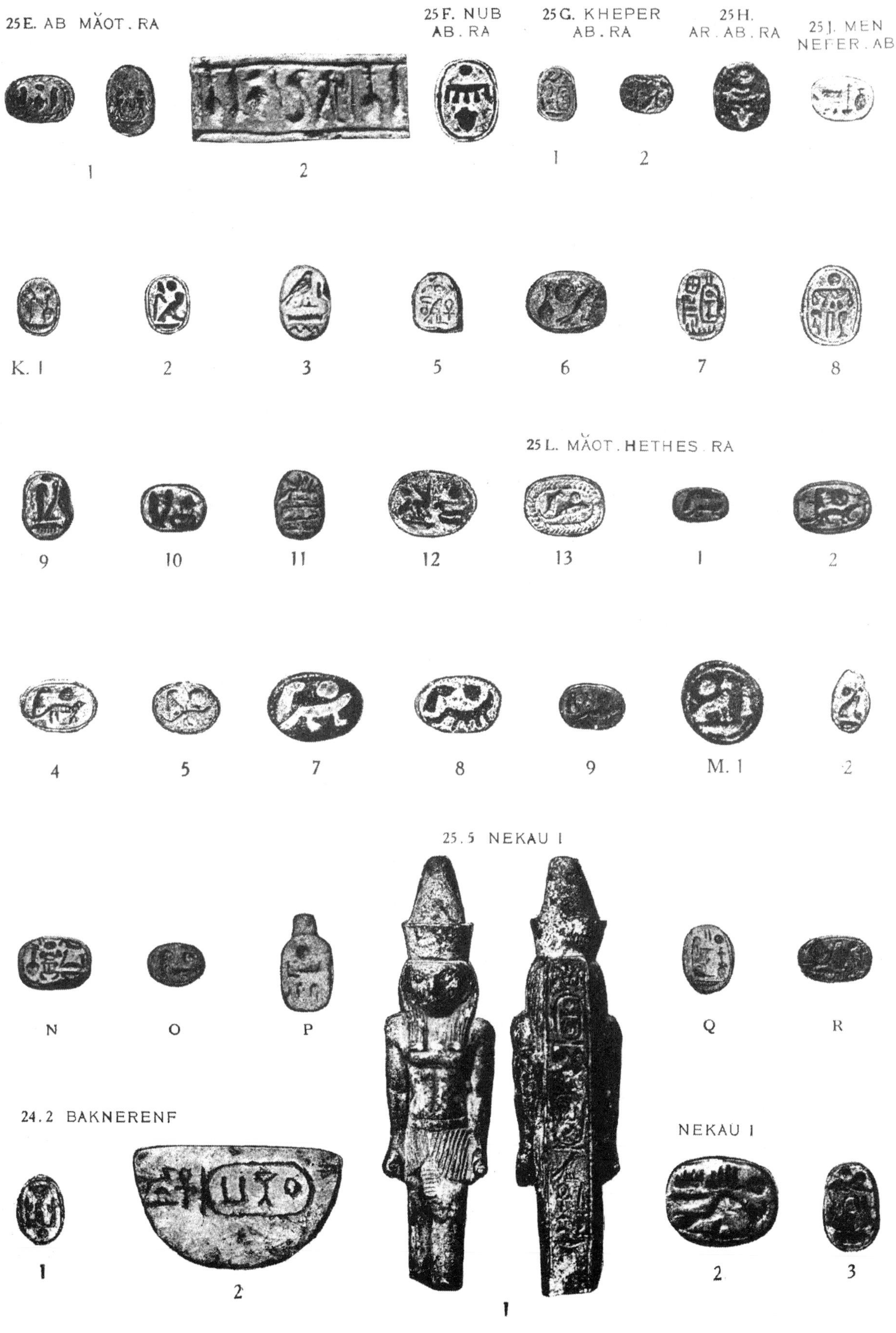

25 E. AB MĂOT. RA — 1, 2

25 F. NUB AB. RA

25 G. KHEPER AB. RA — 1, 2

25 H. AR. AB. RA

25 J. MEN NEFER. AB

K. 1, 2, 3, 5, 6, 7, 8, 9, 10, 11, 12, 13

25 L. MĂOT. HETHES. RA — 1, 2, 4, 5, 7, 8, 9

M. 1, 2

N, O, P, Q, R

25. 5 NEKAU I — 1

24. 2 BAKNERENF — 1, 2

NEKAU I — 2, 3

25·E. RA·AB·MAOT

25·E.

1	RA·AB·MĂOT in rope border; reverse, Hapi and Neferatum joining hands, NEB below	Pottery.	Apple-green	
2	RA·AB·MĂOT NEFER. Standing figure and uraeus		Apple-green	Cylinder

25·F. RA·NUB·AB

25·F.

	RA·NUB·AB	Pottery.	Green	G. 82

25·G. RA·KHEPER·AB

25·G.

1	RA and Lion (vassal of Psamtek ?). RA·KHEPER·AB, MĂOT NEB	Blue paste	N. 20
2	RA·KHEPER·AB. Sphinx seated	Blue paste	N. 20

25·H. RA·AR·AB

25·H.

RA·AR·AB	Pottery, Green	N. 20

25·J. MEN·NEFER·AB

25·J.

MEN·NEFER·AB	Paste.	Yellow	N. 6

25·K. Probable Royal names

25·K.

1	RA·NEFER·UAS·NEB. *Ra the excellent, lord of Thebes*		Light blue	W. 26
2	RA·EM·UAS·NEB. *Ra is lord in Thebes*	Pottery.	Gone white	W. 26
3, 4	HER·MEN. Legs pierced through (another, not figured, gone buff, L. 52)		Green	F. 74
5	ONKH HER, TH·AB (?)		Gone grey	L. 63
6	HER RA·NEFER		Gone red	P. 20
7	RA·NEFER, Seated figure		Gone white	Broken
8	RA·NUB·HEN·S·MĂOT	Pottery.	Gone buff	L. 68
9	RA·MĂOT·NUB		Gone white	G. 68
10	,,		Green	Z. 94
11	NESUT BAT THETET		Gone buff	T. 11
12	RA·MENTH RA·BAT·NEB		Gone brown	T. 33

25·L. RA·MĂOT·HETHES

25·L.

1	RA·MĂOT·HETHES		Gone grey	W. 22
2	,,	Edwards.	Light green	H. 6
3, 4	,, (3 not figured)		Gone buff. Gone grey.	P. 35, P. 65
5, 6	,, (6 not figured)	Both Edwards.	Gone grey. Gone white.	M. 8, F. 59
7	,,	Edwards. Pottery.	Olive	N. 48
8	,,	Pottery.	Olive	N. 48 ?
9	RA·HETHES·AN		Gone buff	J. 5

M·1	RA·MAU·NEB	Pottery.	Burnt brown	Cone
M·2	,,	Edwards. Pottery.	Blue-green	Z. 72
N	RA·KHEPER·NEFER·KA·K (?)		Gone white	E. 77
O	RA·NEB·UAZ	Pottery.	Gone white.	Broken
P	RA·MEN·S uraeus	Pottery.	Blue-green	Flat
Q	RA·NEFER or SEP·NEFER		Gone buff	H. 96
R	NEFER MĂOT SETEP·NE·RA	Pottery.	Gone buff	J. 5

THE PSAMMETICI

24·2. BAKNERENF

24·2.

1	UAH·KA·RA	Gone brown	G. 58
2	RA·UAH·KA, ONKH ZETTA	Foundation deposit plaque. Alabaster	Flat

25·5. NEKAU I (See BM 2529)

25·5.

1	NESUT BAT RA·MEN·KHEPER, SĂ RA NEKAU; HER DA ONKH NEIT NEB SĂU *King Men·kheper·ra, son of Ra, Nekau; the Horus given life by Neit Lady of Sais* Figure of Horus	Pottery. Gone brown	
2	RA·MEN·KHEPER, NEB. Ram of Amen crowned, as in xxvth dynasty (This might belong to Khmeny, but is not like his style.)	Pottery	W. 94
3	RA ZAM (Psemthek I) RA·MEN·KHEPER cartouche adored by Psemthek crowned as king of Upper and Lower Egypt. Posthumous, in honour of Nekau	Light blue	F. 75

XXVIth DYNASTY

26·1. 26·1. PSEMTHEK I

1 RA ZAM (or THAM) PSEMTHEK HER OĂ·AB Pottery. Burnt black H. 88
2 ZAM, PSEM (For the value ZAM or THAM, see list of Edfu, Tanite nome) Gone green-white J. 76
3 RA ZAM on a basis Pottery. Gone brown on white M. 28
4 ,, Teh el Barud. Pottery. Blue, burnt red-brown W. 94
5 ,, on a basis Gone grey J. 99
6, 7, 8 ,, All gone white H. 52, H. 24, E. 59
9 RA ZAM. Lion walking Hard paste. Green E. 75
10 ONKH ZAM. Lion walking Hard paste. Light green G. 22
11 HEZ HER OĂ·AB. *Praise the Falcon name* Gone grey W. 28
12 ,, ,, ,, ,, Gone brown H. 5
13 HER OĂ·AB. Falcon name Grey steatite Z. 35
14 RA·UAH·AB KHO ONKH. King marching. *The living manifestation* Grey steatite W. 20
15 RA-MEN-UAH·AB. Double reading of Psemtek and vassal Men·ab·ra Green, burnt brown J. 47
16 ,, Pottery. Green Z. 86
17 HEZ NEB RA·UAH·AB. *Praise the king* Gone white R. 75
18 HER RA·UAH·AB Hard paste. Gone white M. 32
19 RA·UAH·AB Gone grey-white Z. 5
20 ,, Green K. 90
21 ,, Pottery. Gone white P. 60
22 RA·U·UAH·AB Dark green K. 72
23 ONKH HER·RA PSEMTH blundered Green D. 48
24 RA, MĂOT, NEB; PEMTHEK between feathers Gone grey K. 94
25 RA, MĂOT, NEB, PSEMTHEK. Reverse, RA·SHU·NEB Edwards. Gone white on yellow paste Phot.
26 PSEMTH RA, MĂOT Gone grey W. 28
27 PSEMTHEK. Two feathers Pottery. Olive-green K. 94
28 PSEPEMTHEK, SĂ. Blundered Pottery. Gone drab E. 6
29 PSEMTHEK in plaited border Gone drab. 3 vertical lines on W. 22
30 ,, Gone white. Rude H. 54
31 ,, Edwards. Hard paste. Green J. 87
32 ,, Gone red J. 87
33 ,, TH blundered Green P. 30
34 ,, ,, Pottery. Gone white K. 80
35 PSEM NEB Gone white P. 30
36 ,, Pottery. Pale green L. 69
37 ,, Gone white. Rude H. 54
38 PSEM blundered. Reverse, Head of Hathor Green
39 PSEMTHEK Pottery. Light green Flat
40 PSEMEK blundered. MĂOT seated Gone brown K. 52
41 RA·UAH·AB. Reverse, PSEMTHEK Foundation plaque. Pottery. Olive-green Flat
42 NESUT BAT RA·UAH·AB, SĂ RA PSEMTH(EK). Menat Pottery. Gone white Flat
43 ,, ,, ,, ,, (not figured) Stoneware. Green faded Flat

QUEEN SHEPENAPT, daughter of Amenardas, co-regent with Psemthek

44 NETER DUAT, SHEPENAPT, ONKH. *Divine adorer*, high priestess of Thebes. Foundation block Alabaster
45 NETER NEFER, NEB TAUI, PSEMTHEK, AMEN·RA, KHNEM NEHEH, MER; NETER DUAT SHEPENAPT Heavy silver N. 40

26·A. RA·KHEPER·MĂOT vassal of Psemthek I

46 RA·KHEPER·MĂOT NEB. Reverse, winged sphinx, PEMTHEK between feathers Rope edging. Yellow paste
47 RA·KHEPER·MĂOT Pottery. Gone white N. 66
48 ,, Reverse, Baboon seated Pottery. Olive-green

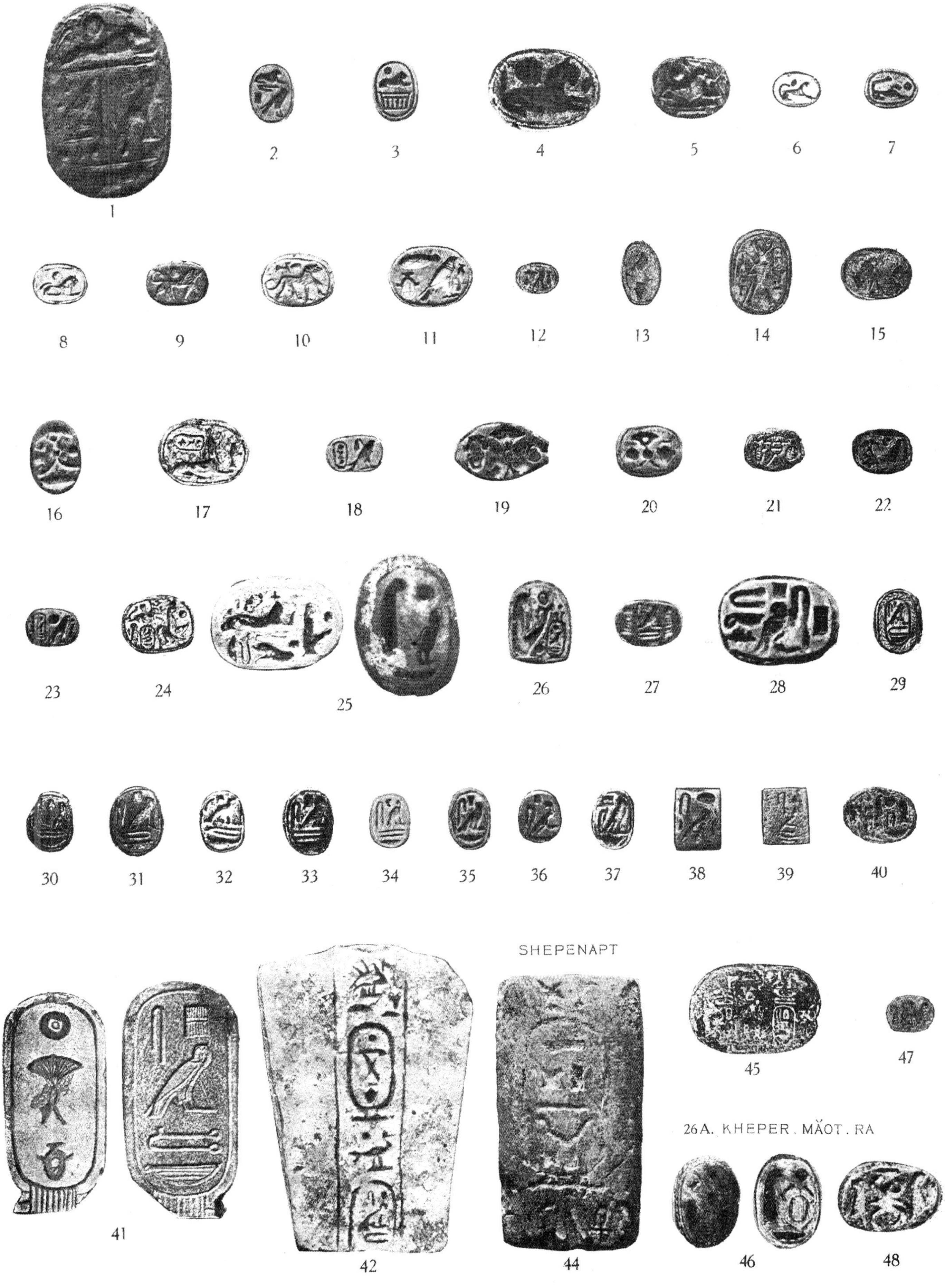
1 2 3 4 5 6 7
8 9 10 11 12 13 14 15
16 17 18 19 20 21 22
23 24 25 26 27 28 29
30 31 32 33 34 35 36 37 38 39 40
SHEPENAPT
41 42 44 45 47
26A. KHEPER. MĂOT. RA
46 48

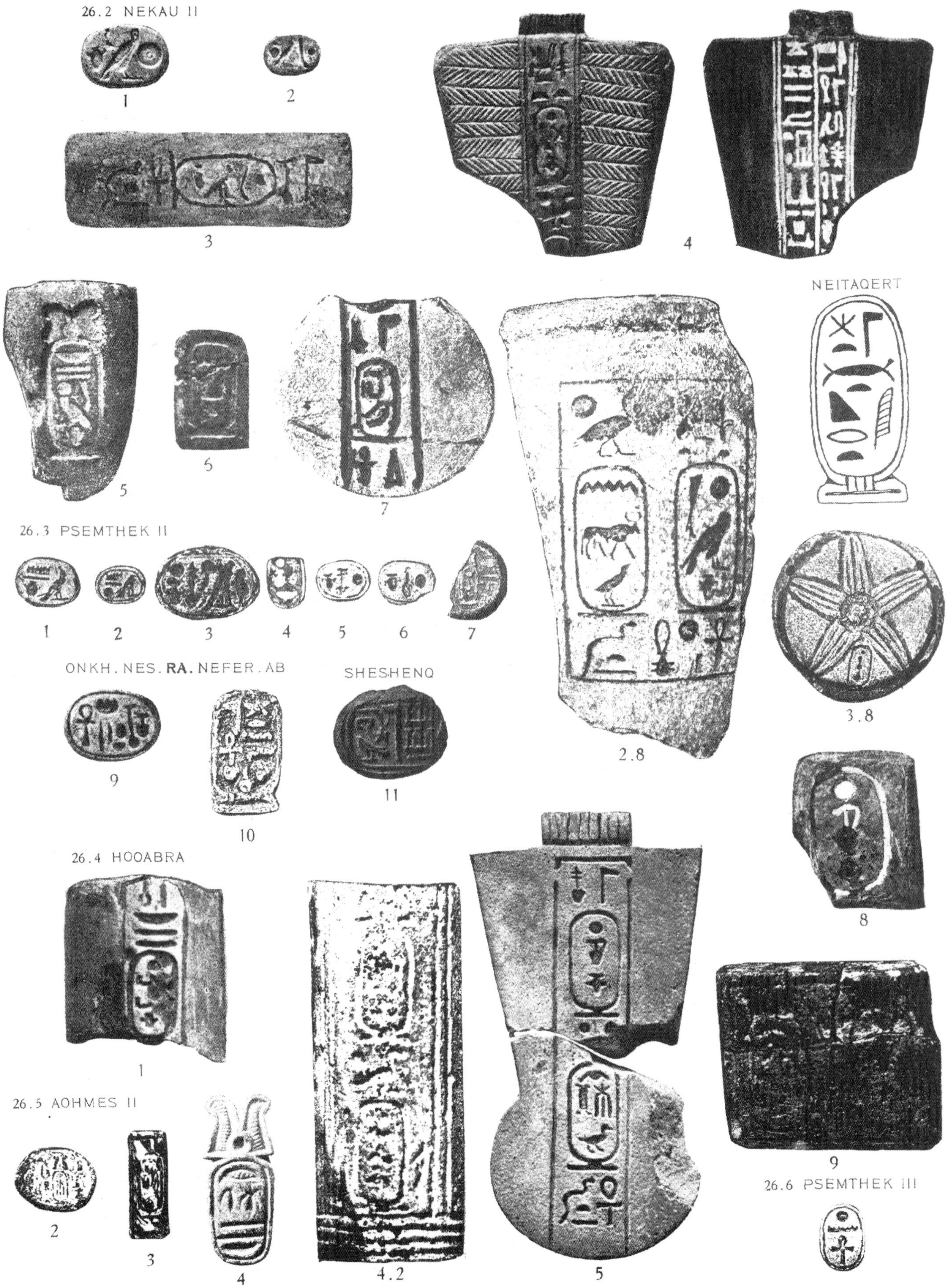
26.2 NEKAU II
1
2
3
4
5
6
7
NEITAQERT
2.8
3.8
26.3 PSEMTHEK II
1 2 3 4 5 6 7
ONKH. NES. RA. NEFER. AB
9
10
SHESHENQ
11
8
26.4 HOOABRA
1
9
26.5 AOHMES II
2
3
4
4.2
5
26.6 PSEMTHEK III

26·2.

26·2. NEKAU II

1 RA·UEHEM·AB — Dark green glaze — W. 20
2 ,, — Yellow paste. Pale green — N. 12
3 NETER NEFER, RA·UEHEM·AB ONKH ZETTA — Limestone — Cylinder
4 NESUT BAT, RA·UEHEM·AB SĂRA NE(KAU) — Menat. Blue paste
Reverse, AMEN NETER HEN, SEM ZED, HER NETER HENU . . . . . (AMEN NEB) NEST TĂUI EM HAT BENBEN PEDA . . . .
Prophet of Amen, priest of the Zed, over the prophets. . . . . Amen lord of the thrones of the lands in Thynabunon, Peda . . .
5 NEB TAUI, RA·UEHEM·AB — Impress on handle of jar
6 NEKAU — Impress in red glass, turned green — Flat
7 NETER NEFER, NEKAU, DA ONKH — End of Menat. Pottery. Apple-green — Rosette
8 NESUT BAT, RA·UEHEM·AB, SĂ RA NEKAU, ONKH RA MA ZETTA. *Living like Ra eternally* — Piece of alabaster vase

26·3.

26·3. PSEMTHEK II

1 HER, MEN(KH)·AB — Pottery. Gone red-brown — K. 52
2 HER MENKH (AB) — Gone white — P. 40
3 MĂOT, HER, RA, RA·NEFER·AB — Gone red-brown — H. 46
4 RA·NEFER·AB, NEB — Green limestone — Z. 86
5 RA·NEFER·AB — Pottery. Green — Worn
6 ,, — Pottery. Blue — Broken
7 . . . . . . RA·NEFER·AB, BA·NE·TEHĂ·HER (see private seal of same, 26 AF, pl. lviii) — Clay sealing
8 RA·NEFER·AB — Star disc to sew on to stuff. Pottery. Green — Flat

ONKH·NES·RA·NEFER·AB, daughter of Psamtek II, queen of Aohmes

9 (NETER) HEMT ONKH·S·RA·NEFER·AB, NEB — (Doubtful.) Pottery. Blue — E.
10 NETER DUAT, ONKH·NES·RA·NEFER·AB — Brand. Copper
11 MER PER UR DUAT NETER, SHESHENQ. *Keeper of the palace of the high priestess, Shesheng* — Clay sealing

26·4.

26·4. UAH·AB·RA (Apries)

1 NETER NEFER, NEB TAUI, RA·HOO·AB. Sistrum handle — Pottery. Yellow-green
2 NESUT BAT, RA·HOO·AB, SĂ RA UAH·AB·RA MERY. Reverse, same. — Sistrum handle. Pottery. Gone white

26·5.

26·5. AOHMES II

1 SĂ RA·KHNEM·AB, NESUT AOHMES·SĂ·NEIT, NEIT MĂOT MER. *Beloved by Neit and Maot.* (See lviii, end) — Memphis. Edwards. Clay sealing
2 NETER HEN PTAH, AOHMES·P·RA SĂ AST. *Prophet of Ptah, Aohmes the sun, Son of Isis.* — Clay impression
3 AOHMES SĂ NEIT — Green — Cylinder
4 AOHMES TAUI NEB — Black steatite — Seal
5 NETER NEFER RA·KHNEM·AB, SĂ RA AOHMES·SĂ·NEIT ONKH ZETTA. — Menat. Pottery. Pale blue — Flat
6, 7 Two fragments of sistrum handles with same names — Pottery. Apple-green. Pale blue
8 RA·KHNEM·AB. Foundation plaque ? — Pottery. Blue — Flat
9 RA·KHNEM·AB, AOHMES·SĂ·NEIT. Pierced from side to side. — Pectoral ? Pottery. Gone white — Flat

26·6.

26·6. PSEMTHEK III

RA·NE·ONKH (for RA·ONKH·KA·NE ; *life of Ra*, for *living one, ka o Ra*) — Pottery. Gone buff — G. 88

27·2. *XXVIIth DYNASTY.* 27·2. DARIUS

1 NETER NEFER, NEBTAUI, ANTARYUASH, DA ONKH ZET(TA). Menat. Pottery. Pale green Flat
2 SĂ (RA) NEB KHOU ANTERUASH Menat. Pottery. Light green with dark inlay Flat

28·1. *XXVIIIth DYNASTY.* 28·1. KHABBASH

KBBAS Palace of Memphis. Edwards. Lead. Sling bullet

29·1. *XXIXth DYNASTY.* 29·1. NĂIFOURUD

BA·RA·NE Gone brown F. 74

29·2. 29·2. HĂKER

RA·MĂOT·(KHNEM). Baboon of Tehuti, Falcon of Ra, Ram of Amen, and illegible Clay sealing

30·1. *XXXth DYNASTY.* 30·1. NEKHT·NEBEF

1 RA·KHEPER·KA. Uraei proceeding from sides of Kheper Pottery. Green F. 57
2 NETER NEFER, RA·KHEPER·KA; SĂ·RA, NEKHT·NEBEF, ONKH RA MA. *Living like Ra.* Foundation block. Alabaster Flat
3 RA·KHEPER·KA Stamp with handle. Pottery. Pale blue Handle
4 . . . . . . NEB TĂUI, RA·KHEPER·KA, SĂ(RA . . . . Handle of sistrum, bent in baking. Stoneware Green and violet
5 SĂ RA, NEKHT·NEBEF, ONKH ZETTA End of Menat. Pale green with grey inlay Flat

30·2. 30·2. ZEHER

NESUT BAT, NEB TĂUI, AR·MĂOT·NE·RA; SĂ RA, NEB KHOU, ZEHER, SETEP·NE·AMEN
MA RA DA ONKH AM PET, SESHEM NETERU . . . . . .
Like the Sun granted life in heaven, leader of the gods. . . . Piece of bowl Memphis. Pottery. Blue

30·3. 30·3. NEKHT·HER·HEB

1 MER·AMEN, NEKHT·HER·HEB Pottery. Blue Flat
2 RA·MER, NEKHT·HER·HEB Clay sealing

31·2. *XXXIst DYNASTY.* 31·2. ARSES

ARSESES Pottery. Light grey-green Jar lid

PTOLEMY I

Head of Ptolemy I as an Egyptian king with short beard Onyx Flat

PTOLEMY III

1 NESUT BAT, OOU NE NETERUI SENUI, SEKHEM ONKH NE AMEN, SETEP NE RA Pottery. Green with grey inlay Flat
2 Same. Reverse, PTULMYS, ONKH ZETTA, PTAH MER Pottery. Green with grey inlay Inscribed

PTOLEMY IV

Head of Ptolemy IV as a seal Gilt bronze Ring

ANTONINUS

ANTUNYNS SEBESTS Impression added here. Probably official ring of prefect. Gold Ring

30 A–U

A RA·HER·NEFER a king? Gone white L. 43
B RA·HER·USER·NEB or HER on NUBTI, RA·USER Blue paste G. 12
C ASAR, NETER HEN NE AMEN·RA NETERU NESUT, MER NUT, ASAR, THAT, NEKHT
The Osiris, prophet of Amen·ra king of the gods, mayor, the Osiris, Vizier, Nekht.
From tomb at Abusir by Lahun, opened by natives 1904 Brown steatite K. 76
D NETER HEN NE RA, MER NUTI, THAT, HER·SĂ·AST *Prophet of Ra, Mayor of both cities, Vizier, Hersa·ast* Green L. 35
E ONKH THAT ZEHUTI. *Living one, Vizier, Tehuti.* Reverse, Baboon Gone brown
F ONKH·RA·UAH·AB. *Onkh·uah·ab·ra* Green jasper. Back lost
G PTAH·HETEP. *Ptah-hetep* Pottery. Gone brown G. 18
HJ PEDA·AMEN. *Peda-amen* Pottery. Apple-green. Gone white G. 92, G. 64
K PEDA·AST. *Peda·ast* Gone white G. 86
LM PEDA·BASTET. *Peda·bast* Pottery. Gone yellow. Pottery. Pale green. Z. 8, W. 60
N PEDA·NEIT. *Peda·neit* Pottery. Bright green W. 20
OP PEDA·RA. *Peda·ra* Gone grey. Gone white. Both G. 90
Q PEDA·KHEPRA. *Peda·khepra* Gone white G. 74
R PEDA·SUKH. *Peda·khonsu* or *sutekh* Black steatite Cone
S MEN·HETEP. *Men·hetep* or *Amen·hetep?* Gone white, broken F.
T NUB·HETEP. *Nub·hetep* or *Nubti·hetep?* Gone light brown P. 30
U ASAR·HAP. *Serapis* Pottery. Gone yellow E. 60

DYNASTIES XXVII TO ROMAN

27.2 DARIUS 1, 2

29.1 NAIFOURUD

29.2 HAKER

30.1 NEKHT. NEBEF 1, 2

28.1 KHABBASH 3, 4, 5

29 3 PSAMUT

30.3 NEKHT. HER. HEB 1, 2

PTOLEMY I

30.2 ZEHER

31.2 ARSES

PTOLEMY III 1, 2

PTOLEMY IV

ANTONINUS

30. A B C D E

F G H J K L M N

O P Q R S T U

V W X Y Z AA AB AC AD

AE AF AG AH AJ AK AL AM

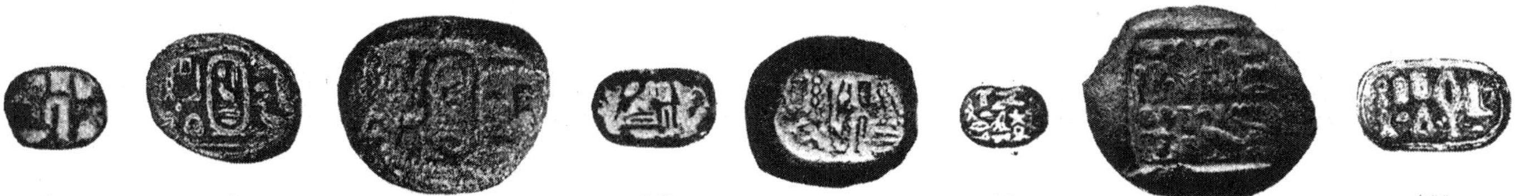

AN AO AP AQ AR AS AT AU

AV AW AY AZ BA BB BC

AX

BD BE BF BG BH BJ BK BL BM

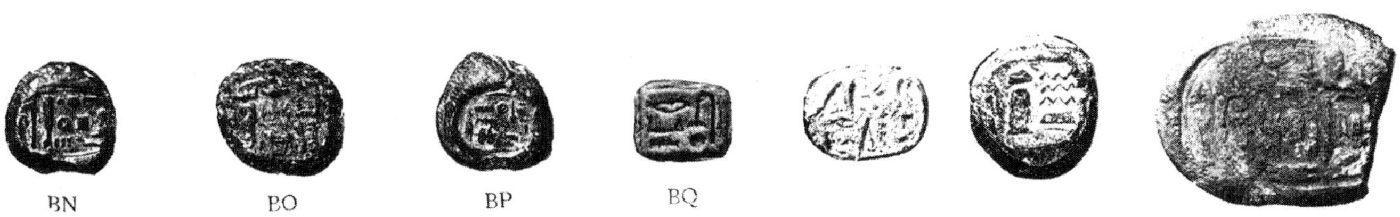

BN BO BP BQ BR BS 26.5.1

V HES HER·PE·KHRED. *Praise Harpokrates* Gone white Broken
W KHERAS Blue paste Broken
X KAREH Gone grey Broken

30 V–BS PRIVATE SEALS AND IMPRESSIONS (in alphabetic order)

Y HEN UR EM OKĂ MU NUT, AOH·TEF·NEKHT. *Chief servant in Schedia* (De Rougé. *Geog.* 21) *Aohtefnekht* Clay sealing
Z AM NETER ONKH·KHRED. *With the god, Onkh·khred* Clay sealing
AA ONKH·HAP. *Onkh·hap* Bronze ring
AB NEIT·UAH·AB, RA·UAH·AB·ONKH. *May Neit increase the heart, Uah abra·onkh* Silver ring
AC . . . . . RA·UAH·AB, MER KHETM, RA·UAH·AB·EM·AĂKHUT. *Keeper of the seal, Uahabra·emaakhut* Clay sealing
AD HEN NEIT ER OHOY, UN·NEFER; SĂ ZET·BASTET·AU·ONKH Apries palace, Memphis. Clay sealing
Servant of Neit at the stele, Unnefer, son of Zetbastauonkh
AE KHER HEB HER TEP UZA, HER HU NET PER. *Chief reciter, Uza, over the food of the temple* Clay sealing
AF HEN HETU, NETER HEN AMEN, BA·NE·TEHA·HER. *Servant of the temples, prophet of Amen, Ba netehaher* Clay sealing
AG KHU SĂ BAKNEF. *Protection behind Baknef* Clay sealing
AH HEN BASTET PE·NEFU·UZAT (?), AMENTI DA BASTET, NETER HEN ASAR. *Servant of Bastet Penefu·uzat, ...* Clay sealing
AJ NEIT SĂ PE·NEF·DA·AST. *Priest of Neit, Penef·da·ast* Clay sealing
AK NEIT SĂ PE·NEF·DA·MĂOT. ,, ,, *Penef·damăot* Clay sealing
AL PTAH, HAP, SĂ, PANEN. *Să priest of Ptah, and Hapi, Pa·nen* Bronze ring
AM HEN KA, SESH . . . . , PENEKHT·MIN. *Servant of the ka, scribe . . . . Penekhtmin* Bronze ring
AN . . . . PSEMEK. . . . . . *Psem(th)ek* Bronze ring
AO KHER HEB HER TEP PSEMTHEK·SĂ·NEIT. *Chief reciter Psemtheksaneit* Clay sealing
AP ,, ,, ,, ,, ,, ,, Larger seal Clay sealing
AQ PSEMTHEK·SĂ·NEIT. *Psemtheksaneit* Silver ring
AR PTAH·TANEN·UN, PSEMTHEK. *Ptah·tanen open to Psemthek* Clay sealing
AS UN AM DUĂT HER ONKH . . . PTAH·AR·DA . . . . . . *Ptahardas* Silver ring
AT HEN NUBT, NESUT SESH O NERE, KHEN HER, PEDAPEP SA NEZNEZA.
Servant of Nubt (Hathor) *Royal scribe of accounts of food* (?) . . . . . *Pedapep son of Nezneza* Clay sealing
AU AST SĂ PEDAPTAH. *Sa-Priest of Isis, Pedaptah* Bronze ring
AV PTAH HEN PEDANEIT. *Servant of Ptah, Pedaneit* Bronze ring
AW UR DUA, KHERP NESTU, PEDANEIT. *High priest of Hermopolis . . . . Pedaneit* Silver ring
AX PEDA·HER·PE·KHRED. *Peda·harpekhroti* Edwards. Limestone seal
AY PEDA·RA·OHĂ, NETER HEN RA NEB NE APT. *Peda·ra·oha, prophet of Ra lord of Karnak* Bronze ring
AZ PTAH SĂ PEDAHER. *Ptah protect Pedaher* Bronze ring
BA MUT·NEB·S. *Mut nebs* Bronze ring
BB AST(?)·HES NE NEB TAUI. *Isis(?) favour the king* (name ?) Silver ring
BC KHETM NETER, NESI·MIN, SĂ AOH·EM·AĂKHUT. *Sealer of the god, Nesimin son of Aoh·-em·aakhut* Bronze ring
BD NETER HEN, UR DUA, KHERP NESTU, NESI·ONKH·HER SĂ UN·NEFER
Prophet, high priest of Hermopolis, ... Nesionkh·her son of Unnefer Bronze stamp
BE . . . . SESH NETER HET, NESIMIN SĂ PSEMTHEK·MENKH·AB. . . . *Scribe of the temple, Nesimin son of Psemthek·menkh·ab* Clay
BF HEN UR UPUAT NESI·HER. *Great priest of Upuat, Nesi·her* Clay sealing
BG . . . . . . NEIT·AR·DAS. . . . . . *Neitandas* Silver ring
BH NETER HEN, UR DUA, KHERP NESTU. . . . . . SEKHMET, BASTET, RU. . . . *Prophet, high priest of Hermopolis. . . .* Silver ring
BJ HER·NEFER SĂ PE·RES·NE·AOH. *Her·nefer son of Peresneaoh* Clay sealing
BK AST SĂ SĂQER, SĂT NETER HEN BASTET, HER. *Protected by Isis, Saqer, daughter of prophet of Bast, Horus* Silver ring
BL AMĂKH PA·BASTET HES HERU. *Devoted in Bubastis, the favoured, Heru* Gold ring
BM HERY. Reverse, same. *Hery* Pottery. Light green Flat
BN SĂ NETER HENU TEKH, HER·PEF. *Order of priests in Denderch, Herpef* Clay sealing
BO Goddess with *semtu* on head. SEN·KA·BA SĂ NEFER. *Senkaba son of Nefer* Clay sealing
BP AMEN ARP, SĂ·NEFER·AB·RA. *Offerer of wine to Amen, Saneferabra* Clay sealing
BQ SEKHMET·AR·DAS. *Sekhmetardas* Limestone. Pyramidal
BR . . . UZT MU. . . . . *stele of waters . . . . . .* Clay sealing
BS HEN NE PTAH, HEN HER, DAT·ASAR. *Priest of Ptah, Priest of Horus, Datasar* Thick bronze seal with back loop

Priestly seal for Aohmes II, described under 26·5·1.

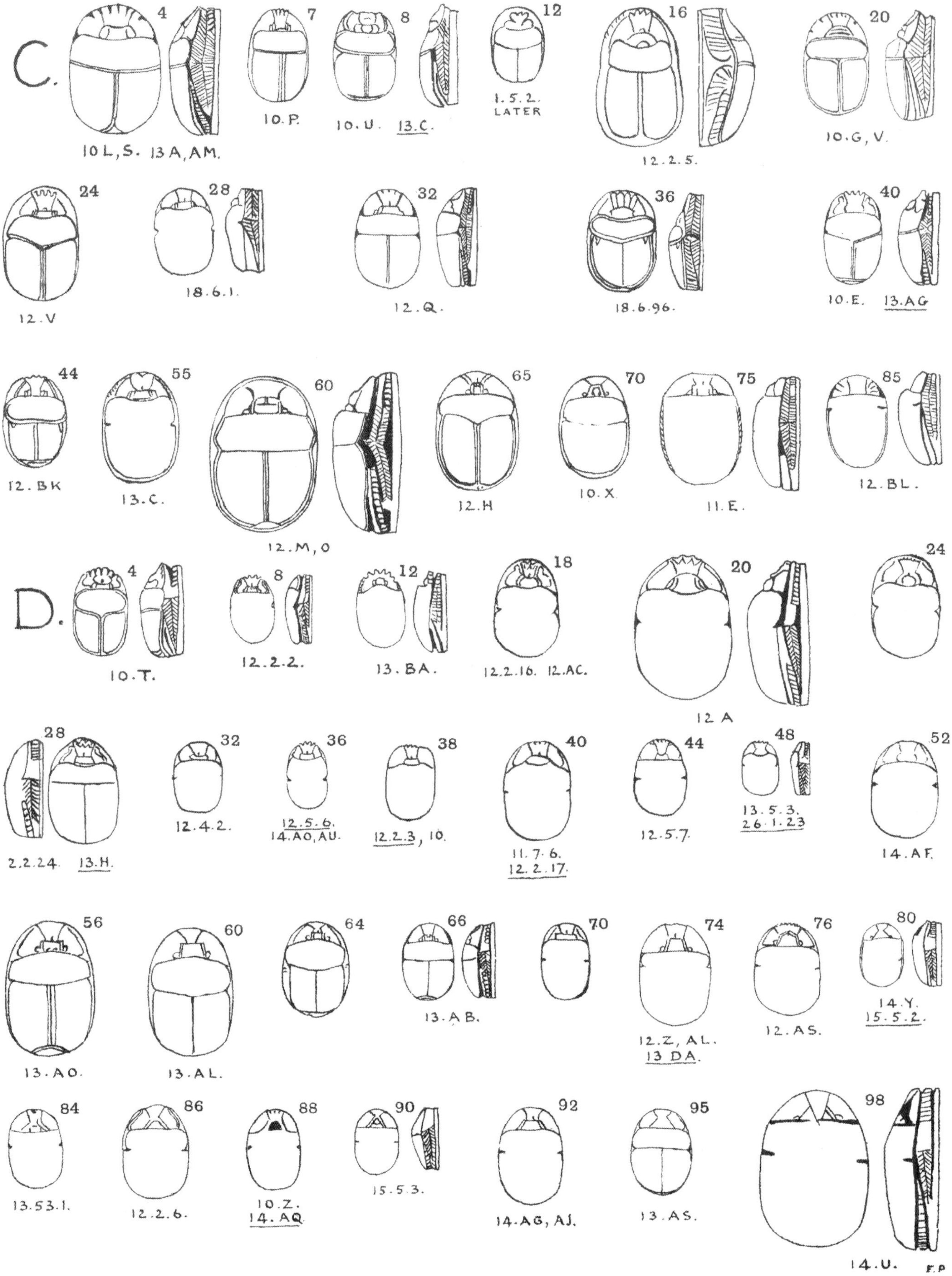
C.
4
10 L, S. 13 A, AM.
7
10. P.
8
10. U. 13. C.
12
1. 5. 2.
LATER
16
12. 2. 5.
20
10. G, V.
24
12. V
28
18. 6. 1.
32
12. Q.
36
18. 6. 96.
40
10. E. 13. AG
44
12. BK
55
13. C.
60
12. M, O
65
12. H
70
10. X
75
11. E.
85
12. BL.
D.
4
10. T.
8
12. 2. 2.
12
13. BA.
18
12. 2. 16. 12. AC.
20
12 A
24
28
2. 2. 24. 13. H.
32
12. 4. 2.
36
12. 5. 6.
14. AO, AU.
38
12. 2. 3, 10.
40
11. 7. 6.
12. 2. 17.
44
12. 5. 7.
48
13. 5. 3.
26. 1. 23
52
14. AF.
56
13. AO.
60
13. AL.
64
66
13. AB.
70
74
12. Z, AL.
13 DA.
76
12. AS.
80
14. Y.
15. 5. 2.
84
13. 53. 1.
86
12. 2. 6.
88
10. Z.
14. AQ.
90
15. 5. 3.
92
14. AG, AJ.
95
13. AS.
98
14. U.
F. P.

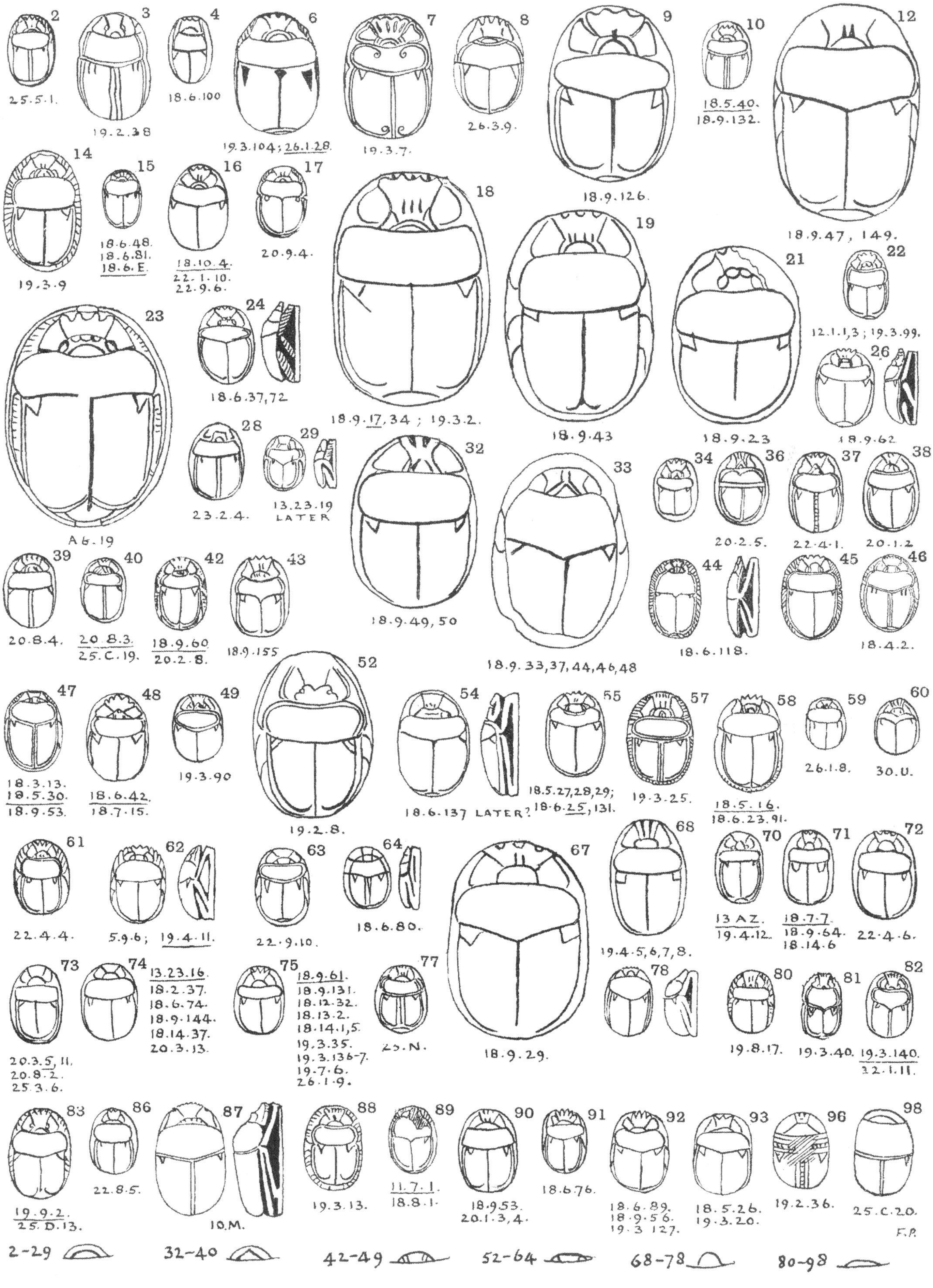

F. SCARABAEUS. V MARKS. DEEP HEAD.

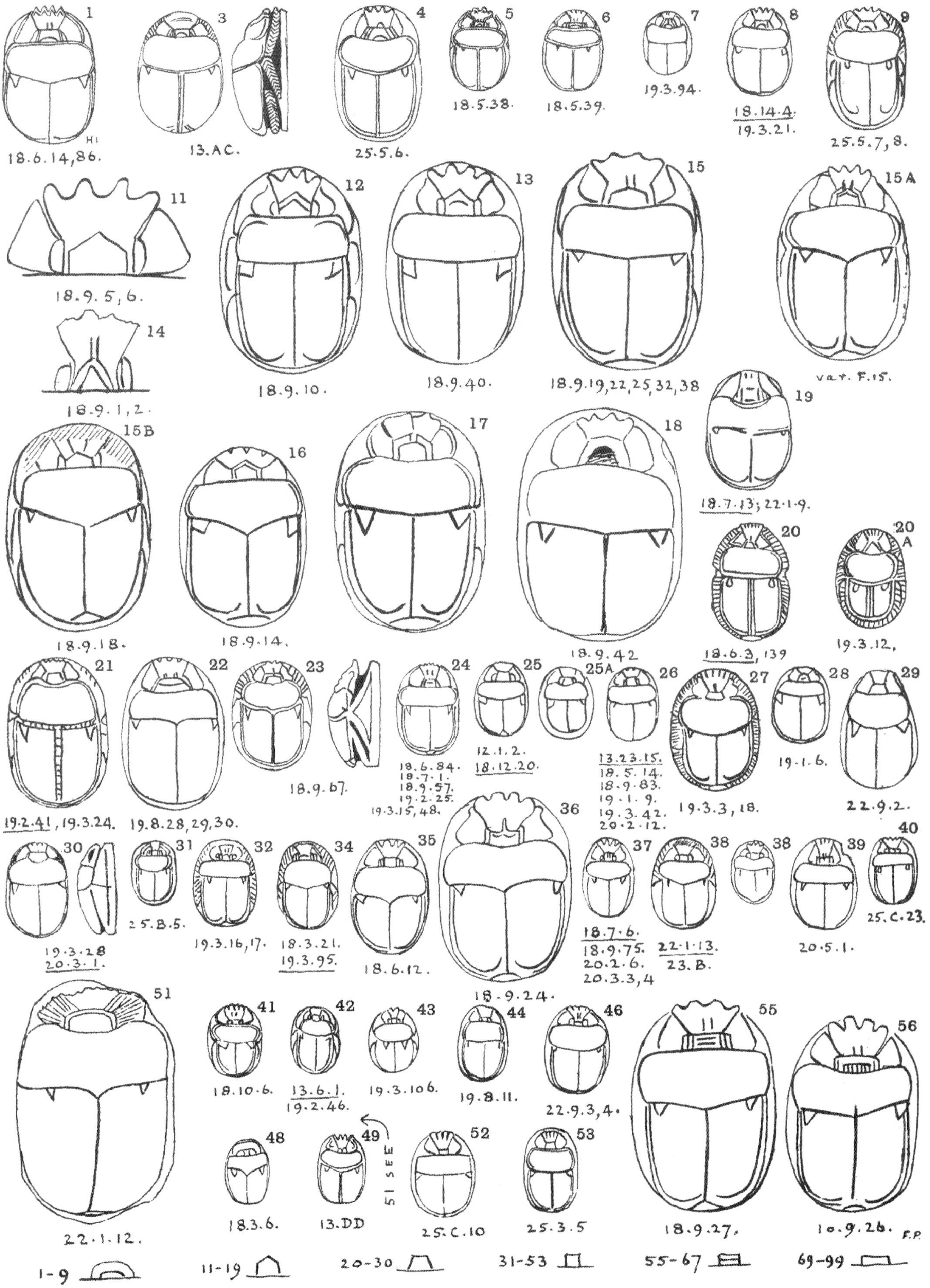

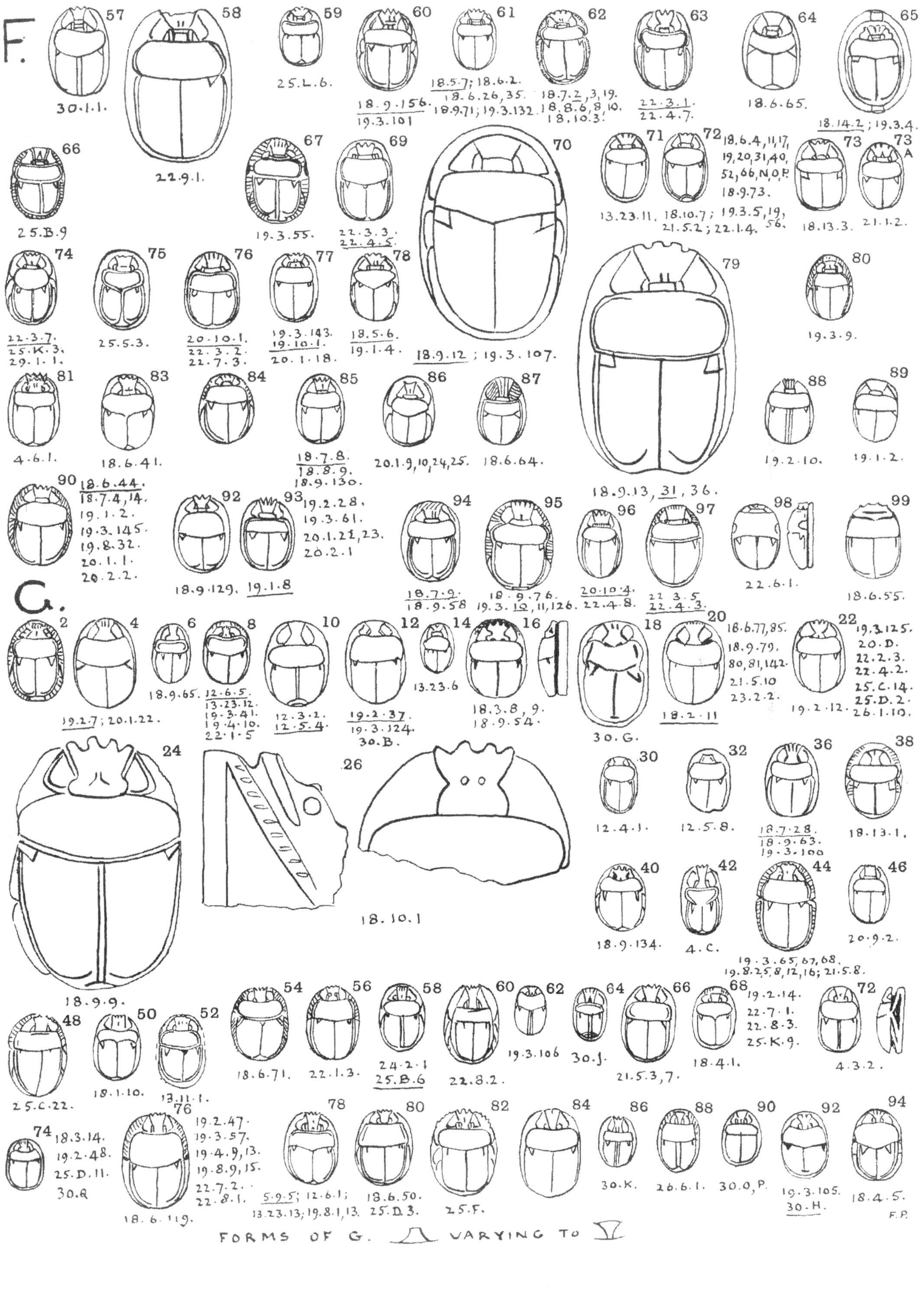

F.
57 30.1.1.
58 22.9.1.
59 25.L.6.
60 18.9.156. 19.3.101
61 18.5.7; 18.6.2. 18.6.26, 35. 18.9.71; 19.3.132.
62 18.7.2, 3, 19. 18.8.6, 8, 10. 18.10.3.
63 22.3.1. 22.4.7.
64 18.6.65.
65 18.14.2; 19.3.4.
66 25.B.9
67 19.3.55.
69 22.3.3. 22.4.5.
70 18.9.12; 19.3.107.
71 13.23.11.
72 18.6.4, 11, 17, 19, 20, 31, 40, 52, 66, N, O, P. 18.9.73. 18.10.7; 19.3.5, 19, 56. 21.5.2; 22.1.4.
73 18.13.3.
73 A 21.1.2.
74 22.3.7. 25.K.3. 29.1.1.
75 25.5.3.
76 20.10.1. 22.3.2. 22.7.3.
77 19.3.143. 19.10.1. 20.1.18.
78 18.5.6. 19.1.4.
79 18.9.13, 31, 36.
80 19.3.9.
81 4.6.1.
83 18.6.41.
84
85 18.7.8. 18.8.9. 18.9.130.
86 20.1.9, 10, 24, 25.
87 18.6.64.
88 19.2.10.
89 19.1.2.
90 18.6.44. 18.7.4, 14. 19.1.2. 19.3.145. 19.8.32. 20.1.1. 20.2.2.
92 18.9.129.
93 19.1.8 19.2.28. 19.3.61. 20.1.22, 23. 20.2.1
94 18.7.9. 18.9.58
95 18.9.76. 19.3.10, 11, 126.
96 20.10.4. 22.4.8.
97 22.3.5 22.4.3.
98 22.6.1.
99 18.6.55.
G.
2 4 19.2.7; 20.1.22.
6 18.9.65.
8 12.6.5. 13.23.12. 19.3.41. 19.4.10. 22.1.5
10 12.3.2. 12.5.4.
12 19.2.37. 19.3.124. 30.B.
14 13.23.6
16 18.3.8, 9. 18.9.54.
18 30.G.
20 18.2.11
18.6.77, 85. 18.9.79, 80, 81, 142. 21.5.10 23.2.2.
22 19.2.12. 19.3.125. 20.D. 22.2.3. 22.4.2. 25.C.14. 25.D.2. 26.1.10.
24 18.9.9.
26 18.10.1
30 12.4.1.
32 12.5.8.
36 18.7.28. 18.9.63. 19.3.100
38 18.13.1.
40 18.9.134.
42 4.C.
44 19.3.65, 67, 68. 19.8.2, 5, 8, 12, 16; 21.5.8.
46 20.9.2.
48 25.C.22.
50 18.1.10.
52 13.11.1.
54 18.6.71.
56 22.1.3.
58 24.2.1 25.B.6
60 22.8.2.
62 19.3.106
64 30.J.
66 21.5.3, 7.
68 18.4.1. 19.2.14. 22.7.1. 22.8.3. 25.K.9.
72 4.3.2.
74 18.3.14. 19.2.48. 25.D.11. 30.R
76 18.6.119. 19.2.47. 19.3.57. 19.4.9, 13. 19.8.9, 15. 22.7.2. 22.8.1.
78 5.9.5; 12.6.1; 13.23.13; 19.8.1, 13.
80 18.6.50. 25.D.3.
82 25.F.
84
86 30.K.
88 26.6.1.
90 30.O, P.
92 19.3.105. 30.H.
94 18.4.5.
F.P.
FORMS OF G. VARYING TO

H. SCARABAEUS. NOTCHED CLYPEUS. LUNATE HEAD. LXIII.

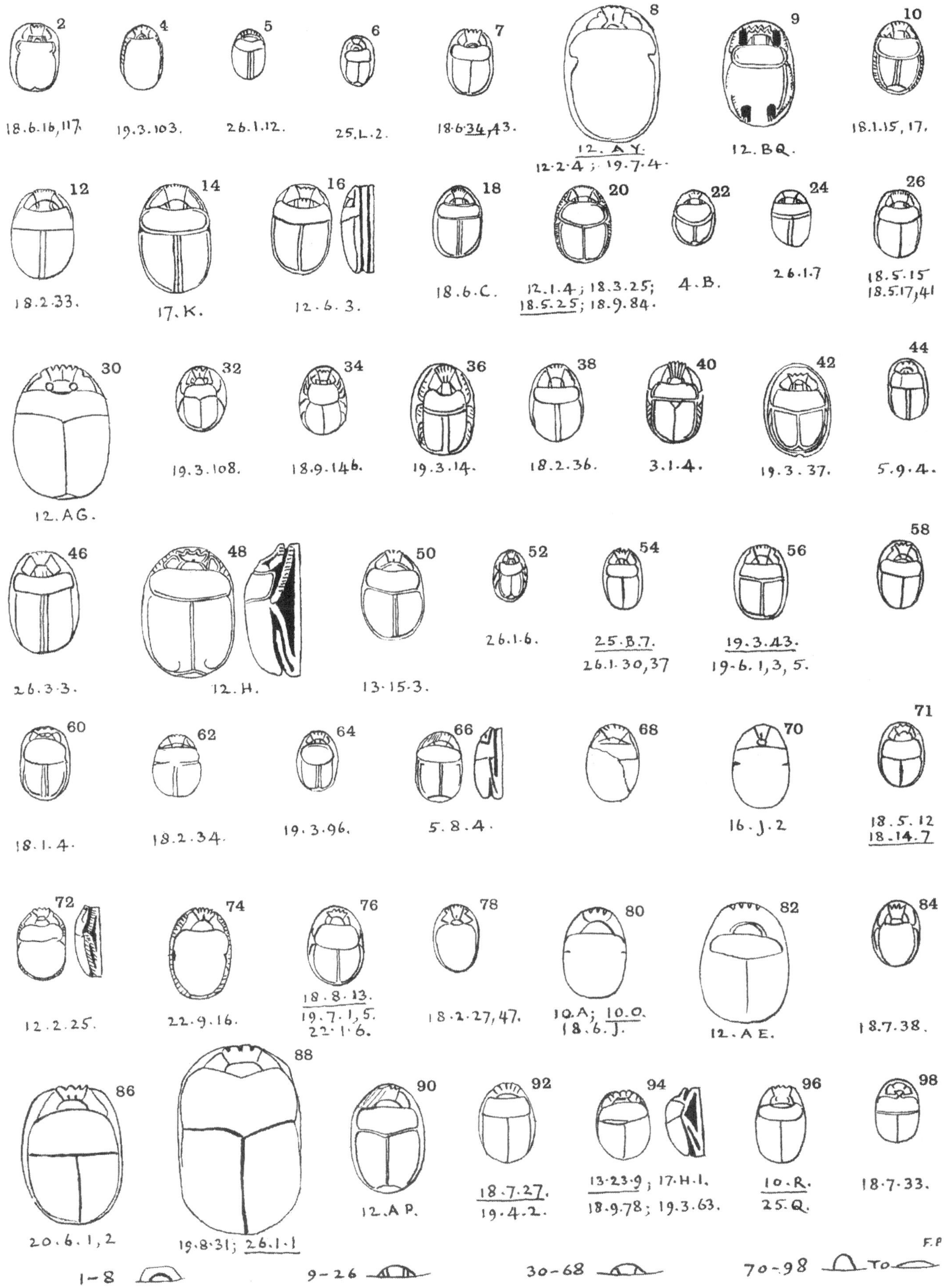

J. SCARABAEUS. NOTCHED CLYPEUS. DEEP HEAD. LXIV.

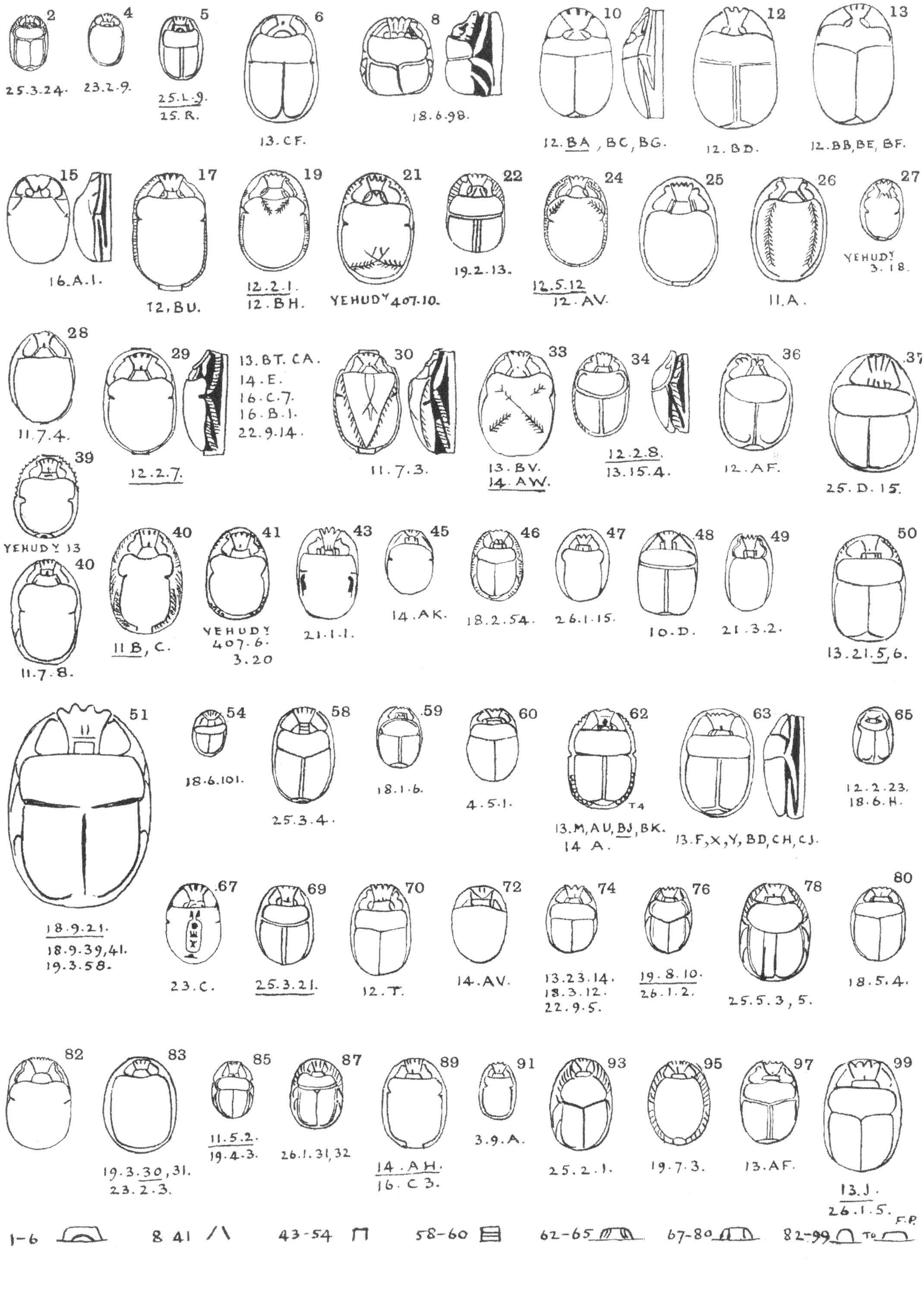

K. SCARABAEUS. NOTCHED CLYPEUS. MERGING HEAD.

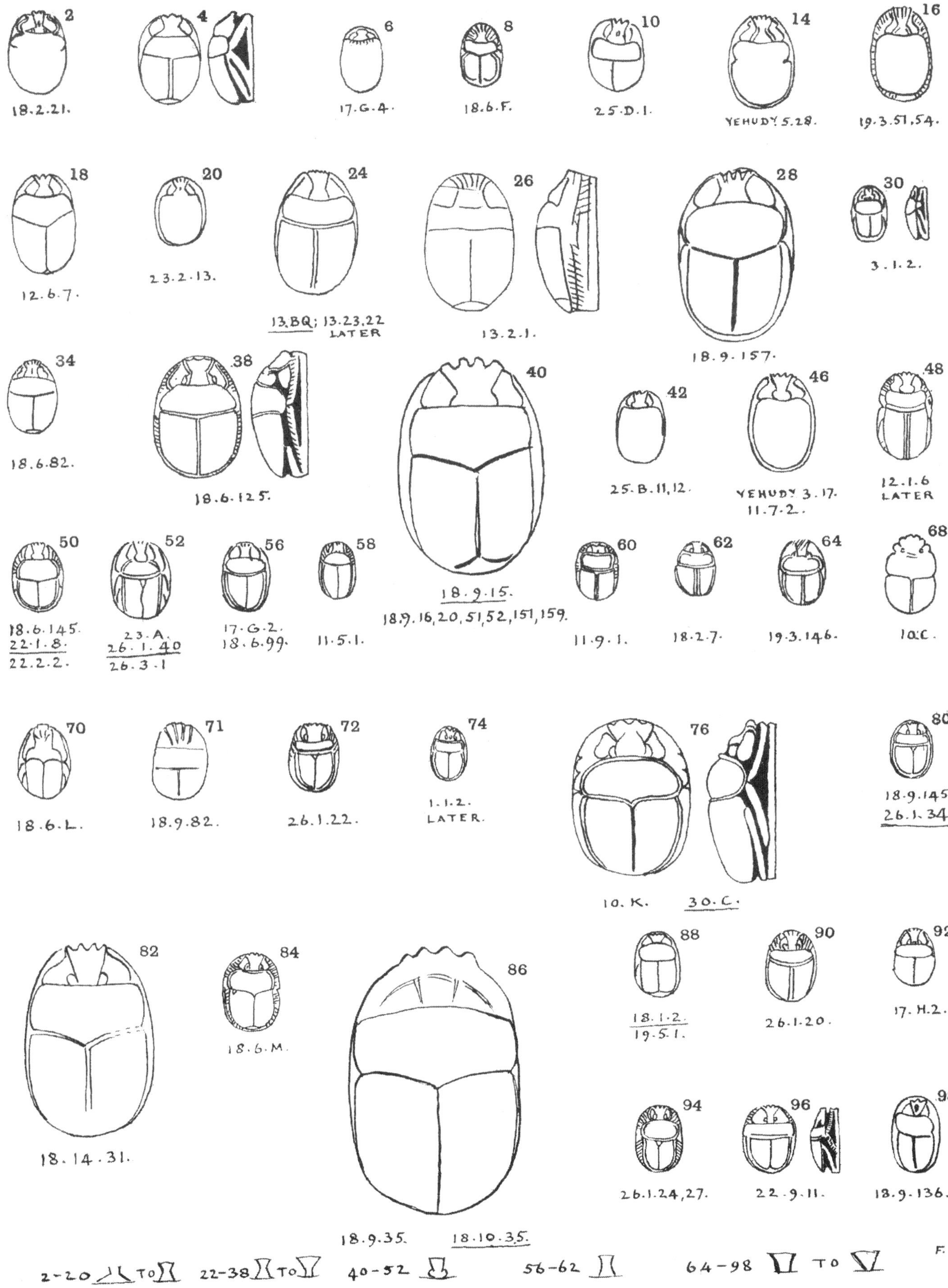

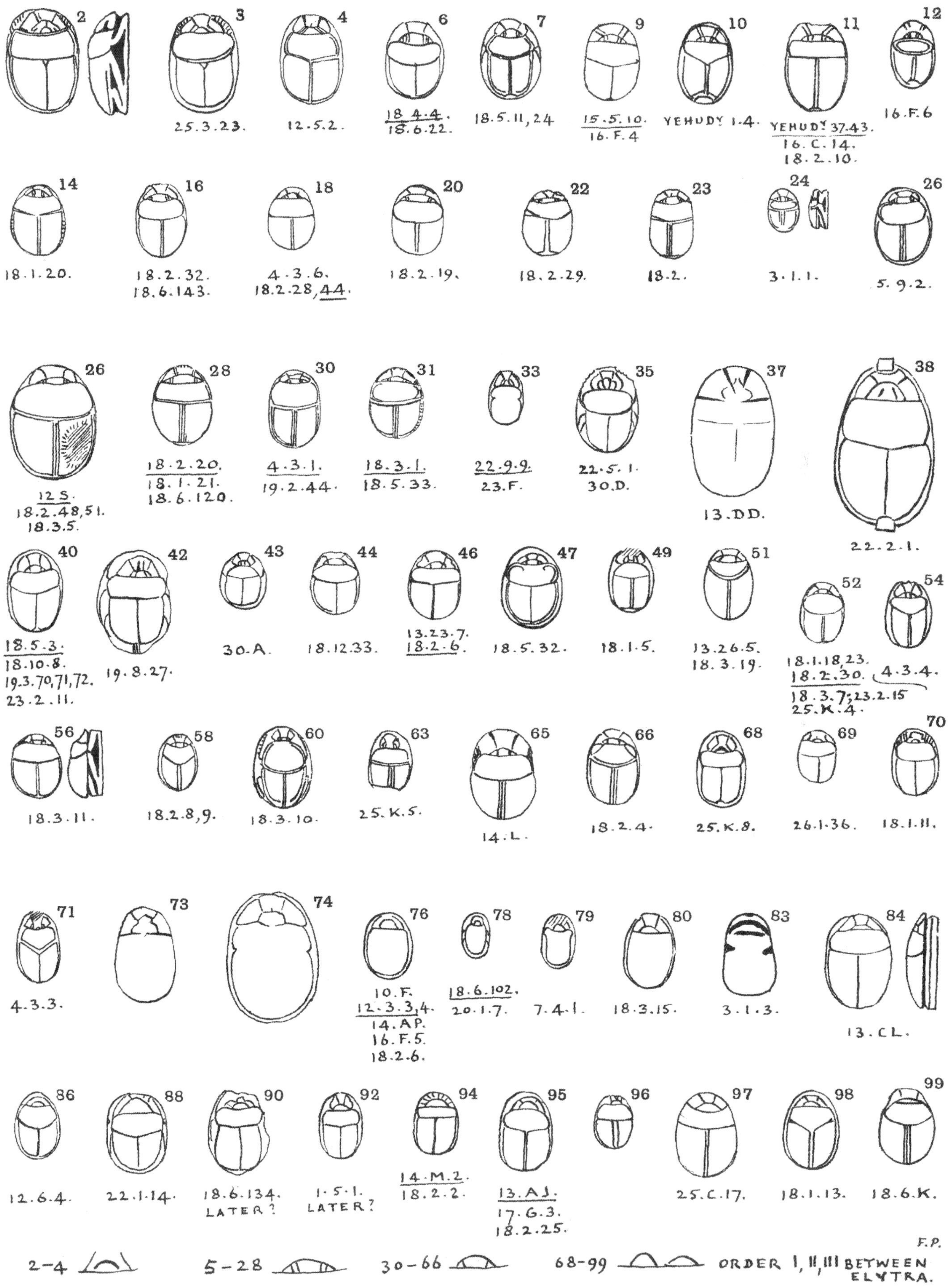
2
3 25.3.23.
4 12.5.2.
6 18.4.4. 18.6.22.
7 18.5.11, 24
9 15.5.10. 16.F.4
10 YEHUDY 1.4.
11 YEHUDY 37.43. 16.C.14. 18.2.10.
12 16.F.6
14 18.1.20.
16 18.2.32. 18.6.143.
18 4.3.6. 18.2.28, 44.
20 18.2.19.
22 18.2.29.
23 18.2.
24 3.1.1.
26 5.9.2.
26 12 S. 18.2.48, 51. 18.3.5.
28 18.2.20. 18.1.21. 18.6.120.
30 4.3.1. 19.2.44.
31 18.3.1. 18.5.33.
33 22.9.9. 23.F.
35 22.5.1. 30.D.
37 13.DD.
38 22.2.1.
40 18.5.3. 18.10.8. 19.3.70, 71, 72. 23.2.11.
42 19.8.27.
43 30.A.
44 18.12.33.
46 13.23.7. 18.2.6.
47 18.5.32.
49 18.1.5.
51 13.26.5. 18.3.19.
52 18.1.18, 23. 18.2.30. 18.3.7; 23.2.15 25.K.4.
54 4.3.4.
56 18.3.11.
58 18.2.8, 9.
60 18.3.10.
63 25.K.5.
65 14.L.
66 18.2.4.
68 25.K.8.
69 26.1.36.
70 18.1.11.
71 4.3.3.
73
74
76 10.F. 12.3.3, 4. 14.AP. 16.F.5. 18.2.6.
78 18.6.102. 20.1.7.
79 7.4.1.
80 18.3.15.
83 3.1.3.
84 13.CL.
86 12.6.4.
88 22.1.14.
90 18.6.134. LATER?
92 1.5.1. LATER?
94 14.M.2. 18.2.2.
95 13.AJ. 17.6.3. 18.2.25.
96
97 25.C.17.
98 18.1.13.
99 18.6.K.
F.P.
2–4
5–28
30–66
68–99
ORDER I, II, III BETWEEN ELYTRA.

M.N. SCARABAEUS. SMOOTH CLYPEUS. M. DEEP HEAD. N. MERGING HEAD. LXVII.

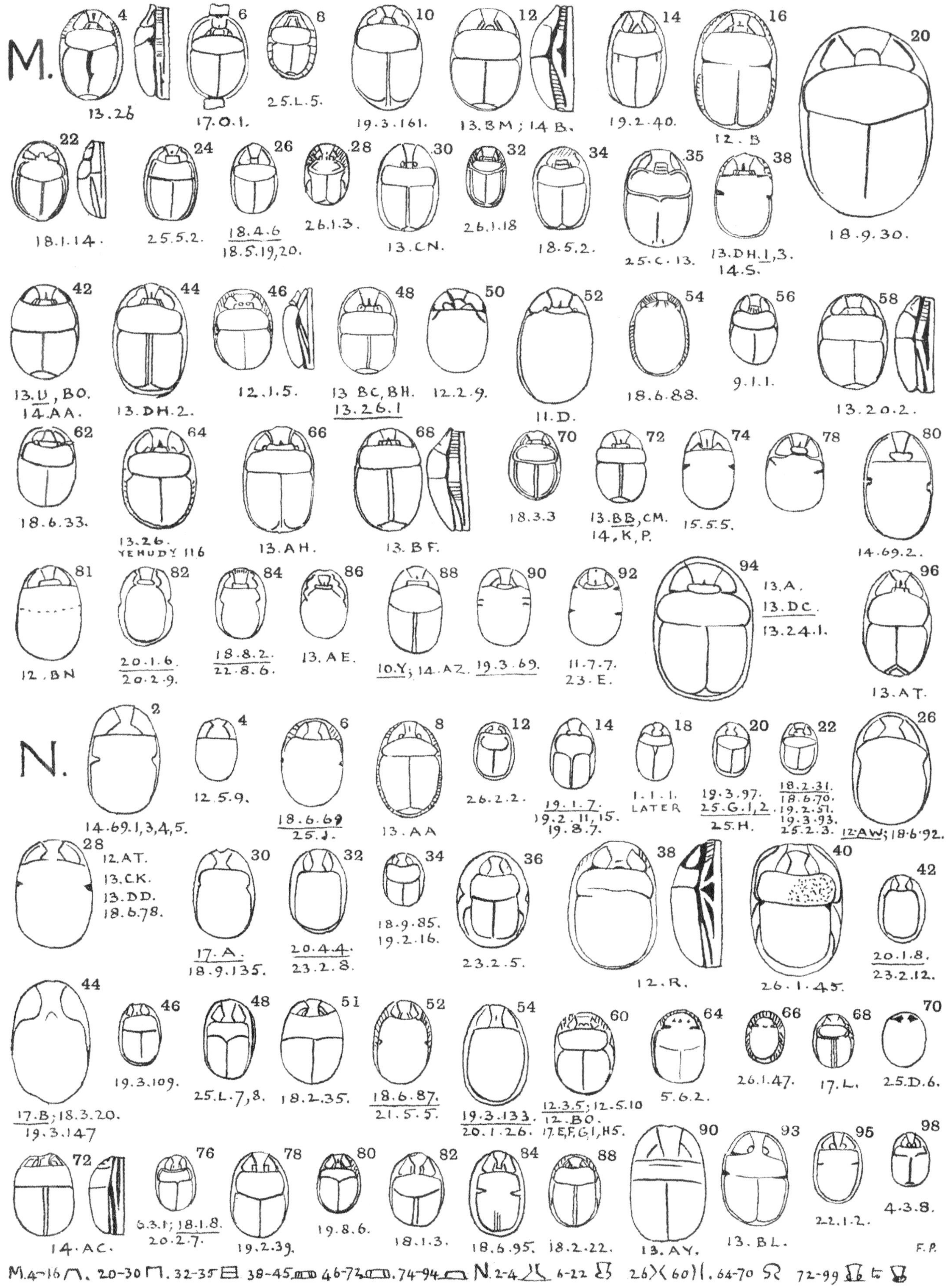

M. 4-16 ⊓. 20-30 ⊓. 32-35 ⊟. 38-45 ▭. 46-72 ▭. 74-94 ▭. N. 2-4 ⅄ 6-22 ⋃ 26)(60)(. 64-70 ☊ 72-99

O. SC. VENERABILIS. P. RIBBED HEAD. Q. CURL. R. MAMMALIAN HEADS. S. CATHARSIUS. LXVIII.

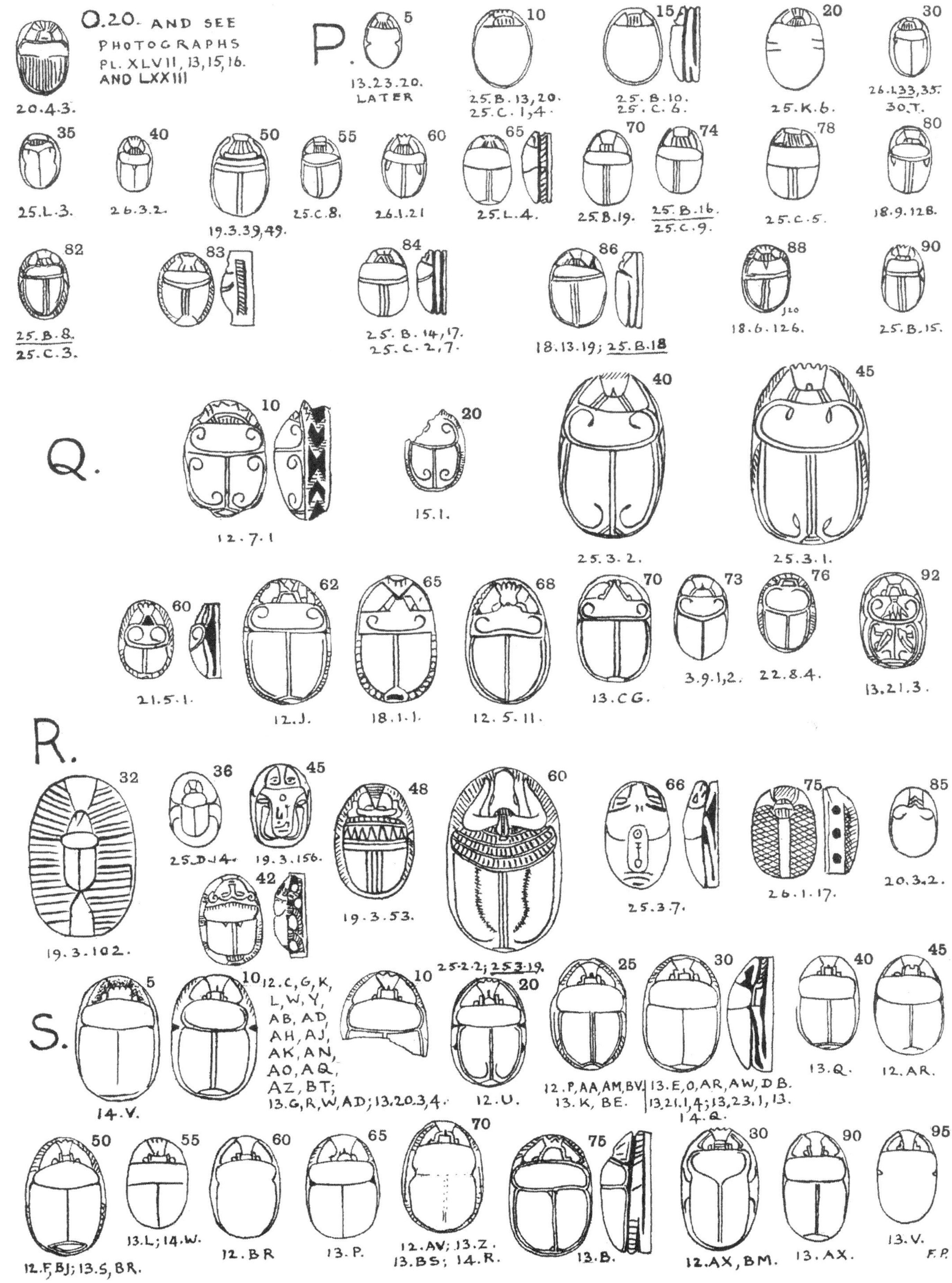

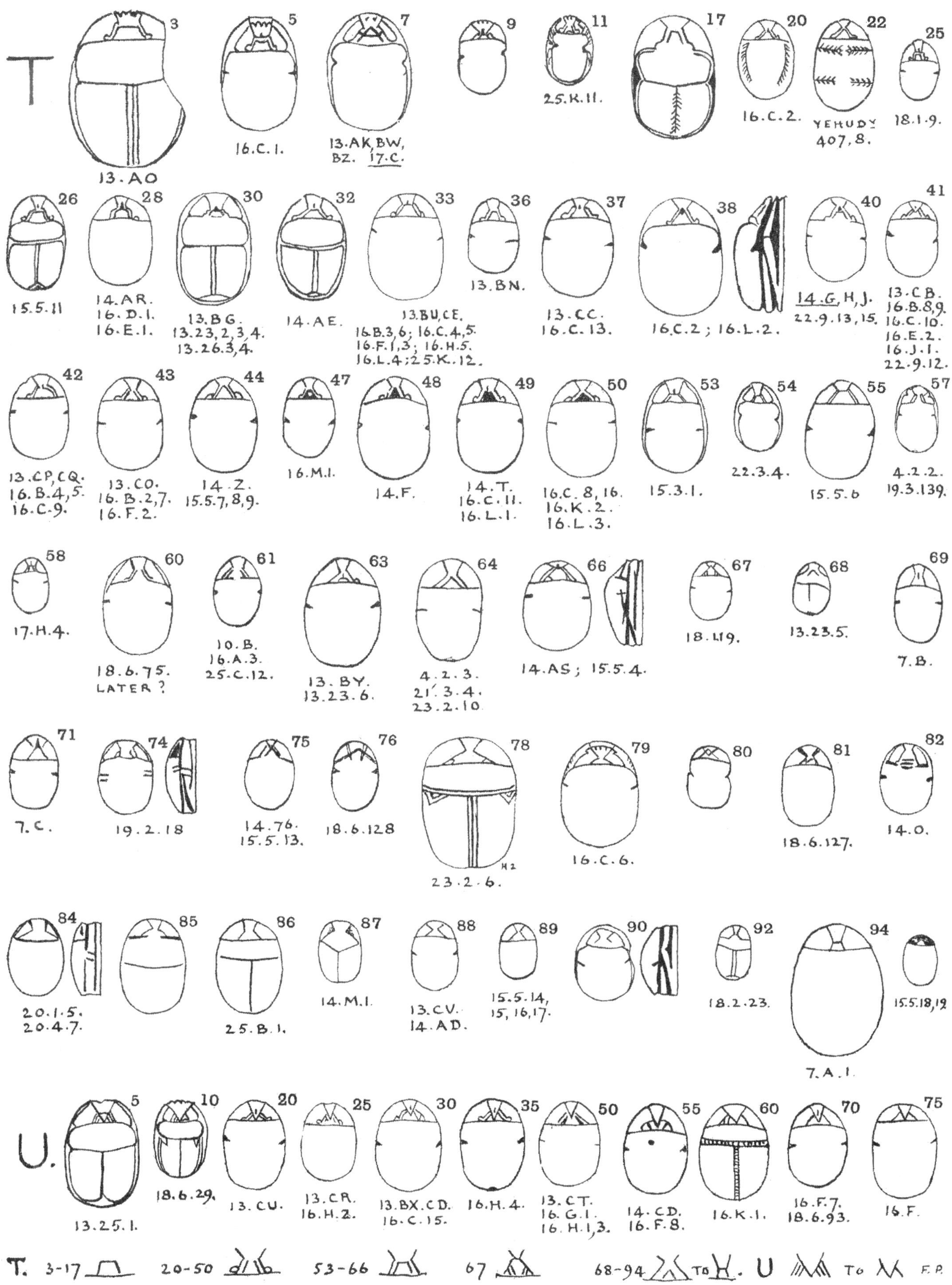
T
3
13.AO
5
16.C.1.
7
13.AK,BW, BZ. 17.C.
9
11
25.K.11.
17
20
16.C.2.
22
YEHUDY 407,8.
25
18.1.9.
26
15.5.11
28
14.AR. 16.D.1. 16.E.1.
30
13.BG. 13.23,2,3,4. 13.26.3,4.
32
14.AE.
33
13.BU,CE. 16.B.3,6; 16.C.4,5. 16.F.1,3; 16.H.5. 16.L.4; 25.K.12.
36
13.BN.
37
13.CC. 16.C.13.
38
16.C.2; 16.L.2.
40
14.G, H, J. 22.9.13,15.
41
13.CB. 16.B.8,9. 16.C.10. 16.E.2. 16.J.1. 22.9.12.
42
13.CP,CQ. 16.B.4,5. 16.C.9.
43
13.CO. 16.B.2,7. 16.F.2.
44
14.Z. 15.5.7,8,9.
47
16.M.1.
48
14.F.
49
14.T. 16.C.11. 16.L.1.
50
16.C.8,16. 16.K.2. 16.L.3.
53
15.3.1.
54
22.3.4.
55
15.5.6
57
4.2.2. 19.3.139.
58
17.H.4.
60
18.6.75. LATER ?
61
10.B. 16.A.3. 25.C.12.
63
13.BY. 13.23.6.
64
4.2.3. 21.3.4. 23.2.10
66
14.AS; 15.5.4.
67
18.L19.
68
13.23.5.
69
7.B.
71
7.C.
74
19.2.18
75
14.76. 15.5.13.
76
18.6.128
78
23.2.6.
79
16.C.6.
80
81
18.6.127.
82
14.O.
84
20.1.5. 20.4.7.
85
86
25.B.1.
87
14.M.1.
88
13.CV. 14.AD.
89
15.5.14, 15,16,17.
90
92
18.2.23.
94
7.A.1.
15.5.18,19
U.
5
13.25.1.
10
18.6.29.
20
13.CU.
25
13.CR. 16.H.2.
30
13.BX.CD. 16.C.15.
35
16.H.4.
50
13.CT. 16.G.1. 16.H.1,3.
55
14.CD. 16.F.8.
60
16.K.1.
70
16.F.7. 18.6.93.
75
16.F.
T. 3-17
20-50
53-66
67
68-94
TO
U
TO
F.P.

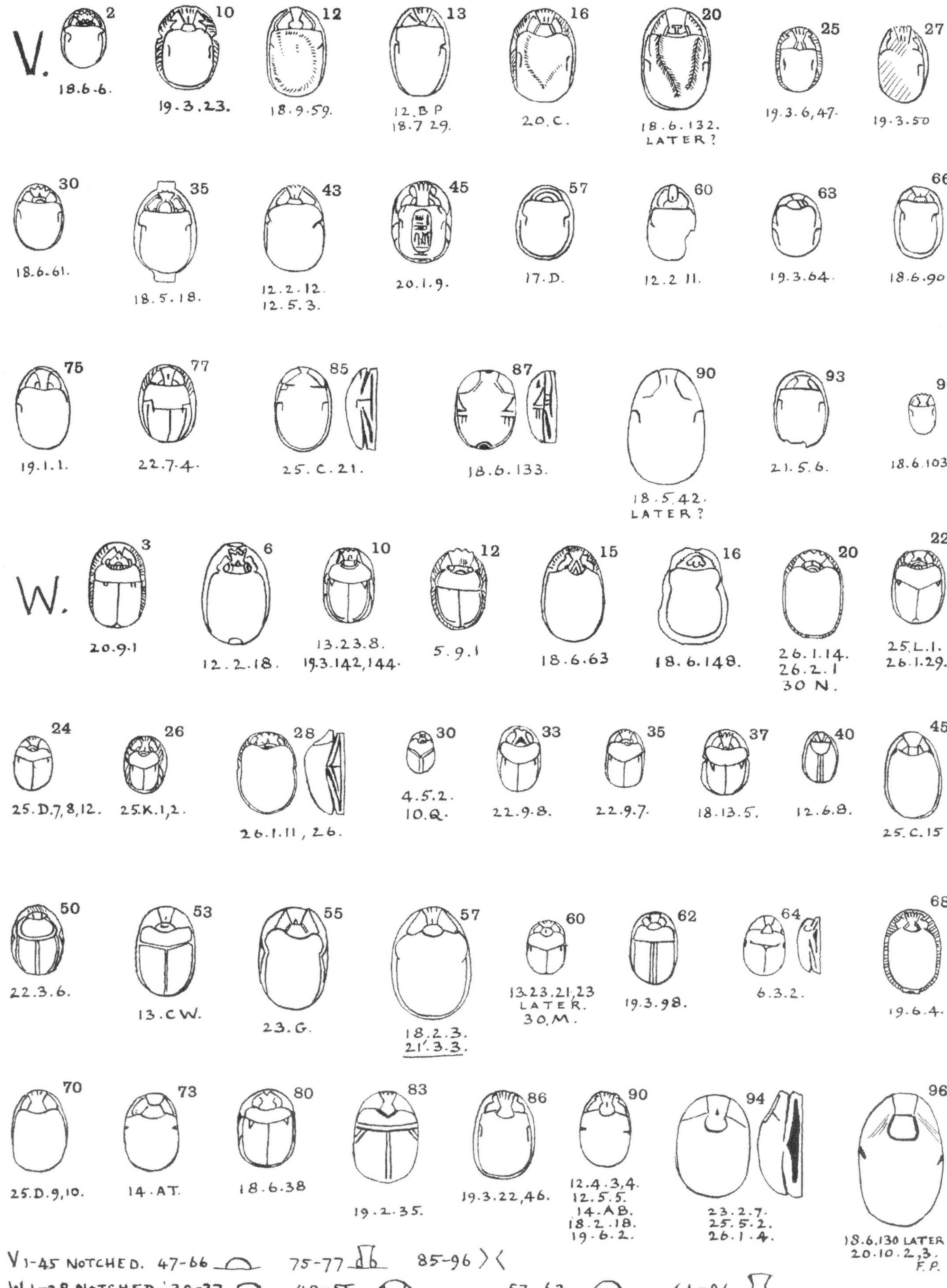
V.
2 18.6.6.
10 19.3.23.
12 18.9.59.
13 12.B P 18.7 29.
16 20.C.
20 18.6.132. LATER?
25 19.3.6,47.
27 19.3.50
30 18.6.61.
35 18.5.18.
43 12.2.12. 12.5.3.
45 20.1.9.
57 17.D.
60 12.2 11.
63 19.3.64.
66 18.6.90
75 19.1.1.
77 22.7.4.
85 25.C.21.
87 18.6.133.
90 18.5.42. LATER?
93 21.5.6.
96 18.6.103.
W.
3 20.9.1
6 12.2.18.
10 13.23.8. 19.3.142,144.
12 5.9.1
15 18.6.63
16 18.6.148.
20 26.1.14. 26.2.1 30 N.
22 25.L.1. 26.1.29.
24 25.D.7,8,12.
26 25.K.1,2.
28 26.1.11, 26.
30 4.5.2. 10.Q.
33 22.9.8.
35 22.9.7.
37 18.13.5.
40 12.6.8.
45 25.C.15
50 22.3.6.
53 13.CW.
55 23.G.
57 18.2.3. 21.3.3.
60 13.23.21,23 LATER. 30.M.
62 19.3.98.
64 6.3.2.
68 19.6.4.
70 25.D.9,10.
73 14.AT.
80 18.6.38
83 19.2.35.
86 19.3.22,46.
90 12.4.3,4. 12.5.5. 14.AB. 18.2.18. 19.6.2.
94 23.2.7. 25.5.2. 26.1.4.
96 18.6.130 LATER 20.10.2,3. F.P.
V 1-45 NOTCHED. 47-66 75-77 85-96 ><
W 1-28 NOTCHED 30-37 40-55 57-62 64-96

X. HYPSELOGENIA. Y. SAME MODIFIED. Z. OVOIDS.

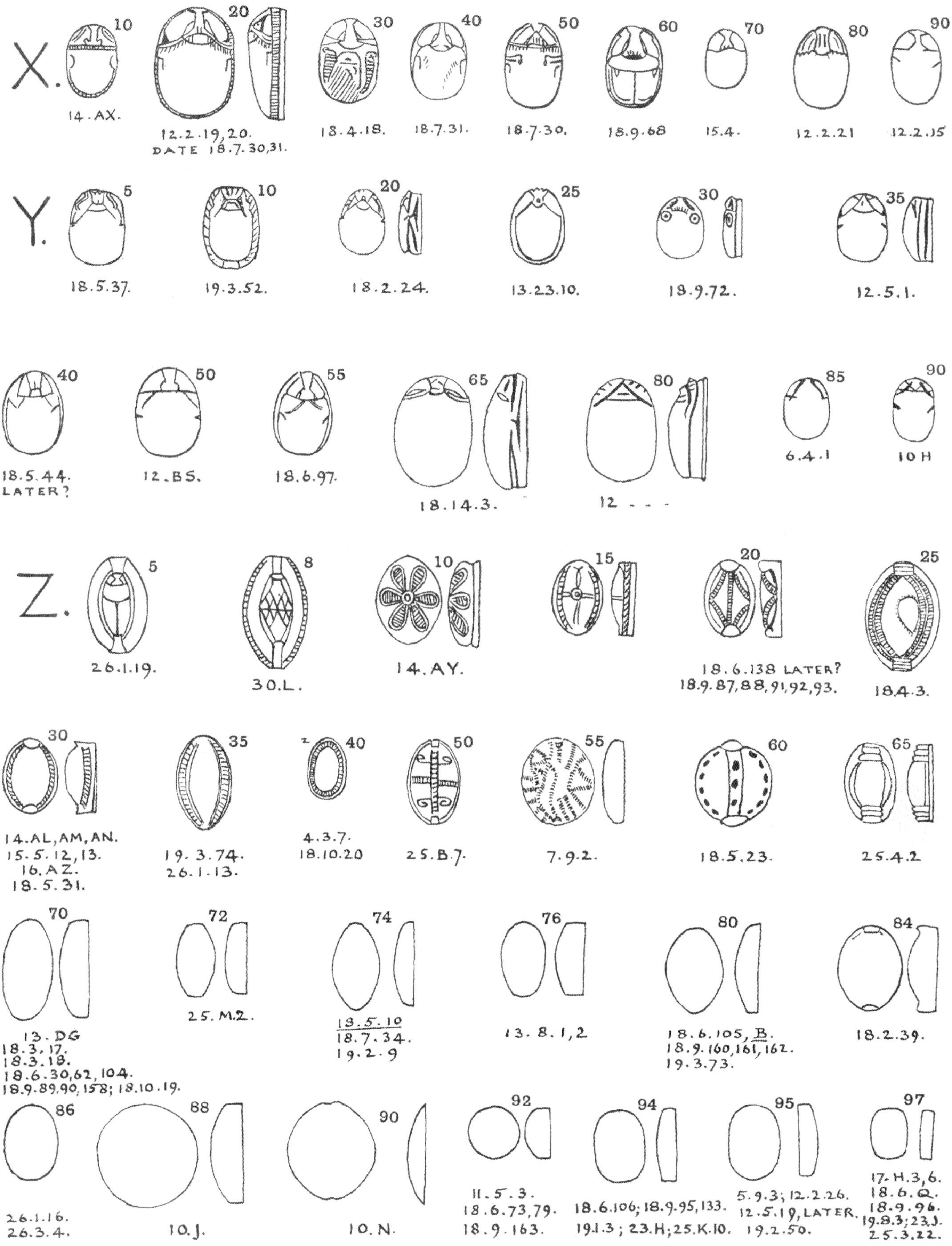

KEMA 13 W 12 AJ SEBEKHETEP II 13 AU 13 AX SEBEKHETEP III

12 AK 13 P

GROOVE DOUBLE OR SINGLE.

13 DB HA·ONKH·F 13 X NEFERHETEP 12 AV SEBEKHETEP III 13 S 14 B 14 K

SEBEKHETEP III 13 BC 13 BH 13 BJ 13 BK 13 CN 13 CF 13 BO AY

WITH WIDE GROOVE.

49 A 108 A 162 A

ADDITIONAL CYLINDERS.

BACKS OF HEART SCARABS IN HISTORICAL ORDER. NUMBERS AS PLS. XLVII. XLVIII.